Advances in
Clinical Child
Psychology

Volume 2

ADVANCES IN CLINICAL CHILD PSYCHOLOGY

A Continuation Order Plan is available for this series. A continuation order will bring delivery of each new volume immediately upon publication. Volumes are billed only upon actual shipment. For further information please contact the publisher.

Advances in
Clinical Child
Psychology

Volume 2

Edited by

Benjamin B. Lahey
University of Georgia, Athens

and

Alan E. Kazdin
Pennsylvania State University, University Park

Plenum Press · New York and London

The Library of Congress cataloged the first volume of this title as follows:

Advances in clinical child psychology. v. 1—

New York, Plenum Press, c1977—

v. ill. 24 cm.
Key title: Advances in clinical child psychology. ISSN 0149—4732

1. Clinical psychology—Collected works. 2. Child psychology—Collected works.
3. Child psychotherapy—Collected works.
RJ503.3.A37   618.9′28′9   77-643411

Library of Congress Catalog Card Number 77-643411

ISBN 0-306-40105-3

© 1979 Plenum Press, New York
A Division of Plenum Publishing Corporation
227 West 17th Street, New York, N.Y. 10011

Printed in the United States of America

*This series is dedicated to
the children of the world, especially*
MEGAN, EDWARD, ERIN, NICOLE, and MICHELLE

Contributors

Robert M. Berland   *Child Behavior Institute, The University of Tennessee at Knoxville, Knoxville, Tennessee*

Gene H. Brody   *Department of Child and Family Development, The University of Georgia, Athens, Georgia*

Robert L. Burgess   *College of Human Development, The Pennsylvania State University, University Park, Pennsylvania*

Thomas D. Coe   *Child Behavior Institute, The University of Tennessee at Knoxville, Knoxville, Tennessee*

Michael Feuerstein   *Stanford Research Institute, Menlo Park, California and Stanford University School of Medicine, Stanford, California*

Daniel P. Hallahan   *Department of Special Education, University of Virginia, Charlottesville, Virginia*

Suzanne Bennett Johnson   *Department of Clinical Psychology, University of Florida, Gainseville, Florida*

James M. Kauffman   *Department of Special Education, University of Virginia, Charlottesville, Virginia*

Thomas R. Kratochwill   *Department of Educational Psychology, The University of Arizona, Tucson, Arizona*

Samuel W. M. LeBaron *Department of Psychology, Stanford University, Stanford, California*

M. Patrick McNees *Luton Community Mental Health Center and Middle Tennessee State University, Murfreesboro, Tennessee*

Barbara G. Melamed *Department of Clinical Psychology, University of Florida, Gainesville, Florida*

Donald Meichenbaum *Department of Psychology, University of Waterloo, Waterloo, Ontario, Canada*

Wayne C. Piersel *Department of Educational Psychology, The University of Arizona, Tucson, Arizona*

Thomas Sajwaj *Luton Community Mental Health Center and Middle Tennessee State University, Murfreesboro, Tennessee*

John F. Schnelle *Luton Community Mental Health Center and Middle Tennessee State University, Murfreesboro, Tennessee*

Robert G. Wahler *Child Behavior Institute, The University of Tennessee at Knoxville, Knoxville, Tennessee*

Marcia M. Ward *Department of Psychology, Ohio State University, Columbus, Ohio*

Preface

The second volume of *Advances in Clinical Child Psychology* continues the high standards set by the contributing authors of Volume 1. The series has been most fortunate in attracting authors who lead the field of applied child and developmental psychology in theory, research, and practice. Their chapters bring together advances from a wide variety of subfields in essays that can legitimately be called "major statements." Often these integrative chapters prove to be more than the sum of their parts, not only bringing together information on the most current topics in the field but pointing to new directions as well.

Donald Meichenbaum summarized current evidence and theory in his chapter on self-control in children. The cognitive and behavioral strategies he outlines offer the promise of effective and convenient treatment methods, but as he points out, much remains to be learned about these methods. Robert Wahler and his associates outline a new model for the study of generalization of child treatment effects. The model views the family as a system that either supports or inhibits generalization. Suggestions for planning treatments within this framework are provided, as well as an outline for extending this analysis to other levels of systems.

James Kauffman and Daniel Hallahan provide a description of the cognitive and behavioral characteristics of learning-disabled and hyperactive children, and critically evaluate available methods of assessment and treatment. Special attention is also paid to the questionable concept of "minimal brain dysfunction." The same concept is addressed by Michael Feuerstein, Marcia Ward, and Samuel Le Baron in their critical appraisal of neuropsychological and neurophysiological approaches to the assessment of children with learning and behavior problems.

Robert Burgess's chapter on child abuse provides a summary of emerging sociological and psychological perspectives on child abuse. Like Wahler, he approaches the abusive family from a systems point of view. Suzanne Johnson and Barbara Melamed summarize and evaluate current evidence on the assessment and treatment of children's fears, and Thomas Kratochwill and his associates update the study of elective mutism. At a different level of analysis, Thomas Sajwaj, Patrick McNees, and John Schnelle compare the advantages and disadvantages of community and clinical (individual-problem-oriented) approaches to the problems of children and youth. Their analysis puts both approaches in better perspective.

Taken together these chapters suggest advances in dealing with children with problems at the level of the individual, the family, and the community. They offer new hope for treatment and suggest new directions for research. We sincerely appreciate the role played by the advisory editors in their suggestions of topics and their editorial comments for volume 2.

BENJAMIN B. LAHEY

ALAN E. KAZDIN

Contents

Child Abuse: A Social Interactional Analysis 5
Robert L. Burgess

Clinical and Community Interventions with Children:
A Comparison of Treatment Strategies
*Thomas Sajwaj, M. Patrick McNees, and
John F. Schnelle* 6

Elective Mutism in Children 7
Thomas R. Kratochwill, Gene H. Brody, and
Wayne C. Piersel

Neuropsychological and Neurophysiological Assessment 8
of Children with Learning and Behavior Problems:
A Critical Appraisal
Michael Feuerstein, Marcia M. Ward,
and Samuel W. M. LeBaron

1   *Teaching Children Self-Control*

Donald Meichenbaum

1. Introduction

An author of a chapter on self-control has to demonstrate just such self-control. In my own case this was necessary for two reasons. The first reason is that I was on sabbatical leave at the University of Hawaii (escaping the Canadian winter) when the completion date for this chapter was approaching. Can you think of a better illustration of a situation that calls for "self-control"?

The second factor contributing to my need for exerting self-control is the variety of approaches one can take to the present topic. Permit me to share the alternatives that I considered. The author of a chapter on self-control may review the literature on specific target populations that by their very nature demonstrate problems in the area of self-control. For example, one could examine the nature of the deficit(s) and treatment interventions for such populations as hyperactive children, acting-out children, or children with low self-esteem. Such an approach has been employed by Camp (1977), Douglas (1972, 1975), and the author (Meichenbaum, 1977). These research approaches attempt to match the specific mode of treatment intervention to the child's specific deficit patterns. A consideration of these studies would entail a careful content analysis of the respective treatment manuals that have been offered to teach children self-control skills (e.g., Bash & Camp, 1975; Fagan, Long, & Stevens, 1975; Spivack & Shure, 1974; Schneider & Robin, 1976). Most of these treatment approaches have *not* been adequately assessed, especially for long-term follow-up. Only promissory notes have been offered. The qualified nature of any conclusions that can be drawn from such treatment studies was nicely highlighted by Paul Karoly in a recent chapter on self-management in children. It is worthwhile to take note of

DONALD MEICHENBAUM • Department of Psychology, University of Waterloo, Waterloo, Ontario, Canada.

1

these limitations at the outset of a chapter on teaching children self-control skills. In reviewing treatment and laboratory studies on children's self-control, Karoly offers the following conclusions:

> It is probably a fair characterization of the field to assert that self-control training has: (1) been conducted mainly in laboratory settings, (2) employed non-clinical populations, (3) neglected individual differences and cognitive developmental variables, (4) failed to apply systematic pretreatment assessment, (5) operated under the assumption of a general skills deficiency (as opposed to possible perceptual, decisional, or motivational deficiencies), (6) attempted to demonstrate the efficacy of a singular (or limited) intervention strategy, (7) focused on a narrow range of self-control responses . . . employed a patient homogeneity myth and (8) failed to pay sufficient attention to issues of maintenance and transfer. (1977, pp. 30-31)

The examination of training studies represents only one approach to a discussion of self-control. Another approach that could be adopted is to examine the nature and development of self-control from an individual difference normative viewpoint. The work by Chess and her colleagues on temperament differences (Chess, Thomas, & Birch, 1968), the work by Jane Loevinger and Jeanne and Jack Black on ego-development, ego-control, and ego-resilience (Loevinger, 1976; Block & Block, 1977), as well as the work on impulsivity (e.g., Kagan, 1966; Messer, 1976; Repucci, 1970; Toner, Holstein, & Hetherington, 1977) can also be conceptualized as falling under the rubric of self-control. One could examine what is known about the development of social cognition and personality and cull guidelines for teaching children self-control.

A somewhat different approach that one could take to this chapter is to consider how self-control skills have been taught to adults in order to determine what lessons can be extended downward to children (e.g., Bellack & Schwartz, 1976; Thoresen & Coates, 1976).

I can continue summarizing other related literatures such as (1) the development of prosocial behavior and moral development (e.g., Staub, 1975; Lickona, 1976), (2) metacognitive development and problem-solving skills (e.g., Flavell, 1977; Spivack, Platt, & Shure, 1976), (3) the self-control lay literature (Klausner, 1965), (4) the literature on theoretical issues such as operant approaches versus social learning regulation models (Mahoney & Thoresen, 1974; Kanfer & Karoly, 1972), (5) the literature on the usefulness of operant approaches in developing self-control in the classroom (e.g., Brownell, 1977; O'Leary & O'Leary, 1976, 1977), and finally (6) the extensive discussions on the component processes that are subsumed under the term *self-control* such as the literature on self-monitoring, standard setting, self-instructions, attributions, and self-reinforcement (e.g., Bandura, 1976; Catania, 1975; Kanfer, 1977;

Masters & Mokros, 1974). In fact one could easily generate a chapter reviewing the literature on any one of these component processes.

It should be apparent that what I have outlined thus far is more a prospectus for a book on self-control than an introduction to a chapter. After having extensively read the literature in each of the above areas, not only am I confused about the nature of self-control but I have reservations about offering specific guidelines for teaching children self-control. (And I thought sabbatical leaves were supposed to help clarify issues.)

The approach that I have chosen is first to examine the kinds of laboratory tasks that have been employed to assess children's self-control, then to note the component skills required to perform these tasks. With such an analysis we can then consider the variety of treatment techniques available to teach each of the component skills. In the case of self-control such a task analysis seems particularly worthwhile since the research has developed around particular experimental paradigms.

2. Self-Control Tasks

Imagine that you have given permission for your child to participate in an experiment to be conducted at his/her school. At the end of the week you ask your child to describe the games he/she was asked to play while in the trailer at the school. In turn, he/she describes the following games the "nice man" asked him/her to play over the course of the week.

First, the child describes some questions the man asked about preferring a small candy bar now or a much larger one in a week. Indeed, your child describes several such questions where he/she was asked to choose between a small reward that could be obtained immediately and a more valuable item that was contingent upon a delay period ranging from 1 to 4 weeks. ("Why were the big ones always later?" your child asks.)

Following these questions your child was left in the trailer with various candies that he/she could have now, or if he/she waited, more candies later. Sometimes, if your child waited a long time before calling in the man he/she could play with the better (more preferred) toy.

On another occasion when your child was left alone in the trailer, he/she was presented with a set of really nice toys "but the man said I could not touch them. If the toy was so fragile and belonged to someone else, why did the man put it out? Also I'm very careful with other people's things."

Then your child had to do some arithmetic problems but there was this "Mr. Clown" toy who kept distracting him/her. Your child had to do the arithmetic problems and disregard this distraction. Most enthusiasm was evident as your child described the scarecrow game when he/she had to imitate a scarecrow by holding his/her arms out at shoulder level for as long as possible.

Finally, the last game was held in the classroom, where the man asked your child to guess, in advance, a number from 0 to 100 that the man would draw on each trial from a lottery box. Each time the children guessed right he/she could get a point. "One thing though, since it is so hard to guess correctly, how come some children get lots of points?

"By the way," your child bemusedly asks, "what was the purpose of all those games?"

What has been briefly described are a battery of tasks that have been employed to assess self-control. The delay-of-gratification task has been extensively employed by Mischel and his colleagues (e.g., Mischel, 1974; Mischel, Ebbesen, & Zeiss, 1972), and the resistance-to-temptation task was at one time a mainstay of social learning research on self-control (e.g., Aronfreed, 1968; Cheyne & Walters, 1970; Lavoie, 1974). The scarecrow game represents a recent innovation in the child self-control literature (Karoly, 1977; Karoly & Dirks, 1977). The guessing game is in the tradition of Hartshorne and May's (1928) classic studies on cheating and it has been employed by Kanfer and Durenfeldt (1968) to study children's self-control. In fact, we could spend the remainder of this chapter just reviewing the host of tasks that have been employed to assess children's self-control. To illustrate, consider the following examples: (1) paper-and-pencil tests designed to assess children's (a) locus of control (Mischel, Zeiss, & Zeiss, 1974; Nowicki & Strickland, 1973), (b) moral reasoning (Kohlberg, 1969), (c) attributional style and motivational orientation (Dweck, 1975; Switzky & Haywood, 1974; Bugental, Whalen, & Henker, 1977), and (d) intrinsic motivation (Deci, 1975); (2) experimental tasks in which children are given instructional prohibitions not to turn around (Hartig & Kanfer, 1973) or, as mentioned above, told to delay responding, not to touch, to persist in the face of distractions, and to withstand aversive consequences; (3) experimental tasks in which children are given opportunities to cheat (O'Leary, 1968; Monahan & O'Leary, 1971) or given opportunities to violate standards that have been conveyed by means of models and/or instructions (Bandura & Perloff, 1967; Masters & Santrock, 1976) or given opportunities to self-reinforce (Kanfer, 1977; Masters & Mokros, 1974).

Parenthetically, it should be noted that one can also view the experimental tasks designed to assess prosocial behaviors within a self-control framework. Such altruistic behaviors as donating, sharing, helping, and rescuing can be viewed as requiring personal denial as in the experimental paradigms employed to assess self-control. In the studies of prosocial behaviors a conflict is established (at least that is the experimenter's intention) between a high-probability behavior that yields immediate personal gains and a low-probability behavior that yields benefits to others.

Common to the many experimental tasks employed to assess self-control is the attempt to place the child in "conflict." Two response tendencies are pitted against one another. Experimental situations are arranged so that compliance with the natural behavioral tendency (playing with the preferred toy, being distracted, dropping one's arms in the scarecrow game) represents, from the experimenter's viewpoint, less self-control. It is not always clear that the children view these experimental challenges as instances requiring self-control. Indeed, one can look upon the variety of self-control tasks as a means of assessing the children's disposition to engage in play behavior (i.e., the ability to engage in fantasy play or the ability to do something else).

These reservations notwithstanding, the basic experimental paradigm to assess children's self-control involves the interruption of a natural sequence of behaviors by means of some instructional demand imposed by the experimenter. That such tasks can generate conflict for children is illustrated by a description of how children behaved in a delay-of-gratification task:

> When the distress of waiting seemed to become especially acute, children tended to reach for the termination signal, but in many cases seemed to stop themselves from signaling by abruptly creating external and internal distractions for themselves. They made up quiet signs . . . hid their heads in their arms, pounded the floor with their feet, fiddled playfully and teasingly with the signal bell, verbalized the contingency ("If I stop now I get . . . , but if I wait I get. . . ."), prayed to the ceiling, and so on. In one dramatically effective self-distraction technique, after obviously experiencing much agitation, a little girl rested her head, sat limply, relaxed herself, and proceeded to fall sound asleep. (Mischel et al., 1972, p. 215)

A second commonality across several of the experimental self-control tasks is for the experimenter to expose children to some standard performance by means of instructions or models and to assess the child's compliance with the standard.

It should be apparent from a description of these tasks that self-control does *not* represent a unitary process but instead represents a multidimensional process involving situational, perceptual, cognitive, behavioral, attitudinal, and motivational components. In the various laboratory studies each of these components has been manipulated (see Karoly, 1977 for a review of these studies). Moreover, consistency of self-regulatory behavior across a variety of tasks has *not* been demonstrated in children. In fact, the research by Anderson, Fodor, and Alpert (1976), Robin (1966), and Toner *et al*. (1977) indicates that self-control is not a unitary process or trait. Instead, self-control behaviors are markedly influenced by situational demands, so that there is a need to provide specific treatment approaches appropriate to specific self-control goals. Given that self-control is a complex process, the present conceptualization is to view it as a set of separate teachable and learnable skills. These skills will be described below and guidelines for teaching them to children will be noted. We will examine the various literatures cited above for guidelines as to how the respective component skills can be taught to children.

The discussion thus far indicates that the construct of self-control has been applied in a variety of situations that require the individual to (a) demonstrate behavioral restraint such as delay of gratification or show persistence; (b) eliminate maladaptive responses; (c) establish adaptive approach responses that aid in the tolerance of unpleasant, strenuous, or difficult situations that carry the long-term promise of reward (i.e., short-range unpleasant, but long-range positive consequences); (d) demonstrate behavior patterns that are contrary to the conspicuous environmental consequences. In short, as Kanfer (1977) has indicated, self-control applies when the probability of a response with initial high likelihood of occurrence is decreased and the probability of a response with initially low likelihood is increased by the execution of self-generated behaviors. Self-control refers to behavior initiated by the individual, where such behavior is relatively free from external constraints.

In order to further identify the component skills that contribute to self-control, it is useful to examine briefly the several conceptualizations that have been offered to describe and explain self-control.

3. Conceptualizations of Self-Control

Although one can find many historical forerunners to B. F. Skinner's discussion of self-control, such as William James's, it is to Skinner's credit that in 1953 in *Science and Human Behavior* he suggested how a person could use specific skills to change his/her own behavior. Before citing Skinner's suggestions it is worthwhile to note William James's advice. In 1918, in discussing "habits," James stated that an individual must

> accumulate all the possible circustances which shall re-enforce the right motives; put yourself assiduously in conditions that encourage the new way;

> make engagements incompatible with the old; take a public pledge, if the
> case allows; in short envelope your resolution with every aid you know.

See Mahoney and Thoresen (1974), Thoresen and Mahoney (1974), and Thoresen, Gray-Kirmil, and Crosbie (1977) for additional examples of historical forerunners prior to Skinner who discussed ways of establishing self-control.

According to Skinner's operant conditioning model of self-control, one controls his/her own behavior in precisely the same way that he/she controls the behavior of anyone else, through manipulation of the variables of which the behavior is a function. For example, for one to decrease an undesirable behavior in oneself, one makes the undesirable response less probable by the rewards on which it depends. Goldiamond (1965) aptly summarizes this approach by stating: "If you want a specific behavior from yourself, set up the conditions which you know will control it."

Since the focus of this chapter is the teaching of self-control it is worthwhile to list briefly the techniques Skinner offered in 1953 that are available to the individual to exercise self-control. (1) Employing physical restraint and physical aids that help the individual to avoid some form of punishment or to achieve some reward more easily (e.g., removing the child from the situation). (2) Changing the stimulus involves identifying the eliciting or discriminative stimuli for the desired/ undesired response and seeing that they are presented or removed from the situation (e.g., changing situations where temptations are removed). (3) Directly applying deprivation and satiation to the response to be elicited or extinguished, or applied to the competing response. Skinner offers several examples of self-satiation or self-deprivation. For example, an individual who has a habit of nail-biting is instructed to intentionally bite his nails to the point of satiation. (4) Manipulating emotional conditions involves a variety of measures, both physical and symbolic, which lead to changes in emotional states (e.g., getting oneself in a good mood or rehearsing past punishments, or counting to 10 when angry). (5) Using aversive stimulation is offered in both concrete and symbolic forms for controlling behavior (e.g., setting alarm clocks, emitting self-statements such as "get up," and making public commitments are but a few of the examples offered by Skinner). In short, we engineer our environment to increase the likelihood that self-control behaviors will be emitted. To quote Skinner:

> We prepare aversive stimuli which will control our own future behavior
> when we make a resolution. This is essentially a prediction concerning our
> own behavior. By making it in the presence of people who supply aversive
> stimulation when a prediction is not fulfilled, we arrange consequences

which are likely to strengthen the behavior resolved upon. Only by behaving
as predicted can we escape the aversive consequences of breaking our resolu-
tion. (1953, p. 237)

I quote Skinner because this passage is a harbinger of issues to be
discussed below on the correspondence between the verbal and behavior repertoire or the link between what one says and what one does.

The remaining suggestions offered by Skinner include operant conditioning, punishment, drugs, and "doing something else." It is interesting to juxtapose Skinner's list with the set of controlling responses
the children used in the delay-of-gratification task as cited above in the
quote of Mischel *et al*. It should be indicated that although one can view
the several procedures Skinner has described from a number of different
perspectives (e.g., see Mahoney, 1974; Meichenbaum, 1977), Skinner's
list does provide a motif against which to consider alternative conceptualizations of self-control.

Kanfer (1977) has offered a model of self-control involving (1) making a commitment to change a behavior (2) setting a standard or criterion of behavior change as a goal (3) self-monitoring and self-evaluating
the behavior in question, and (4) self-rewarding when the behavior
reaches the standard or criterion. Kanfer distinguishes two stages of
self-control, namely, decisional self-control and protracted self-control.
The first stage of decisional self-control is characterized by the requirement "for a clear and momentary decision to choose among alternatives." Decisional self-control takes place when the individual is presented with two or more choices and in the situation only a single response needs to be made. But once a decision has been made, the consequences to the individual are no longer under his control. By contrast,
protracted self-control involves self-monitoring, self-evaluating, and
self-rewarding the desired changes in one's behavior over time.

The heuristic value of a sequential component model of self-control
is illustrated in a study by Spates and Kanfer (1977). They tested the
relative contributions of the self-monitoring, criterion-setting, self-
evaluation, and self-reinforcement components in the learning of a simple arithmetic task in first-graders. Training consisted of teaching the
children to generate different self-instructions while doing the task. The
results indicated that the inclusion of criterion setting in training was
the most significant feature. Training in additional components, i.e.,
self-reinforcement and self-monitoring plus criterion setting, yielded no
further significant reduction in arithmetic errors. At least in this study
the suggestion is offered that the establishment of a criterion against
which a child can assess his current performance is a critical element in
the use of self-control to improve performance. (See Greiner and Karoly,
1976, for an example of this dismantling research strategy with adults.)

A related model of self-control has been offered by Thoresen and his colleagues (Thoresen & Coates, 1976; Thoresen & Mahoney, 1974; Thoresen *et al.*, 1977). Like the Kanfer model, the Thoresen model emphasizes the role of self-monitoring, self-evaluation, and self-reinforcement; however, it does not draw any distinction along the time dimension between decisional and protracted self-control. Consistent with the notions of Mischel (1973), Thoresen and his colleagues highlight the role of mediational processes as a critical feature of self-control. Such concepts as "contingency rules" are embraced to explain the guidance of behavior in the absence of, or sometimes despite, contrary pressures from the external situation. These contingency rules or plans tell the person what kinds of behavior are appropriate or expected under particular conditions, what performance levels (standards) the behavior must achieve, and the consequences for reaching or failing to reach stated standards. In short, from this more cognitive view Thoresen *et al.* (1977) describe self-control as a problem involving conscious effort made in trying to implement a choice between options having conflicting consequences. The Thoresen *et al.* model thus highlights the role of decision making and problem solving as contributing to self-control. Table 1, taken from Thoresen and Coates (1976), conveys the sequential mediational processes involved in self-control.

From a different vantage point I have also highlighted the role of cognitive processes in the self-control process (Meichenbaum, 1976). I argued that in order to bring about behavioral change (including self-control) a sequential mediating process must be established. The first step in the change process is the individual's becoming an observer of his own behavior. Through heightened awareness and deliberate attention, the individual must monitor with increased sensitivity the target behaviors, be they thoughts, feelings, and/or interpersonal behaviors. In order to develop self-control the individual must interrupt the sequence of behaviors and thoughts preceding a maladaptive response and must produce incompatible self-instructions, images, and behaviors. The maladaptive behaviors that are habitual in nature (i.e., not premeditated) must first be returned to a "de-automatized" condition; that is, the "target" behaviors should be preceded by deliberate cognitions. Such "forced mediation" increases the likelihood of interrupting a chain of events that would otherwise lead to the maladaptive response. As I will highlight below in the section on self-instructional training, the development of self-control will be enhanced if the inhibition of impulses can occur at a low level of intensity or at an incipient stage. The goal is to teach the child to identify the impulse early and to have him/her attempt to control it at that incipient stage and then to practice self-control responses at increasingly greater levels of intensity. Thus, by teaching chil-

TABLE 1
Strategies of Self-Control[a]

Strategy 1: Developing and maintaining commitment
   a. Substitute more adaptive self-attributions about nature of problem.
   b. What "if-then" relationships do you see between certain actions and particular outcomes?
   c. Identify and systematically anticipate several positive outcomes of your new behavior.

Strategy 2: Observing one's activities
   a. What do you say to yourself about
      (i) the behavior you want to change?
      (ii) your ability to change it?
      (iii) your progress?
   b. Under what circumstances do you currently engage in the behavior you want to change?
   c. How frequently or how much do you currently engage in the behavior you want to change?

Strategy 3: Planning the environment
   a. Establish a supportive environment: Teach family, friends, and/or associates how you would like them to help.
   b. Modify the stimuli or cues that evoke the behavior you want to change.
      (i) external: Rearrange your physical environment.
      (ii) internal: Alter undesirable internal cues such as thoughts and images.
   c. Develop a contract that specifies goals, behavior needed to attain those goals, and consequences for success and failure.

Strategy 4: Arranging consequences (behavioral programming)
   a. Self-reward
      (i) covert: Plan positive thoughts to follow successful actions.
      (ii) overt: Plan to give yourself or have someone give you a reward for success (e.g., playing golf on Saturday, a gift.
   b. Self-punishment
      (i) covert: Plan negative thoughts and/or images to follow immediately undesired actions.
      (ii) overt: Withold a selected pleasant activity (e.g., watching your favorite TV show) or take away something you have (e.g., fine yourself $1 for each occurrence of undesirable behavior.

---

[a] From Thoresen and Coates (1976).

dren (1) to recognize and label their impulses and the cues that instigate them at different levels of intensity and (2) to spontaneously employ cognitive and behavioral coping responses, they will develop self-control.

Thus, the first stage in developing self-control is increased awareness and self-monitoring. In order to perceive the subsequent stages, consider the example of someone interrupting you and then drawing your attention to some aspect of your behavior. What is likely to happen when such an interruption occurs? I would suggest that you are quite likely to engage in some "internal dialogue" (i.e., a set of thoughts and images that you are, or can be, made aware of). A variety of factors will influence the content of your internal dialogue at that specific moment following interruptions. Your internal dialogue—namely, appraisals, attributions, expectations—will influence your behavior. What you do, vis-à-vis the individual who interrupted you, will in turn elicit his/her reactions and this in turn will affect your internal dialogue as well as your behaviors, and so forth. Thus, a cycle is established involving your behavior, the interpersonal consequences that follow your behavior, and your accompanying internal dialogue. In the same way that someone else can interrupt you to affect your mode of behavior you can similarly interrupt yourself. Such an interruption leads to an internal dialogue and this internal dialogue influences whether or not you will emit self-controlling responses. Therefore, from the viewpoint of teaching self-control, it will be argued that it is important to influence the nature of the internal dialogue that is emitted as part of the self-control process. From this viewpoint, the individual's cognitions play a central role in the development of self-control. (See Meichenbaum, 1976, 1977, for a more complete discussion of these issues.)

Whereas the operant approach focuses attention on the rearrangement of the external environment to help establish self-control, the more cognitive conceptualization of self-control (e.g., Mahoney, Thoresen, Meichenbaum) supplements the operant approach by helping individuals to alter their internal environments (i.e., thoughts, images, mood states). Note that both the operant and cognitive approaches to self-control often overlap in their specific advice concerning the teaching of self-control, but they differ mainly in how they describe their respective efforts and their respective starting points, and in where they would focus their intervention efforts.

4. Training Procedures

Most accounts of the self-control literature suggest that how we conceptualize self-control influences how we attempt to study and how we teach it. I would suggest that more often the reverse occurs. The practical problems of teaching self-control often alter the way we conceptualize the processes of self-control. The bidirectional influences between theory and practice will become more evident as we turn our attention to the training procedures that have been employed to teach children self-control.

Four major training procedures will be discussed, namely, operant conditioning, modeling, self-instructional training, and problem-solving training. It should be noted at the outset that in many (if not most) cases these procedures are administered in combination. Few, if any, comparative studies have been conducted on the respective training procedures with children.

4.1. Operant Conditioning

The thrust of the research on operant conditioning with children has been to demonstrate clearly that the manner and frequency with which peer and adult behavioral consequences follow a child's behavior have a significant impact on that child's behavior. A review of this literature is beyond the scope of the present chapter. The interested reader should see Kazdin (1977) and O'Leary and O'Leary (1976, 1977). Instead, the present review will briefly examine the use of operant procedures as a means of fostering children's self-control.

Two major concerns have given impetus to the work on self-control by operant conditioners. One source is the whole issue of treatment generalization and how such generalization can be enhanced (Stokes & Baer, 1977). The second concern involves the touchy issue of "control" that has enveloped the use of operant procedures, especially as applied to the classroom (O'Leary, Poulous, & Devine, 1972; Winnett & Winkler, 1972). Closely akin to these social-ethical arguments are empirical concerns about the impact operant programs have on children's motivational systems (de Charmes, 1968; Deci, 1975; Steiner, 1970). In an attempt to humanize the operant procedures and in the search for greater treatment efficacy a number of operant studies have been conducted where the child is treated as a collaborator in the implementation of the operant procedures. The child's contribution to the operant program may be at any or all of the following points: (1) self-determination of goals and reinforcement standards (2) self-evaluation and (3) self-reinforcement. Illustrative studies and summary findings for each of these stages will be offered.

4.1.1. Goals and Reinforcement Standards

Two examples where children have contributed to the self-determination of goals and reinforcement standards will be described. The first example is a laboratory study, conducted by Bandura and Perloff (1967) in which they investigated self- versus external-imposition of standards of reinforcement. Children in one condition selected their own reinforcement criteria for work on a motor task (wheel cranking), and the children administered their own rewards upon reaching those standards. A yoked group had rewards imposed upon them and were given rewards by the experimenter. Bandura and Perloff found that external-imposition subjects and self-determination subjects performed significantly better than control subjects, but they did not differ from each other. These results have been replicated under similar experimental conditions (Liebert, Spiegler, & Hall, 1970; Switzky & Haywood, 1974), as well as under academic conditions (Felixbrod & O'Leary, 1973, 1974).

As part of their operant training program (i.e., Achievement Place), Phillips, Phillips, Fixsen, and Wolf (1972) taught adolescents rule development. The adolescents initially had rules imposed and were in turn taught how to (1) establish new rules and modify old rules, (2) give reasons for each rule, and (3) establish consequences for rule violations. While the focus of the Achievement Place program was on the manipulation of environmental consequences, the rule-development aspect of the program aided the adolescents in learning how to determine goals.

Recent evidence that contingent reinforcement is more effective when performance standards were self-determined than when standards were externally imposed has been offered by Brownell, Colletti, Ersner-Hershfield, Hershfield and Wilson (1977). The Brownell *et al.* results must be qualified as the differential benefits of self-determination of standards was found with one dependent measure (time at task while doing arithmetic problems), while the other dependent measure (number of correct solutions) showed equal effectiveness for both self-determination and external imposition of standards.

After reviewing the literature on self-determination of goals and reinforcement standards O'Leary and O'Leary (1976) conclude:

> With few exceptions, one can conclude from present evidence that a self-determined reinforcement standard results in productivity equivalent to an externally determined reinforcement standard. (p. 494)

They also offer a caveat:

> As long as children realize that there are no aversive consequences for imposing very lenient standards of reinforcement, they will often do so. In brief, if relatively high standards of reinforcement are to be maintained, some surveillance and social reinforcement for high standard setting generally must be maintained. (p.494)

4.1.2. Self-Evaluation

The concerns O'Leary and O'Leary raise are also evident in children's involvement in self-evaluation as well as self-reinforcement. Note that the operant approach is attempting to teach self-control behaviors, yet the absence of self-control responses may often mitigate the implementation of that very operant program. A study by Santogrossi, O'Leary, Romanczyk, and Kaufman (1973) examined ways to handle the child's accuracy in self-recording and self-evaluating performance. Some of the problems that are involved are illustrated by Felixbrod and O'Leary (1973), who found that children initially tended to impose stringent standards on themselves but became more lenient over time in the absence of social surveillance.

Perhaps the best study on self-evaluation was conducted by Drabman, Spitalnik, and O'Leary (1973), who taught emotionally disturbed children to evaluate their own behavior in a token program on a 1-10 rating scale. In order to teach accurate self-evaluations, the children's self-evaluations were checked with those of the teacher and points were subtracted or awarded depending upon how closely the children's ratings matched the teacher's ratings. The self-evaluative token program was effective in reducing the children's classroom disruptive behavior and, most importantly, the effects generalized to a generalization (non-token) period. Turkewitz, O'Leary, and Ironsmith (1975) replicated the Drabman et al. study even though in this study both teacher surveillance and backup reinforcers were faded. These results, in concert with other findings by Santogrossi et al. (1973) and Kaufman and O'Leary (1972), have indicated that self-control interventions can be effective in maintaining behavior change previously elicited by an external reinforcement system. Indeed, Broden, Hall, and Mitts (1971) reported that when children were given an opportunity to record their own inattentive and disruptive behavior in the classroom, these behaviors improved even though no external consequences were provided. The full potential of using self-monitoring procedures with children has not yet been fully explored. (See Kunzelmann, 1970, for some innovative attempts to have children learn to self-monitor their behavior.)

4.1.3. Self-Reinforcement

Although there is some controversy (e.g., Bandura, 1976; Brigham, 1977; Catania, 1975) about the conceptual basis of self-reinforcement, several studies, conducted primarily in the classroom, have shown that children can reward themselves with tokens and that their behavior usually improves as a result (e.g., Bolstad & Johnson, 1972; Felixbrod & O'Leary, 1973, 1974; Lovitt & Curtiss, 1969; McLaughlin & Malaby, 1974). Other studies have shown that teacher-determined and self-determined token reinforcements are equally effective (Felixbrod & O'Leary, 1973, 1974; Glynn, 1970; Glynn, Thomas, & Shee, 1973).

In our lab, Helen Best (1973) examined the maintenance of kindergarten children's persistence behavior in a simple match-to-sample discrimination task following a reinforcement training, where the reinforcement was either self-administered or externally administered by the experimenter. A second variable examined in the study was whether the reinforcement was social (praise) or material (edibles). Using an ABA design she found that the social-self condition was most effective in combating extinction effects. In order to have the children self-praise their performance (social self-condition, for example, "good," "fine," or "I'm doing a good job"), Best included the instruction "It's kind of like being your own teacher and telling yourself what a good job you are doing." Children complied with this instruction and readily evaluated and socially reinforced themselves. The instruction to act as if you are your own teacher helped to mitigate the embarrassment that often accompanies social self-praise, especially when spoken aloud.

Parenthetically, it is interesting to note that one can find innumerable instances in which individuals castigate or verbally punish themselves aloud, but within our culture to praise oneself aloud is usually viewed as socially unacceptable.

In fine, the operant research on maximizing long-term maintenance has only recently begun. As with the other approaches for establishing children's self-control, the operant procedures can only offer promissory notes. Any attempts to train maintenance of behavior change would do well to take heed of the advice offered by Stokes and Baer (1977), who indicate that we need an implicit technology of generalization, and that the concept of generalization as it is applied across settings, persons, and time needs to be reconceptualized.

The effort to develop operant programs that include self-control elements is appealing, not only because of its efficiency, in terms of teachers' time, but because it includes the added incentive of involving the children and providing them with choice and opportunities for decision making that in itself likely has reinforcing aspecs (e.g., see Brigham, 1977). As the children become involved in the operant program they learn skills that they can use to change their own environments. The potential of these procedures will be evident as we examine the more cognitively based attempts to teach children self-control.

4.2. Modeling

It is mainly within the last 10 years that the full therapeutic potential of behavioral, cognitive, and imaginal modeling has begun to be realized (Rosenthal, 1976). Part of the impetus for this has been the growing realization that modeling or observational learning should *not* be equated with mimicry or exact matching or superficial imitation. Instead, the exposure to a modeling display permits the discrimination and organized memory of relatively complex and integrated behavior chains that may then be retrieved to satisfy environmental demands. Bandura (1969) has emphasized that the information that observers gain from models is converted to covert perceptual-cognitive images and covert mediating rehearsal responses that are retained by the observer and later used by him/her as symbolic cues to overt behaviors.

Bandura's work has been a prototype for laboratory studies of how modeling can be employed to establish and enhance children's self-control behaviors. Within the laboratory context a whole host of children's self-control behaviors have been increased as a result of exposure to either live or symbolic child or adult models. Some of the self-controlling behaviors that have been successfully modeled within a laboratory context include self-imposed delay of reward (Bandura & Mischel, 1965), adoption of self-evaluative standards (Allen & Liebert, 1969), patterns of self-reinforcement (Bandura & Kupers, 1964), moral reasoning (Bandura & MacDonald, 1963), and reflective thinking behaviors (Debus, 1970). Moreover, if the modeling displays are accompanied by the observing children's emitting task-relevant verbalizations (Wolf, 1973) or persuasive arguments supportive of delay (Staub, 1972), or if the children are permitted to practice requisite responses (White, 1972), then self-control performance is even further augmented.

The translation of these laboratory findings to clinical and pedagogical application of teaching children self-control has been quite limited. As in the case of operant conditioning, the potential of the modeling procedures has not been realized. Some beginnings, however, have been offered by Stumphauzer (1972), Fry (1972), and Prentice (1972), who have experimented on a short-term basis with the use of modeling procedures to teach delay of gratification to adolescent delinquents. Perhaps the best demonstration of how modeling (plus behavioral rehearsal) can be employed to teach children self-control responses has been offered by Sarason and Ganzer (1973), who successfully taught delinquent boys a host of self-control as well as interpersonal problem-solving skills. A recent example of how modeling of self-control can be employed with younger children was offered by Goodwin and Mahoney (1975). In a series of case studies, they used a circle game to alter behavior in aggressive hyperactive boys between the ages of 6 and 11. The circle game involves having children taunt a child who is in the center of the circle. Prior to a child's taking a turn in the center he is exposed to a videotaped model with dubbed-in thoughts and instructional commentary that cognitively models how to cope with such provocations. The therapist supplements the modeling with coaching and practice.

The potential of using modeling to enhance children's self-control (as in the case of overcoming a fear) was recognized some time ago. Consider the following quote:

> Your child shrieks and runs away at the sight of a frog, let another catch it, and lay it down at a good distance from him; at first accustom him to look upon it; when he can do it directly, following you, to come nearer to it, and see it leap without emotion; then to touch it directly, when it is held fast in another's hand; and so on until he can come to handle it confidently as a butterfly, or sparrow.

This quote is not from a study by Bandura and his colleagues on participant modeling with a phobic child but was instead offered in 1693 by John Locke. The quote nicely reminds us that the various self-control procedures reviewed in this chapter reach back over the centuries. Perhaps such observations will lessen our moments of pretentiousness.

Finally, if self-control is viewed as a multicomponent set of subskills, then modeling in conjunction with other procedures may have much pedagogical and clinical potential. This potential will be evident as we now turn to a consideration of self-instructional training.

4.3. Self-Instructional Training

Since both the empirical research and clinical data on self-instructional training with children has recently been reviewed in detail (Craighead, Craighead-Wilcoxon, & Meyers, 1978; Karoly, 1977; Kendall, 1977; Meichenbaum, 1977), the present focus will be on the developmental research and theory that gave impetus to the self-instructional procedure. With this as background information we can then summarize the empirical studies that have evaluated the efficacy of the self-instructional training regimen.

Developmental research on a number of related problems has contributed to the burgeoning interest in self-instructional training. One prominent research area has been the self-control laboratory-based investigation of children's self-mediated cognitive strategies. For example, Mischel and his colleagues have examined specific types of cognitive variables involved in children's ability to delay gratification. In the Mischel paradigm, nursery school children are placed alone before a less preferred but immediate reward and asked to wait for a more preferred but delayed reward. Mischel (1974) has found that effective self-generated strategies reduce frustration. These include:

1. *Not* focusing attention on the actual rewards, but instead thinking about the rewarding qualities of an equally pleasurable, but unavailable reward. The actual contents of the children's distracting cognitions proved important (e.g., "think fun" was more effective than "think

sad"). Masters and Santrock (1976) have reported similar findings in a children's persistence task. They report that children persist less when they become self-critical instead of self-praising.

Cognitively transforming the rewards to minimize their motivational arousal. Even when the actual tantalizing objects were in front of the children the strategy of cognitively transforming the objects was effective in increasing delay of gratification. (For example, the children imagined the pretzel sticks as "little brown logs" or the marshmallows as "fluffy white clouds.") Moore, Mischel, and Zeiss (1976) have recently demonstrated that the manner in which the child cognitively represents rewards is a much more potent determiner of his/her delay behavior than is the actual reward stimulus in front of the child.

3. Using individually oriented self-instructions and cognitive activities such as self-praise, overt repeating of the experimental contingency, and spontaneous self-instructional strategies (e.g., "If I just wait a little more, I'll get it for sure—yes he'll come back soon now").

The series of studies by Mischel and his colleagues using the delay-of-gratification task as well as a perseverance task (e.g., see Patterson & Mischel, 1975, 1976) underscores the powerful role of cognitive appraisal in children's self-control. Kanfer and his colleagues, using different experimental tasks of tolerance for exposure to total darkness in 5- and 6-year-olds (Kanfer, Karoly, & Newman, 1975) and children's transgression latencies in a resistance-to-temptation situation (Hartig & Kanfer, 1973), also found that the content of the children's self-statements significantly influenced performance.

A second major impetus to the work in self-instructional training was the developmental theorizing and research conducted by the Soviet psychologists Vygotsky (1962) and Luria (1961, 1969). Luria proposed three stages by which the initiation and inhibition of voluntary motor behaviors come under verbal control. During the first stage, the speech of others, usually adults, controls and directs a child's behavior. In the second stage, the child's own overt speech becomes an effective regulator of his behavior. Finally, the child's covert or inner speech assumes a self-governing role. (See Meichenbaum, 1975; Meichenbaum & Goodman, 1978; Wozniak, 1972, for more detailed presentations of the Soviet position.)

In an attempt to combine the developmental social learning literature (as exemplified by Mischel, Kanfer) and the Soviet developmental theory, Meichenbaum and Goodman (1971) developed a self-instructional training regimen that was composed of combinations of modeling, overt and covert rehearsal, prompts, feedback, and social reinforcement. In short, a multifaceted training format was developed in order to teach hyperactive children to "think before they act," to become more reflective in their behavior, to develop self-control. The training regimen included the following procedural steps: (1) An adult model performed a task while talking to himself out loud (cognitive modeling); (2) the child performed the same task under the direction of the model's instructions (overt, external guidance); (3) the child performed the task while instructing himself aloud (overt self-guidance); (4) the child whispered the instructions to himself as he went through the task (faded, overt self-guidance); and finally (5) the child performed the task while guiding his performance via private speech (covert self-instruction).

Over a number of training sessions the package of self-statements modeled by the experimenter and rehearsed by the child (initially aloud and then covertly) was enlarged by means of response chaining and successive approximation procedures. For example, in a task that required the copying of line patterns, the examiner performed the task while cognitively modeling as follows:

> Okay, what is it I have to do? You want me to copy the picture with the different lines. I have to go slowly and carefully. Okay, draw the line down, down, good; then to the right, that's it; now down some more and to the left. Good, I'm doing fine so far. Remember, go slowly. Now back up again. No, I was supposed to go down. That's okay. Just erase the line carefully. . . . Good. Even if I make an error I can go on slowly and carefully. I have to go down now. Finished. I did it! (Meichenbaum & Goodman, 1971, p. 117)

In this thinking-out-loud phase, the model displayed several performance-relevant skills: (1) problem definition ("what is it I have to do?"); (2) focusing attention and response guidance ("carefully . . . draw the line down"); (3) self-reinforcement ("Good, I'm doing fine"): and (4) self-evaluative coping skills and error-correcting options ("That's okay. . . . Even if I make an error I can go on slowly").

A variety of tasks was employed to train the child to use self-instructions to control his nonverbal behavior. The tasks varied from simple sensorimotor abilities to more complex problem-solving abilities. The sensorimotor tasks, such as copying line patterns and coloring figures within boundaries, provided first the model, then the child, with the opportunity to produce a narrative description of the behavior, both preceding and accompanying performance. Over the course of a training session the child's overt self-statements on a particular task were faded to the covert level. The difficulty of the training tasks was increased over the training sessions, using more cognitively demanding activities. Hence, there was a progression from tasks such as reproducing designs and following sequential instructions taken from the Stanford-Binet intelligence test, to completing such pictorial series as on the Primary Mental Abilities test, to solving conceptual tasks such as Raven's Matrices. The experimenter modeled appropriate self-verbalizations for each of these tasks and then had the child follow the fading procedure.

The self-instructional training procedure, relative to placebo and assessment control groups, resulted in significantly improved performance on Porteus Maze, performance IQ on the WISC, and increased cognitive reflectivity on the Matching Familiar Figures test (MFF). The improved performance was evident in a 1-month follow-up. Moreover, it was observed that 60% of the self-instructionally trained impulsive children spontaneously were talking to themselves in the posttest and follow-up sessions.

The self-instructional paradigm has now been used successfully to establish inner speech control over the disruptive behavior of hyperactive children (Douglas, Parry, Marton, & Garson, 1976), by aggressive children (Camp, Blom, Hebert, & van Doorninck, 1977), by disruptive preschoolers (Bornstein & Quevillon, 1976), over cheating behavior in kindergarteners, and first-graders (Monahan & O'Leary, 1971), on Porteus Maze performance of hyperactive boys (Palkes, Stewart, & Freedman, 1972; Palkes, Stewart, & Kahana, 1968), on the conceptual tempo of emotionally disturbed boys (Finch, Wilkinson, Nelson, & Montgomery, 1975) as well as on normal children (Bender, 1976; Meichenbaum & Goodman, 1971).

The Douglas *et al.* study nicely illustrates the general treatment approach, as the hyperactive children were initially exposed to a model who verbalized the following cognitive strategies, which the child could in turn rehearse, initially aloud and then covertly. The cognitive strategies included stopping to define a problem and the various steps within it; considering and evaluating several possible solutions before acting on any one; checking one's work throughout and calmly correcting any errors; sticking with a problem until everything possible has been tried to solve it correctly; and giving oneself a pat on the back for work well done. Verbalizations modeled by the trainer to illustrate these strategies included:

> "I must stop and think before I begin." "What plans can I try?" "How would it work out if I did that?" "What shall I try next?" "Have I got it right so far?" "See, I made a mistake there—I'll just erase it." "Now let's see, have I tried everything I can think of?" "I've done a pretty good job! (Douglas *et al.*, 1976, p. 408)

The cognitive training was applied across tasks in order to ensure that the children did *not* just develop task-specific response sets but instead developed cognitive representations. This latter point needs to be underscored. The process by which socialized (or external) speech develops into egocentric (or internal) speech and then into inner speech requires much considerations. As Vygotsky (1962) noted in *Thought and Language*, this process of internalization and abbreviation should *not* be viewed merely as a process of faded speech; instead the transformation from interpersonal speech to thought represents qualitative differences in structure. How interpersonal instructions modeled by a therapist, teacher, or parent change into the child's own private speech and thought is a major theoretical and practical question. The answer to this question will have major implications for the potential of self-instructional training with children. (See Meichenbaum, 1977, for a discussion of these issues.)

Recent studies have been conducted to dismantle the complex self-instructional regimen in order to discern the active ingredient(s). For example, Alkus (1977) examined the relative contributions of problem-solving versus coping self-statements versus reattribution training (as in Dweck, 1975) in aiding second-graders in classroom academic performance. The training was conducted in the classroom. The problem-solving group focused on definition of problem and self-guiding self-statements. The coping group focused on error-correcting strategies that included identification of errors and normalizing self-statements of a self-reinforcing nature. In terms of treatment generalization Alkus found that a self-instructional training regimen that teaches children strategies for dealing specifically with errors and concomitant frustration/failure experiences seemed critical to achieving generalization. The Alkus study represents one of several studies that have attempted to examine the components of self-instructional training (see Bender, 1976; Bugental *et al.*, 1977; Denney, 1975; Jakibchuk & Smeriglio, 1976; Kanfer *et al.*, 1975; Meichenbaum & Goodman, 1971).

Of the studies cited, the study by Bugental *et al.* deserves special mention because they examined the interaction between the children's motivational style and the particular mode of treatment intervention. Hyperactive boys were individually tutored for 2 months in a classroom setting: Half were instructed in self-instructional training and half received an operant social reinforcement program. Significant interactive effects were found between the intervention approach and children's attributional style. "Luck" attributors showed greater improvement following the reinforcement method, whereas "effort" attributors benefited from self-instructional training. The Bugental *et al.* study highlights the potential value of matching a child's attributional style with attributional assumptions in an intervention package ("different strokes for different folks").

Elsewhere (Meichenbaum, 1977), I have described a host of clinical suggestions as to how self-instructional training can be conducted with children. These included (1) using the child's own medium of play to initiate and model self-talk; (2) using tasks that have a high "pull" for the use of sequential cognitive strategies; (3) using peer teaching by having children cognitively model while performing for another child; (4) moving through the program at the child's own rate, and building up the package of self-statements to include self-talk of a problem-solving variety as well as coping and self-reinforcing elements; (5) guarding against the child using the self-statements in a mechanical noninvolved fashion; (6) including a therapist who is animated and responsive to the child; (7) learning to use the self-instructional training with low-intensity responses; (8) supplementing the training with imagery practice such as the "turtle technique" (Schneider & Robin, 1976); (9) supplementing the self-instructional training with correspondence training (Risley, 1977; Rogers-Warren & Baer, 1976); (10) supplementing the self-instructional training with operant procedures such as a response-cost system (Kendall & Finch, 1976, 1978; Nelson, 1976; Robertson & Keeley, 1974).

Of the many clinical suggestions that I have listed, two bear special mention, namely, the use of correspondence training and the use of play.

4.3.1. Correspondence Training

The objective of the self-instructional training approach is *not* to focus overly on language but rather to bring the child's behavior in alignment with his verbal statements or, in other words, to establish some correspondence between what he says (word) and what he does (deed). Using the scarecrow game, Karoly and Dirks (1977) found that if preschoolers were contingently reinforced upon matching verbal report to actual performance then their self-control improved. Consistent with the findings of others (Israel & O'Leary, 1973; Kurtz, Neisworth, Goeke, & Hanson, 1976; Risley & Hart, 1968), Karoly and Dirks found that the level of correspondence exhibited was greater for the say-do group than a do-say group. Thus, if you elicit from the child a detailed specification of his/her intention and then provide explicit feedback as to whether he/she has complied with the previous intentional statement, correspondence training will be established. If such intention-execution sequences are contingently reinforced then self-control increases. Risley (1977) nicely illustrated the potential of correspondence training in a study of preschool children. The target behavior was picking up litter in the school yard. During the initial phase of the study, the children's intention statements that they would pick up the litter were reinforced. Like those of some adults, the children's verbal statements did not alter their litter-picking-up behavior (e.g., note the questionable effects of

New Year's Eve's resolutions on adult behaviors). However, when children's discussion sessions were also used as an opportunity to give feedback on the correspondence between the verbal commitment and the actual behaviors on the playground, the picking-up-better behaviors began to occur. Writers with an operant viewpoint tend to describe the correspondence training in terms of mediated generalization (e.g., Stokes & Baer, 1977) or they view the intention statement (saying) as a verbal operant for execution of the intention behavior (doing). I am partial to my mother's description of correspondence training: eliciting guilt ("You said you were going to do it, but you didn't do it, etc.").

4.3.2. Use of Play

Whereas the focus of this section has been on the use of language to enhance children's self-control, a growing literature has indicated that imagery and fantasy procedures can also be successfully employed. An important study that gave impetus to the use of fantasy play for altering children's behavior was conducted by Smilansky (1968). Smilansky found that as a result of the role-playing behavior in sociodramatic play, children were less aggressive and impulsive; they emitted more positive affect; they increased their use of parts of speech and in general increased their verbal communications. Freyberg (1973) essentially replicated Smilansky's approach and noted that enhanced fantasy play proved to be associated with greater verbal communication, longer and more complex sentence usage, more sensitive responding to the cues of other children, increased attention span, and more positive expression of emotions. Saltz and Johnson (1974) and Saltz, Dixon, and Johnson (1977) compared what they call thematic fantasy play with Smilansky's sociodramatic-play approach. The thematic fantasy play focuses the children's play and role enactment on fairy tales, whereas the sociodramatic approach uses the children's daily common experiences. The preliminary results suggest that the addition of the pretend elements in the form of thematic fantasy adds to the training package.

These studies, as well as the work by Singer, Nahmettuang, and Wheaton (1976), underscore the observation by Feitelson and Ross (1973) that play as a means of socialization (and I would add as a means of teaching children self-control) has been a neglected factor. This should *not* be the case when one considers that the thrust of the use of imagery and play is consistent with the suggestions of both Piaget (1951) and Vygotsky (1967), that imitation and pretend play are basic aspects of cognitive development, and that such play is instrumental to the development of internal systems of representation. Such internal representations free the child from the control of external stimulation and permit thinking about objects and events that are not immediately present. The development of such representation systems will contribute to the expression of self-control. The problem-solving training procedures to which we now turn our attention are designed to explicity teach such representation systems and rule-generative behaviors.

4.4. Problem-Solving Training

As in the case of the previous training procedures that have been described, the problem-solving approach to teaching children self-control has received attention only recently, and extensive comparative studies with adequate follow-up are infrequent. The problem-solving training approach attempts to teach children to become sensitive to interpersonal problems, to develop the ability to generate alternative solutions, to understand means-end relationships and the effect of one's social acts on others (D'Zurilla & Goldfried, 1971). That children with behavior problems require such training is evidenced by the research by Spivack *et al.* (1976), who found that emotionally disturbed and behaviorally disruptive schoolchildren, relative to matched controls, tend to show problem-solving deficits.

These deficits include selecting the first solution the child thinks of without developing alternatives or examining consequences, thus failing to conceptualize alternative options of action.

In order to compensate for these deficiencies Spivack and Shure (1974) provided training in two types of social reasoning over some 30 lessons. One type of reasoning involved the child's thinking of alternative solutions to simple conflict situations with peers. A related ability was the child's prediction of likely consequences should his solution be put into effect. The focus of the training, which takes the form of a variety of games, was not *what* to think but rather *how* to think about interpersonal problems. The initial games dealt with developing specific language and attentive skills, identifying emotions, thinking about how people have different likes and dislikes, and learning to gather information about other people. Final games posed the problem of finding several alternative solutions to interpersonal problems and evaluating cause and effect in human relationships. The training resulted in significant increases in social reasoning abilities and most importantly—and uniquely for a training study—it showed significant and enduring positive effects on social behaviors with peers, changes that were maintained at a 1-year follow-up in kindergarten. From a clinical implementation viewpoint, a most important aspect of the training program is that positive results were obtained when teachers trained children and when mothers trained their own children. In a personal communication, Spivack described his training as follows:

> Training reduces socially maladaptive behavior by enhancing certain mediating interpersonal cognitive skills of direct relevance to social adjustment. . . . These skills involve the capacity to generate alternative solutions and consequences, and in older individuals the ability to generate means-ends thought.

Recently, a number of programs tailored after Spivack and Shure have been developed to teach children a variety of skills including self-control. These programs include Allen, Chinsky, Larcen, Lochman, and Selinger (1976), Gesten, Flores-de-Apodaca, Rains, Weissberg, and Cowen (1978), Elardo (1974), Russell and Thoresen (1976), Poitras-Martin and Stone (1977), and Stone, Hinds, and Schmidt (1975).

The initial promising results reported by Spivack and Shure (1974) have not been replicated by Allen et al. (1976), who used somewhat older children. By the time Allen et al. conducted a 4-month follow-up, the differences between the control group and the problem-solving group had dissipated. The Connecticut group of Allen et al. are continuing to improve their assessment and problem-solving training package. Similar innovative attempts are being made at Rochester (Cowen, 1977) and at Arkansas (Elardo, 1974). Table 2, taken from Gesten et al. (1978), illustrates the component skills that are central to many of the social problem-solving training programs. In order to teach such skills several teaching modes are used, including verbal, behavioral, videotape, cartoon-workbook, poster-pictorial, and flash-card activities. A similar multifaceted training program was employed by Stone et al. (1975) to teach children to distinguish between facts, choices, and solutions. In each of the problem-solving training studies thus far conducted, with the exception of the Spivack and Shure (1974) study, and to a lesser degree Gesten et al. (1978), the results hold more promise than thus far evidenced.

Consistent with this promissory theme is the recent problem-solving training approach of Russell and Thoresen (1976). In a residential treatment home they taught decision-making skills to acting-out preadolescents. Using both audiotape and written materials, the children were taught to identify problems, generate alternatives, collect information, recognize personal values, make a decision, and then review that decision at a later time. As with the other problem-solving studies, controlled evaluation is now underway.

These early beginnings represent a harbinger for what we should see in the future, namely, curricula to teach children self-control and interpersonal skills. To achieve this goal the full clinical and pedagogical

TABLE 2
Components of Problem-Solving Training[a]

Prerequisite skill	(Pre)	Look for signs of upset, or "not so good," feelings.
Problem definition	(1)	Know exactly what the problem is.
Goal statement	(2)	Decide on your goal.
Impulse delay	(3)	Stop and think before you act.
Generation of alternatives	(4)	Think of as many solutions as you can to solve your problem.
Consideration of consequences	(5)	Think of the different things after each solution.
Implementation	(6)	When you think you have a really good solution, try it.
Recycle	(Post)	If your first solution doesn't work be sure to try again.

[a]From Gesten, Flores-de-Apodaca, Rains, Weissberg, and Cowen (1978).

armamentarium will be required. The present review suggests that the elements for such a curriculum are available.

5. A Closing Caveat

The focus of this chapter has been on the variety of techniques and skills that are available to teach children self-control. But the expression of self-control behaviors always occurs in some context and it would be short-sighted for a training program to focus only on the child. The bidirectional nature of interpersonal behavior should sensitize us to the need to assess both the situational context and any significant others before implementing a self-control training program. The extensive research on teaching parents behavior modification skills has implications for how we can involve parents in teaching their children self-control.

In order to illustrate my concern, permit me to leave you, the reader, with a task. As I was writing this chapter and reading all of the laboratory studies on self-control, I began informally to conduct an observational study of my own four children, ages 18 months to 10 years. My task was to identify all those situations and behavioral occurrences that I would characterize as requiring self-control. My problem is that while observing my children's interactions with each other as well as with my wife and myself, I discovered more situations that required self-control on the part of the parents than of the children. In short, the task simply is to conduct a naturalistic study of children (any age) and determine how many instances fit our laboratory paradigms and theoretical concepts of self-control. The task is to determine exactly when we infer the presence or absence of self-control. From such an observational study we will better learn how to teach children self-control.

6. References

Alkus, S. *Self-regulation and children's task performance: A comparison of self-instruction, coping and attribution approaches*. Unpublished doctoral dissertation, University of California, Los Angeles, 1977.

Allen, G., Chinsky, J., Larcen, S., Lochman, J., & Selinger, W. *Community psychology and the schools: A behaviorally oriented multi-level preventive approach*. Hillsdale, N.J.: Lawrence Erlbaum Associates, 1976.

Allen, M., & Liebert, R. Effects of live and symbolic deviant-modeling cues on adoption of a previously learned standard. *Journal of Personality and Social Psychology*, 1969, *11*, 253-260.

Anderson, L., Fodor, I., & Alpert, M. A comparison of methods for training self-control. *Behavior Therapy*, 1976, *7*, 649-658.

Aronfreed, J. *Conduct and conscience*. New York: Academic Press, 1968.

Bandura, A. *Principles of behavior modification*. New York: Holt, Rinehart & Winston, 1969.

Bandura, A. Self-reinforcement: Theoretical and methodological considerations. *Behaviorism*, 1976, *4*, 135-155.

Bandura, A., & Kupers, C. Transmission of patterns of self-reinforcement. Through modeling. *Journal of Abnormal and Social Psychology*, 1964, *69*, 1-9.

Bandura, A., & MacDonald, F. Influence of social reinforcement and the behavior of models in shaping children's moral judgments. *Journal of Abnormal Social Psychology*, 1963, *67*, 274-281.

Bandura, A., & Mischel, W. Modification of self-imposed delay of reward through experience to live and symbolic models. *Journal of Personality and Social Psychology*, 1965, *2*, 698-705.

Bandura, A., & Perloff, B. Relative efficacy of self-monitored and externally imposed reinforcement systems. *Journal of Personality and Social Psychology*, 1967, *7*, 111—116.

Bash, M., & Camp, B. *Think aloud program: Group manual*. Unpublished manuscript, University of Colorado Medical School, Denver, 1975.

Bellack, A., & Schwartz, J. Assessment for self-control programs. In M. Hersen & A. Bellack (Eds.), *Behavioral assessment: A practical handbook*. New York: Pergamon Press, 1976.

Bender, N. Self-verbalization versus tutor verbalization in modifying impulsivity. *Journal of Educational Psychology*, 1976, *68*, 347-354.

Best, H. *The maintenance of behavior through self-reinforcement*. Unpublished doctoral dissertation, University of Waterloo, Ontario, 1973.

Block, J., & Block, J. *The developmental continuity of ego-control and ego-resiliency*. Paper presented at the meeting of the Society for Research in Child Development, New Orleans, 1977.

Bolstad, O., & Johnson, S. Self-regulation in the modification of disruptive classroom behavior. *Journal of Applied Behavior Modification*, 1972, *5*, 443-454.

Bornstein, P., & Quevillon, R. The effects of a self-instructional package on overactive preschool boys. *Journal of Applied Behavior Analysis*, 1976, *9*, 176-188.

Brigham, T. Some speculations about self-control. In T. Brigham & A. Catania (Eds.), *The handbook of applied behavior research: Social and instructional processes*. New York: Irvington Press, 1977.

Broden, M., Hall, R., & Mitts, B. The effect of self-recording on the classroom behavior of two eighth-grade students. *Journal of Applied Behavior Analysis*, 1971, *4*, 191-199.

Brownell, K., Colletti, G., Ersner-Hershfield, S., Hershfield, H., & Wilson, T. Self-control in school children: Stringency and leniency in self-determined and externally imposed performance standards. *Behavior Therapy, 1977, 8*, 442-55.

Bugental, D., Whalen, C., & Henker, B. Causal attributions of hyperactive children and motivational assumptions of two behavior-change approaches: Evidence for an interactionist position. *Child Development*, 1977, *48*, 874-884.

Camp, B. Verbal mediation in young aggressive boys. *Journal of Abnormal Psychology*, 1977, *86*, 145-153.

Camp, B., Blom, G., Hebert, F., & van Doorninck, W. "Think aloud": A program for developing self-control in young aggressive boys. *Journal of Abnormal Child Psychology*, 1977, *5*, 157-169.

Catania, A. The myth of self-reinforcement. *Behaviorism*, 1975, *3*, 192-199.

Chess, S., Thomas, A., & Birch, H. Behavioral problems revisited. In S. Chess & H. Birch (Eds.), *Annual progress in child psychiatry and child development*. New York: Brunner Mazel, 1968.

Cheyne, J., & Walters, R. Punishment and prohibition: Some origins of self-control. In T. Newcomb (Ed.), *New directions in psychology*. New York: Holt, Rinehart & Winston, 1970.

Cowen, E. Baby steps toward primary prevention. *American Journal of Community Psychology*, 1977, *5*, 1-22.

Craighead, E., Craighead-Wilcoxon, L., & Meyers, A. New directions in behavior modification with children. In H. Hersen, R. Esler, & P. Miller (Eds.), *Progress in behavior modification* (Vol. 6). New York: Academic Press, 1978.

Debus, R. Effects of brief observation of model behavior on conceptual tempo of impulsive children. *Developmental Psychology*, 1970, *2*, 22-32.

de Charmes, R. *Personal causation: The internal determinants of behavior*. New York: Academic Press, 1968.

Deci, E. *Intrinsic motivation*. New York: Plenum Press, 1975.

Denney, D. The effects of exemplary and cognitive models and self-rehearsal on children's interrogative strategies. *Journal of Experimental Child Psychology, 1975, 19*, 476-488.

Douglas, V. Stop, look and listen: The problem of sustained attention and impulse control in hyperactive and normal children. *Canadian Journal of Behavioral Science*, 1972, *4*, 259-281.

Douglas, V. Are drugs enough?—to treat or to train the hyperactive child, *International Journal of Mental Health*, 1975, *5, 199-212*.

Douglas, V., Parry, P., Marton, P., & Garson, C. Assessment of a cognitive training program for hyperactive children. *Journal of Abnormal Child Psychology*, 1976, *4*, 389-410.

Drabman, R., Spitalnik, R., & O'Leary, D. Teaching self-control to disruptive children. *Journal of Abnormal Psychology*, 1973, *82*, 10-16.

Dweck, C. The role of expectations and attributions in the alleviation of learned helplessness. *Journal of Personality and Social Psychology*, 1975, *31*, 674-685.

D'Zurilla, T., & Goldfried, N. Problem solving and behavior modification. *Journal of Abnormal Psychology*, 1971, *78*, 107-126.

Elardo, P. *Project AWARE: A school program to facilitate social development of children*. Paper presented at the Fourth Annual Blumberg Symposium, Chapel Hill, No. Carolina, 1974.

Fagan, D., Long, I., & Stevens, R. *Teaching children self-control*. Columbus, Ohio: Charles E. Merrill, 1975.

Feitelson, D., & Ross, G. The neglected factor—play. *Human Development*, 1973, *16*, 202-223.

Felixbrod, J., & O'Leary, K. Effects of reinforcement on children's academic behavior as a function of self-determined and externally imposed contingencies. *Journal of Applied Behavior Analysis*, 1973, *6*, 241-250.

Felixbrod, J., & O'Leary, D. Self-determination of academic standards by children. *Journal of Educational Psychology*, 1974, *66*, 845-850.

Finch, A., Wilkinson, M., Nelson, W., & Montgomery, L. Modification of an impulsive cognitive tempo in emotionally disturbed boys. *Journal of Abnormal Child Psychology*, 1975, *3*, 49-52.

Flavell, J. Metacognitive development. Paper presented at the NATO Advanced Study Institute in structured process theories of complex human behavior. Banff, Alberta, Canada, 1977.

Freyberg, J. Increasing imaginative play of urban disadvantaged kindergarten children through systematic training. In J. Singer (Ed.), *The child's world of make believe*. New York: Academic Press, 1973.

Fry, P. Self-imposed delay of gratification as a function of modeling. *Journal of Counseling Psychology*, 1972, *19*, 234-237.

Gesten, E., Flores-de-Apodaca, R., Rains, M., Weissberg, R., Cowen, E. Promoting peer related social competence in school. In M. Kent & J. Roff (Eds.), *The primary prevention of psychopathology, Vol. 3: Promoting social competence and coping in children*. Hanover, N.H.: University Press of New England, 1978.

Glynn, E. Classroom applications of self-determined reinforcement. *Journal of Applied Behavior Analysis*, 1970, *3*, 123-132.

Glynn, E., Thomas, J., & Shee, S. Behavioral self-control of on task behavior in an elementary classroom. *Journal of Applied Behavior Analysis*, 1973, *6*, 105-113.

Goldiamond, I. Self-control procedures in personal behavior problems. *Psychological Reports*, 1965, *17*, 851-868.

Goodwin, S., & Mahoney, M. Modification of agression via modeling: An experimental probe. *Journal of Behavior Therapy and Experimental Psychiatry*, 1975, *6*, 200-202.

Greiner, J., & Karoly, P. Effects of self-control training on study activity and academic performance: An analysis of self-monitoring, self-reward, and systematic planning components. *Journal of Counseling Psychology*, 1976, *23*, 495-502.

Hartig, M., & Kanfer, F. The role of verbal self-instructions in children's resistance to temptation. *Journal of Personality and Social Psychology*, 1973, *24*, 259-267.

Hartshorne, H., & May, M. *Studies in deceit*. New York: Macmillan, 1928.

Israel, A., & O'Leary, D. Developing correspondence between children's words and deeds. *Child Development*, 1973, *44*, 575-581.

Jakibchuk, Z., & Smeriglio, U. The influence of symbolic modeling on the social behavior of preschool children with low levels of social responsiveness. *Child Development*, 1976, *47*, 838-841.

James, W. *The principles of psychology*. New York: Dover Publications, 1918.

Jones, R., Nelson, R., & Kazdin, A. The role of external variables in self-reinforcement: A review. *Behavior Modification*, 1977, *1*, 147-178.

Kagan, J. Reflection-impulsivity: The generality and dynamics of conceptual tempo. *Journal of Abnormal Psychology*, 1966, *71*, 17-24.

Kanfer, F. The many faces of self-control or behavior modification changes its focus. In R. Stuart (Ed.), *Behavioral self-management*. New York: Brunner/Mazel, 1977.

Kanfer, F., & Durenfeldt, P. Age, class standing and commitment as determinants of cheating in children. *Child Development*, 1968, *39*, 545-557.

Kanfer, F., & Karoly, P. Self-control: A behavioristic excursion into the lion's den. *Behavior Therapy*, 1972, *3*, 398-416.

Kanfer, F., Karoly, P., & Newman, A. Reduction of children's fear of the dark by competence related and situational threat related verbal cues. *Journal of Consulting and Clinical Psychology*, 1975, *43*, 251-258.

Karoly, P. Behavioral self-management in children: Concepts, methods, issues and directions. In M. Hersen, R. Eisler, & P. Miller (Eds.), *Progress in behavior modification* (Vol. 5). New York: Academic Press, 1977.

Karoly, P., & Dirks, M. Developing self-control in preschool children through correspondence training. *Behavior Therapy*, 1977, *8*, 398-405.

Kaufman, K., & O'Leary, D. Reward, cost, and self-evaluation procedures for disruptive adolescents in a psychiatric hospital school. *Journal of Applied Behavior Analysis*, 1972, *5*, 293-310.

Kazdin, A. *The token economy*. New York: Plenum Press, 1977.

Kendall, P. On the efficacious use of verbal self-instructional procedures with children. *Cognitive Therapy and Research*, 1977, *1*, 331-343.

Kendall, P., & Finch, A. A cognitive-behavioral treatment for impulse control: A case study. *Journal of Consulting and Clinical Psychology*, 1976, *44*, 852-857.

Kendall, P., & Finch, A. A cognitive-behavioral treatment for impulsivity. A group comparison study. *Journal of Consulting and Clinical Psychology*, 1978, *46*, 110-118.

Klausner, S. (Ed.). *The quest for self-control: Classical philosophies and scientific research*. New York: Free Press, 1965.

Kohlberg, L. Stage and sequence: The cognitive-developmental approach to socialization. In D. Goslin (Ed.), *Handbook of socialization theory and research*. New York: Rand McNally, 1969.

Kunzelmann, H. (Ed.). *Precision teaching*. Seattle: Special Child Publications, 1970.

Kurtz, P., Neisworth, J., Goeke, K., & Hanson, M. Training verbal-nonverbal correspondence. *Journal of Applied Social Psychology*, 1976, *6*, 314-321.

Lavoie, J. Cognitive determinants of resistance to deviation in seven-, nine-, and eleven-year old children of low and high maturity of moral judgment. *Developmental Psychology*, 1974, *10*, 393-403.

Lickona, T. (Ed.). *Moral development and behavior*. New York: Holt, Rinehart & Winston. 1976.

Liebert, R., Spiegler, M., & Hall, W. Effects of the value of contingent self-administered and non-contingent externally imposed reward on children's behavioral productivity. *Psychonomic Science*, 1970, *18*, 245-246.

Loevinger, J. *Ego development*. San Francisco: Jossey-Bass, 1976.

Lovitt, T., & Curtiss, K. Academic response rate as a function of trainer and self-imposed contingencies. *Journal of Applied Behavior Analysis*, 1969, *2*, 49-53.

Luria, A. *The role of speech in the regulation of normal and abnormal behaviors*. New York: Liveright, 1961.

Luria, A. Speech and formation of mental processes. In M. Cole & I. Maltzman (Eds.), *A handbook of contemporary Soviet psychology*. New York: Basic Books, 1969.

Mahoney, M. *Cognition and behavior modification*. Cambridge, Mass.: Ballinger, 1974.

Mahoney, M., & Thoresen, C. *Self-control: Power to the person*. Monterey, Cal.: Brooks/Cole, 1974.

Masters, J., & Mokros, J. Self-reinforcement processes in children. In H. Reese (Ed.), *Advances in child development and behavior* (Vol. 9). New York: Academic Press, 1974.

Masters, J., & Santrock, J. Studies in the self-regulation of behavior: Effects of contingent cognitive and affective events. *Developmental Psychology*, 1976, *12*, 334-348.

McLaughlin, T., & Malaby, J. Increasing and maintaining assignment completion with teacher and pupil controlled individual contingency programs: Three case studies. *Psychology*, 1974, *11*, 1-7.

Meichenbaum, D. Theoretical and treatment implications of developmental research on verbal control of behavior. *Canadian Psychological Review*, 1975, *16*, 22-27.

Meichenbaum, D. Toward a cognitive theory of self-control. In G. Schwartz & D. Shapiro (Eds.), *Consciousness and self-regulation* (Vol. 1). New York: Plenum Press, 1976.

Meichenbaum, D. *Cognitive-behavior modification: An integrative approach*. New York: Plenum Press, 1977.

Meichenbaum, D., & Goodman J. Training impulsive children to talk to themselves: A means of developing self-control. *Journal of Abnormal Psychology*, 1971, *77*, 115-126.

Meichenbaum, D., & Goodman, S. Critical questions and methodological problems in studying children's private speech. In G. Zivin (Ed.), *Development of self-regulation through speech*. New York: Wiley, 1978.

Messer, S. Reflection-impulsivity: A review. *Psychological Bulletin*, 1976, *83*, 1026-1052.

Mischel, W. Toward a cognitive social learning reconceptualization of personality. *Psychological Review*, 1973, *80*, 252-283.

Mischel, W. Processes in delay of gratification. In L. Berkowitz (Ed.), *Advances in experimental social psychology* ((Vol. 7). New York: Academic Press, 1974.

Mischel, W., Ebbesen, E., & Zeiss, A. Cognitive and attentional mechanisms in delay of gratification. *Journal of Personality and Social Psychology*, 1972, *21*, 204-218.

Mischel, W., Zeiss, R., & Zeiss, A. Internal-external control and persistence: Validation and implications of the Stanford Preschool Internal-External Scale. *Journal of Personality and Social Psychology*, 1974, *29*, 265-278.

Monahan, J., & O'Leary, D. Effects of self-instruction on rule-breaking behavior. *Psychological Reports*, 1971, *29*, 1059-1066.

Moore, B., Mischel, W., & Zeiss, A. Comparative effects of the reward stimulus and its cognitive representation in voluntary delay. *Journal of Personality and Social Psychology*, 1976, *34*, 419-424.

Nelson, M. *Cognitive-behavioral strategies in modifying an impulsive cognitive style*. Unpublished doctoral dissertation, Virginia Commonwealth University, 1976.

Nowicki, S., & Strickland, B. A locus of control of scale for children. *Journal of Consulting and Clinical Psychology*, 1973, *40*, 148-154.

O'Leary, K. D. The effects of self instruction of immoral behavior. *Journal of Experimental Child Psychology*, 1968, *6*, 297-301.

O'Leary, K. D., & O'Leary, S. *Classroom management: The successful use of behavior modification* (2nd ed.). New York: Pergamon Press, 1977.

O'Leary, K. D., Poulous, R., & Devine, W. Tangible reinforcers: Bonuses or bribes? *Journal of Consulting and Clinical Psychology*, 1972, *38*, 1-8.

O'Leary, S., & O'Leary, K. D. Behavior modification in the school. In H. Leitenberg (Ed.), *Handbook of behavior modification and behavior therapy*. Englewood Cliffs, N.J.: Prentice-Hall, 1976.

Palkes, H., Stewart, M., & Freedman, J. Improvement in maze performance on hyperactive boys as a function of verbal training procedures. *Journal of Special Education*, 1972, *5*, 337-342.

Palkes, H., Stewart, M., & Kahana, B. Porteus maze performance after training in self-directed verbal commands. *Child Development*, 1968, *39*, 817-826.

Patterson, C., & Mischel, W. Plans to resist distraction. *Developmental Psychology*, 1975, *11*, 369-378.

Patterson, C., & Mischel, W. Effects of temptation-inhibiting and task-facilitating plans on self-control. *Journal of Personality and Social Psychology*, 1976, *33*, 209-217.

Phillips, E., Phillips, A., Fixsen, D., & Wolf, N. *The teaching-family handbook*. Lawrence: University of Kansas Printing Service, 1972.

Piaget, J. *Play, dreams, and imitation in childhood*. New York: Norton, 1951.

Poitras-Martin, D., & Stone, G. Psychological education: A skills-oriented approach. *Journal of Counseling*, 1977, *24*, 153-157.

Prentice, N. The influence of live and symbolic modeling on promoting moral judgment of adolescent delinquents. *Journal of Abnormal Psychology*, 1972, *80*, 157-161.

Reppucci, N. Individual differences in the consideration of information among two-year-old children. *Developmental Psychology*, 1970, *2*, 240-246.

Risley, T. *The social context of self-control*. Paper presented at the Banff Conference on behavior modification, 1977.

Risley, T., & Hart, B. Developing correspondence between nonverbal and verbal behavior of preschool children. *Journal of Applied Behavior Analysis*, 1968, *1*, 267-281.

Robertson, D., & Keeley, S. *Evaluation of a mediational training program for impulsive children by a multiple case study design*. Paper presented at the American Psychological Association, 1974.

Robin, D. *Delay of gratification in children*. Unpublished doctoral dissertation, Columbia University, 1966.

Rogers-Warren, A., & Baer, D. Correspondence between saying and doing: Teaching children to share and praise. *Journal of Applied Behavior Analysis*, 1976, *9*, 335-354.

Rogers-Warren, A., Warren, S., & Baer, D. A component analysis: Modeling, self-reporting, and reinforcement of self-reporting in the development of sharing. *Behavior Modification*, 1977, *3*, 307-322.

Rosenthal, T. Modeling therapies. In M. Hersen, R. Eisler, & P. Miller (Eds.), *Progress in behavior modification* (Vol. 2). New York: Academic Press, 1976.

Russell, M., & Thoresen, C. Teaching decision-making skills to children. In J. Krumboltz & C. Thoresen (Eds.), *Counseling methods*. New York: Holt, Rinehart & Winston, 1976.

Saltz, E., Dixon, D., & Johnson, J. Training disadvantaged preschoolers on various fantasy activities: Effects on cognitive functioning and impulse control. *Child Development*, 1977, *48*, 367-380.

Saltz, E., & Johnson, J. Training for thematic-fantasy play in culturally disadvantaged children: Preliminary results. *Journal of Educational Psychology*, 1974, *66*, 623-630.

Santogrossi, D., O'Leary, D., Romanczyk, R., & Kaufman, K. Self-evaluation by adolescents in a psychiatric hospital school token program. *Journal of Applied Behavior Analysis*, 1973, *6*, 277-288.

Sarason, I., & Ganzer, V. Modeling and group discussion in the rehabilitation of juvenile delinquents. *Journal of Counseling Psychology*, 1973, *20*, 442-449.

Schneider, M., & Robin, A. The turtle technique: A method for the self-control of impulsive behavior. In J. Krumboltz & C. Thoresen (Eds.), *Counseling methods*. New York: Holt, Rinehart & Winston, 1976.

Singer, D., Nahmettuang, L., & Wheaton, A. *Imaginative play training interventions with emotionally disturbed children: An evaluation study*. Paper presented at the Eastern Psychological Association, New York, 1976.

Skinner, B. F. *Science and human behavior*. New York: Macmillan, 1953.

Smilansky, S. *The effects of sociodramatic play on disadvantaged children*. New York: Wiley, 1968.

Spates, C., & Kanfer, F. Self-monitoring, self-evaluation and self-reinforcement in children's learning: A test of a multistage self-regulation model. *Behavior Therapy*, 1977, *8*, 9-16.

Spivack, G., Platt, J., & Shure, M. *The problem solving approach to adjustment*. San Francisco: Jossey-Bass, 1976.

Spivack, G., & Shure, M. *Social adjustment of young children: A cognitive approach to solving real life problems*. San Francisco: Jossey-Bass, 1974.

Staub, E. Effects of persuasion and modeling on delay of gratification. *Developmental Psychology*, 1972, *6*, 166-177.

Staub, E. *The development of prosocial behavior in children*. Morristown, N.J.: General Learning Press, 1975.

Steiner, I. Perceived freedom. In L. Berkowitz (Ed.), *Advances in experimental social psychology* (Vol. 5). New York: Academic Press, 1970.

Stokes, T., & Baer, D. An implicit technology of generalization. *Journal of Applied Behavior Analysis*, 1977, *10*, 349-367.

Stone, G., Hinds, W., & Schmidt, G. Teaching mental health behaviors to elementary school children. *Professional Psychology*, 1975, *6*, 34-40.

Stumphauzer, J. Increased delay of gratification in young prison inmates through imitation of high delay peer models. *Journal of Personality and Social Psychology*, 1972, *21*, 10-17.

Switzky, H., & Haywood, H. Motivational orientation and the relative efficacy of self-monitored and externally imposed reinforcement systems in children. *Journal of Personality and Social Psychology*, 1974, *30*, 360-366.

Thoresen, C., & Coates, T. Behavioral self-control: Some clinical concerns. In M. Hersen, R. Eisler, & P. Miller (Eds.), *Progress in behavior modification* (Vol. 2). New York: Academic Press, 1976.

Thoresen, C., Gray-Kirmil, K., Crosbie, P. *The processes of self-control: A working model*. Unpublished manuscript, Stanford University, 1977.

Thoresen, C., & Mahoney, M. *Behavioral self-control*. New York: Holt, Rinehart & Winston, 1974.

Toner, I., Holstein, R., & Hetherington, E. M. Reflection-impulsivity and self-control in preschool children. *Child Development* 1977, *48*, 239-245.

Turkewitz, H., O'Leary, D., & Ironsmith, M. Producing generalization of appropriate behavior through self-control. *Journal of Consulting and Clinical Psychology*, 1975, *43*, 577-583.

Vygotsky, L. *Thought and language*. New York: Wiley, 1962.

Vygotsky, L. Play and its role in the mental development of the child. *Soviet Psychology*, 1967, *5*, 6-18.

White, G. Immediate and deferred effects of model observation and guided and unguided rehearsal on donating and stealing. *Journal of Personality and Social Psychology*, 1972, *21*, 139-148.

Winnett, R., & Winkler, R. Current behavior modification in the classroom: Be still, be quiet, be docile. *Journal of Applied Behavior Analysis*, 1972, *5*, 499-504.

Wolf, T. Effects of televised modeled verbalizations and behavior on resistance to deviation. *Developmental Psychology*, 1973, *8*, 51-56.

Wozniak, R. Verbal regulation of motor behavior: Soviet research and non-Soviet replications. *Human Development* 1972, *15*, 13-57.

2   *Generalization Processes in Child Behavior Change*

ROBERT G. WAHLER,
ROBERT M. BERLAND,
AND THOMAS D. COE

The concept *generalization* has always been a prevalent feature of discussions on human behavior. Since the earliest psychological writings, theorists have guessed at the process by which people appear to transcend boundaries that supposedly govern their actions. Arguments concerning the process have usually run something like this: Human behavior is best understood as a set of specific units;—units of overt responses, units of measurable internal events, and units of environmental events. Some interacting combination of these units provides our understanding of why people do what they do. But, in addition to this focus on the specific units and their combinations, somthing *general* or nonspecific must be brought into this understanding. While one might draw useful conclusions through mapped-out unit combinations shown to govern behavior, there always seem to be instances in which the organism acts beyond the confines of this mapping. For example, consider a child who is taught to attach the letter *S* to a group of nouns referring to more than one object. As that learned group expands in number, the child begins to apply this rule of thumb to nouns not included in the group. The child's use of the plural for the original group is understandable through a reinforcement process; the generalization, however, is not "explained" by the process. Rather, this by-product of the learning experience is a descriptive phenomenon—a capacity of the organism not governed by the learning process. Man's efforts to explain this capacity have taken very different directions over the years. There are those who have speculated on the presence of hypothetical structures within the organism (e.g., Piaget, Freud) and those who have taken a more empiri-

ROBERT G. WAHLER, ROBERT M. BERLAND, AND THOMAS D. COE • Child Behavior Institute, The University of Tennessee at Knoxville, Knoxville, Tennessee. This research was supported by the National Institute of Mental Health, Crime and Delinquency Section, MH 18516.

cal bent (e.g., Guthrie, Hull, Skinner). This chapter represents a selective look at the latter strategy—the efforts of behaviorists to understand generalization and to derive principles that would make the phenomenon a predictable process. In line with the child-clinical focus of this book, our coverage will be aimed primarily at those investigations in which troubled children are the subjects of study. Therefore, our intent is to understand generalization as it occurs (or fails to occur) in reference to clinical intervention procedures. But we also believe that such understanding will require a careful examination of studies geared to generalization as a *natural* phenomenon of childhood. This naturalistic-developmental orientation could provide useful guidelines in the study of generalization as an outcome of clinical treatment procedures.

1. Generalization as a Treatment Product

When caretakers believe that a child is psychologically troubled, and thus in need of help, the task these people face is complex. First of all, a decision on helper and type of helping procedure must be made. Since the caretakers are usually not knowledgeable enough to make such a decision, a "grapevine" network identical to that in the medical arena is typically employed. That grapevine usually says nothing about the helping procedure; rather, it reflects on the supposed skill of the helper. Unknown to the caretakers, there may be differences in how the helper views generalization as a facet of the helping operation. Before discussing these differences, let us outline the sorts of generalization that are relevant to clinical treatment:

1. Generalization across behaviors. Here, the child's repertoire of behaviors is the dimension of concern. Most troubled children attract clinical attention because of multiple problem behaviors, and it is important to realize that some of these behaviors will be difficult to deal with in any direct fashion. Those behaviors likely to occur outside the scope of caretaker or clinician detection make them difficult to deal with as they emerge. Thus, behaviors such as stealing, fighting, truancy, and property destruction are usually not amenable to direct intervention. In behavioristic forms of treatment, either a long-term contingency is arranged or efforts are made to deal directly with those problem behaviors occurring within the immediate scope of detection. In both cases, it is presumed that the treatment contingency will generalize across the dimension of behaviors common to that child.

2. Generalization across settings. This form of generalization is related to that just discussed. The child's global environment is obviously composed of numerous stimulus settings, such as "at home with parent," "at home alone," "in neighborhood with peers," "in the school

classroom." This stimulus dimension interacts with the child-behavioral dimension in a yet undocumented, but intuitively obvious manner. The child's repertoire of behaviors is spread in some fashion across those settings composing that individual's environment. Thus, a troubled child is apt to display deviant behavior in a variety of stimulus settings, and it may not be feasible to cover all of these settings in terms of a clinical intervention program. To some degree it must be assumed that therapeutic changes will generalize across the stimulus dimension comprising these settings.

3. Generalization across time. The durability or maintenance of therapeutic change is highlighted in this case. Time is a nebulous dimension involving both the child's behavior repertoire and the stimulus settings in which these behaviors occur. As time passes, changes are bound to occur in stimulus context and in the developing child's repertoire. Thus it would seem that the durability of therapeutic change will be some function of interactions between these two factors. Whatever the function, any treatment procedure must consider the time dimension as well as the preceding two dimensions.

The current behavioristic helping procedures for children differ in their assumptions about the three classes of generalization. We believe that the majority of these procedures can be arranged into three types. First, consider those that emphasize placing the troubled child in a specially constructed therapeutic setting—a setting not common to the child's natural environment. Treatment programs such as *Achievement Place* (Phillips, 1968) or *Re-Ed.* (Hobbs, 1966) are examples of such an intervention strategy. These programs are geared to rapid changes in the children, particularly in reference to their deficiencies in social and academic behaviors. It is presumed that equipping the children with new behavioral alternatives will combat a resumption of their problem behaviors once they return to their natural environments. In addition, the caretakers in the natural environments are also "reeducated" so that they are prepared to set supporting contingencies for their children's newfound behaviors. Obviously, these programs depend heavily on planned and unplanned generalization across settings and time. Generalization across the behaviors of a child is not so important because of the close stimulus control imposed by the planned therapeutic setting.

Another popular intervention strategy attempts to lean less heavily on unplanned setting generality. In this orientation, the clinical program is moved directly into the natural environments of troubled children. The goals here center on intensive reeducation of caretakers—to enable these adults (usually parents and teachers) to circumvent the reinforcement traps that appear to maintain the children's behavior problems (e.g., Patterson, 1974). Typically, the child's home and family comprise the focal setting for intervention, although the public school classroom is also a common target. Obviously, the clinician will have less control over these sorts of settings than is true of the strategy discussed earlier. Thus generalization across behaviors, as well as time, is an important consideration.

More recent in development is a therapeutic strategy that attempts to solve generalization problems by equipping the troubled child with *self-management* skills (e.g., Mahoney, 1974). In essence, the child is taught to keep track of his or her behavior, as well as the environmental consequences of that behavior. Along with these tracking skills, the child is shown the importance of goal setting—efforts to arrange the environment in such a manner as to ensure obtaining desired reinforcers and avoiding aversive consequences. For example, the child may be taught a set of behaviors that are known to result in approval by a classroom teacher. Clearly, self-management strategies depend heavily on the child's capacity to alter those environmental contingencies that currently support problem behavior. In contrast to the preceding two strategies, this one views the child as capable of some actions independent of environmental control. Thus, since the clinician does not provide direct rearrangement of the environment, this strategy relies heavily on unplanned generalization of all three types.

2. Generalization as a Natural Phenomenon

It is our contention that generalization as a therapeutic product can be best fostered by an understanding of how this phenomenon occurs in the natural development of children. The field of developmental psychology has made ample reference to generalization phenomena as obvious features of the growing child. It then makes sense to examine those environment-behavior interactions that appear to produce such phenomena. Given an understanding of the ecological underpinnings of generalization, clinicians might be able to construct better treatment programs.

Behavioristic views have traditionally emphasized learning paradigms in discussing natural generalization. Most recently, the notions of response class and stimulus class (see Skinner, 1953) have been employed to account for the phenomenon. The earlier "habit family hierarchy" (see Hull, 1943) was a similar explanatory model.[1] According to the *class* concept, behavioral events and environmental events will

---

[1] The Skinnerian and Hullian concepts differ sharply in predicting response generalization. While the Hullian notion views the organism's responses as ordered in habit

become grouped into functional clusters following the principles of operant learning. Stimuli will become related functionally if they are discriminative for a common response and its reinforcement. Responses likewise will form into a functional covarying class if they share a common discriminative and/or reinforcing stimulus.

First, consider the stimulus class concept—essentially, a means of accounting for stimulus generalization. Imitation is perhaps the best known example of this natural process, and it has been the focus of a good many developmental studies. Baer and Sherman (1964) provide the classic empirical demonstration of imitation as a phenomenon of generalization. According to their view, imitative behavior is best understood as a response controlled by a class of stimuli—namely, the presentation of behaviors by a model or a number of models. If the child is reinforced for imitating some of the model's behaviors, a functional class of modeling stimuli is formed in reference to the child. In the Baer and Sherman study, a set of modeling stimuli were made discriminative for a child's imitative behavior. Once this was accomplished through systematic reinforcement of the child's appropriate matching behavior, modeling stimuli not belonging to the discriminative set also controlled the child's imitation. Despite the fact that these latter stimuli were *never* discriminative for reinforced imitation, the child reliably emitted imitative behavior when the stimuli were presented. Baer and Sherman had clearly demonstrated a predictable pattern of stimulus generalization. In this case, the dimension of relevance was the cueing behavior of a model.

Of equal interest is the Baer and Sherman explanation for the generalization process. According to them, secondary reinforcement may have developed as a result of pairing the external reinforcers with the stimulus dimension of *similarity*—similarity of model and child behavior. Since imitation constitutes a matching of model behaviors by the imitator, it is possible to view such a stimulus dimension as produced by the child's behavior. Thus, all modeling stimuli become discriminative for reinforcement; the crucial maintaining reinforcers are external, while those responsible for the stimulus generalization are produced through stimulus properties of the child's imitative behavior. Considering the similarity dimension of these properties as secondary reinforcers places the generalization phenomenon within the framework of operant learning.

Learning-theory views on response generalization follow a pattern

---

strength, or the likelihood of occurring in the presence of a stimulus, Skinnerian views do not argue any sort of hierarchical ordering of response probability. In other words, the Skinnerian response *class* concept contains no assumptions concerning organizational relationships among responses. The same is true of Skinner's stimulus class concept.

typical of that just discussed in reference to stimulus generalization. Again, it is assumed that the events of interest (in this case, responses) become grouped into functional classes because they are controlled by common stimuli in the child's environment. Thus, predictable covariations across a number of a child's behaviors might be due to the fact that all share the same discriminative and/or reinforcing stimuli. As in the case of stimulus generalization, there are laboratory examples of this developmental process.

Lovaas (1961) provided one of the earliest illustrations of response class phenomena in children. His interest was aimed at documenting covariations across verbal and nonverbal aggressive behaviors as a function of reinforcement principles. To do so, Lovaas reinforced children's aggressive verbal statements directed toward a doll (e.g., "Bad doll!"). As expected, frequencies of these commonly reinforced statements increased. Then, the children were allowed access to another laboratory setting in which the children's manipulation of a lever would result in a mechanical puppet hitting another puppet with a stick. Results showed predictable covariations between the reinforced verbal aggressive statements and the nonreinforced lever pressing. As the verbal statements increased in frequency, so did the nonverbal aggressive behavior. It was also found that reinforcement of the children's nonaggressive verbal statements led to a reduction in the "aggressive" lever pressing. Clearly, each child's verbal and nonverbal aggressive responses were members of a common class, and this response membership was spread across at least two stimulus settings of the laboratory. A similar response—response generalization phenomenon—was demonstrated by Sherman (1964). This investigator found that reinforcing children's positive statements about a particular food affected their choice of foods to eat in another setting. As in the Lovaas study, the latter behavior (food choice) could be predicted by its verbal descriptor reinforced in the first setting.

In the above studies, inferences about the obtained response classes were as follows: Some verbal and non-verbal responses probably share common likelihoods of reinforcement. In the case of aggressive behavior, the child's natural environment is somehow arranged to foster a sequential linking of verbal and nonverbal behavior. When the child is reinforced for verbal aggression, this episode is discriminative for reinforcement following nonverbal aggression. In other words, a child reinforced for verbal aggression is also likely to be reinforced for nonverbal aggression. The same process would, of course, account for other sorts of response-response linkings (e.g., food statements and preferences).

Obviously, none of the laboratory studies of stimulus and response generalization provide empirical proof of how the process operates. We have discussed these studies merely to illustrate a conceptual model commonly employed in learning-theory explanations of natural generalization. The functional class model has been, and continues to be, a useful means of understanding generalization across time, settings, and behaviors. We believe that the model, in a global sense, will eventually yield an integration of natural and treatment-produced generalization. By global, we refer to the notion that stimulus and response generalization are some function of associations between child behaviors and stimulus events in the child's environment. An exact description of the mappings of these associations has yet to be achieved—there is little empirical reason to argue a Skinnerian, Hullian, Guthrian, or any other version. Our intent at this point is to orient the reader to a broad view of the functional class concept. As we view the concept, child behaviors and stimulus events in that child's environment become organized into predictable patterns. These yet unknown patterns govern the process of stimulus and response generalization—both the natural variety and that produced as a product of clinical treatment. The latter type may well depend on our understanding of the former. This understanding might best be pursued by tracing those efforts of basic and applied researchers aimed at a mapping of generalization precesses. To do so we must turn back the clock a bit.

3. Movements from the Laboratory to the Real World: The Followers of Theory

When human behavior was largely a topic of laboratory science, generalization was as important an issue as it is today in the clinical arena. The phenomenon bore a variety of labels, depending on the theorist and whether the focus was on response or stimulus generalization. Response generalization was usually referred to as *transfer* and stimulus generalization as *induction* or simply *generalization*.

Early work was largely based on suppositions and data emanating from the laboratories of Hull and Spence. Their focus on generalization was noteworthy for the time (1940s) because they offered the field a readily testable model of transfer and induction. Based on the Hull-Spence notion of habit and inhibition (see Spence, 1942), it proved possible to scale the expected outcomes of reinforcing a particular stimulus-response combination. The generalization process for both stimuli and responses should follow a mathematical curve along a dimension of physical similarity in reference to the reinforced S-R pair. In the instances in which physical similarity could not be used (e.g., linguistic responses), a hypothetical dimension based on the organism's proprioceptive stimuli was advanced (see secondary generalization, Hull, 1943). While the Hull-Spence model of generalization was repeatedly criticized by other learning theorists (Tolman and Guthrie), it attracted the bulk of attention in the clinical field.

Attempts to utilize the Hull-Spence model of generalization in the clinical field were led by Hull's own colleagues at Yale. Dollard and Miller (1950) proposed that the laboratory-derived model could account for some important aspects of human psychopathology (e.g., phobias), and it could generate predictions on therapeutic changes following a Hullian-based treatment strategy. Approach-avoidance curves of generalization were often cited in these clinical efforts to explain the development of behavior problems, as well as therapeutic efforts to solve the problems. With childhood problems as the usual examples, the Dollard-Miller strategy seemed a likely means of integrating the natural phenomenon of generalization and that expected by clinical treatment. Studies of children's fears—still laboratory in nature—were cited as evidence of how the Hullian model could account for both developmental and treatment aspects of generalization (Watson & Raynor, 1920).

Despite the immense popularity of the Hull-Spence model of generalization, and the Dollard-Miller efforts to promote its use in the clinical field, application of the model to child treatment never materialized. Clinicians, taught to expect the emergence of generalization as a set of classes inherent in the organism, perhaps found little to support this hope. The deductively produced model of generalization as an expect by-product of clinical treatment turned out to be a dead end.[2]

Laboratory endeavors following the Hull-Spence group shied away from the deductive construction of models. Most noteworthy for the clinical field was the work of Skinner (1953) and his group of followers concerned with applied matters (Bijou & Baer, 1961). Skinner, intent on bypassing hypothetical states of the organism, interpreted generalization as a problem to be solved through inductive research. For him, the issue of response generalization as "transfer" was a pseudoproblem and he said so in his pioneering book, *Science and Human Behavior* (1953, p.94). According to Skinner, scientists and clinicians should not be surprised at their inability to predict generalization across the behavior repertoire of an organism. Since the prevalent view of the term *response* centered on units dictated by theory (at that time, Hullian), the scientist was in essence constructing the expected generalization dimension. As Skinner noted: "We divide behavior into hard and fast units and are then surprised to find that the organism disregards the boundaries we have set" (1953, p.94). Skinner clearly rejected any *a priori* notions concerning the nature of response generalization.

---

[2] It must be noted that the Hull-Spence model has led to useful clinical applications for adult behavior problems. Wolpe's (1958) efforts to utilize the model within the framework of respondent conditioning culminated in a set of treatment procedures

Equally inductive in perspective was Skinner's view on stimulus generalization: If we are to understand the impact of environmental factors on behavior, we must study the stimulus context of that environment. This kind of statement underscored Skinner's belief that the organism's interpretation of environmental stimuli is of little use in determining how that environment operates. Thus he notes: "When Romeo compares Juliet to the sun, we need not suppose that he is engaging in an act of creative imagination; we need only suppose that Juliet's effect upon him shares some of the properties of the effect of the sun and that the verbal response 'sun' is therefore strengthened" (1953, p. 133). For Skinner, there was no single known gradient to describe stimulus generalization. Functional relationships among stimuli must be empirically determined and therefore the generalization process can be known only by thorough study of how environmental stimuli affect the organism.

If one were to follow Skinner's more inductive approach to the study of generalization, the operating strategy is obvious: One must monitor the widest possible range of an organism's responses as well as the widest possible range of stimuli composing that organism's environment. Skinner's own laboratory studies of stimulus generalization were exemplary instances of exploring the latter range. Through his empirical work and arguments on research strategy the stage was once again set for a hoped-for transition from the laboratory to the real world.

In contrast to the Hullian movement, the clinical proponents of Skinner's views did construct real-world translations of the Skinnerian strategy. However, scme sins of strategic omission accompanied these translations. The proponents adhered closely to Skinnerian principles concerning the strengthening and weakening of behavior (reinforcement and extinction); but their early work largely ignored the strategy concerning generalization. For example, Williams (1959) reported one of the first applications of reinforcement principles to a child-clinical problem. In this case, Williams was called upon to help deal with the frequent bedtime tantrum behaviors of a two-year-old child. Reasoning that the child's tantrums were under the social reinforcement control of his parents, Williams instructed the parents to ignore these outbursts. Data reported in the study were number of minutes of crying over 10 bedtime observations. As expected, the child's crying declined in duration along an extinction curve typical of that seen in the laboratory. Now, in reference to generalization phenomena, it is significant to note Williams's recognition of this issue. He writes: "No further tantrums at

---

shown to produce specific and general therapeutic results. Since the Wolpean techniques have yet to be used extensively with children, we have not included this clinical strategy in our review.

bedtime were reported during the next two years"—and "No unfortunate side or aftereffects of this treatment were observed." In these two
sentences Williams made reference to generalization over time and
across the behavior repertoire of the child. *But, attempts to measure these
phenomena were never conducted.*

Following the Williams study, the child-clinical field witnessed a
plethora of similar studies—most pointing to a remarkable therapeutic
success of reinforcement procedures. While generalization issues were
addressed in most of these studies, they were rarely documented with
hard data. For example, Rickard and Mundy (1965) treated a child's
verbal stuttering through reinforcement procedures applied in a clinic
setting. Generalization across stimulus settings was promoted by eventually using the child's parents as therapists, but parent-dispensed social stimuli were not measured; nor was the child's stuttering outside the
clinic measured. Response generalization was not considered and
generalization over time was merely alluded to through subjective reports. A similar lack of documentation and analysis of generalization
phenomena was seen in another clinic-based study of parents as
therapists (Wahler, Winkel, Peterson, & Morrison, 1965).

In 1964 and 1967, two clinical studies by three investigators set a
promising example for implementing the Skinnerian search for generalization. These studies of an autistic child by Wolf, Risley, and Mees (1964)
and Wolf, Risley, Johnston, Harris, & Allen (1967) measured multiple
problem behaviors of the child and included observational data on the
child's behavior in a second stimulus setting (home), as well as over time
in the home setting. Most of the clinical procedures were applied in an
institutional setting, although the child's parents were brought into this
setting to promote generalization to the home setting. All response-
generalization phenomena were planned through systematic contingencies for the problem behaviors (e.g., head banging and bedtime tantrums), thus making it impossible to evaluate natural by-products of
treatment. Generalization across settings and time also involved
planned training of the child's parents; although parent behavior was
not measured, the child's home behavior was documented—a notable
first effort in the field.

Unfortunately, the Wolf, Risley, and Mees example of documenting
generalization phenomena did not affect the field. Most of the child-
clinical studies in that time frame did not follow suit on the methodological requirements necessary to examine generalization processes. Rather,
the aim of most clinical researchers appeared geared to repeated demonstrations of how reinforcement principles could change child behavior.
Thus, the bulk of studies in the 1960s measured only single child behaviors, were based in only one stimulus setting, and rarely included

follow-up measures. Witness the frequently quoted preschool studies by Harris, Johnston, Kelley, and Wolf (1964), Hart, Allen, Buell, Harris, and Wolf (1964), and Allen, Hart, Buell, Harris, and Wolf (1964).

The late 1960s marked the beginning of more serious efforts to evaluate generalization phenomena. A few investigators began to provide direct observational data on child behavior over time and in more than one environmental setting. However, these developments were rare. The major impetus in this direction centered on the study of response generalization. With the work of G. R. Patterson and his colleagues at the Oregon Research Institute, a number of studies on the topic appeared. When the Patterson group announced their use of a coding system for multiple child and adult behaviors (Patterson, Ray, Shaw, & Cobb, 1969), the Skinnerian-oriented clinical field finally took notice. Two aspects of this new focus on response generalization were apparent: (1) The behavioral outcomes of child treatment were studied in terms of multiple criteria of success (e.g., a variety of behaviors in the child's repertoire, parent impressions of child behavior change, the child's status in the community). (2) Investigators took greater interest in the baseline phases of clinical study. That is, the organization of child behavior repertoires and their relationship to the environment became topics of study. This look at *natural* generalization led to some useful guidelines in the search for treatment-produced generalization. Unfortunately, or perhaps fortunately (depending on one's belief system), such an expanded look at the worlds of troubled children produced doubts about the simplistic use of reinforcement procedures in clinical treatment. The Skinnerian theoretical principles behind such procedures were likewise questioned.

4. Anomalies

The early clinical extrapolations of Skinner's operant model lent an appealing simplicity to the quest for treatment generalization. This quest was spearheaded by two developmental psychologists whose two-volume text presented a brilliant application of operant (and respondent) principles to child development. For Sidney Bijou and Donald Baer (1961, 1965), child behavior was viewed largely as a function of its immediate stimulus consequences and antecedents. By and large, the bulk of those clinical studies reviewed earlier were stimulated by the Bijou-Baer formulations. Inherent in these formulations were at least three assumptions concerning generalization:

1. Deviant child behaviors are under the social reinforcement control of people who live with the child. Therefore, the treatment strategy of choice should entail shifting these reinforcement contingencies to

child behaviors deemed desirable by the child's family, school, and other natural groups. Granted this assumption, an effective shifting of contingencies ought to ensure generalization of treatment effects over time. That is, when the troubled child emits behaviors valued by members of a natural group, these members will be reinforced for using those social contingencies that developed the valued behaviors. In other words, the child's newfound desirable behaviors will serve to reinforce appropriate behaviors by the child's parents, teachers, and peers. Such reinforcement cycles should thus be self-perpetuating.

2. In the course of a child's natural development, that individual's behavior repertoire will become organized into functional classes. In addition, the social and physical stimuli composing the child's natural environment will likewise become grouped into functional classes (see pp. 38-41). In both cases, the resultant classes are understandable as operants. The response groupings are held together by common discriminative and reinforcing stimuli; the stimulus sets are related through a common response and its reinforcement contingencies.

The functional class assumption leads one to expect treatment-produced generalization across responses. When a clinician teaches a troubled child's caretakers to shift their reinforcement contingencies to a desirable child behavior, the impact of that shift should extend beyond the targeted behavior. If that behavior falls within a class of behaviors, then all behavioral members of the class should be altered in frequency. Thus, if we discover that a child's hitting and screaming are commonly reinforced by a parent, contingency management of hitting ought to affect screaming as well.

3. In those cases where a child's various problem and desirable behaviors are functionally independent, generalization must be programmed (see Baer, Wolf, & Risley, 1968). The "programming" notion ties directly into the previous two assumptions. If child behavior indeed follows the laws of operant and respondent pyschology, one ought to be able to induce stimulus generalization by setting common reinforcement contingencies for the independent behaviors. For example, suppose we find that a child's work behaviors at school and home are functionally independent (as did Wahler, 1969). By then ensuring that the child's parents and teachers apply common reinforcement contingencies to these behaviors, the two stimulus settings will become joined as a functional class—both will set the occasion for the child's work behavior. Maintenance of such setting generality over time would be expected through the social reinforcement cycle outlined in assumption number 1.

It may well be that the conceptual comfort offered by assumptions 1 and 2 fostered the casual examinations of generalization as seen in the early clinical studies. Generalization across time and behaviors ought to follow an operant-based intervention. If not, then one must take the pains to set contingencies that will produce the phenomenon. Since the operant is supposedly a natural unit of child behavior, its organizational properties should ensure therapeutic generalization.

4.1. The Impact of Behavior Ecology

At the time that the early operant clinical studies were under way, another group of child development investigators had already taken a different conceptual look at children. This group, usually referred to as the "behavior ecologists," shared the operant group's focus on children's natural environments. However, the conceptual guidelines for behavior ecology were broader than those steering the operant workers. The Lewinian concepts fostered by Roger Barker and Herbert Wright (e.g., Barker & Wright, 1954) led these pioneers to cover a wide range of child behaviors as well as multiple environments. While the behavior ecologists had little interest in clinical intervention, their observational findings had some important messages for the generalization-seeking operant group. Unfortunately, although major proponents of both groups were located at the same university (Kansas), functional communication between them was minimal.

In essence, findings of the behavior ecologists painted a rather pessimistic picture with respect to any easy road to clinical generalization. Perhaps the highlights in this respect could be centered on a "predictability" factor in the Barker-Wright data. First, the observational findings were clear in showing that the molar context of an environment was a good predictor of any child's behavioral pattern. Thus, school classrooms, playgrounds, drugstores, and homes yielded distinctly different styles of behavior for the same child. This independence of environmental settings underscored the importance of the "programming" assumption of the operant group.

Now, while the functional independence of child environments would not have surprised the operant-oriented clinical workers, ecological findings within these environments probably would have. Predictable relationships between child behavior and stimulus events composing environmental context were hard to come by, leading the behavior ecologists to emphasize repeatedly the complexity of child-environment interchanges. No doubt some of this complexity was due to the broad observational units employed in these ecological analyses. Nevertheless, a failure to find one-to-one relationships between child behaviors and environmental stimuli could be taken as a disquieting lack of support for the operant as a basic unit of interbehavioral analysis—if any degree of communication had existed between the two groups.

In the late 1960s, a single member of the behavior ecology movement attempted to bridge the communication gap between his group and the clinical-operant group. Edwin Willems's classic paper of 1968 voiced some obvious concerns about operant interpretations of how behavior-environment relationships are organized. His focus in this paper centered on natural generalization across behaviors. Willems took issue with the operant contention that child behaviors are tied together in any simple manner, such as through short-term stimulus contingencies (i.e., common reinforcers and discriminative stimuli). He noted the lack of evidence to suggest *any* extra-laboratory knowledge about the organizational properties of human behavior.

The essence of Willems's message to operant-clinical workers was a warning: a warning that generalization phenomena might turn out to be more detrimental than beneficial. He urged the clinicians to obtain better understandings of human ecology before pushing further advances in their intervention technology. However, in the absence of relevant data, Willems could only cite examples from the field of biology (e.g., detrimental unintended effects on water wildlife following river dam construction). Not surprisingly, Willems's arguments had little impact on operant technology at that time.

4.2. Anomalies in Operant Interventions

Perhaps indirectly, the behavior ecology movement did lead a few operant-oriented clinicians to broaden their research perspectives. Certainly the later papers in behavior ecology had such impact (see Warren & Rogers-Warren, 1977). As an added impetus in this direction, the operant workers were themselves becoming increasingly aware of their failures to examine generalization phenomena (e.g., Tharp & Wetzel, 1969, p.126; O'Leary, Becker, Evans, & Saudargas, 1969). The broadening or procedural expansion within the field grew in three directions: (1) The research population of troubled children and their social surroundings (e.g., families) became more heterogeneous. Up until the late 1960s, much of the operant-clinical work had been restricted to minor childhood problems (e.g., shyness) in social settings conducive to operant intervention (e.g., operant-oriented preschools). (2) The measurement of child behavior broadened from one or two responses to multiple responses. As noted earlier in this chapter, the development and use of coding systems for multiple child behaviors (Patterson *et al.*, 1969) was a major impetus in these procedural expansions. (3) Measurement was expanded across child environments and across time. This development was, of course, an obvious requirement to evaluate setting and maintenance generality.

Let us first consider the impact of sampling a wider variety of troubled children and their social environments. Up until the late 1960s, the most common means of changing problem behavior consisted of differential social attention. Consistent with operant assumption number 1 (p. 45), child behavior change and its maintenance over time ought to occur if the child's caretakers were to attend primarily to the child's desirable behaviors. Now, while the maintenance issue was seldom subjected to empirical scrutiny, the efficacy of differential attention in producing therapeutic change was substantiated in over 80 studies (Sajwaj & Dillon, 1977). However, continued efforts to apply the technique led to some very puzzling results—possibly due to some combination of differing subject samples studied in these later years. Wahler (1968) used the technique with the families of five severely oppositional children. While the mothers of these children correctly applied differential attention (approval) to the children's cooperative behavior, no therapeutic changes were evident over a period of 4 weeks. Likewise, Sajwaj and Hedges (1971) documented a similar failure with a 6-year-old oppositional child in a family setting. In this case, the lack of therapeutic change was observed over a 5-month time period. Strangely enough, when this child's parent (father) then praised the child's oppositional behavior, that behavior declined to zero frequency in just 6 days! Consistent with these procedural anomalies, Herbert, Pinkston, Hayden, Sajwaj, Pinkston, Cordua, and Jackson (1973) found that maternal attention following the problem behaviors of four children actually reduced the frequencies of these behaviors. Prior to these findings, the authors discovered consistent and stable increments in the children's problem behaviors when differential attention was used according to usual practice.

As of yet, no consistent pattern of behavioral, subject, or social setting characteristics has been shown to account for the anomalies just reviewed. Probably, some combination thereof will eventually prove to predict such treatment failures. At this point, one must wonder about the likelihood that a standard operant technique (differential attention) can lead to generalization across time. If the procedure sometimes fails to produce even short-term therapeutic results, what of long-term outcomes ?

In view of these failures, it is logical to look now at the more broadly expected outcomes of operant intervention—generalization across time and environmental settings. Recall that operant assumptions would predict generalization over time following an effective intervention, although an intervention may have to be programmed in more than one environmental setting to produce such maintenance.

The necessity of programming treatment generalization across settings is now quite obvious. Studies by Meichenbaum, Bowers and Ross (1968), Wahler (1969), Redd and Birnbrauer (1969), and Miller and Sloane (1976) all point to a compelling specificity of child behavior. Homes, schools, playgrounds, institutions, and other settings comprising a troubled child's community present remarkably "tough" boundaries as far as natural generalization is concerned. To even "program" setting generalization, one must realize the monumental effort that probably lies ahead. For example, Wahler, Berland, and Leske (1975) evaluated a simple programming effort to induce generalization from an institution to homes and public school settings. In this endeavor, the programming involved several hours of counseling the troubled children's parents and teachers in principles of contingency management. Despite these attempts to bridge environments, 82% of the children resumed their problem behaviors within 6 months of leaving the institutional facility.

The crucial necessity of pursuing an environmental programming strategy is not only seen in the previously reviewed studies. More recent treatment studies suggest that *detrimental* effects can occur in those child environments not covered by a treatment program. For example, if a clinical intervention is based in only one setting (e.g., home), therapeutic changes in that setting may be accompanied by a worsening of child behavior in another setting (e.g., school). These findings, while highly tentative and unpredictable, have been reported in three studies thus far (Skinrud, 1972; Walker, Hops, & Johnson, 1975; Wahler, 1975). Such procedural outcomes must be ranked as anomalies along with the previously cited puzzling effects of differential attention. These across-setting effects come as a total surprise in the face of extensive prior data pointing to the functional independence of common child environments. It is of interest to note, however, that a similar across-setting effect has already been well documented in the animal laboratory. "Behavioral contrast," as the phenomenon is usually called, refers to an inverse relationship in responding between two independently controlled stimulus settings (see Malone & Staddon, 1973; Reynolds, 1961). Thus, when a pigeon's disk pecking is controlled under two independent reinforcement schedules, planned changes in one schedule will not only alter the pecking rate under that schedule; the pigeon's rate will also shift in an opposite direction under the second, unchanged schedule. The anomalous nature of this sort of generalization has been noted by Malone (1975): "The interesting aspect of contrast effects, then, is that they seem to transcend the confines of operant discrimination learning; if traditional mechanisms cannot deal with them, then it is time to question the sufficiency of these mechanisms and, if necessary, seek others which are more appropriate."

When one turns next to an examination of generalization over time, another bleak picture of therapeutic outcomes is presented. While a few short-term follow-up studies suggest a self-perpetuating maintenance of treatment gains (Walker & Buckley, 1972; Herbert & Baer, 1972; Johnson & Christensen, 1975), the majority of child treatment studies have side-stepped the question by not including follow-up phases. In fact, a recent article by Forehand and Atkeson (1977) shows an inverse relationship between the rigor of follow-up assessment and evidence of treatment durability. Perhaps the most thorough follow-up study yet published (Patterson's 1-year assessment of treated families, 1974) points clearly to the fact that not all families are able to maintain therapeutic changes without continued help. As Wahler, Leske, and Rogers (1977) discovered, the reinforcement cycle that supposedly guarantees therapeutic maintenance (operant assumption number 1) may not be functional with poorly motivated caretakers who are pressed by financial problems, interference by extended family members, and crowded, unpleasant living conditions. These caretakers and their children might well prove extremely resistant to therapeutic generalization over time as well as settings. In highlighting this possibility, all child clinicians should become acquainted with a nonoperant, highly intensive therapeutic effort with a large sample of such families in the 1930s. The Cambridge-Sommerville counseling project for potentially delinquent children involved a comparison between two randomly selected groups of such youth (McCord, 1978). While the treated group judged the counseling to be helpful, a 30-year follow-up evaluation of all children revealed some shocking outcomes. On a wide variety of outcome measures (e.g., criminal convictions, employment status), the treated children suffered adolescent and adult problems more severe than those of the control children! In view of today's very limited and partially negative generalization of operant intervention techniques, it seems fair to conclude that the field has considerable cause to worry about the natural outcomes of this technology.

If, as the above studies suggest, there is little basis to trust natural generalization over settings and time, it would appear that a systematic programming strategy is called for. This view has been recently discussed by Stokes and Baer (1977), who provide a technological elaboration of the programming position outlined earlier by Baer *et al.* (1968). Also, there is limited evidence that such a strategy might lead to therapeutic generalization in terms of settings and time (Walker, Hops, & Johnson, 1975; Jones & Kazdin, 1975). However, one bothersome question not addressed by the programming advocates is this: What if the natural environments of children are organized in ways that eventually compete with technologically imposed contingencies (Willems, 1974)? Of course, there are good reasons to adopt a "try it and see" attitude (Baer, 1974)—particularly if the question were to impede needed intervention for troubled children. But, at the same time, it seems reasonable to argue that the nature-versus-technology question must be pursued. If the recent survey article by Keeley, Shemberg, and Carbonell (1976) is at all representative, we simply do not yet know how effectively clinicians can program generalization. Of the 146 studies reviewed, only 2.1% examined long-term setting generalization, and 5.4% provided "hard" data on maintenance generalization (at least 6 months follow-up). Clearly, there is reason to voice doubts about the outcomes of mixing imposed (programmed) contingencies within the natural contingencies of environments.

Questions regarding the natural and imposed structure of children's environments are probably best viewed within the topic of across-response generalization. Recall that this type of generalization presumes a child's behavior repertoire to be organized in such a way that planned changes in one of the child's responses will also affect other aspects of his or her behavior. Furthermore, it is assumed (by behaviorists) that environmental context plays an important role in the nature of this organization. From an operant viewpoint, the previously discussed response and stimulus *class* concepts describe the supposed hows and whys of behavior-environment relationships.

If the study of response generalization is to provide information on the natural structure of behavior-environment relationships, at least two criteria must be met: (1) Multiple child behaviors and their stimulus associations must be measured as they occur over time. (2) At some time, one or more of the child's behaviors must be altered in frequency through some kind of planned intervention. Through the procedures described in (1), it should then prove possible to examine response generalization and to evaluate the role of environmental factors (stimuli) in that process.

In recent years, a number of empirical studies have addressed the above generalization topic. As a group, these studies clearly document the reliable occurrence of across-behavior generalization. However, as was true of the previously cited investigations on setting and time generalization, factors instrumental to the process proved elusive. One of the earliest demonstrations of response generalization was reported by Wahler, Sperling, Thomas, Teeter, and Luper (1970). In this study, two children referred for help because of dysfluent speech were also found to present other, nonverbal behavior problems. When the children's mothers were trained to set social contingencies to remedy these latter problems, unexpected improvements also occurred in their speech problems. While experimental test probes proved that the two problem behaviors were functionally related, it was not possible to "explain" the relationship on the basis of stimuli in the children's environments. That is, the covarying behaviors did not share common discriminative or reinforcing stimuli. Likewise, Sajwaj, Twardosz, and Burke (1972) discovered that contingency management of one behavior produced generalization effects across behaviors. These investigators taught teachers to ignore a child's excessively adult-oriented behavior. The behavior declined in frequency as expected. In addition, the child interacted more frequently with peers, played less often with girls' toys, and he became more oppositional and disruptive in group settings. Once again, a search for environmental stimuli that might account for these united behaviors proved fruitless.

More intensive efforts to understand across-behavior generalization were employed by Wahler (1975) and Kara and Wahler (1977). In these studies, correlational analyses of lengthy baseline periods were implemented, as well as experimental test probes to evaluate possible generalization outcomes. The correlational analyses were viewed as hopeful ways of predicting generalization effects, and as a means to describe the process by which such effects occur. Both studies revealed that some aspects of across-behavior generalization can be predicted. However, none of the three children studied behaved in ways that made their covarying behaviors understandable. Stimuli that might have controlled the generalization process could not be discovered.

At this point in our discussion, it seems obvious that generalization phenomena are perplexing, elusive, and not always desirable aspects of treatment outcomes. The anomalies discussed suggest that we should hold off any firm commitment to conceptual models specifying the operating characteristics of child-environment relationships. While the popular operant model has proven to be a useful means of constructing child-treatment procedures, the model's efficacy in guiding our search for generalization is yet unclear. Changes in child behavior do occur when man-made contingencies are set; changes also occur during the child's natural development. But, like it or not, the behavioristic penchant to account for these changes through simple associations with environmental events has not yet produced a holistic understanding of child behavior. Although specific alterations in a child's behavior are understandable as a function of shifts in that behavior's stimulus antecedents and/or consequences, the larger response pattern affecting that behavior does not appear related to stimuli in any simple fashion. In other words, the organizational properties of a child's behavior repertoire are poorly understood; the organization is tied somehow to environmental settings (e.g., home), and on some occasions to more than one setting (e.g., home and school). However, just how these environment-behavior ties operate is unclear.

5. Self-Management: Generalization Directed from Within

Anomalies emerging in the search for generalization have bolstered a view of child behavior as partly a self-directed process. This more recent position on generalization phenomena is seen by some as a concerted effort to combine principles of operant psychology with selected aspects of "cognitive" psychology (e.g., Mahoney, 1974). Proponents of self-management (self-control, self-reinforcement) argue that traditional operant notions tend to minimize the two-way or bidirectional quality of child-environment relationships (see Bandura, 1971). That is, operant strategies usually orient the clinician to examine stimulus control of the child's behavior. One could just as well examine the child's control of those stimulus sources (e.g., parents and teachers)—and, as Goldiamond (1976) has pointed out, this alternate view is completely consistent within the operant concept. But a majority of operant-based clinical studies have chosen to follow a one-way path in examining stimulus control. Possibly, this selective attention by most operant clinicians has led the self-management group to seek "cognitive" guidance in a continued search for generalization. While the utility of this extraoperant guidance is hotly contested (see Mahoney, 1976; Goldiamond, 1976), there is little doubt that self-management has become a new look in child treatment.

If troubled children are capable of analyzing, setting, and modifying their environmental contingencies, a means of transcending the nebulous stimulus boundaries discussed earlier might be at hand. However, if such a strategy is to yield better generalization scores than the traditional operant approach, the troubled child must possess a powerful potential to direct the generalization process. Not only must the child be capable (through training) of accomplishing the tasks usually reserved for the operant-oriented clinician, that youthful person's efforts must also have more extensive and more sustained impact than has been true of adult-directed efforts. Thus, as was the case in developing traditional operant procedures, behavior change is only the first-sought criterion of clinical success; generalization looms ahead as the tougher criterion.

Although self-management procedures for troubled children are recent developments in the behavioristic helping field, there is already ample evidence that children can accomplish the standard clinical tasks leading to their own behavior change. Children can conduct their own behavioral assessments (Ballard & Glynn, 1975; Johnson & White, 1971), they can specify desired changes in their behaviors and set environmental contingencies to help produce these changes (Lovitt & Curtiss, 1969; Glynn, Thomas, & Shee, 1973), and they can identify and modify those environmental contingencies that support their problem behaviors (Seymour & Stokes, 1976). While all of these tasks require child training by a knowledgeable second party, it is clearly the child who carries out the tasks. There is little doubt that the self-management strategy now occupies a significant role in the child-clinical arena. In fact, it also seems clear that this strategy may be as effective as the traditional operant approach (Frederiksen & Frederiksen, 1975; Felixbrod & O'Leary, 1973).

Unfortunately, when one turns to an examination of the generalization outcomes of self-management, a picture at least as bleak as that produced by traditional operant procedures is evident. There are a few studies that show limited generalization over time (Drabman, Spitalnik, & O'Leary, 1973) and settings (Turkewitz, O'Leary, & Ironsmith, 1975), just as one can cite for the traditional operant approach. Also true of the early operant studies, the population of children and environments under self-management study has been rather limited in terms of problems (largely work behavior) and also restricted to a standard setting (usually regular school classrooms). An expanding of this population might well be followed by the anomalous findings characterized by previously discussed operant studies. Suggestions that this state of affairs might well be the case is seen in a recent study dealing with "disruptive" students in special school settings (Santogrossi, O'Leary, Romanczyk, & Kaufman, 1973). In this study, the generalization of treatment effects over time was quite short-lived (i.e., several days).

In summary, generalization evidence for self-management procedures is no more compelling than that cited for the external control of child problem behavior. But, then again, it is probably erroneous to think of these two procedural strategies as separate entities. If operant-clinical workers were to preserve the bidirectional properties of the operant, it is likely that the two strategies would be pursued *together*. Witness Bandura's succinct conclusion in this respect:

> Acquisition of self-reinforcement functions does not create an invariable control mechanism within the organism. Informal evidence indicates that activation of self-reinforcement is under discriminative control. In humans, for example, the same behavior is not uniformly self-rewarded or self-punished irrespective of the circumstances under which it is performed. Self-reinforcement contingencies that are customarily applied to certain classes of behavior can be temporarily suspended by exonerative justifications and environmental arrangements that obscure or distort the relationship between actions and the effects they produce. Moreover, people learn to discriminate

between situations in which self-reward is made contingent upon performance and those in which it is appropriate to reward oneself noncontingently. (Bandura, Mahoney, & Dirks, 1976, p. 1)

It is tempting to believe that some combination of self-management and a concerted analysis and modification of the troubled child's external environment might be a keystone set of procedures for generalization. But, while both approaches used independently have produced documented changes in problem behavior, neither has led to dependable generalization. Why then should a combination hold more promise? It is our contention that a conceptual base common to both strategies can be filtered from the empirical findings thus far. That base, composed of two global factors, sets a combination of guidelines seldom followed together in generalization research:

(Factor 1). Organizational properties of the child's behavior repertoire. This factor has emerged as an important consideration in the traditional operant-clinical camp. As we argued earlier, successful programming of generalization over time and stimulus settings will probably depend on the ways in which a child's various behaviors are naturally organized. If one were then to strip away "cognitive" software of the self-management strategy, it appears that this same factor emerges as a central consideration. *Self-observation, self-instructions,* and *self-recording* are terms crucial to the operations of self-management. All are potentially documented behaviors and, as such, they represent components of the child's behavior repertoire. The task at hand from a self-management viewpoint is to determine how these selected behaviors might alter other aspects of the child's own repertoire. Thus, regardless of whether the clinical strategy emphasizes self- or external control, both have reason to focus on covariations within the troubled child's behavior repertoire.

(Factor 2). Closely related to factor 1 is the role of environmental context and its interplay with the child's behavior repertoire. Recall that this factor has been examined in pursuit of an operant explanation for across-behavior generalization. While such an explanation has yet to emerge, available findings strongly suggest some sort of functional ties between environmental context and the child's repertoire of responses. Both the environmental specificity findings (e.g., Wahler, 1969) and the tentative behavior contrast findings (e.g., Walker, Hops, & Johnson, 1975) indicate a perplexing but definite connection between context and behavior. Of course, an equal interest in environmental context is shared by self-management proponents. Contrary to the label implications, most workers in this area argue against the "self" as an autonomous governor of behavior (e.g., Bandura *et al.,* 1976). As in traditional operant findings, results from self-management studies point to complex and yet unknown dependencies between the child's behavior repertoire and environmental context.

It is our contention that future behavioristic attempts to understand generalization can best be fostered with the ambiguous guidance of the above two factors. We believe that more specific guidelines are simply unwarranted in view of our primitive understanding of child-environment relationships. In line with the early views of Skinner (1953), it is time for broad empirical studies that are largely inductive in strategy.

6. An Inductive Look at Ecobehavioral Networks

This final section is devoted to our view of future trends in generalization research—trends that follow the sparsely outlined notions encompassed in factors 1 and 2. We refer to these trends as inductive because of the minimal conceptual guidance offered by the factors; they are ecobehavioral in the sense that broad views of child behavior in natural settings are emphasized. Recently, such trends can be seen in the child-oriented work of Patterson (1977), Risley (1977), and Wahler, Berland, Coe, and Leske (1977). This work may be generally referred to as a "behavioral systems" orientation and, briefly, involves the following notions. The child is viewed as a behavioral system operating within a nested hierarchy of ever-encompassing behavioral systems, such as the family, the block, the neighborhood, and the community. Each of these systems is a level within which component elements are interdependent in the way they function. A given level of behavioral system is affected by the dynamics of levels above and below it. For instance, the family's functioning would be considered a function of the dynamics within each member's repertoire, among family members, and between family members and the outside world, both individually and collectively. The interdependency within a given level (e.g., the family) would mean that changes wrought on one element of that system would affect the other elements in the system, and the other elements in the system would be expected to exert a potent influence on the individual. This type of model for human behavior is like that of mathematical systems theory and can be found to be in use in nearly all scientific fields (Sutherland, 1973).

The behavioral systems model, then, emphasizes the importance of relations among behaviors within a given level, and the importance of the context within which a system functions. A correlational strategy presented by Wahler, House, and Stambaugh (1976) is one way of describing these relations among behaviors and environmental stimuli. In this strategy, the events of interest would be depicted as quantified covariations both within levels and between levels of system operation. At present, the term *covariation* or *correlation* refers to relations in a global—but quantifiable—sense. For example, Lichstein's correlational analysis of an autistic child's behavior repertoire revealed some systematic patterns made up of self-stimulation, and nonsocial responses (Lichstein & Wahler, 1976). While this response class proved stable over time, the correlational analysis could not discern more precise temporal or sequential connections among its members. To do so would have required a more fine-grained ethological strategy typical of that employed by Patterson and his co-workers (Patterson *et al.*, 1969). This approach to the same phenomena would entail the use of conditional probability analyses describing sequential dependencies among these variables (Patterson, 1977). Obviously, one's strategy of choice in "systems analysis" is somewhat arbitrary; the molar strategy has the advantage of yielding a broad picture of system operation; the more molecular ethological strategy, while usually missing the big picture, is more likely to determine the underpinnings of *how* the system operates. Ideally, of course, both approaches would be employed. Presently, however, little research of either type has appeared in the child-clinical arena. Thus our choice of material to present from this point on will necessarily be restrictive, primarily encompassing our own molar correlational strategy.

The previously reviewed response class findings within child repertoires, together with the behavioral systems model, suggest the possibility of similar behavior covariations among family members' behaviors. Berland (1976) investigated this question and found complex networks of behavior covariations among family members' repertoires. As an example, a child's problem behaviors were found to correlate over time with parental and sibling behaviors directed to the child—as one might expect. But of greater interest was the fact that some of these predictive parental and sibling behaviors were themselves significantly intercorrelated. Thus a parent's behavior directed to the child appeared to be a function of more than just that child's behavior. As the second-order correlations would suggest, parent-parent and parent-sibling interchanges contributed *indirectly* to a parent's child-directed behaviors. Similary, Patterson and Maerov (1976) and Moore and Patterson (1977) were able to discern brief but stable classes of parent-child and child-parent response sequences. As was true for individual children, family response classes were found to include a variety of social, nonsocial, deviant, nondeviant, active, and idle behaviors. These findings serve to verify the behavioral systems model and emphasize the complexity and inclusiveness of relations among family members' behaviors.

An extension of this kind of analysis to relations between the family and its community was recently suggested by Wahler, Leske, and Rogers (1977). They have proposed to examine an "Insularity Hypothesis" by looking for correlations between exchanges within the home and interactions by family members outside the home. According to the hypothesis, families showing little evidence of treatment generalization may have patterns of extrafamily interactions that compete with therapeutic change (insularity). An insular family ought to display a different set of community interchanges than would be true of a noninsular family. And, on a correlational level, such outside-the-family social contacts should show impact on how these families operate. Recent findings by Leske, Afton, Rogers, and Wahler (1978) provide confirmation. Parents of families who were poor bets to show treatment generalization also produced very low rates of community interaction, and those produced were primarily with kinfolk and helping agency representatives. Now, it was also found that rate of outside contact was highly correlated *inversely* with parent-child problem interchanges (the lower the rate of extrafamily contacts by a parent, the higher the rate of parent-child problems). To a lesser extent, kinfolk and helping agency contacts were also correlated (positively) with parent-child problem interchanges. In essence then, family member interactions at the community level must be considered part of the overall social system affecting a child's adaptive and maladaptive behaviors.

The types of findings mentioned in the paragraphs above demonstrate the appropriateness of the general behavioral systems model for describing social environmental determinants of individual child behavior. They also depict the utility of the correlational strategy for investigating and describing child behavior in its family and community contexts. These studies are only the most initial forays into this type of research, of course, describing very little of behavior structure at the various levels. While they confirm the importance of interbehavioral relations to generalization research, they have investigated only a limited number of behaviors, or tried to verify only limited generalization research concepts (e.g., insularity) thus far. However, there have been some clinical applications developed for the correlational findings. The first of these entails the assessment and prediction of treatment generality effects across behaviors in the child's repertoire (Kara & Wahler, 1977). Anticipation of these effects might make the clinical worker's job easier and the troubled family's therapeutic transition more painless.

A second application of behavior correlation findings is the possibility of "indirect modification" procedures. If two behaviors covary across baseline and treatment conditions when only one of them is being modified, then it should be possible to target one behavior and change a problem covariate. More than just an interesting trick, this procedure would make it possible to modify low-rate child behavior problems that are nearly impossible to monitor and modify directly. Examples of such behaviors include lying, thievery, fighting away from home, truancy, and similar problems commonly found in oppositional children.

The present authors' study of behavior covariations has revealed findings differing greatly among children within and across settings. However, a relatively uniform sample of high-risk oppositional children we examined did show a common set of covariations that reduced essentially to an inverse relationship between low-rate problems and sustained, independent work in the school; the same correlational match was revealed between low-rate problems and sustained independent toy play in the home (Wahler & Moore, 1975). A relatively simple procedure designed to increase rates of independent toy play at home through behavioral contracts was then examined. The aim, of course, was to indirectly reduce rates of the inversely related low-rate problem behaviors. In the two preliminary samples of high-risk chronic oppositional families investigated, the stable families with more regular (though deviant) daily behavior patterns showed measurable improvements with this procedure, while unstable families were not favorably affected (Berland, Resch, & Wahler, 1977). Of the successful families, 50% were prior failures with traditional home-based behavioral contracting. The improvements generalized beyond the predicted improvements in low-rate problems. Decreases in high-rate problems and improvements in parent attitudes and parent-child interactions were also present in these families. Of interest in the context of this chapter is the fact that these multiple behaviors were assessed; it is hoped that the patterns of change in these behaviors and others will make apparent the mechanism generating success with this procedure.

The clinical applications made so far of behavior covariation studies have been largely the result of concern with behavioral generality, or effects on it. The suggestion has been made that these contextual influences in behavioral systems may have a significant bearing on the generality of treatment changes over time, i.e., the durability of these changes following intervention. Though ground-breaking efforts at best, these studies are examples of generality measurement and research generating changes, or innovations in treatment procedures. They also exemplify the notion of an interplay between descriptive studies of naturally occurring relations among behaviors and intervention, or change-inducing investigations. We see these two approaches as being essential to the development of effective generalization research and research products. We will emphasize and elaborate them in the rest of our discussion.

The notion that generality research should affect treatment development is central to the proposed shift in generalization research being called for in this chapter. The view evident in the material reviewed by Forehand and Atkeson (1977) and Stokes and Baer (1977) is that the origins of treatment strategies are usually considered independently from the origins of "generalization strategies." According to this view, generalization programming should occur following the successful implementation of treatment procedures. However, we believe that factors controlling generalization are not usefully studied on their own. While there are certainly different stages of treatment development that may require different research strategies, examples have already been given of how descriptive and intervention studies of generalization can be integrated with therapeutic procedures. Changes following treatment may be favorable or undesirable and involve problem and nonproblem behaviors. It is this broadened perspective that is necessary to account for the real-world changes that result from treatment. The perspective can and should affect the kinds of behaviors chosen for treatment, the nature of the strategies used, and the criteria and behaviors assessed for outcome and generality.

This becomes more apparent when one begins viewing child referrals from a behavioral systems perspective. Treatment and generality need to be dealt with at various systems levels simultaneously. When you look, you quickly begin to see that what is initially the referral of an oppositional child often involves more complex problems within the family. Typically, other children in the family also pose problems, both at home and in other settings. In many of these families (up to 85% according to Johnson & Lobitz, 1974), the parents are having marital difficulties as well as child management problems. One or both parents is also usually having difficulties in the community ouside the home, either with neighbors, on the job, with public agencies, or with friends and relatives. Often any one of these kinds of problems might disrupt family function, and treating one to the exclusion of the others would leave deviant influences in the system, threatening treatment success.

These other kinds of problems are among the environmental factors controlling the generality of improvements in deviant children. Environmental factors figure highly in the other problems, too. Increasingly complicated measurement at various levels in the family system (not necessarily all by the same investigator) will begin to form a picture of these influences. From this picture, mechanisms controlling problem phenomena should begin to emerge. Treatment programs utilizing these mechanisms to best advantage should increasingly overcome environmental countereffects on treatment-induced change. While at an early stage, the type of family described above might have to be treated in a piecemeal fashion to manage each of the various problems; keystone factors, which control several problems at one time, will ideally begin to be discovered. The interdependent nature of families, already verified empirically, suggests the likelihood of this possibility. Treatments derived from such factors would be more efficient and effective.

How far-ranging these measurement and treatment procedures need to be remains an open question. Evidence of community influences on child and family behavior has already been cited, and influences among community components and upon the community from outside are being investigated as possible sources of problem maintenance or propagation. As these influences are verified and analyzed, their role in treatment strategies may increase. Some forms of community-wide treatment are not farfetched notions even now and may be found to be necessary in the so-called high-risk communities discussed by Wahler and Moore (1975). Certainly the various behavioral relations within the family need further, more detailed examination. These are pressing because of the prominent role the family plays in the life of the child. Relations among behaviors within each child's repertoire have been examined, although the ground has been barely broken. Relations among children in a family need examination. These would include direct influences on one child's behavior(s) by those of one or more other children, and influences on changes or patterns within one child's repertoire by behaviors in siblings. The same kinds of influence on children by parents, and on one parent by another, need examination and analysis. Direct influence on various behaviors, or influence on changes in relations among behaviors within the individual's repertoire by events outside the home, need study for each family member. The possible complexities in such research grow by leaps and bounds with very little imagination. Very quickly, bivariate analyses would give way to all manner of multivariate investigations. Correlational and sequential analyses would include increasingly diverse and indirect kinds of relations. However, before the reader, especially the clinical practitioner, throws his or her hands up in despair and claims that this is fine in theory but is unlikely to ever occur, note some real limits and qualifications on these suggestions.

To begin with, these analyses and the accumulating knowledge of individual and group response structures will grow slowly over time. No call is being made to give up all intervention research until all behavioral relations have been described and analyzed. Intervention studies will and should continue right along with more descriptive studies of naturally occurring relations. Such intervention studies will be necessary because of our continual press to find new and better ways to help families in distress. These studies will also be useful because they will likely suggest other intervention and descriptive studies. Many behavioral phenomena do not become apparent until manipulations are made or pressures put on behavioral systems to change. The effect on much intervention research might just be inclusion of more measurement at various levels of family behavioral systems. To be sure, we believe there is an immediate need to take a multilevel approach to treatment, as described above, if effectiveness is to begin improving. The measurement and complete analyses of these levels can only come with time, however.

Note also that not every investigator will examine every level so closely. Some will develop concepts pertaining to multiple levels, but others may study concepts applying only within one level, or between only two levels. The field as a whole would piece together the picture of various behavioral systems and the inter- and intrarelations. What is being described in this chapter, while specific in many ways, is also in many ways a general frame of reference for generalization research. As such, it should not pose a threat to clinical practitioners or researchers. Clinical treatment need not include many of these facets being called for in clinical research. While the scope of clinical practice would, one hopes, expand in response to a continuing accumulation of evidence supporting this view, the immense burden of complete measurement would not be typically part of this practice. Practitioners should only be more aware of the results and implications of this type of research.

For researchers expanding their perspective to a behavioral systems view, there are a number of methodological issues that should not be overlooked. Space limitations permit only brief mention to be made of some of these: (1) The molecularity or molarity of the behaviors to be studied will vary according to the circumstances and issues under investigation. (2) The question of whether to do intervention or descriptive research will vary with the individual investigator and the nature of the behavior problem. The issue may grow to be one of degree toward one or the other as the field progresses. (3) There are many existing and potential criteria for choosing behaviors to be measured and analyzed. Clearly in the forefront of these criteria is clinical relevance, but as the research expands, this criterion will take on new meaning itself. The independent toy play research described earlier already demonstrates the range of behaviors beyond problem responses that may take on clinical relevance. (4) In promoting a view of child-clinical research that emphasizes environmental determinants of behavior, the discussion has revolved primarily around the measurement of social stimuli. This does not mean that physical stimuli do not figure highly in an individual or family's response patterns. Environmental psychology has begun measuring a wide range of such stimuli. For instance, Risley and his co-workers have conducted a number of such analyses of day-care environments (Risley, 1977). These investigators have already provided data concerning beneficial arrangements of sleeping areas and play equipment. Such might also be true for families in their homes, possibly affecting child-adult problems and their elimination. (5) Population, setting, and problem differences may affect the choices made of behaviors to study. (6) The type of measurement is another important issue. Observational measurement, generally preferred by behavioral researchers, is not always feasible. Balance must be made between psychometric limitations of other types of measures, and their utility in exploring behavioral phenomena inaccessible to direct observation. Combinations and cross-verifications with various measures will probably be the route investigators will have to take. (7) A final example is the possibility of effects on choice of design in intervention studies. For instance, the behavioral systems model may pose limitations on the multiple-baseline design. Hall and Fox (1977) describe this design as involving the generation of concurrent baseline measures of behavior across behaviors, subjects, and settings. A change is made in one behavior with the expectation that the other behaviors will stay the same if the change is due to the manipulation made on the targeted response. In effect, it is assumed that the behaviors being measured are all under direct environmental control and operate in isolation, completely independent of one another. These assumptions are contradicted by numerous findings already available. The independent toy play contracting research cited above is one example. Research designs will have to recognize and accommodate this interdependency.

An overview of this chapter must leave one with a sense of frustration. From the laboratory era to the present-day ecobehavioral orientation, the child-clinical field has not gained a great deal of useful information on generalization phenomena. There is no doubt that some sort of process or processes govern those general outcomes of man-made and natural changes in child behavior. But we are just beginning to unearth the network behind these outcomes. Despite our own frustration at this state of affairs, we must also voice a guarded optimism for the future. Clinicians will (and should) continue their intervention efforts as if it were now possible to ensure appropriate generalization effects. In our view, the current ecobehavioral research emphasis will gradually add techniques and conceptual guidelines to these efforts. As long as clinicians realize that their work in promoting generalization is in dire need of research support, the clincial field will grow with substance.

7. References

Allen, K. E., Hart, B., Buell, J., Harris, F., & Wolf, M. M. Effects of social reinforcement on isolate behavior of a nursery school child. *Child Development*, 1964, *35*, 511-518.

Baer, D. M. A note on the absence of a Santa Claus in any known ecosystem: A rejoinder to Willems. *Journal of Applied Behavior Analysis*, 1974, *7*, 167-170.

Baer, D. M., & Sherman, J. A. Reinforcement control of generalized imitation in young children. *Journal of Experimental Child Psychology*, 1964, *1*, 37-49.

Baer, D. M., Wolf, M. M., & Risley, T. R. Some current dimensions of applied behavior analysis. *Journal of Applied Behavior Analysis*, 1968, *1*, 91-97.

Ballard, K. D., & Glynn, T. Behavioral self-management in story writing with elementary school children. *Journal of Applied Behavior Analysis*, 1975, *8*, 387-398.

Bandura, A. Vicarious and self-reinforcement processes. In R. Glaser (Ed.), *The nature of reinforcement*, New York: Academic Press, 1971. pp. 228-278.

Bandura, A. *Aggression: A social learning analysis.* Englewood Cliffs, N.J.: Prentice-Hall, 1973.

Bandura, A., Mahoney, M. J., & Dirks, S. J. Discriminative activation and maintenance of contingent self-reinforcement. *Behaviour Research and Therapy*, 1976, *14*, 1-6.

Barker, R. G., & Wright, H. F. *Midwest and its children: The psychological study of an American town*. Evanston, Ill.: Row, Peterson Publishers, 1954.

Berland, R. M. *The family social system and child deviancy: A comparison of deviant and non-deviant families*. Unpublished doctoral dissertation, University of Tennessee, Knoxville, 1976.

Berland, R. M., Resch, E. E, & Wahler, R. G. *Independent toy play: A keystone behavior in the treatment of oppositional children*. Summary of an APA symposium presentation: Applied research on response generalization: Progress and perspectives, San Francisco, August 1977.

Bijou, S. W., & Baer, D. M. *Child Development* (Vol. 1). New York: Appleton-Century-Crofts, 1961.

Bijou, S. W. & Baer, D. M. *Child Development* (Vol. 2). New York: Appleton-Century-Crofts, 1965.

Bolstad, O., & Johnson, S. Self-regulation in the modification of disruptive classroom behavior. *Journal of Applied Behavior Analysis*, 1972, *5*, 443-454.

Dollard, J., & Miller, N. E. *Personality and psychotherapy*. New York: McGraw-Hill, 1950.

Drabman, R. S., Spitalnik, R. & O'Leary, K. D. Teaching self-control to disruptive children. *Journal of Abnormal Psychology*, 1973, *82*, 10-16.

Felixbrod, J. F. & O'Leary, K. D. Effects of reinforcement on children's academic behavior as a function of self-determined and externally imposed contingencies. *Journal of Applied Behavior Analysis*, 1973, *6*, 241-250.

Forehand, R., & Atkeson, B. M. Generalization of treatment effects with parents as therapists: A review of assessment and implementation procedures. *Behavior Therapy*, 1978, *8*, 575-593.

Frederiksen, L. W., & Frederiksen, C. B. Teacher determined and self determined token reinforcement in a special education classroom. *Behavior Therapy*, 1975, *6*, 310-314.

Glynn, E. L., Thomas, J. D., & Shee, S. M. Behavioral self-control of on-task behavior in an elementary classroom. *Journal of Applied Behavior Analysis*, 1973, *6*, 105-113.

Goldiamond, I. Self-reinforcement. *Journal of Applied Behavior Analysis*, 1976, *9*, 509-514.

Hall, R. V., & Fox, R. G. Changing criterion designs: An alternate applied behavior analysis procedure. In B. Etzel, J. LeBlanc, & D. M. Baer (Eds.), *New developments in behavioral research: Theory, method and application*. Hillsdale, N. J.: Lawrence Erlbaum Associates, 1977.

Harris, F. R., Johnston, M. K., Kelley, C. W., & Wolf, M. M. Effects of positive social reinforcement on regressed crawling of a nursery school child. *Journal of Educational Psychology*, 1964, *55*, 35-41.

Harris, F. R., Wolf, M. M., & Baer, D. M. Effects of adult social reinforcement on child behavior. *Young Children*, 1964, *20*, 8-17.

Hart, B. M., Allen, K. E., Buell, J. S., Harris, F. R., & Wolf, M. M. Effects of social reinforcement on operant crying. *Journal of Experimental Child Psychology*, 1964, *1*, 145-153.

Herbert, E. W., & Baer, D. M. Training parents as behavior modifiers: Self recording of contingent attention. *Journal of Applied Behavior Analysis*, 1972, *5*, 139-149.

Herbert, E. W., Pinkston, E. M., Hayden, M. L, Sajwaj, T. E., Pinkston, S., Cordua, G., & Jackson, C. Adverse effects of differential parent attention. *Journal of Applied Behavior Analysis*, 1973, *6*, 15-30.

Hobbs, N. Helping disturbed children: Psychological and ecological strategies. *American Psychologist*, 1966, *21*, 1105-1115.

Hull, C. L. *Principles of behavior.* New York: Appleton-Century-Crofts, 1943.

Johnson, S. M., & Christensen, A. Multiple criteria follow-up of behavior modification with families. *Journal of Abnormal Child Psychology*, 1975, *3*, 135-154.

Johnson, S. M., & Lobitz, G. K. *The personal and marital adjustment of parents as related to observed child deviance and parenting behaviors.* Unpublished manuscript, University of Oregon, Eugene, 1974.

Johnson, S. M., & White, G. Self-observation as an agent of behavior change. *Behavior Therapy*, 1971, *2*, 488-497.

Jones, R. T. & Kazdin, A. E. Programming response maintenance after withdrawing token reinforcement. *Behavior Therapy,* 1975, *6*, 153-164.

Kara, A., & Wahler, R. G. Some organizational properties of a young child's behavior. *Journal of Experimental Child Psychology,* 1977, *24*, 24-39.

Keeley, S. M., Shemberg, K. M., & Carbonell, J. Operant clinical intervention: Behavior management or beyond? Where are the data? *Behavior Therapy*, 1976, *7*, 292-305.

Leske, G., Afton, A., Rogers, E. S., & Wahler, R. G. The interpersonal functioning of insular and non-insular families: Factors related to treatment success and failure. Unpublished paper.

Lichstein, K. & Wahler, R. G. The ecological assessment of an autistic child. *Journal of Abnormal Child Psychology*, 1976, *4*, 31-54.

Lovaas, O. I. Interaction between verbal and nonverbal behavior. *Child Development*, 1961, *32*, 329-336.

Lovitt, T. C., & Curtiss, K. A. Academic response rate as a function of teacher and self-imposed contingencies. *Journal of Applied Behavior Analysis*, 1969, *2*, 45-53.

Mahoney, M. J. *Cognition and behavior modification.* Cambridge, Mass.: Ballinger, 1974.

Mahoney, M. J. Terminal terminology: A self-regulated response to Goldiamond. *Journal of Applied Behavior Analysis*, 1976, *9*, 515-517.

Malone, J. C. The integration of operant behaviors. NIMH grant proposal (page 11), 1975.

Malone, J. C., & Staddon, J. E. R. Contrast effects in maintained generalization gradients. *Journal of the Experimental Analysis of Behavior*, 1973, *19*, 167-179.

McCord, J. A thirty year follow-up of treatment effects. *American Psychologist,* 1978, *33*, 284-289.

Meichenbaum, D. H., Bowers, K. S., and Ross, R. R. Modification of classroom behavior of institutionalized female adolescent offenders. *Behavior Research and Therapy*, 1968, *6*, 343-353.

Miller, S. J., & Sloane, H. N. The generalization effects of parent training across stimulus settings. *Journal of Applied Behavior Analysis*, 1976, *9*, 355-370.

Moore, D. R., & Patterson, G. R. *Behavior structure in deviant family systems.* Summary of presentation at APA symposium: Applied research on response generalization: Progress and perspectives, San Francisco, August 1977.

O'Leary, K. D., Becker, W. C., Evans, M. B., & Saudargas, R. A. A token reinforcement program in a public school: A replication and systematic analysis. *Journal of Applied Behavior Analysis*, 1969, *2*, 3-13.

Patterson, G. R. Intervention for boys with conduct problems: Multiple settings, treatments and criteria. *Journal of Consulting and Clinical Psychology*, 1974, *42*, 471-481.

Patterson, G. R. A three-stage functional analysis for children's coercive behaviors: A tactic for developing a performance theory. In B. Etzel, J. LeBlanc, & D. Baer (Eds.), *New developments in behavioral research: Theory, method and application*. Hillsdale, N. J.: Lawrence Erlbaum Associates, 1977.

Patterson, G. R., & Maerov, S. *Functional analysis of stimuli controlling coercive behaviors in two settings*. Paper presented at the Association for the Advancement of Behavior Therapy, New York, December 1976.

Patterson, G. R., Ray, R. S., Shaw, D. A., & Cobb, J. A. *A manual for coding family interactions, sixth revision*, 1969. Available from ASIS National Auxiliary Publications Service, in care of CCM Information Service, Inc., 90 Third Avenue, New York, N.Y. 10022. Document # 01234.

Phillips, E. L. Achievement place: Token reinforcement procedures in a home-style rehabilitation setting for "pre-delinquent" boys. *Journal of Applied Behavior Analysis*, 1968, *1*, 213-223.

Redd, W. H., & Birnbrauer, J. S. Adults as discriminative stimuli for different reinforcement contingencies with retarded children. *Journal of Experimental Child Psychology*, 1969, *1*, 440-447.

Reynolds, G. S. Behavioral contrast. *Journal of the Experimental Analysis of Behavior*, 1961, *4*, 57-71.

Rickard, H. C., & Mundy, M. B. Direct manipulation of stuttering behavior: An experimental-clinical approach. In L. P. Ullman & L. Krasner (Eds.), *Case studies in behavior modification*. New York: Holt, Rinehart & Winston, 1965.

Risley, T. R. The ecology of applied behavior analysis. In A. Rogers-Warren, & S. F. Warren, *Ecological perspectives in applied behavior analysis*. Baltimore: University Park Press, 1977.

Sajwaj, T., & Dillon, A. Complexities of an "elementary" behavior modification procedure: Differential adult attention used for children's behavior disorders. In B. Etzel, J. LeBlanc, & D. M. Baer, (Eds.), *New developments in behavioral research: Theory, methods and application*. Hillsdale, N. J.: Lawrence Erlbaum Associates, 1977.

Sajwaj, T. E., & Hedges, D. Functions of parental attention in an oppositional, retarded boy. *Proceedings of the 79th Annual Convention of the American Psychological Association*, 1971, 697-698.

Sajwaj, T., Twardosz, S., & Burke, M. Side effects of extinction procedures in a remedial preschool. *Journal of Applied Behavior Analysis*, 1972, *5*, 163-175.

Santogrossi, D. A., O'Leary, K. D., Romanczyk, R. G., & Kaufman, K. F. Self-evaluation by adolescents in a psychiatric hospital school token program. *Journal of Applied Behavior Analysis*, 1973, *6*, 277-287.

Seymour, F. W., & Stokes, T. F. Self-recording in teaching girls to increase work and evoke staff praise in an institution for offenders. *Journal of Applied Behavior Analysis*, 1976, *9*, 41-54.

Sherman, J. A. Modification of nonverbal behavior through reinforcement of related verbal behavior. *Child Development*, 1964, *35*, 717-723.

Skinner, B. F. *Science and human behavior*. New York: Macmillan, 1953.

Skinrud, K. *Generalization of treatment effects from home to school settings*, Unpublished manuscript, Oregon Research Institute, Eugene, 1972.

Spence, K. W. The basis of solution by chimpanzees of the intermediate size problem. *Journal of Experimental Psychology*, 1942, *31* , 257-271.

Stokes, T. F., & Baer, D. M. An implicit technology of generalization. *Journal of Applied*

Behavior Analysis, 1977, *10*, 349-367.

Sutherland, J. W. *A general systems philosophy for the social and behavioral sciences*. New York: George Braziller, 1973.

Tharp, R. G., & Wetzel, R. J. *Behavior modification in the natural environment*. New York: Academic Press, 1969.

Turkewitz, H., O'Leary, K. D., & Ironsmith, M. Producing generalization and maintenance of appropriate behavior through self-control. *Journal of Consulting and Clinical Psychology*, 1975, *43*, 577-583.

Wahler, R. G. *Behavior therapy for oppositional children: Love is not enough*, Paper presented at the Eastern Psychological Association Convention, Washington, D. C., 1968.

Wahler, R. G. Setting generality: Some specific and general effects of child behavior therapy. *Journal of Applied Behavior Analysis*, 1969, *2*, 239-246.

Wahler, R. G. Some structural aspects of deviant child behavior. *Journal of Applied Behavior Analysis*, 1975, *8*, 27-42.

Wahler, R. G., Berland, R. M., Coe, T. D., & Leske, G. Social systems analysis: Implementing an alternative behavioral model. In A. R. Warren & S. F. Warren (Eds.), *Ecological perspectives in behavior analysis*, Baltimore: University Park Press, 1977, pp. 211-228.

Wahler, R. G., Berland, R. M., and Leske, G. *Environmental boundaries in behavior modification: Problems in residential treatment of children*, Unpublished manuscript, Child Behavior Institute, University of Tennessee, Knoxville, 1975.

Wahler, R. G., House, A. E. & Stambaugh, E. E. *Ecological assessment of child problem behavior*. New York: Pergamon Press, 1976.

Wahler, R. G., Leske, G., & Rogers, E. S. The insular family: A deviance support system for oppositional children. *Banff International Conference on Behavior Modification*, 1977.

Wahler, R. G., & Moore, D. M. *School-home behavior change procedures for oppositional children*, Paper presented at the Association for the Advancement of Behavior Therapy, San Francisco, 1975.

Wahler, R. G., Sperling, K., Thomas, M., Teeter, N., & Luper, H. The modification of childhood stuttering: Some response-response relationships. *Journal of Experimental Child Psychology*, 1970, *9*, 411-428.

Wahler, R. G., Winkel, G. H., Peterson, R. F., & Morrison, D. C. Mothers as behavior therapists for their own children. *Behaviour Research and Therapy*, 1965, *3*, 113-124.

Walker, H. M., & Buckley, N. K. Programming generalization and maintenance of treatment effects across time and across settings. *Journal of Applied Behavior Analysis*, 1972, *5*, 209-224.

Walker, H. M., Hops, H., & Johnson, S. M. Generalization and maintenance of classroom treatment effects. *Behavior Therapy*, 1975, *6*, 188-200.

Warren, S. F., & Rogers-Warren, A. *Ecological perspectives in behavior analysis*, Baltimore: University Park Press, 1977.

Watson, J. B., & Raynor, R. Conditioned emotional reactions. *Journal of Experimental Psychology*, 1920, *3*, 1-14.

Willems, E. P. An ecological orientation in psychology. *Merrill-Palmer Quarterly*, 1968, *11*, 317-343.

Willems, E. P. Behavioral technology and behavioral ecology. *Journal of Applied Behavior Analysis*, 1974, *7*, 151-160.

Williams, C. The elimination of tantrum behavior by extinction procedures. *Journal of Abnormal and Social Psychology*, 1959, *59*, 269.

Wolf, M. M., Risley, T., & Mees, H. L. Application of operant conditioning procedures to the behavior problems of an autistic child. *Behaviour Research and Therapy*, 1964, *1*, 305-312.

Wolf, M. M., Risley, T., Johnston, M., Harris, F. R., & Allen, K. E. Application of operant conditioning procedures to the behavior problems of an autistic child: A follow-up and extension. *Behaviour Research and Therapy*, 1967, *5*, 103-111.

Wolpe, J. P. *Psychotherapy by reciprocal inhibition*. Stanford: Stanford University Press, 1958.

3 Learning Disability and Hyperactivity (with Comments on Minimal Brain Dysfunction)

JAMES M. KAUFFMAN
AND DANIEL P. HALLAHAN

Practitioners in the child-care professions—especially clinical psychologists, pediatricians, psychiatrists, and educators—are very frequently called upon to deal with children who have serious academic difficulty in school and/or behave in ways that exasperate adults. The recognition, clinical description, and treatment of such children are not recent developments. On the contrary, clear descriptions of such children and a variety of treatment methods can be found in the 19th-century literature on idiocy (mental retardation), insanity (behavior disorders), and child care (Hallahan & Kauffman, 1977; Kauffman, 1976, 1977). However, in recent decades new labels have been suggested for the problems some of these children present: *minimal brain dysfunction* (MBD), *hyperactivity* (HA), and *learning disability* (LD). In brief, the labels are used to refer to children who are thought to have intelligence above the retarded range but who are suspected of having brains that do not function properly (MBD), show high rates of socially inappropriate behavior (HA), and achieve academically at a level far below what one would predict on the basis of their IQs (LD). In the 15 years since S. A. Kirk introduced the term *LD* in the early 1960s, there has been much stormy debate about

JAMES M. KAUFFMAN AND DANIEL P. HALLAHAN • Department of Special Education, University of Virginia, Charlottesville, Virginia. Preparation of this chapter was supported in part by a contract (300-77-0495) from the Bureau of Education for the Handicapped of the U.S. Office of Education, Department of Health, Education and Welfare, for a Learning Disabilities Research Institute. Also, a portion of this chapter was prepared while the second author was the Priorsfield Fellow at the University of Birmingham, Birmingham, England.

what the labels mean and how the children to whom the labels refer should be treated (see Bosco & Robin, 1976; Cruickshank & Hallahan, 1975a, 1975b; Hallahan & Cruickshank, 1973; Hallahan & Kauffman, 1976; Kauffman & Hallahan, 1976; Ross, 1976; Ross & Ross, 1976).

1. Minimal Brain Dysfunction

As pointed out elsewhere, MBD has been tied to the concepts of LD and HA since the early 1960s (Hallahan & Kauffman, 1976; Ross & Ross, 1976). The term *MBD* was thought to be a good replacement for the term *minimal brain damage* because, although *damage* to the brain could not be demonstrated, it was reasoned that brain *dysfunction* could be safely inferred from children's behavioral characteristics. That is, the notion was fostered that behavioral characteristics such as high rates of socially inappropriate behavior (especially tantrums, impulsivity, and inattention or distractibility), motor incoordination or awkwardness, reversals or poor performance on paper-and-pencil tasks (often referred to as "perceptual" problems), and academic underachievement—in the absence of an immediately obvious causal factor such as frank brain damage or extreme environmental deprivation—point clearly to a dysfunction of the brain that cannot be detected by currently available neurological assessment techniques.

It is our considered judgment that the term *MBD* is not only entirely useless (except for historical interest) but potentially damaging to children and likely to inhibit progress in clinical practice. The term should be abandoned because (a) the "evidence" linking the behavioral characteristics associated with the term to any known dysfunction of the brain is, in the vast majority of cases, purely circumstantial and speculative; (b) identifiable damage to the brain does not reliably produce the behavioral characteristics associated with the term; (c) there are no implications for clinical treatment based on the "diagnosis" of MBD; (d) use of the term may result in misattribution of behavior to causal factors that are neither demonstrable nor alterable, rather than to contributing factors the clinician and clients can identify reliably and alter directly; and (e) there is a considerable body of empirical research showing the effectiveness of clinical methods in which the concept of MBD is irrelevant. We base these statements on research we (Hallahan & Kauffman, 1976) and others (e.g., Freeman, 1976; Koupernik, MacKeith, & Francis-Williams, 1975; Ross, 1976; Ross & Ross, 1976; Sprague, 1973; Werry, 1972) have reviewed. At this point clinicians will be well advised to heed the straightforward remarks of Koupernik *et al*. (1975):

> Increasingly it is more and more widely realized that MBD is an empty term, used to save us the trouble of thinking clearly about what we are talking

> about. . . . We do not need or want labels which have no clinical relevance. No increasing of our understanding comes from the continued use of the MBD group of labels. (p. 125)

Certainly, the psychologist or other nonmedical child-care specialist has a professional responsibility to see that the child's neurological status is adequately assessed, but we do not want to leave the impression that the findings of a neurological examination will often have implications for the clinical psychologist's work. As Koupernik *et al.* comment:

> Where the brain lesion or disorder is a nonprogressive one, there is often no advantage in treatment to identifying the cause or the anatomical or physiological disorder. All the child's various abilities and disabilities must be evaluated and then treatment given for his visual, auditory, language, motor, learning, emotional, and social deficits; his pre-, peri-, or postnatal insult is in the past and is untreatable. (p. 114)

2. Hyperactivity

The term *HA* appears to have more substance than the term *MBD* because it refers to behavior that can be measured directly: i.e., HA is what the child *does*, not a supposed cause of behavior. Unfortunately, HA is a term that still sparks volatile debate because (a) there is not much agreement among researchers or among clinicians regarding the measurement of behavior or the specific behaviors or behavioral rates that comprise activity that is "hyper"; (b) the causes of HA are anything but clear, and some clinicians and researchers still invoke the MBD hypothesis when referring to HA; and (c) there is a great controversy regarding the best methods of treating HA, especially when psychoactive drugs or behavior modification techniques are considered. The literature on HA has become voluminous during the past two decades (see Bosco & Robin, 1976; Ross & Ross, 1976), but it is accurate to say that only a small percentage of that literature has added knowledge or clarity to the confusion. About all we can state with confidence today are the following: HA refers not to high rates of activity *per se*, but rather to high rates of *socially inappropriate* responses; HA appears to be accompanied frequently by attentional problems (distractibility), impulsivity, and academic retardation, although these additional disorders are not invariably linked to HA and the actual statistical relationship among HA and these disorders has not yet been determined; there is as yet no convincing evidence that any of the hypothesized causes of HA are in actuality causally related to HA in all cases; and the most common and, apparently, most effective therapeutic approaches to HA are the use of psychoactive drugs (especially central nervous system stimulants) and behavior modification techniques. Our view, which we have elaborated elsewhere (Hallahan & Kauffman, 1975, 1976), is that HA should be considered by the clinical psychologist as a deficit in social learning. Approaching HA as a social-learning problem does not attribute the cause of the behavior to any particular etiological agent, but it does have the advantage of focusing clinical intervention on the manipulation of the child's social-emotional environment, the stock-in-trade of child psychologists. Furthermore, it results in viewing HA as one of several specific learning disabilities, and therefore connects HA clearly to LD.

3. Learning Disability

Of the three terms—MBD, HA, and LD—we believe LD is the most viable. In its short history, LD has been defined most often as a deficit in academic learning, a lag in perceptual-motor skills, and/or hyperactivity and distractibility which can *not* be explained on the basis of such factors as sensory impairment, mental retardation, emotional disturbance, or environmental disadvantage. In other words, LD has typically been attributed to unknown causal agents or to brain damage or to brain dysfunction (whether or not damage or dysfunction could be demonstrated empirically). In other work (Hallahan & Kauffman, 1976, 1977, 1978), we have stated our position that LD is valuable as a *concept* (not as a label for children)—as the idea that children of whatever "diagnostic" or classifying label may have learning problems in one or more areas of development or ability. To be brief, the way we will treat LD in this chapter is as failure (for whatever reason) to learn at a rate commensurate with one's ability—a learning failure that may or may not include HA.

The first task of the clinician, then, is to describe and measure precisely whatever learning problem(s) the child presents. Whether the child is labeled LD, emotionally disturbed, or mentally retarded, or not labeled anything at all, is irrelevant to the *concept* of LD. The important consideration is that the child has deficits in learning that must be assessed accurately and functionally. While space does not permit us to provide a detailed description of appropriate assessment procedures, we do wish to stress that direct observation and measurement of behavior is an essential component of clinical competence (see Bijou & Grimm, 1975; Gelfand & Hartmann, 1975; Kazdin, 1975; Lovitt, 1977; O'Leary, 1972; White & Liberty, 1976, for more details). As Bijou and Grimm (1975) have stated, "Diagnosis [from the viewpoint of behavioral analysis] is . . . *oriented toward determining the conditions that would probably develop new behavior and modify the problem behavior*" (p. 164). There must be continuous, objective assessment of the child's response (or lack of response) that *is* the problem. Direct daily measurement is called for so that exactly what the child does in response to academic and social demands can be determined. In the case of academic responses, the assessment must be done by the person who teaches the child; social behavior may be observed and measured by the teacher or another individual (e.g., clinician, teacher's aide, parent). Anecdotal reports, interviews, standardized tests, behavioral inventories, and rating scales may be useful, but direct measurement of target behaviors is indispensable (see Evans & Nelson, 1977). To achieve competence in dealing with LD, the clinician simply must avail himself of opportunities to learn the skills required for behavioral assessment—learn them well enough to be able to teach them to teachers and parents of the children he serves.

Given that LD is conceptualized as a learning problem, learning principles can be invoked as the logical beginning point in clinical management. Indeed, a very large body of research could be reviewed showing that behavioral methods are effective in resolving LD (see, for example, Hallahan & Kauffman, 1976; Kauffman, 1975; Lahey, 1976; Lovitt, 1975, 1977). The scope of this chapter does not permit a review of basic learning principles or their application to LD in general, and such reviews are readily available in sources already cited. Our purpose in the remainder of the chapter, therefore, is to deal with concepts and studies related to two important recent developments: the use of behavior modification techniques as an alternative or supplement to medication and the development of cognitive-behavior modification for use with children.

4. Comparison of Treatment Approaches: Behavior Modification and Drugs

4.1. Necessity of Comparing Behavior Modification and Drugs

Perhaps there is no more controversial and frequently discussed topic related to HA and LD than the use of drugs. Extensive reviews of research findings and discussions of issues concerning the medication of children have been written (e.g., Bosco & Robin, 1976; Ross & Ross, 1976; Sroufe, 1975). Many unresolved problems remain, among them the following: unreliable prediction of the response of children to various drugs (Barkley,1976); serious questions regarding the safety and side effects of medications (Sprague & Boileau, 1973; Sverd, Hurwic, David, & Winsberg, 1977); undesirable causal attributions and motivational changes associated with drug use (Bugental, Whalen, & Henker, 1977; Whalen & Henker, 1976); failure to make provision for precise measurement of drug effects, including effects on classroom behavior and academic learning (Sprague & Baxley, in press; Sulzbacher, 1972; Weithorn & Ross, 1976); and inadequate experimental design of drug studies

(Marholin & Phillips, 1976). Thus, although drugs are often suggested as the treatment of choice for HA, there are ample reasons for seeking effective alternatives.

In the years since Patterson and his colleagues (Patterson, 1965; Patterson, Jones, Whittier, & Wright, 1965) first demonstrated the application of operant conditioning techniques to the behavior of children labeled HA, there have been numerous studies showing that disruptive, inattentive behavior can be brought under control by manipulating its consequences (see Ayllon & Rosenbaum, 1977). However, behavior modification techniques have sometimes been known to fail, and there are criticisms that behavior modification requires an excessive expenditure of time and effort or fosters dependence on contrived, externally programmed consequences. Thus, although the efficacy of behavior modification has been demonstrated repeatedly, there are good reasons for seeking both the variables that govern its success and failure and the factors that indicate its potential strength relative to other treatments.

Lately, it has become popular to suggest, in the context of data showing the susceptibility of HA to operant control, that behavior modification is indeed an effective *alternative* to medication, even though the data have not been derived from research involving direct comparisons between behavioral and medical interventions (e.g., Alabiso, 1975; Rosenbaum, O'Leary, & Jacob, 1975; Weissenberger & Loney, 1976). Although these suggestions regarding behavior modification are not unreasonable, neither are they convincing; the studies they are based on do not provide a sound foundation for clinical practice because they do not directly address the question of *comparative* efficacy by assessing the independent and combined effects of drugs and behavior modification on the same subjects or comparable groups of children.

Fortunately, there is a growing (but still small) number of studies in which experimental comparisons between the two interventions have been made, and it is to these studies and their implications that we now turn. We have chosen to restrict our discussion to studies that compare behavior modification and drugs not only because several previous reviews have addressed the independent effects of one of these interventions on LD and HA but also because at this time advances in clinical practice await examination of the *interactive* effects of combined treatments or direct comparisons of their relative efficacy (see Bugental *et al.*, 1977; Sprague & Baxley, in press).

4.2. Comparative Studies

One strategy of comparison has been to obtain baseline data with the child on his usual dose of medication and then gradually withdraw the drug, simultaneously (or subsequently) instituting a program of behavior therapy. Pelham (1977) followed this plan in the case of a 9-year-old boy who had been taking 30 mg of methylphenidate (Ritalin) daily for 18 months. Treatment consisted of initiating a behavior modification program in the home and concurrently lowering the dosage of the drug until it was withdrawn completely. Pelham's data, which consisted of weekly ratings by the child's teacher (using the Conners Abbreviated Teacher Rating Scale) and behavioral ratings by teacher and mother before and after therapy, showed continued improvement when the drug dosage was reduced to 10 mg daily and, finally, completely supplanted by the behavioral intervention. Unfortunately, no direct measurement of behavior was included in Pelham's study; and the research design allows no conclusions regarding the relative efficacy of the two interventions, although it is clear that for this child the behavior modification program alone was sufficient to maintain improvement following combined use of behavioral and drug treatment. A follow-up contact 11 months after treatment was terminated seemed to indicate continued improvement without medication.

Stableford, Butz, Hasazi, Leitenberg, and Peyser (1976) conducted two case studies in which behavior therapy was successfully used as a replacement for chemical therapy. In the first case, an 8-year-old boy taking 15 mg of methylphenidate daily was gradually withdrawn from the drug by substituting (in 5-mg steps of 1 week's duration each) a placebo for the active ingredient. Direct measurement of classroom behavior showed no decline in appropriate on-task responses while the active drug was being phased out; but when no pills were given (no drug, no placebo), the child's behavior deteriorated. This result suggested a definite placebo effect. Subsequently, a behavior modification program (points earned for good behavior and exchangeable for rewards) was instituted in the classroom and appropriate behavior returned to the high level maintained during drug treatment. The second case was experimentally more rigorous than the first. The child was an 11-year-old boy taking 25 mg of dextroamphetamine (Dexadrine) daily. Behavior was measured directly in school by an observer and at home by the boy's mother. A behavior modification program (point system) was instituted at home and run for 25 days before any reduction in drug dosage. When the point system for positive behavior was introduced at home, negative behavior dropped considerably compared to its baseline level. Although the boy's behavior was recorded at school, no behavior modification procedures were used there. During drug-reduction phases, in which the active drug was replaced by a placebo in 5-mg increments, the child's behavior was maintained at acceptable levels both at home and at school, even when neither the active drug nor the placebo were any longer given. Clearly, drugs were not necessary for the management of these two children, but it is not clear to what extent the behavior modification procedures used were indispensable. In Case #1, it appears that a placebo alone may have been sufficient to maintain appropriate behavior; in Case #2, data were not presented regarding the child's behavior at school when behavior modification was not being used, nor was the point system ever withdrawn during the study.

In another study of the use of behavior therapy following withdrawal of stimulant medications, O'Leary and Pelham (1978) worked with seven elementary-age boys taking methylphenidate, dextroamphetamine, or magnesium pemoline (Cylert) in varying doses. Measurement included direct observation of off-task behavior in the classroom and teachers' and mothers' ratings of behavior. During pretreatment off-medication sessions, the treatment group of seven children showed a much higher off-task level than a comparison group of same-sex peers. Following pretreatment assessment of the children both on and off medication, drugs were withdrawn (immediately or gradually, depending on the individual case) and an individualized behavior modification program involving both teachers and parents was implemented. The behavior therapy program ran for 4 months. One month after the program was terminated, posttreatment data were obtained. Although the responses of individual children to both drugs and behavior modification varied, the treatment group's average percent off-task behavior was similar to their pretreatment on-medication average percentage and to the off-task behavior shown by the comparison group. The parent and teacher ratings also showed significant treatment effects for the behavior modification procedures when mean posttreatment off-medication ratings were compared to pretreatment off-medication ratings. Most, but not all, children showed improvement on all measures during treatment. Individual variations in classroom environments and parental commitment to the behavior therapy program apparently determined the level of success, pointing to the necessity of single-subject evaluation in such research.

Another research strategy is comparing the effects of drugs plus behavior modification to behavior modification or drugs alone in alternating experimental phases. Christensen and Sprague (1973) compared the effects of behavior modification (contingent light flashes and points exchangeable for money) and drugs (.30 mg/kg of methylphenidate or placebo) alone and combined on the in-seat movement of 12 children during 20-min experimental sessions. Movement was measured by means of stabilimetric cushions on the seats of the subjects' chairs. Following a pretreatment assessment phase, half the children received the active drug and half received placebo; next both the active-drug and placebo groups received behavior modification in addition; then the behavior modification was withdrawn for both groups and reinstated for both groups; and finally both groups received behavior modification plus placebo. Behavior modification reduced in-seat activity for both active-drug and placebo groups, but the activity level of the active-drug group was consistently lower than that of the placebo group, especially during nonreinforcement sessions. The results suggest that the combination of drugs and behavior modification provides the best effect, but this conclusion must be tentative due to the narrowly defined dependent variable, the small sample, the absence of individual-subject analyses, the short duration of the study, and the contrived setting in which behavior was measured.

Shafto and Sulzbacher (1977) compared reinforcement (food and praise contingent on appropriate play) alone, methylphenidate alone in varying doses, and a combination of behavior modification and methylphenidate in controlling HA and other inappropriate responses of a 4½-year-old boy. Several behaviors were directly observed and recorded in the preschool classroom, including hyperactivity (defined as changes of activity), isolate play, wandering, compliance, and verbalization. Baseline (no drug, no behavior modification) sessions were followed by a phase in which the child was given 10 mg of methylphenidate daily. Subsequently, behavioral intervention, consisting of food and praise from the teacher for sustained appropriate play, was added to the drug. After a return to baseline conditions, methylphenidate alone (varying from 5 to 15 mg daily) and behavioral intervention alone were tried; finally, there was a third baseline phase. Methylphenidate alone had no appreciable effect on activity changes, but behavior modification alone and combined with the drug reduced hyperactivity. At the highest dosage (15 mg daily) the child's parents noted that methylphenidate had a side effect (insomnia) and requested curtailment of the study, preventing investigation of various dosage levels and a placebo. Although medication seemed to increase the child's attention to tasks, it seemed to make him less responsive to the teacher's instructions, increase his isolate play, and increase his inappropriate verbalizations, especially at the 15-mg dosage level.

Methylphenidate, a placebo, and behavior modification were compared by Wulbert and Dries (1977) in their work with a boy 8 yr 11 mo of age. The boy's ritualistic behavior and aggression were recorded at home by his mother; these same behaviors plus accuracy on visual and auditory tasks, eye contact, and distractibility were recorded during 90-min clinic sessions. Methylphenidate (40 mg daily) and a placebo were given (in a double-blind design) in successive 2-week blocks, and baseline and treatment (behavior modification) phases of the study included an equal number of active-drug and placebo weeks. The mother carried out a token reinforcement system at home throughout the study; token reinforcement was alternated with nonreinforcement in clinic sessions. At home, methylphenidate produced low levels of aggression but high levels of ritualistic behavior. In the clinic, the drug did not affect any of the behaviors recorded, but token reinforcement decreased ritualistic behavior and increased task accuracy. The salutary effects of reinforcement did not generalize to unreinforced behaviors or to settings in which reinforcement was not programmed, and there was no interaction between reinforcement and medication.

Christensen (1975) obtained results similar to those of Wulbert and Dries with 16 institutionalized retarded youngsters; i.e., adding methylphenidate to behavior modification procedures had few advantages in producing appropriate classroom behavior. Using ratings by teachers and direct measurement of several behaviors in addition, Christensen assessed behavior during baseline phases and alternating sessions in which behavior modification plus methylphenidate or behavior modification plus placebo were used. The behavior modification procedures consisted of token reinforcement and social praise. As Christensen himself points out, his study has several serious limitations: lack of analysis of effects for individuals; standardized (.3 mg/kg) rather than individualized dosage; absence of phases in which active drug, placebo, and behavior modification were applied alone; and a relatively restricted range of environmental conditions.

Strong, Sulzbacher, and Kirkpatrick (1974) also found active medication and a placebo to have practically no influence on target responses. They recorded facial grimaces of a 5-year-old boy and found that these behaviors could be decreased very effectively by having the boy record his own grimaces and by providing praise and candy as reinforcers for not grimacing. Subsequently they found that 12.5-mg and 25-mg doses of diphenhydramine hydrochloride (Benadryl) and a placebo were ineffective in decreasing grimacing and that neither the active drug nor the placebo affected the child's arithmetic performance. Unfortunately, the design of the study does not allow rigorous comparisons of the relative effects of behavioral and chemical interventions.

Wolraich, Drummond, Salomon, O'Brien, and Sivage (1978) set up two special classes in a public school in which a special teacher and an aide did individual and group work with children four afternoons per week for 6 weeks. There were 10 children in each class, and children were matched on age, IQ, grade level, and teacher rating of hyperactive behavior. One member of each matched pair was assigned to an active drug (.3 mg/kg/day of methylphenidate) or placebo condition. All persons directly involved with the classrooms were blind to the drug-placebo condition. The design of the study was an ABA sequence with 2 weeks of baseline, 2 weeks of a behavior modification program (token reinforcement), and a return to baseline conditions for 2 weeks. The drug conditions (methylphenidate or placebo) were superimposed on the ABA design so that all the children were taking pills each day throughout the study. Pills were administered at the beginning of each afternoon session. Behavior was coded daily by observers beginning 30-40 minutes after medication. Observations were made during group work and during individual work, and daily samples of academic work were taken. Only data from the last week of each experimental phase were analyzed. Finally, the teacher or aide rated each child's behavior twice each week using the Conners Abbreviated Teacher Behavior Rating Scale.

No analyses were made of individual children's data by Wolraich *et al.* Group statistical comparisons were interpreted to mean that there were no interactions between medication and behavior modification, that both medication and behavior modification were effective in decreasing undesired behaviors in certain situations (behavior modification being most effective during group work and drugs being most effective during individual seat work), that only behavior modification was effective in improving academic performance, and that teacher ratings were unaffected. The data may be viewed with caution, not only because of the absence of analysis of individual effects but also because in some cases behaviors became worse during behavior modification than during baseline (e.g., nonattending and peer interaction during group work) and the statistically significant changes associated with the behavior modification program were primarily increases in inappropriate behavior during the second baseline phase. Furthermore, the short duration of the study and the contrived nature of the classrooms should be considered.

A group statistical design employed by Gittelman-Klein, Klein, Abikoff, Katz, Gloisten, and Kates (1976) yielded results contradictory to the findings of several studies just reviewed. Gittelman-Klein *et al.* compared methylphenidate alone, methylphenidate plus behavior therapy, and placebo plus behavior therapy and found that all treatments produced significant clinical improvement in 34 6- to 12-year-old children. The active drug combined with behavior therapy was the best treatment; methylphenidate alone was next best; behavior therapy plus placebo was least effective; however, there were no significant differences between medication alone and medication plus behavior therapy, although behavior therapy with placebo was significantly less effective than either of the other two treatments. Behavior therapy consisted of individually designed procedures involving both home and school.

Measurement consisted of direct behavioral observation in the classroom and behavioral ratings by teachers, mothers, and psychiatrists as well. However, it should be noted that comparisons were made between groups of subjects; no experimental analyses were made for single subjects. Furthermore, dosage of the active drug began at 10 mg daily and was increased weekly (up to 60 mg daily) if undesirable behavior persisted, with the average after 8 weeks of drug treatment being 35.6 mg daily for the 12 children in the drug-only group and the 13 children in the behavior-therapy-plus-drug group (there were 9 children who received placebo plus behavior therapy). Differences between this and other studies in the way dosage was determined could have alone accounted for the conflicting results. In addition, the study suffers from a lack of placebo-only and behavior-therapy-only comparison groups, and the authors are under the misimpression that "only investigations with random assignment and concurrent treatment groups allow for valid conclusions regarding the relative merits of interventions" (p. 374). As Hersen and Barlow (1976) point out, appropriate single-subject research designs do allow rigorous comparison of relative treatment effects and are, in fact, preferable to group statistical designs in most cases (see also Marholin & Phillips, 1976, for discussion of the advantages of single-case methodology for assessing drug effects).

Ayllon, Layman, and Kandel (1975) used a multiple-baseline design across two behaviors (reading and math) to evaluate changes in three elementary-age children's academic performance and hyperactive behavior when medication (methylphenidate) was withdrawn and reinforcement was instituted. This is the only study to date involving a comparative analysis for single subjects of the effects of drugs and behavior modification on both hyperactive behavior and academic performance in the classroom. Baseline data were first recorded while the children were on medication, the dependent measures for each child consisting of direct observation of hyperactive behaviors and performance on reading and math assignments. Following baseline, medication was withdrawn and, after 3 days, a token reinforcement program was instituted during math assignments. Six days later, the reinforcement program was extended to reading assignments as well as math. The results were strikingly consistent for each of the three subjects: Withdrawal of medication resulted in dramatic increases in hyperactive behavior and slight improvements in academic performance; reinforcement for academic work produced dramatic improvements in performance and reduced hyperactive behaviors to their baseline (on-medication) level. Clearly, behavior modification was an effective substitute for medication for these subjects, at least for the short duration of the study, and methylphenidate appeared to have a negative influence on academic performance. However, there was no placebo control, and the combined effects of medication and behavioral treatment were not examined.

The 11 studies just reviewed did not yield consistent results—one cannot conclude from them as an aggregate that drugs, behavior therapy, or some combination of these two interventions is an indispensable part of treatment or is always the most effective component of treatment of HA. One can only conclude from the available data that (a) medication alone is effective for some children in some settings; (b) behavior therapy alone is effective for some children in some settings; (c) sometimes a combination of medication and behavior therapy is effective, although in such cases the relative effects of the two interventions is unclear; (d) medication is general in its influence on behavior, whereas behavior therapy tends to be specific in its effects; and (e) analysis of target responses for individuals is an essential aspect of evaluating the efficacy of both medication and behavior therapy, since responsiveness to both types of treatment and their combination tends to be idiosyncratic. Studies to date have dealt with diverse populations, employed a variety of drugs and dosages, used a variety of behavior modification techniques, and relied upon a wide array of research designs. Consequently, generalizations beyond the five we have listed must be tentative. We are of the opinion that the best designed comparisons so far (Ayllon *et al.*, 1975; Shafto & Sulzbacher, 1977; Wulbert & Dries, 1977) support the argument that behavior therapy is indeed a preferable alternative to drug therapy in some (perhaps many or most) cases, particularly those cases in which the objective of therapy is to teach the child adaptive responses, not just to keep misbehavior under control. One must consider the fact that drugs cannot be counted upon to produce desirable behavior change in the absence of appropriate environmental support, whereas behavior therapy is by definition environmental support for learning and often does not depend on drug-induced physiological states.

It is worth noting that not one of the 11 studies reviewed has included any attempt to develop a model for predicting the differential effects of drugs and behavior modification with different types of children and environments. Yet, if drugs are the treatment of choice with children having certain characteristics and for certain settings, while behavior modification is the best treatment for others, as seems very likely, then studies exploring the child characteristics and environments associated with differential responsiveness to interventions would be particularly helpful.

4.3. Possible Relationship of Cognitive Factors to Therapeutic Outcome

One recent experiment did address the issue of differential effects of behavioral interventions depending on specific child characteristics and whether or not drugs were being taken. Bugental et al. (1977) compared the effects of self-controlling speech (one type of cognitive-behavioral intervention we discuss in the next section) and contingent social reinforcement during tutoring sessions for 36 elementary-age boys who exhibited HA. Half the boys received the self-control intervention in which they were taught to give themselves instructions, half the contingent social reinforcement. Half the boys in each of these groups were taking methylphenidate, half no medication. The dependent measures were qualitative error scores on the Porteus Mazes and scores on the Conners Abbreviated Teacher Rating Scale. In addition, the children's attributions of personal causation for academic success and failure—the extent to which they believed they themselves or external factors were responsible for their academic performance—were measured by means of a structured interview. The findings after 2 months of treatment revealed that how well children responded to an intervention depended on an interaction between their attributions of success and their medication status. No significant differences were found for teacher ratings, but on Porteus Mazes significantly greater mean error reduction was produced by the self-control intervention for children who were not taking medication *and* were high in perceived personal causality, whereas significantly greater mean error reduction was produced by the social reinforcement intervention for children who were medicated *and* low in perceived personal causality.

In these results and the recent work of others (e.g., Bandura, 1977) we see a suggestion (not a conclusion) that cognitive factors may be a key determinant of how children respond to interventions of various sorts, including the chemical and behavioral methods we have been discussing. Conclusions must be based on additional research, including careful analysis of direct behavioral measures for individuals. As Bugental et al. speculate, however, it may be that the most effective intervention is one with implicit causal attributions (e.g., the high personal causation implied by self-control techniques) that match the causal attributions of the child (e.g., the child's idea that he is personally responsible for his actions and the consequences he receives). A highly structured environment in which externally applied consequences are consistent and salient may be necessary for HA and LD children who attribute events primarily to external causal factors—necessary not only to establish control over their behavior initially but also for the eventual development of the self-regulatory functions that are the ultimate goal of behavior therapy. Self-control may, perhaps, be attainable by LD children only after they have experienced consistent consequences arranged by others, for as Bandura (1977) notes, performance accomplishments typically outweigh vicarious experience, verbal persuasion, and physiological states in inducing behavioral change. Pill-taking and psychological states induced by drugs seem unlikely to foster personal causal attributions or to provide a reliable experiential foundation for self-control.

5. An Emerging Treatment Approach for LD: Cognitive-Behavior Modification

In the past few years, there has been a rapid growth in the use of cognitive-behavior modification with LD children. Cognitive-behavior modification is a blending of two schools of thought—cognitive and behavioral psychology—that had previously been viewed as incompatible. Behaviorists, because of their emphasis on changing *observable* behaviors, have been leery of those cognitive theorists who deal with such unobservable behaviors as thought processes. While many behavioral and cognitive psychologists are still at odds with each other, a growing literature in the field reflects the fact that many have viewed the marriage between the two as a positive event. Even a cursory glance at the various relevant journals reveals that cognitive-behavior modification is being tried with a variety of psychopathological conditions, including LD.

What is interesting with regard to our earlier discussion concerning the relative efficacy of medication and behavior modification is that cognitive-behavior modification has received much of its impetus from clinicians' dissatisfaction with *both* of these approaches. We have already noted the frequently cited disadvantages of using medication with LD children. Douglas and her colleagues have perhaps been the ones who have most seriously questioned the use of behavior modification for HA. While recognizing the general effectiveness of behavior modification, they have argued for the use of cognitive-behavior modification over more traditional operant techniques because of what they perceive to be some important limitations in the latter:

> Nevertheless, several considerations suggest that it would be unwise to rely solely on operant techniques to train hyperactive children. Thus far, there

have been few attempts to document resistance to extinction or to establish the long-term effectiveness of these methods. Our own concern about the exclusive use of contingency management was also raised by investigations in which the first author and her colleagues studied the effect of several different reinforcement parameters on the performance of hyperactive children on a variety of tests. The findings suggest that these children respond to reinforcement contingencies in unique ways. Their performance is more disrupted than that of normal children by partial and noncontingent reinforcement and extinction. It also appears that positive reinforcement may increase impulsivity and attract their attention away from the task and toward the reinforcement or the reinforcing adult (Cohen, 1970; Douglas, 1975; Firestone, 1974; Firestone & Douglas, 1975; Friebergs & Douglas, 1969; Parry, 1973; Parry & Douglas, in press). (Douglas, Parry, Marton, & Garson, 1976, p. 390)

Because a cognitive-behavior modification program varies considerably depending upon who is planning it and with whom it is being implemented, it is not easy to define. There are, however, two features that are included in most such educational programs. (For a more thorough discussion of the components of cognitive-behavior modification, see Meichenbaum, 1977.) First, the child is provided direct instruction and/or modeling by an adult. The focus of such instruction or modeling is usually on teaching the child a particular strategy for performing more appropriately. The strategy may either be as simple as a verbal reminder to "slow down" or a relatively elaborate set of instructions for solving a complex problem. Second, the child is usually taught to verbalize to himself a set of instructions or strategies. Normally, these self-instructions are practiced overtly at first and then are faded so that they become covert.

Relevant to the field of LD, cognitive-behavior modification methods have been used for two general problem areas—behavioral and academic problems. Thus far, the major emphasis has been on the former. In particular, a number of investigations have examined the use of cognitive-behavior modification, or other highly similar approaches, for the control of impulsive and/or hyperactive behavior (e.g., Bem, 1967; Bender, 1976; Blackwood, 1970; Bornstein & Quevillon, 1976; Camp, Blom, Hebert, & van Doorninck, 1977; Douglas *et al.*, 1976; Egeland, 1974; Finch & Kendall, 1978; Giebink, Stover, & Fahl, 1968; Hartig & Kanfer, 1973; MacPherson, Candee, & Hohman, 1974; Meichenbaum & Goodman, 1969, 1971; Palkes, Stewart, & Freedman, 1972; Palkes, Stewart, & Kahana, 1968; Patterson & Mischel, 1975, 1976; Ridberg, Parke, & Hetherington, 1971; Zelniker & Oppenheimer, 1973). Although not unanimous in their findings, these studies have generally documented the value of cognitive-behavior modification techniques.

Using Kagan's (1965, 1966) conceptualization of impulsive versus reflective cognitive tempos as a basis, most of these studies have concentrated on changing the behavior of impulsive problem-solvers. In particular, many of these investigators have focused their efforts on encouraging children who respond impulsively (high errors and fast response times) to adopt a more reflective (low errors and slow response times) problem-solving strategy as assessed by Kagan's Matching Familiar Figures (MFF) test. While many researchers have stayed within the laboratory setting, enough studies have now been successfully conducted in the applied arena (e.g., Blackwood, 1970; Bornstein & Quevillon, 1976; Camp et al., 1977; Douglas et al., 1976; Giebink et al., 1968) to conclude that such an approach holds promise for the control of impulsivity and HA within the classroom setting. Because of the high incidence of impulsivity and HA among children classified as LD (Hallahan, 1975; Hallahan & Kauffman, 1975, 1976; Hallahan, Kauffman, & Ball, 1973; Heins, Hallahan, Tarver, & Kauffman, 1976; Keogh & Donlon, 1972) and because many of the studies using cognitive-behavior modification for the control of impulsivity and HA have used LD subjects, there is a great deal of support for the use of cognitive-behavior modification with LD children.

With regard to the remediation of *academic* and learning problems through such an approach, however, there has been much less research conducted. As we have already noted elsewhere (Hallahan & Cohen, 1977; Hallahan & Kauffman, 1976; Kauffman, 1977), it is the exception rather than the rule to find children with purely learning *or* social-behavioral problems. The difficulties associated with the differential diagnosis of LD versus emotional disturbance is evidence of the overlap between these two categories of special education. Nevertheless, in order to assess fully the impact of procedures such as strategy and self-verbalization training, it is necessary to examine their value in ameliorating academic deficits in children. The remainder of this chapter will thus be devoted to a discussion of the merits of cognitive-behavior modification techniques for *academic* problems. First, however, it is of interest to explore the rationale behind such an approach to the learning problems of LD children. In other words, one might ask if there is any evidence that would lead us to believe that strategy and self-verbalization training would be particularly effective with LD children.

5.1. Rationale for the Use of Cognitive-Behavior Modification with LD

In the past few years a number of basic research studies have explored the basic learning processes of LD subjects. Two areas that have perhaps received the most intensive study are memory and attention. Not only have these investigations compared LD with normal children but they have also looked at the specific learning processes characteristic of LD children. In other words, not only have these studies confirmed the clinical impressions that LD children have poor memory and attentional abilities but they have also reached consistent conclusions regarding some of the underlying *reasons* for these areas of poor performance. There is evidence that LD children are not deficient in attention and memory abilities *per se* as much as they are lacking in task-approach skills. They appear to be at a disadvantage in knowing how to go about engaging in tasks that require attention and memory skills. Once provided with appropriate task strategies by an adult, however, they perform at a level comparable to that of their normal peers.

5.1.1. Studies of Memory

It was first noted within the normal child development literature that children, with age, develop strategies for performing memory tasks. Relevant to our discussion of cognitive-behavior modification, it has been observed that, in particular, children develop the ability to use overt and covert verbal mediators. Reese (1962), one of the first investigators in this area, posited that young children exhibit a "verbal mediation deficiency." He hypothesized that older children, when presented with a serial memory task, are able to use verbal rehearsal in order to help them remember the serially presented stimuli. For younger children, however, he hypothesized that verbal responses fail to act as mediators. Further refinements of Reese's conceptualizations were made by Flavell and his colleagues (Flavell, Beach, & Chinsky, 1966; Keeney, Cannizzo, & Flavell, 1967). They noted that a more appropriate designation for the younger child's inabilities would be "production deficiency." The production-deficiency hypothesis states that young children (before the age of about 8 years), when given a memory task, fail to produce words at the appropriate time but perform quite capably when *instructed* to rehearse verbally. This is in contrast to the mediation-deficiency hypothesis, which assumes that the verbal responses are made by young children but that they fail to function as mediators.

There are numerous studies supporting the production-deficiency hypothesis over the mediation-deficiency hypothesis (e.g., Flavell *et al.*, 1966; Hagen, Hargrave, & Ross, 1973; Hagen & Kail, 1973; Hagen & Kingsley, 1968; Keeney *et al.*, 1967). Keeney *et al.* (1967), for instance, took 6- and 7-year-olds who were nonrehearsers and instructed them to rehearse. The subsequent recall of the instructed group equaled that of spontaneous rehearsers. The work of Hagen and his colleagues on the effects of rehearsal on the accuracy of recall and serial position curves also supports the production-deficiency hypothesis. Their results have shown that not only do older compared to younger children recall more information from all positions in a series but that they do especially well at remembering the first few items in the series. For example, if presented with the following series of pictures or words—cat, bird, dog, horse, camel, raccoon, monkey—the older child typically remembers the first (e.g., cat and bird) and last (e.g., raccoon and monkey) items presented better than he does the middle items (e.g., dog, horse, and camel). The younger child, however, may recall the last items (e.g., raccoon and monkey) better than the rest but generally is no more proficient on the first than the middle stimuli. The younger child is said to exhibit a *recency effect* (good recall of last items presented), but the older child evidences both a recency and a *primacy effect* (good recall of first items presented). The existence of a primacy effect is interpreted as evidence that the child is engaging in a verbal rehearsal strategy.

The findings that (a) the serial memory differences between older and younger children are largely due to the latter's failure to evidence a primacy effect and (b) instructions to rehearse verbally result in the child's showing a primacy effect are generally consistent with the notion that older children have learned to adopt a more efficient strategy for remembering than have their younger peers.

Relevant to our discussion in this chapter are studies of memory abilities of LD children. These studies have shown that LD children perform similarly to their younger normal peers (Bauer, 1977; Freston & Drew, 1974; Parker, Freston, & Drew, 1975; Ring, 1976; Swanson, 1977; Torgesen & Goldman, 1977). In other words, LD children do not spontaneously use strategies that normal children of the same age use to help them on recall tasks. For example, Bauer (1977), using an auditory task, found a lack of primacy effect for 10-year-old LD children. Swanson (1977) found the same absence of a primacy effect for two-dimensional visual materials, but did find a primacy effect and no differences between LD and normal subjects when three-dimensional items were used. Swanson suggests that LD children may be influenced to rehearse when redundant cues (present in a three-dimensional format) are available. That failure of LD children to rehearse is a function of a production rather than a mediation deficiency has been shown by Torgesen and Goldman (1977), who compared normal and poor readers. They found that poor readers were inferior to normal readers in recall except when instructions to label the stimuli were provided. In other words, when instructed to do so, the poor readers were able to verbalize and thus recall as well as normal readers.

Other studies of memory abilities in LD children have found them deficient in the use of other learning strategies besides verbal rehearsal. Freston and Drew (1974) and Parker *et al.,* (1975) found that LD children are unable to take advantage of organizational cues. When presented with lists of words to remember, they, unlike normal children, do as well on randomized lists as when the words are organized into categories such as animals, geometric shapes, flowers, and foods. Even though they do not take advantage of lists organized on the basis of conceptual categories, Ring (1977) found that temporally grouped lists do produce an advantageous effect on recall. Apparently, LD children are able to make use of a strategy like temporal grouping because it is a relatively primitive method of organization, whereas, as Ring notes, conceptual organization is more linguistically and conceptually complex.

5.1.2. Studies of Selective Attention

In addition to poor memory abilities, there is a plethora of evidence indicating that LD children are deficient in their ability to focus on relevant and ignore irrelevant information (Dawson, 1977; Deikel & Friedman, 1976; Hallahan, 1975; Hallahan, Gajar, Cohen, & Tarver, 1978; Hallahan, Kauffman, & Ball, 1973; Hallahan, Tarver, Kauffman, & Graybeal, in press; Mondani & Tutko, 1969; Pelham & Ross, 1977; Tarver, Hallahan, Cohen, & Kauffman, 1977; Tarver, Hallahan, Kauffman, & Ball, 1976). Furthermore, many of these studies point to inefficient use of strategies such as verbal rehearsal and clustering as being at the root of the LD child's selective attention problems (Dawson, 1977; Hallahan, Tarver, Kauffman, & Graybeal, in press; Pelham & Ross, 1977; Tarver et al., 1977; Tarver et al., 1976).

The majority of research on selective attention in LD children has used the central-incidental experimental paradigm developed by Hagen (1967). The experimenter on each trial shows the child a series of cards, each of which contains the picture of an animal and a household object. The child is told to pay attention to the position of the animals in the array. Each card is shown for about 2 seconds and then turned face down. After all the cards are face down in front of the child, the experimenter shows the child a cue card containing the picture of one of the animals. The child is to point to the card in the face-down array that contains the picture of the animal on the cue card. The number correct over a number of these trials is referred to as the child's central learning score. After the child responds to the central task, he is presented with the incidental task, on which he is given cards each containing an animal and cards each containing a household object. He is required to match the animals to the household objects with which each had always appeared during the central task. The total number of correct pairings is termed *incidental recall*—incidental in the sense that the child had not been instructed to pay attention to the incidental information, i.e., household objects. In a variety of experimental situations with normal children, it was found that there is a developmental increase in the ability to attend to central information and to ignore incidental stimuli (Druker & Hagen, 1969; Hagen, 1967; Hagen & Sabo, 1967; Hallahan, Kauffman, & Ball, 1973; Hallahan, Stainback, Ball, & Kauffman, 1973; Maccoby & Hagen, 1965). The major increase in selective attention has usually occurred at about 12 to 13 years of age, when, although the recall of central information continues to increase uniformly, incidental recall generally drops off. In addition, there is a positive correlation between central and incidental recall at younger ages and a negative correlation between the two at about 12 years of age. The different directions of these correlations implies that older children have developed a strategy for giving up incidental information in order to recall central material.

Studies using Hagen's central-incidental task with LD children have found them to be deficient in selective attention-ability relative to normal chronological age mates (Dawson, 1977; Hallahan, Gajar, Cohen, & Tarver, 1978; Hallahan, Kauffman, & Ball, 1973; Hallahan, Tarver, Kauffman, & Graybeal, in press; Tarver et al., 1977; Tarver et al., 1976). In fact, these studies have consistently found LD children to be about 2 years behind normal children in the ability to attend selectively. These studies, in a similar manner to the memory studies discussed earlier, have also found that one of the keys to the LD child's inability to attend on this task is his lack of a verbal rehearsal strategy. When provided with such a strategy, he exhibits a primacy effect on the central task and demonstrates selective attention ability comparable to his normal peers.

5.1.3. Relevance of Memory and Attention Studies

It is interesting to note that studies investigating memory and attentional abilities in LD children have reached essentially the same conclusions. The LD child's problem is not so much one of learning per se as it is one of using the appropriate learning strategies. The normal child learns certain problem-solving shortcuts that make him a better learner; the LD child is delayed about 2 years in the application of these strategies.

Torgesen (1977), in his review of memory studies, has reached essentially the same conclusions in his conceptualization of the LD child as a passive rather than an active learner. Instead of concentrating on looking for specific disabilities, as is the general practice, he recommends that we should consider the possibility that there are more general cognitive deficits such as inappropriate strategies that adversely affect the performance of LD children on a variety of tasks. He points out that Flavell's (1971) concept of meta variables may be helpful in explaining the performance deficits of LD children:

> Given the central role of subject activity in the various cognitive processes
> . . . , how do investigators explain individual differences in the use of effi-

cient strategies or activity on a given task: Some have invoked *meta* variables. These variables describe certain relationships which exist between the subject and his task environment, and *between the subject and his own cognitive processes.* . . .

As two examples of *meta* variables which influence performance in memory tasks, Hagen (1971) offers "awareness that memory is possible and desirable," and "awareness of himself as an actor in his environment" (p. 267). Such variables as the child's awareness of his abilities vis-à-vis a given task, and his appreciation of the qualities which make certain tasks hard or easy also are seen to relate to the use of efficient strategies in any task situation that involves the deliberate attempt to learn something for later recall (Flavell, 1971). Norman (1969) has emphasized that purposive learning requires a plan of action so that an "intent to learn" is crucial to performance on a broad variety of learning tasks. Finally, Gibson (1973, p. 2) has suggested that "increasing ability *to be aware of one's own cognitive processes*" is a very important variable in the attainment of complex skills like reading. (p. 29, italics added)

If one of the primary problems exhibited by the LD child is his lack of awareness of his own cognitive processes, then it seems logical that treatment should consist of helping the child to make better use of cognitive strategies available to him. Since this is one of the basic aims of cognitive-behavior modification, it seems that this approach should be particularly effective with LD children.

5.2. Studies Using Cognitive-Behavior Modification with Academic Deficits

While there have been numerous studies assessing the efficacy of a cognitive-behavioral approach to social and behavioral problems such as HA and impulsivity, there have been relatively fewer involving academic behaviors (Bower, 1975; Camp *et al.*, 1977; Douglas *et al.*, 1976; Egeland, 1974; Epstein, 1975; Grimm, Bijou, & Parsons, 1973; Lovitt & Curtiss, 1968; Parsons, 1972; Robertson & Keeley, 1974; Robin, Armel, & O'Leary, 1975; Wozniak & Nuechterlein, 1973). Even some of these fall only loosely under the general rubric of "cognitive-behavior modification" in that they involve common elements such as self-instruction (Grimm *et al.*, 1973; Lovitt & Curtiss, 1968; Parsons, 1972). In addition, some of these studies have included measures of academic progress as only secondary to other problems such as impulsivity or HA (e.g., Camp *et al.*, 1977; Douglas *et al.*, 1976; Egeland, 1974; Robertson & Keeley, 1974). It is therefore difficult to draw many definitive conclusions regarding the value of the cognitive-behavioral approach for the remediation of academic disabilities. There are, however, a few tentative conclusions that can be forwarded.

Before turning to these conclusions, we will present brief summaries of each of these studies. Since our focus here is on the effects of treatment on academic work, we will only report results of dependent measures assessing academic abilities.

Two of the investigations under consideration have been large-scale projects studying the effects of cognitive-behavior modification procedures on a broad spectrum of behaviors (Camp *et al.*, 1977; Douglas *et al.*, 1976). Both studies dealt with similar samples in that the former involved aggressive and the latter HA children. Treatment procedures used were highly similar to those used by Meichenbaum and Goodman (1971) in that they emphasized the modeling and self-verbalization of cognitive strategies. For example, Camp *et al.* trained children to develop answers to four basic questions: "What is my problem?"; "What is my plan?"; "Am I using my plan?"; and "How did I do?" Both groups of investigators were only moderately successful in terms of increasing children's academic abilities. Camp *et al.*, administering only one measure of academic achievement—the *Wide Range Achievement Test,* Reading subtest—found improvement at the .10 level. Douglas *et al.* found that immediately upon completion of the program, there was significant improvement in the experimental group compared to a control group on the *Durrell Analysis of Reading Difficulty*, Listening Comprehension subtest, and significant gains at the .10 level on the Spelling and Oral Comprehension subtests. No differences were obtained on the Oral Reading subtest or the WRAT Arithmetic subtest. In a follow-up 3 months later, the results changed somewhat but with no effect on the overall assessment of the efficacy of the program for academic achievement: i.e., significant differences were found for the Oral Reading and Oral Comprehension subtests only.

In a completely different vein from that of the above two studies, three of the studies (Grimm *et al.*, 1973; Lovitt & Curtiss, 1968; Parsons, 1972) employed single-subject designs. While these experiments were not specifically designated as investigations of the cognitive-behavioral approach, each of them was concerned with the influence of self-verbalization on arithmetic achievement. Also unlike the two large-scale group studies, these three single-subject investigations found self-verbalization to be highly effective. Lovitt and Curtiss (1968), for example, gave the following rationale for their study:

> The current study was prompted by a student who exhibited extreme variability in responding to mathematics materials. His teacher had noted that at times he could answer certain problems correctly, but at other times would err when presented the same facts. The teacher had further observed that occasionally, when the subject verbalized the problem before writing the answer, the probability of correct responding was increased. The purpose of the present investigation was to assess experimentally the function of a popular remediation suggestion of teachers and parents, that children "think before they do." More specifically, this study was designed to determine the effects

of simply writing the answers to mathematics problems *versus* verbalizing the problems before making a written response. (pp. 329-330)

The studies by Grimm *et al.* (1973) and Parsons (1972) combined teaching the child to self-verbalize and to break down math problems into component processes. This task analysis/self-verbalization approach was quite successful in improving math performance. Parsons, for example, found that having the child name the appropriate sign (+ or −) and circle it was more effective than circling it alone. Grimm *et al.* reinforced children for verbalizing steps in a problem-solving chain as they computed arithmetic problems.

In addition to the above studies that have been large-scale projects or single-subject experiments focusing on specific academic problems, the remaining investigations can be considered intermediate in terms of breadth of focus. They have dealt with groups of children for relatively short periods of time. One way in which they have differed from one another is whether the remediation has involved the use of academic materials themselves or tasks not *concretely* related to academics, such as the Matching Familiar Figures test. While Bower (1975), Robertson and Keeley (1974), Robin *et al.* (1975), and Wozniak and Nuechterlein (1973) made some attempt to include at least some training with academic content, Epstein (1975) and Egeland (1974) trained children using the MFF and a perceptual match-to-sample task, respectively. It is important to point out that, in general, the latter two studies were not as successful as the previous four investigations; Epstein found no effects on arithmetic performance and Egeland found significant effects for reading comprehension only and no effects for two measures of vocabulary and word and paragraph reading. Although the four studies using academic training materials were not overwhelmingly successful, some positive results were obtained. Bower, for example, who adapted Meichenbaum and Goodman's (1971) training techniques directly to math and reading work sheets, found significant differences over a control group on reading work sheets and borderline significance ($p < .10$) on math work sheets. No significant differences were obtained on standardized measures of arithmetic and reading. Wozniak and Nuechterlein found borderline significance on a standardized measure of reading but no differences on standardized measures of word discrimination and word knowledge. Robertson and Keeley, using standardized measures, found improvement in spelling, "some" (the term *some* was used by the investigators, who used criteria other than traditional significance levels) improvement in reading, and no improvement in arithmetic. Robin *et al.* successfully taught kindergartners identified as having handwriting problems to use self-instructions to improve their printing. However, the effects did not generalize to letters that had not been used in training. A potential problem mitigating against finding positive effects, however, was that some of the children may not have needed much instruction in the first place. Fifteen children in each of two kindergarten classes were selected on the basis of a pretest. This appears to be a rather high percentage of children being identified for instruction.

5.3. Conclusions Regarding Cognitive-Behavior Modification with Academic Deficits

It would be hazardous to draw many definitive conclusions based on the research thus far; too few studies have been conducted and many of the findings are contradictory. A few generalizations, however, can be tentatively forwarded. The most obvious conclusion that emerges from the data so far is that the more one uses academic materials in the training process, the more likely one is to find gains in academic achievement. This generally consistent finding that the probability of changing academic behavior is increased when training is academic in nature should alert future researchers of the need to adapt training strategies to academic tasks themselves. In fairness to the authors of many of the studies we have reviewed, achievement gains were not always the major focus of the project, but rather, effects on achievement scores were tangential to other dependent measures such as impulsivity or hyperactivity. Douglas *et al*. (1976), for instance, working with hyperactive children, noted the limitations of their study with regard to academic gains:

> There also is little evidence for effects of training on the arithmetic test of the Wide Range Achievement Test. It seems likely that training specifically geared to arithmetic computations would have to be added to our training program in order to produce significant changes on achievement tests measures. It should also be stressed that similar advice is in order in the area of reading skills. Although the trained group improved on some tests of the Durrell Analysis of Reading Difficulty, the lack of improvement on the remaining Durrell comparisons suggest that training in specific reading and spelling skills should be added to the programs of children who have difficulties in these areas. (p. 405)

The most interesting aspect of the above conclusion is that it seems an obvious one even before any data are collected. It appears that the illogic of not using academic tasks to train academic abilities should be obvious. Such an error in logic, however, is not unusual in the field of special education. Learning-disabilities professionals, in particular, have frequently trained children on other than academic materials, expecting (or, perhaps, just hoping) that there will be generalization to academic achievement. A considerable amount of debate has raged concerning the efficacy of using perceptual-motor and psycholinguistic training with learning-disabled children. Advocates of this "process"-oriented approach, for example, engage the child in perceptual training on nonacademic materials. Although there is some limited evidence that such training improves perceptual-motor skills, there is no solid support for the notion that it leads directly to academic gains (Hallahan & Cruickshank, 1973; Hallahan & Kauffman, 1976; Hammill & Larsen, 1974).

There is a sense, however, in which it is unfair to make a direct analogy between the perceptual-motor training literature and the cognitive-behavior modification literature that concentrates on training attentional abilities or reflectivity. While there are few data to support the idea of a relationship between perceptual-motor abilities and academics, there is considerable evidence that we have already cited supporting the relationship between attentional abilities and reflectivity, on the one hand, and academic achievement on the other. Thus, it may be that training to increase these kinds of processes may be at least a necessary if not a sufficient condition for children who have attentional and/or impulsivity problems.

Another generalization that can be tentatively forwarded is that studies using a single-subject design are generally more successful. This is probably due to the fact that single-subject designs allow the experimenter the freedom to draw up a specific remediational program for individual children. In addition, these single-subject studies have also placed more emphasis on breaking the task down into its component parts so that the child can learn the various elements that make up the problem-solving sequence. The difficulty in using academic tasks in the remediation process that we mentioned above may thus be minimized to a certain degree if one adopts a task-analytic orientation within a single-subject design. In other words, rather than attempting to design remediational activities for large groups of children, it may prove more beneficial to construct a general program for the group but then make individual modifications as required. A passing thought in connection with our discussion is the observation that most of the studies adopting such a task-analytic strategy have used arithmetic as the subject matter. It is no doubt relatively easy to spell out to the child the sequence of behaviors necessary to solve math problems, whereas it is much more difficult to analyze reading into an observable sequence of behaviors.

Before concluding, a few statements should be made about the possible reasons why those studies reporting positive results have been successful. While it is undoubtedly premature to claim that there is overwhelming evidence favoring the efficacy of a cognitive-behavior modification orientation to academic problems, there are enough positive data to warrant some mention of possible critical factors. If nothing else, such a discussion might suggest further areas for study.

As should be obvious by now, *cognitive-behavior modification* is not a term that can be easily defined. The rubric of cognitive-behavior modification covers a very broad range of treatment techniques. (As we have already noted, some of the studies we reviewed were not specifically identified by their authors as being cognitive-behavior modification studies but did contain certain elements that were similar to such an approach.) Even our limited coverage of literature pertaining only to academic deficits reveals considerable differences in treatment procedures. (If one considers the vast literature pertaining to the use of cognitive-behavior modification with such diverse conditions as alcoholism, depression, and obesity, the variety of treatment procedures is even more pronounced.) This broad range of procedures makes it extremely difficult to specify what factors are responsible for gains when they are found.

Given the fact that a strong case can be made for the LD child's possessing a passive rather than an active approach to problem solving, one treatment variable that must be high on the list of possible critical ones is that of providing the child with direct instruction in how to go about solving a particular type of problem. In addition to instruction in appropriate strategies, however, another possible critical variable is that of self-verbalization, both overt and covert. There are at least three ways in which having the child overtly verbalize his problem-solving steps might be an effective technique. First, when the child overtly verbalizes as he solves a problem he is making "observable" the thought processes he is engaging in. Thus, the adult is provided with a way of knowing what strategies the child is or is not using at various stages of the problem-solving sequence. In the usual classroom situation, for example, the teacher may ask the child to compute an arithmetic problem. The child attempts to solve the problem and all that the teacher observes is the child's final product—a correct or incorrect answer. While the teacher may, from the nature of the error made, be able to figure out the child's faulty thought processes when he makes an error, this will not always be an easy task. If, however, he has the child overtly verbalize his thoughts as he engages in them, the chances are perhaps greater that the teacher will be able to pinpoint the location of the child's erroneous thinking in the problem-solving sequence.

The other two ways in which overt verbalization may be influential have been summarized by Lovitt and Curtiss (1968):

> The current study, which experimentally assessed the function of a popular remediation theory—that verbalizing a problem aids in solving it—revealed data supporting this theory. . . . One possible explanation is that the subject's increased accuracy when the problem was verbalized was a function of adding a second stimulus dimension to the mathematics problem—orally reciting the problem as well as seeing it. The theoretical basis for such a thesis,

that learning proceeds at a more rapid rate under multisensory conditions, has historically been supported by numerous educators.

An alternative explanation . . . could be that he simply became more deliberate. A pupil, when required merely to write an answer to a problem, could regard the cost of making a pencil mark as extremely minimal. However, when required to state a problem verbally, then write a solution, the increase in cost and/or complexity could have functioned to make the child more deliberate. (p. 332)

6. Summary and Conclusions

Minimal brain dysfunction is a term that is not useful to clinicians, educators, or researchers. *Hyperactivity* refers to high rates of socially inappropriate behavior and is most usefully conceptualized as a type of learning disability—as a deficit in social learning. *Learning disability* is most appropriately considered as failure (for whatever reason) to learn at a rate commensurate with one's ability. A recent line of research is the comparison of psychoactive drugs and behavior modification techniques in treating hyperactivity and learning disability. Only a few comparative studies, differing widely in subject selection, design, and methodology, have been reported so far. While only tentative conclusions can be made on the basis of existing data, it appears that behavior modification is often highly effective with or without drugs and often has certain advantages: It tends to be specific in its effects, encourages a focus on teaching adaptive behavior in addition to reducing misbehavior, and requires appropriate environmental changes. In addition, it was noted that the success of behavior change techniques may depend on certain cognitive factors and that pill-taking probably does not foster attribution of behavior change to personal causal factors. Another emerging area of research involves cognitive-behavior modification. This intervention approach, which is an attempt to reconcile certain aspects of cognitive and behavioral psychology, includes teaching children problem-solving strategies and self-instruction techniques. A strong rationale for the use of cognitive-behavior modification with learning disability can be built on the basis of extensive literature showing learning-disabled children to be deficient in memory strategies and selective attention. Not many studies of cognitive-behavior modification with learning-disabled children have been reported yet, and only a handful of experiments have given attention to the effects of these techniques on academic responses. The available data suggest that cognitive-behavior modification may be a particularly useful strategy for dealing with academic deficits if academic responses themselves, not other responses tapping supposedly related "cognitive process" performances, are used in training and if training is highly individualized. Three possible explanations for the success of cognitive-behavior modification techniques are suggested: The procedures make the child's cognitive processes open to some extent to direct observation and analysis, multisensory experience is required, and the child must become more deliberate or focus his attention more acutely. In both the emerging areas of research we have reviewed, the most useful data are those obtained from careful single-subject analyses of intervention strategies.

7. References

Alabiso, F. Operant control of attention behavior: A treatment for hyperactivity. *Behavior Therapy*, 1975, *6*, 39-42.

Ayllon, T., Layman, D., & Kandel, H. J. A behavioral-educational alternative to drug control of hyperactive children. *Journal of Applied Behavior Analysis*, 1975, *8*, 137-146.

Ayllon, T., & Rosenbaum, M. S. The behavioral treatment of disruption and hyperactivity in school settings. In A. E. Kazdin & B. B. Lahey (Eds.), *Advances in clinical child psychology* (Vol. 1). New York: Plenum, 1977.

Bandura, A. Self-efficacy: Toward a unifying theory of behavioral change. *Psychological Review*, 1977, *84*, 191-215.

Barkley, R. A. Predicting the response of hyperkinetic children to stimulant drugs: A review. *Journal of Abnormal Child Psychology*, 1976, *4*, 327-348.

Bauer, R. H. Memory processes in children with learning disabilities: Evidence for deficient rehearsal. *Journal of Experimental Child Psychology*, 1977, *24*, 415-430.

Bem, S. L. Verbal self-control: The establishment of effective self-instruction. *Journal of Experimental Psychology*, 1967, *74*, 485-491.

Bender, N. N. Self-verbalization versus tutor verbalization in modifying impulsivity. *Journal of Educational Psychology*, 1976, *68*, 347-354.

Bijou, S. W., & Grimm, J. A. Behavioral diagnosis and assessment in teaching young handicapped children. In T. Thompson & W. S. Dockens (Eds.), *Applications of behavior modification*. New York: Academic Press, 1975.

Blackwood, R. O. The operant conditioning of verbally mediated self-control in the classroom. *Journal of School Psychology*, 1970, *8*, 251-258.

Bornstein, P. H., & Quevillon, R. P. The effects of a self-instructional package on overactive preschool boys. *Journal of Applied Behavior Analysis*, 1976, *9*, 179-188.

Bosco, J. J., & Robin, S. S. (Eds), The hyperactive child and stimulant drugs: Definitions, diagnosis, and directives. *School Review*, 1976, *85*(1), 1-175.

Bower, K. B. *Impulsivity and academic performance in learning and behavior disordered children*. Unpublished doctoral dissertation, University of Virginia, 1975.

Bugental, D. B., Whalen, C. K., & Henker, B. Causal attributions of hyperactive children and motivational assumptions of two behavior change approaches: Evidence for an interactionist position. *Child Development*, 1977, *48*, 874-884.

Camp, B. W., Blom, G. E., Hebert, F., & van Doorninck, W. J. "Think Aloud": A program for developing self-control in young aggressive boys. *Journal of Abnormal Child Psychology*, 1977, *5*, 157-169.

Christensen, D. E. Effects of combining methylphenidate and a classroom token system in modifying hyperactive behavior. *American Journal of Mental Deficiency*, 1975, *80*, 266-276.

Christensen, D. E., & Sprague, R. L. Reduction of hyperactive behavior by conditioning procedures alone and combined with methylphenidate (Ritalin). *Behaviour Research and Therapy*, 1973, *11*, 331-334.

Cohen, N. J. *Physiological concomitants of attention in hyperactive children*. Unpublished doctoral dissertation, McGill University, 1970.

Cruickshank, W. M., & Hallahan, D. P. (Eds.), *Perceptual and learning disabilities in children. Vol. 1: Psychoeducational practices*. Syracuse: Syracuse University Press, 1975. (a)

Cruickshank, W. M., & Hallahan, D. P. (Eds.), *Perceptual and learning disabilities in children. Vol. 2: Research and theory*. Syracuse: Syracuse University Press, 1975. (b)

Dawson, M. C. *The effect of reinforcement and verbal rehearsal on selective attention in learning disabled children*. Unpublished doctoral dissertation, University of Virginia, 1977.

Deikel, S. M., & Friedman, M. P. Selective attention in children with learning disabilities. *Perceptual and Motor Skills*, 1976, *42*, 675-678.

Douglas, V. S. Are drugs enough? To train or to treat the hyperactive child. *International Journal of Mental Health*, 1975, *5*, 199-212.

Douglas, V. S., Parry, P., Marton, P., & Garson, C. Assessment of a cognitive training program for hyperactive children. *Journal of Abnormal Child Psychology*, 1976, *4*, 389-410.

Druker, J. F. & Hagen, J. W. Developmental trends in the processing of task irrelevant information. *Child Development*, 1969, *40*, 371-382.

Egeland, B. Training impulsive children in the use of more efficient scanning techniques. *Child Development*, 1974, *45*, 165-171.

Epstein, M. H. *Modification of impulsivity and arithmetic performance in underachieving children*. Unpublished doctoral dissertation, University of Virginia, 1975.

Evans, I. M., & Nelson, R. O. Assessment of child behavior problems. In A. R. Ciminero, K. S. Calhoun, & H. E. Adams (Eds.), *Handbook of behavioral assessment*. New York: Wiley, 1977.

Finch, A. J., & Kendall, P. C. Impulsive behavior: From research to treatment. In A. J. Finch & P. C. Kendall (Eds.), *Treatment and research in child psychopathology*, Hollinswood, N.Y.: Spectrum Publications, 1978.

Firestone, P. *The effects of reinforcement contingencies and caffeine on hyperactive children*. Unpublished doctoral dissertation, McGill University, 1970.

Firestone, P., & Douglas, V. S. The effects of reward and punishment on reaction times and autonomic activity in hyperactive and normal children. *Journal of Abnormal Child Psychology*, 1975, *3*, 201-216.

Flavell, J. H. What is memory development the development of? *Human Development*, 1971, *14*, 272-278.

Flavell, J. H., Beach, I. R., & Chinsky, J. M. Spontaneous verbal rehearsal in a memory task, as a function of age. *Child Development*, 1966, *37*, 283-299.

Freeman, R. D. Minimal brain dysfunction, hyperactivity, and learning disorders: Epidemic or episode? *School Review*, 1976, *85*(1), 5-30.

Freibergs, V., & Douglas, V. S. Concept learning in hyperactive and normal children. *Journal of Abnormal Psychology*, 1969, *74*, 388-395.

Freston, C. W., & Drew, C. J. Verbal performance of learning disabled children as a function of input organization. *Journal of Learning Disabilities*, 1974, *7*, 424-428.

Gelfand, D. M., & Hartmann, D. P. *Child behavior: Analysis and therapy*. New York: Pergamon, 1975.

Gibson, E. J. *Trends in perceptual development: Implications for the reading process*. Paper presented at the Minnesota Symposium on Child Development, Minneapolis, October 1973.

Giebink, J. W., Stover, D. O., & Fahl, M. A. Teaching adaptive responses to frustration to emotionally disturbed boys. *Journal of Consulting and Clinical Psychology*, 1968, *32*, 366-368.

Gittelman-Klein, R., Klein, D. F., Abikoff, H., Katz, S., Gloisten, A. C., & Kates, W. Relative efficacy of methylphenidate and behavior modification in hyperkinetic children: An interim report. *Journal of Abnormal Child Psychology*, 1976, *4*, 361.

Grimm, J. A., Bijou, S. W., & Parsons, J. A. A problem-solving model for teaching remedial arithmetic to handicapped young children. *Journal of Abnormal Child Psychology*, 1973, *1*, 26-39.

Hagen, J. W. The effect of distraction on selective attention. *Child Development*, 1967, *38*, 685-694.

Hagen, J. W. Some thoughts on how children learn to remember. *Human Development*, 1971, *14*, 262-271.

Hagen, J. W., Hargrave, S., & Ross, W. Prompting and rehearsal in short-term memory. *Child Development*, 1973, *44*, 201-204.

Hagen, J. W., & Kail, R. V. Facilitation and distraction in short-term memory. *Child Development*, 1973, *44*, 831-836.

Hagen, J. W., & Kingsley, P. R. Labeling effects in short-term memory. *Child Development*, 1968, *39*, 113-121.

Hagen, J. W. & Sabo, R. A developmental study of selective attention. *Merrill-Palmer Quarterly*, 1967, *13*, 159-172.

Hallahan, D. P. Distractibility in the learning disabled child. In W. M. Cruickshank & D. P. Hallahan (Eds.), *Perceptual and learning disabilities in children, Vol. 2: Research and theory*. Syracuse: Syracuse University Press, 1975.

Hallahan, D. P., & Cohen, S. B. Learning disabilities: Problems in definition. *Behavioral Disorders*, 1977, *2*, 132-135.

Hallahan, D. P., & Cruickshank, W. M. *Psychoeducational foundations of learning disabilities*. Englewood Cliffs, N.J.: Prentice-Hall, 1973.

Hallahan, D. P., Gajar, A. H., Cohen, S. B., & Tarver, S. G. Selective attention and locus of control in learning disabled and normal children. *Journal of Learning Disabilities*, 1978, *11*, 231-236.

Hallahan, D. P., & Kauffman, J. M. Research on the education of distractible and hyperactive children. In W. M. Cruickshank & D. P. Hallahan (Eds.), *Perceptual and learning disabilities in children, Vol. 2: Research and theory*. Syracuse: Syracuse University Press, 1975.

Hallahan, D. P., & Kauffman, J. M. *Introduction to learning disabilities: A psycho-behavioral approach*. Englewood Cliffs, N.J.: Prentice-Hall, 1976.

Hallahan, D. P., & Kauffman, J. M. Categories, labels, behavioral characteristics: ED, LD, and EMR reconsidered. *Journal of Special Education*, 1977, *11*, 139-149.

Hallahan, D. P., & Kauffman, J. M. *Exceptional children: Introduction to special education*. Englewood Cliffs, N.J.: Prentice-Hall, 1978.

Hallahan, D. P., Kauffman, J. M., & Ball, D. W. Selective attention and cognitive tempo of low achieving and high achieving sixth grade males. *Perceptual and Motor Skills*, 1973, *36*, 579-583.

Hallahan, D. P., Stainback, S., Ball, D. W., & Kauffman, J. M. Selective attention in cerebral palsied and normal children. *Journal of Abnormal Child Psychology*, 1973, *1*, 280-291.

Hallahan, D. P., Tarver, S. G., Kauffman, J. M., & Graybeal, N. L. A comparison of the effects of reinforcement and response cost on the selective attention of learning disabled children. *Journal of Learning Disabilities*, in press.

Hammill, D. D., & Larsen, S. The effectiveness of psycholinguistic training. *Exceptional Children*, 1974, *41*, 5-15.

Hartig, M., & Kanfer, F. H. The role of verbal self-instructions in children's resistance to temptation. *Journal of Personality and Social Psychology*, 1973, *25*, 259-267.

Heins, E. D., Hallahan, D. P., Tarver, S. G., & Kauffman, J. M. Relationship between cognitive tempo and selective attention in learning disabled children. *Perceptual and Motor Skills*, 1976, *42*, 233-234.

Hersen, M., & Barlow, D. H. *Single case experimental designs*. New York: Pergamon, 1976.

Kagan, J. Impulsive and reflective children: Significance of conceptual tempo. In J. D. Krumboltz (Ed.), *Learning and the educational process*. Chicago: Rand McNally, 1965.

Kagan, J. Developmental studies in reflection and analysis. In A. H. Kidd & J. H. Rivoire (Eds.), *Perceptual development in children*. New York: International Universities Press, 1966.

Kauffman, J. M. Behavior modification. In W. M. Cruickshank & D. P. Hallahan (Eds.), *Perceptual and learning disabilities in children, Vol. 2: Research and theory*. Syracuse: Syracuse University Press, 1975.

Kauffman, J. M. Nineteenth century views of children's behavior disorders: Historical contributions and continuing issues. *Journal of Special Education*, 1976, *10*, 335-349.

Kauffman, J. M. *Characteristics of children's behavior disorders*. Columbus, Ohio: Charles E. Merrill, 1977.

Kauffman, J. M., & Hallahan, D. P. (Eds.), *Teaching children with learning disabilities: Personal perspectives*. Columbus, Ohio: Charles E. Merrill, 1976.

Kazdin, A. E. *Behavior modification in applied settings*. Homewood, Ill.: Dorsey Press, 1975.

Keeney, T. J., Cannizzo, S. R., & Flavell, J. H. Spontaneous and induced verbal rehearsal in a recall task. *Child Development*, 1967, *38*, 953-966.

Keogh, B. K., & Donlon, G. M. Field-independence, impulsivity, and learning disabilities. *Journal of Learning Disabilities*, 1972, *5*, 331-336.

Koupernik, C., MacKeith, R., & Francis-Williams, J. Neurological correlates of motor and perceptual development. In W. M. Cruickshank & D. P. Hallahan (Eds.), *Perceptual and learning disabilities in children, Vol. 2: Research and theory*. Syracuse: Syracuse University Press, 1975.

Lahey, B. B. Behavior modification with learning disabilities and related problems. In M. Hersen, R. Eisler, & P. Miller (Eds.), *Progress in behavior modification* (Vol. 3). New York: Academic Press, 1976.

Lovitt, T. C. Applied behavior analysis and learning disabilities. *Journal of Learning Disabilities*, 1975, *8*, 432-443, 504-518.

Lovitt, T. C. *In spite of my resistance—I've learned from children*. Columbus, Ohio: Charles E. Merrill, 1977.

Lovitt, T. C., & Curtiss, K. A. Effects of manipulating an antecedent event on mathematics response rate. *Journal of Applied Behavior Analysis*, 1968, *1*, 329-333.

Maccoby, E. E., & Hagen, J. W. Effects of distraction upon central versus incidental recall: Developmental trends. *Journal of Experimental Child Psychology*, 1965, *2*, 280-289.

MacPherson, E. M., Candee, B. L., & Hohman, R. J. A comparison of three methods for eliminating disruptive lunchroom behavior. *Journal of Applied Behavior Analysis*, 1974, *7*, 287-297.

Marholin, D., & Phillips, D. Methodological issues in psychopharmacological research: Chlorpromazine—a case in point. *American Journal of Orthopsychiatry*, 1976, *46*, 477-495.

Meichenbaum, D. *Cognitive-behavior modification*. New York: Plenum Press, 1977.

Meichenbaum, D., & Goodman, J. Reflection-impulsivity and verbal control of motor behavior. *Child Development*, 1969, *40*, 785-797.

Meichenbaum, D., & Goodman, J. Training impulsive children to talk to themselves: A means of developing self-control. *Journal of Abnormal Psychology*, 1971, *77*, 115-126.

Mondani, M. S., & Tutko, T. A. Relationship of academic underachievement to incidental learning. *Journal of Consulting and Clinical Psychology*, 1969, *33*, 558-560.

Norman, D. A. *Memory and attention*. New York: Wiley, 1969.

O'Leary, K. D. The assessment of psychopathology in children. In H. C. Quay & J. S. Werry (Eds.), *Psychopathological disorders of childhood*. New York: Wiley, 1972.

O'Leary, S. G., & Pelham, W. E. Behavior therapy and withdrawal of stimulant medication with hyperactive children. *Pediatrics*, 1978, *61*, 211-217.

Palkes, H., Stewart, M., & Freedman, J. Improvement in maze performance of hyperactive boys as a function of verbal-training procedures. *Journal of Special Education*, 1972, *5*, 337-342.

Palkes, H., Stewart, N., & Kahana, B. Porteus maze performance of hyperactive boys after training in self-directed verbal commands. *Child Development*, 1968, *39*, 817-826.

Parker, T. B., Freston, D. W., & Drew, C. J. Comparison of verbal performance of normal and learning disabled children as a function of input organization. *Journal of Learning Disabilities*, 1975, *8*, 386-393.

Parry, P. *The effect of reward on performance of hyperactive children*. Unpublished doctoral dissertation, McGill University, 1973.

Parry, P., & Douglas, V. S. The effect of reward on the performance of hyperactive children. *Journal of Abnormal Child Psychology*, in press.

Parsons, J. A. The reciprocal modification of arithmetic behavior and program development. In G. Semb (Ed.), *Behavior analysis and education–1972*. Lawrence: University of Kansas, Department of Human Development, 1972.

Patterson, C. J., & Mischel, W. Plans to resist distraction. *Developmental Psychology*, 1975, *11*, 369-378.

Patterson, C. J., & Mischel, W. Effects of temptation-inhibiting and task-facilitating plans on self-control. *Journal of Personality and Social Psychology*, 1976, *33*, 209-217.

Patterson, G. R. An application of operant conditioning techniques to the control of a hyperactive child. In C. P. Ullmann & L. Krasner (Eds.), *Case studies in behavior modification*. New York: Holt, Rinehart & Winston, 1965.

Patterson, G. R., Jones, R. W., Whittier, J. E., & Wright, M. A. A behavior modification technique for the hyperactive child. *Behaviour Research and Therapy*, 1965, *2*, 217-226.

Pelham, W. E. Withdrawal of a stimulant drug and concurrent behavioral intervention in the treatment of a hyperactive child. *Behavior Therapy*, 1977, *8*, 473-479.

Pelham, W. E., & Ross, A. O. Selective attention in children with reading problems: A developmental study of incidental learning. *Journal of Abnormal Child Psychology*, 1977, *5*, 1-8.

Reese, H. W. Verbal mediation as a function of age level. *Psychological Bulletin*, 1962, *59*, 502-509.

Ridberg, E., Parke, R., & Hetherington, E. M. Modification of impulsive and reflective cognitive styles through observation of film mediated models. *Developmental Psychology*, 1971, *5*, 369-377.

Ring, B. C. Effects of input organization on auditory short-term memory. *Journal of Learning Disabilities*, 1977, *9*, 591-595.

Robertson, D. U., & Keeley, S. M. *Evaluation of a mediational training program for impulsive children by a multiple case study design*. Paper presented at the American Psychological Association Convention, 1974.

Robin, A. L., Armel, S., & O'Leary, K. D. The effects of self-instruction on writing deficiencies. *Behavior Therapy*, 1975, *6*, 178-187.

Rosenbaum, A., O'Leary, K. D., & Jacob, R. G. Behavioral intervention with hyperactive children: Group consequences as a supplement to individual contingencies. *Behavior Therapy*, 1975, *6*, 315-323.

Ross, A. O. *Psychological aspects of learning disabilities and reading disorders*. New York: McGraw-Hill, 1976.

Ross, D. M., & Ross, S. A. *Hyperactivity: Research, theory, and action*. New York: Wiley, 1976.

Shafto, F., & Sulzbacher, S. I. Comparing treatment tactics with a hyperactive preschool child: Stimulant medication and programmed teacher intervention. *Journal of Applied Behavior Analysis*, 1977, *10*, 13-20.

Sprague, R. L. Minimal brain dysfunction from a behavioral viewpoint. *Annals of the New York Academy of Sciences*, 1973, *205*, 349-361.

Sprague, R. L., & Baxley, G. B. Drugs used for the management of behavior in mental retardation. In N. R. Ellis (Ed.), *Handbook of mental deficiency* (2nd ed.). Hillsdale, N.J.: Erlbaum Associates, in press.

Sprague, R. L., & Boileau, R. A. Are drugs safe? In R. L. Sprague (chm.), *Psychopharmacology of children with learning disabilities*. Symposium presented at the American Psychological Association, Montréal, Québec, Canada, 1973.

Sroufe, L. A. Drug treatment of children with behavior problems. In F. D. Horowitz (Ed.), *Review of child development research* (Vol. 4). Chicago: University of Chicago Press, 1975.

Stableford, W., Butz, R., Hasazi, J., Leitenberg, H., & Peyser, J. Sequential withdrawal of stimulant drugs and use of behavior therapy with two hyperactive boys. *American Journal of Orthopsychiatry*, 1976, *46*, 302-312.

Strong, C., Sulzbacher, S. I., & Kirkpatrick, M. A. Use of medication versus reinforcement to modify a classroom behavior disorder. *Journal of Learning Disabilities*, 1974, *7*, 214-218.

Sulzbacher, S. I. Behavior analysis of drug effects in the classroom. In G. Semb (Ed.), *Behavior analysis and education—1972*. Lawrence: University of Kansas, Department of Human Development, 1972.

Sverd, J., Hurwic, M. J., David, O., & Winsberg, B. G. Hypersensitivity to methylphenidate and dextroamphetamine: A report of two cases. *Pediatrics*, 1977, *59*, 115-117.

Swanson, H. L. Nonverbal visual short-term memory as a function of age and dimensionality in learning-disabled children. *Child Development*, 1977, *48*, 51-55.

Tarver, S. G., Hallahan, D. P., Cohen, S. B., & Kauffman, J. M. The development of visual selective attention and verbal rehearsal in learning disabled boys. *Journal of Learning Disabilities*, 1977, *10*, 491-500.

Tarver, S. G., Hallahan, D. P., Kauffman, J. M., & Ball, D. W. Verbal rehearsal and selective attention in children with learning disabilities: A developmental lag. *Journal of Experimental Child Psychology*, 1976, *22*, 375-385.

Torgesen, J. K. The role of nonspecific factors in the task performance of learning disabled children: A theoretical assessment. *Journal of Learning Disabilities*, 1977, *10*, 27-34.

Torgesen, J. & Goldman, T. Verbal rehearsal and short-term memory in reading-disabled children. *Child Development*, 1977, *48*, 56-60.

Weissenberger, F. E., & Loney, J. Hyperkinesis in the classroom: If cerebral stimulants are the last resort, what is the first resort? *Journal of Learning Disabilities*, 1976, *10*, 339-347.

Weithorn, C. J., & Ross, R. Stimulant drugs for hyperactivity: Some additional disturbing questions. *American Journal of Orthopsychiatry*, 1976, *46*, 168-173.

Werry, J. S. Organic factors in childhood psychopathology. In H. C. Quay & J. S. Werry (Eds.), *Psychopathological disorders of childhood*. New York: Wiley, 1972.

Whalen, C. K., & Henker, B. Psychostimulants and children: A review and analysis. *Psychological Bulletin*, 1976, *83*, 1113-1130.

White, O. R., & Liberty, K. A. Behavioral assessment and precise educational measurement. In N. G. Haring & R. L. Schiefelbusch (Eds.), *Teaching special children*. New York: McGraw-Hill, 1976.

Wolraich, M., Drummond, T., Salomon, M. K., O'Brien, M. L., & Sivage, C. Effects of methylphenidate alone and in combination with behavior modification procedures on the behavior and academic performance of hyperactive children. *Journal of Abnormal Child Psychology*, 1978, *6*, 149-161.

Wozniak, R. H., & Nuechterlein, P. Reading improvement through verbally self-guided looking and listening, summary report. University of Minnesota Research, Development and Demonstration Center in Education of Handicapped Children, 1973.

Wulbert, M., & Dries, R. The relative efficacy of methylphenidate (Ritalin) and behavior-modification techniques in the treatment of a hyperactive child. *Journal of Applied Behavior Analysis*, 1977, *10*, 21-31.

Zelnicker, T., & Oppenheimer, L. Effect of different training methods on perceptual learning in impulsive children. *Child Development*, 1976, *47*, 492-497.

4 The Assessment and Treatment of Children's Fears

SUZANNE BENNETT JOHNSON
AND BARBARA G. MELAMED

While fear is a necessary and often "healthy" response to a wide variety of situations, at times it can become so debilitating as to be maladaptive. Careful distinctions involving terms such as *fear*, *phobia*, and *anxiety* are not always made. However, there seems to be some general consensus that fear connotes a differentiated response to a specific object or situation. Anxiety is a more diffuse, less focused response, perhaps best described as apprehension without apparent cause. A phobia is a special form of fear that (1) is out of proportion to the demands of the situation, (2) cannot be explained or reasoned away, (3) is beyond voluntary control, and (4) leads to avoidance of the feared situation (Marks, 1969).

From a practical standpoint, it is questionable whether careful distinctions between terms have any real significance. Certainly from a behavioral perspective, the clinician must assess what are the stimulus conditions leading to the child's negative affective state regardless of the descriptive terms employed. Admittedly, such an assessment might take longer for the child presenting with diffuse anxiety than for the child with a specific fear or phobia. The goals of the assessment procedure, however, would remain the same (i.e., specifying the discriminative stimuli eliciting the anxious or phobic reaction).

Fear can be manifested in a variety of ways. These include behavioral avoidance responses, verbal self-report, and physiological reactions. No one response necessarily connotes fear and often there is inconsistency between response domains. This is further complicated by the time at which the fear response is assessed. Any rigorous definition of fear seems to require a broad multidimensional analysis with care taken to specify when measures are of anticipation anxiety, actual reaction to stress, or recovery from a frightening experience.

SUZANNE BENNETT JOHNSON AND BARBARA G. MELAMED • Department of Clinical Psychology, University of Florida, Gainesville, Florida.

1. Scope of the Review

The definition of fear is complex and its etiology is not well understood. In fact, it would be naive to assume that all fears are generated in
the same manner. The current review focuses on children between the
ages of 4 and 12, with an emphasis on debilitating fears that interfere
with daily functioning or social development. A critique of the available
assessment devices stresses the need for demonstrated reliability and
validity of the instruments; assessment is a critical tool for accountability
and cannot be overlooked.

Treatment approaches are evaluated with an emphasis on what we
know about the likely success for the different approaches given a specific fear constellation. The need for longitudinal studies that take personality variables, as well as treatment mode into account is indicated.

Implications for the researcher as well as the practitioner are presented.

2. Incidence and Content of Children's Fears

It is clear that fear is a universal experience in normal child development. MacFarlane, Allen, and Honzik (1954) report that 90% of the
children they studied had at least one specific fear between the ages of 2
and 14. Forty-three percent of the normal children studied by Lapouse
and Monk (1959) were described as having seven or more fears, a finding similar to that reported by Pratt (1945). The content of children's
fears, however, seems to change with age; some fears are outgrown
while others appear, although younger children generally have more
fears than older children. Very young children show fears of loud
noises, depth, and strangers, which are replaced by fears of animals in
2- and 3-year-olds and fears of darkness, nightmares, and imaginary
creatures in 4- and 5-year-olds (Jersild & Holmes, 1935). In fact, a recent
study by Bauer (1976) found 74% of kindergartners to be fearful of
monsters, ghosts, and nightmares. In contrast, sixth-graders in the
same study rarely reported fears of imaginary creatures; their primary
fear was of bodily injury or physical danger, fears hardly ever mentioned
by kindergartners.

While there is a tendency to consider children's fears as focused on
a variety of inanimate dangers (e.g., water, darkness), animals, or imaginary creatures (e.g., ghosts, nightmares), they clearly experience a
variety of other, interpersonally related fears (Simon & Ward, 1974).
School phobia, of course, is a common example. Social withdrawal and
elective mutism often stem from children's interpersonal fears. Fears of
doctors and dentists are also frequently reported. A factor-analytic study
by Miller, Barrett, Hampe, and Noble (1972b) offers a useful means of

categorizing the content of children's fears. Factor I consists of fears of physical injury or personal loss (e.g., being kidnapped, having an operation, divorce of parents, death of a family member). Factor II is characterized by natural and supernatural dangers (e.g., storms, ghosts, the dark). Factor III reflects what the authors termed "psychic stress" and includes fears of exams, making mistakes, school, social events, doctors, and dentists.

A recurrent finding in the literature is that girls express more fears than boys (Bauer, 1976; Lapouse & Monk, 1959; Pratt, 1945; Simon & Ward, 1974). However, as Bauer (1976) has pointed out, girls and younger children may be more willing to admit their fears due to a variety of social and cultural factors.

While the incidence of fears in normal children is very high, the incidence of excessive fears for which the child needs treatment is more difficult to assess. Marks (1969) and Poznanski (1973) report that phobic disorders account for only 3-4% of all referrals to child psychiatrists. School phobia occurs in only 1-2% of all child cases seen in psychiatric clinics (Chazan, 1962; Eisenberg, 1958) and in 3.8% of all "neurotic" children seen (Smith, 1970). Estimates of incidence in the general population range from 1.7% (Kennedy, 1965) to 5-8% (Kahn & Nursten, 1962). Factor-analytic studies of the behavioral and emotional characteristics of disturbed children have repeatedly isolated a cluster of symptoms that have been variously named "personality problems," "withdrawn," "disturbed-neurotic," "overinhibited," "manifest anxiety" (see Quay, 1979). These symptoms include anxiety, self-consciousness, social withdrawal, crying, worrying, hypersensitivity, and seclusiveness. Taken together, they seem to be describing an overly fearful child in whom avoidance is a primary mode of response. Wolff (1971) reports that 26% of their child clinic population fit this description. Similar data have been reported by Frommer, Mendelson, and Reid (1972). In other words, the incidence of children treated for very specific fears and phobias is low. But the incidence of children who suffer from a cluster of symptoms including excessive anxiety and social withdrawal is relatively high.

Even fewer data are available as to the course of excessive fears through the child's development. We know that most fears in children are short-lived and there is some tentative evidence that excessive fears are more persistent (Poznanski, 1973). Even so, Agras, Chapin, and Oliveau (1972) report that 100% of untreated phobic children improved over a 5-year period; this did not occur for phobic adults. Agras et al. (1972) also note that the more specific and focused the fear, the better the prognosis. Follow-up studies on children treated for school phobia often describe continued adjustment problems later in life (Waldron, 1976; Coolidge, Brodie, & Feeney, 1964). However, distinctions have been made between Type I School Phobia typified by acute onset in younger children and Type II School Phobia, which involves more gradual, chronic episodes of school refusal usually in older children (Coolidge, Hahn, & Peck, 1957; Kennedy, 1965). Prognosis is considered better for the first type. Data reported by Rodriquez, Rodriquez, and Eisenberg (1959) in a follow-up of 41 children treated for school phobia support this conclusion. However, the spontaneous remission rate of school phobia is unknown.

3. Etiology

Fear most likely has multiple determinants. Some theories attempt to explain the development of phobic behavior as a defense mechanism protecting an inadequate ego. These are difficult to test as they interpret behavior on the basis of unobservable processes. Learning theories employ principles of classical and operant conditioning and modeling to specify the necessary conditions under which fear behaviors are likely to develop. We can prove them inadequate or demonstrate where they seem to account for the variability in the behaviors observed. However, for any theory to adequately explain the development of fear, it must answer the following questions:

1. Why do some fears extinguish without any specific treatment?
2. Why do some fears develop and persist even in the absence of actual exposure to the feared situation?
3. Why are some children predisposed to react with fear to intense or unpredictable stimuli, whereas others may respond with anger or curiosity?
4. Why are some situations or objects more likely to elicit fearful responses than others?

Initially, radical behaviorists such as John B. Watson argued that fears were developed by a simple classical conditioning paradigm. In their classic experiment, Watson and Raynor (1920) exposed a 9-month-old child, Albert, to a loud noise that consistently made the child tremble and cry. Subsequently, Albert was repeatedly presented with a white rat followed by the loud noise. Soon he began to show distress, crying when the rat was presented alone. This fear seemed to generalize to other similar objects such as cotton wool, a white rabbit, and a fur coat. One month later, although Albert shoed less extreme responses to these stimuli, some fearfulness remained.

Although some fears may develop under similar circumstances, most fears probably cannot be explained so simply. Solyom, Beck, Solyom, and Hugel (1974) extensively studied 47 phobic patients and compared them on a number of variables to 47 matched "normal" controls. They specifically note that a precipitating traumatic event leading to the patient's phobia was a relatively rare event. Characteristics of the phobic patients that differentiated them from normals included greater numbers of fears in childhood and adulthood and higher levels of general anxiety, tension, and dependency. Phobic patients more often had psychiatric disturbances in their families and/or mothers or fathers who were also phobic.

Currently, several factors are considered important to the development of excessive or maladaptive fears. Trauma, of course, remains an important causal variable although it does not explain all or even most of children's fears. The notion of "stimulus prepotency"—certain stimuli induce fear more easily than others—was discussed by Thorndike as early as 1935. At that time English (1929) had been unable to condition fear to a child's toy duck using a paradigm similar to Watson and Raynor's (1920). Bregman (1934) had also reported no acquisition of fear when a variety of objects (e.g., wooden triangle, ring, cloth curtains) were used as stimuli. The fact that the content of children's fears is unusually consistent and age-related also suggests that certain stimuli more easily elicit fear at varying developmental stages (see Seligman & Hagar, 1972, for a more thorough discussion of this issue).

Modeling, of course, is an additional contributory variable. Children often experience the same kind and number of fears as their mothers (Hagman, 1932). The Solyom et al. (1974) study noted that 30% of the mothers of phobic patients and 3% of their fathers were also phobic. Similar findings have been reported by Bandura and Menlove (1968) with dog-phobic children; 35% had parents who were also fearful. Other studies have found maternal anxiety to be related to children's stress reactions in dental or medical settings (Heffernan & Azarnoff, 1971; Johnson, 1971; Shaw, 1975; Wright & Alpern, 1971; Wright, Alpern & Leake, 1973).

Individual differences in arousal and habituation should also be taken into consideration. Thomas, Chess, Birch, Hertzig, and Korn (1963) have provided evidence that even at birth, children differ widely in their response to external stimuli. Some are distressed with seemingly little provocation, others are not bothered by what appears to be moderate to high levels of negative stimulation. Several authors have reported that patterns of arousal and habituation in the "personality problem" or "neurotic-disturbed" child are different from those seen in normal or conduct-disordered youngsters (Borkovec, 1970; DeMeyer-Gapin & Scott, 1977; Mueller & Shamsie, 1967; Whitehill, DeMeyer-Gapin, & Scott, 1976).

Before leaving considerations regarding the acquisition of children's fears, it is probably worth noting that fear reactions can be maintained or intensified by the responses of significant others in the child's environment. For example, parents of school-phobic children are often described as permitting the child to remain at home, watching television and engaging in a number of activities that might be more entertaining than going to school (Ayllon, Smith, & Rogers, 1970; Kennedy, 1965). Concurrent with avoiding the feared situation, the child is sometimes given additional rewards, which further encourage maintenance of his phobic reaction. In helping a child deal with a stressful situation, there are some data to suggest that parents who use positive reinforcement, modeling, and reassurance have children with better coping skills than parents who use force, punishment, or criticism (Zabin, 1975).

4. Assessment

Fear is considered to be a tripartite construct involving verbal, motor, and physiological components (Lang, 1968). Various attempts have been made to measure children's fears within each component although self-report is the most frequent assessment procedure used.

4.1. Self-Report Measures

Self-report measures of children's fears and anxieties can be classified into two categories: measures of anxiety as a trait and measures of specific fears. The Children's Manifest Anxiety Scale (CMAS) is an example of the former; the Test Anxiety Scale for Children (TASC) and the Fear Survey Schedule for Children (FSS-FC) are examples of the latter. The State-Trait Anxiety Inventory for Children (STAIC) is a more recent attempt to measure both state and trait anxiety with one instrument.

4.1.1. Children's Manifest Anxiety Scale

This scale, which was developed by Castaneda, McCandless, and Palermo (1956), consists of 42 anxiety items and 11 additional items that constitute a Lie Scale. It is assumed to measure the child's tendency to experience a general or chronic state of anxiety across a whole variety of situations. Test-retest reliability has ranged from $r = .70$ to $r = .94$ for normals (Castaneda *et al.*, 1956; Holloway, 1958) and $r = .77$ for emotionally disturbed children (Finch, Montgomery, & Deardorff, 1974a). Correlations with other scales purportedly designed to measure the same thing, such as the Anxiety-State measure of the STAIC are only moderate ($r = .38$ reported by Finch & Nelson, 1974; $r = .47$ reported by Montgomery & Finch, 1974). Similar correlations have been reported between CMAS scores and the total number of fears checked on the FSS-FC ($r = .49$, Scherer & Nakamura, 1968) and other self-report measures of anxiety ($r = .34$, Kutina & Fisher, 1977). The Kutina and Fisher (1977) study, however, reported no correlation between CMAS scores and either teacher or observer ratings of anxiety.

Validity studies indicate that children in adjustment classes and in residential treatment for emotional and behavioral disorders do receive significantly higher scores than normal children of the same sex and age (Kitano, 1960; Montgomery & Finch, 1974). At least two studies have reported the CMAS to be relatively insensitive to situational stress (Kaplan & Hafner, 1959; Melamed & Siegel, 1975).

Girls typically score higher than boys (Castaneda *et al.*, 1956; Coleman, Mackay, & Fidell, 1972; Finch & Nelson, 1974; Holloway, 1961; Scherer & Nakumura, 1968; Ziv & Luz, 1973). Norms are available for both sexes and different age groups but standardization data vary considerably across different geographical areas (Coleman *et al.*, 1972).

A factor-analytic study of 245 children by Finch, Kendall, and Montgomery (1974) reported that the Anxiety Scale of CMAS seems to be composed of three primary factors: (1) Anxiety: Worry and Oversensitivity (e.g., I worry most of the time; my feelings are easily hurt), (2) Anxiety: Physiological (e.g., I have trouble swallowing; often I feel sick to my stomach), and (3) Anxiety:Concentration (e.g., It's hard for me to keep my mind on my schoolwork; I have trouble making up my mind). Two factors have been reported by Scherer and Nakamura (1968): (1) Anxiety-Worry, similar to the first factor of Finch *et al.* (1974) and (2) Anxiety-Neurosis, which seems to include items from the second and third factors of Finch *et al.* (1974).

4.1.2. State-Trait Anxiety Inventory for Children

This instrument consists of two independent 20-item self-report scales developed by Speilberger (1973) to measure both transitory anxiety that varies over time and across situations (A-State) and more stable anxiety similar to what is presumably tapped by the CMAS (A-Trait). In addition to the information available in the test manual, there are several studies reporting reliability and validity data. Finch, Montgomery, and Deardorff (1974b) found good split-half reliability ($r = .89$ for A-State and $r = .88$ for A-Trait) but poor test-retest reliability over a 3-month period ($r = .63$ for A-State and $r = .44$ for A-Trait). Poor reliability would be expected for the A-State measure but not for the A-Trait measure. Same-day test-retest reliabilities are somewhat higher ($r = .72$ for A-State and $r = .65$ for A-Trait; Finch, Kendall, Montgomery, & Morris, 1975), but only Bedell and Roitzsch (1976) have reported high reliability for A-Trait ($r = .94$).

Correlations with other instruments designed to measure state or trait anxiety have not consistently supported the state-trait distinction on the STAIC. One would expect, for example, that the A-Trait measure would clearly correlate higher with the CMAS than the CMAS with A-State, or A-State with A-Trait; studies have not found this to be consistently the case (Finch & Nelson, 1974; Montgomery & Finch, 1974). However, other validity data suggest that emotionally disturbed children score higher on both dimensions than normal children (Finch *et al.*, 1974b; Finch & Nelson, 1974; Montgomery & Finch, 1974). In addition, Gaudry and Poole (1972) provide evidence that A-State scores do increase in response to situational stress. Bedell and Roitzsch (1976) and Newmark, Wheeler, Newmark, and Stabler (1975) also found that experimentally increasing the demands placed on a child led to increases in A-State scores but, as predicted, not in A-Trait scores. However, Bedell and Roitzsch (1976) did not report any differences in A-State or A-Trait between their normals and their emotionally disturbed or delinquent subjects. And, one study did not report differential increases in A-State and A-Trait scores in response to experimentally induced stress (Finch *et al.*, 1975).

Consistent with the general anxiety literature, female children often score higher than male children (Finch & Nelson, 1974). However, not all investigators have found this to be the case (Newmark *et al.*, 1975). Norms are available in the test manual, although there is no careful assessment of their stability across various geographical regions. A factor-analytic study has been recently reported by Finch, Kendall, and Montgomery (1976) using the responses of 120 emotionally disturbed and 126 normal children to the STAIC. The A-State factors found were bipolar, depicting worry, feelings of tension, and nervousness, on the one hand, and pleasantness, relaxation, and happiness on the other. Two trait factors also emerged, one dealing with worry and the other with indecisiveness and rumination. An additional trait factor depicting difficulty sleeping and sweaty hands emerged in normals. Perhaps most interesting was the finding that A-State factors accounted for most of the variance among emotionally disturbed children while normals had nearly an equal proportion of variance accounted for by A-State and A-Trait factors. Unfortunately, the emotionally disturbed children were grouped together as a whole and no separate consideration was given to children with different types of psychological disturbance (e.g., conduct disorders, personality disorders). One might expect, for example, that conduct-disordered children would have lower A-Trait scores than personality-problem children. But since this kind of data was not presented, it is difficult to explain these particular results.

4.1.3. Text Anxiety Scale for Children

This is a 30-item test, developed by Sarason, Davidson, Lighthall, Waite, and Ruebush (1960), which is read to the child. The items range from questions about worries specific to taking tests to more general school-related anxieties. The child simply circles "yes" or "no" on an answer sheet after each question is read. Similar to the CMAS, an 11-item Lie Scale is also available.

Split-half reliability is reported to be high, r = .88 to .90 (Mann, Taylor, Proger, & Morrell, 1968; Sarason, Davidson, Lighthall, & Waite, 1958) and test-retest reliability to be moderate, r = .67 (Sarason *et al.*, 1960).

Few studies of construct or convergent validity have been published, although a low correlation (r = .20) has been reported between teacher ratings of children's classroom anxieties and their TASC scores (Sarason *et al.*, 1960). Most studies have focused on concurrent or predictive validity particularly with regard to intelligence tests and measures of achievement. Both are consistently reported to be low to moderately related to TASC scores, with high-anxious children performing more poorly (Cotler & Palmer, 1970; Hill & Sarason, 1966; Kestenbaum & Weiner, 1970; Mann *et al.*, 1968; Milgram & Milgram, 1977; Sarason *et al.*, 1960; Young & Brown, 1973). Poor performance is considered to be the result of interfering effects of anxiety rather than a consequence of inadequate intelligence. For example, perseverative, rigid problem-solving strategies and other task-irrelevant behavior is presumed to be anxiety-induced, leading to overall poor task performance. Recent work by Sieber, Kameya, and Paulson (1970), Dusek, Mergler, and Kermis (1976), and Nottelmann and Hill (1977) seems to support this position.

In general, however, more studies have focused on various hypothetical correlates of TASC scores rather than its adequacy as a measure of test-anxiety. Girls often acknowledge more anxiety than boys (Hill & Sarason, 1966; Sarason *et al.*, 1960; Young & Brown, 1973) but well-standardized norms are not readily available. The usual approach is to give a large number of children the TASC and then to classify children as low or high test-anxious by a median split or to divide the children into thirds, labeling the groups low, medium, and high test-anxious.

4.1.4. Fear Survey Schedule for Children

Modeled after Wolpe and Lang's (1964) Fear Survey Schedule for adults, this 80-item scale consists of specific fears related to the following categories: school, home, social, physical, animal, travel, classical phobia, and miscellaneous. Sometimes, the total number of fears a child ascribes to is used to measure his chronic anxiety as well. Although split-half reliability of the FSS-FC seems quite acceptable (r = .94 reported by Scherer & Nakamura, 1968), test-retest reliability has not been reported. One of the few studies in the area found that ratings by five adolescents on the adult version of the FSS showed very low or no agreement with the same ratings carried out by parents or care-takers who were also asked to rate the adolescents' fears (Mermis & Ross, 1971).

As noted previously, the total number of fear items checked has correlated moderately ($r = .49$) with the CMAS (Scherer & Nakamura, 1968). Girls are reported to admit to more fears than boys (Scherer & Nakamura, 1968) but no norms are available. There are almost no validity data on this instrument, although Melamed and her colleagues (Melamed, Hawes, Heiby, & Glick, 1975; Melamed, Weinstein, Hawes, & Katin-Borland, 1975; Melamed, Yurcheson, Fleece, Hutcherson, & Hawes, 1978) note some sensitivity of the measure to treatment manipulations. The differences, however, were statistically significant in only one of the studies cited (Melamed et al., 1978).

A factor-analytic study (Scherer & Nakamura, 1968) of responses to the instrument by normal 9-to 12-year-olds reports factors very much in keeping with the Miller et al. (1972b) categorization of children's fears into (1) fear of physical injury and personal loss, (2) fear of natural and supernatural danger, and (3) fears related to psychic stress (school, doctors, tests, etc.).

4.2. Behavioral Measures

Behavioral measures of children's fears fall into four categories: behavioral avoidance tests (BAT), observational codes, behavior checklists, and global behavioral ratings.

4.2.1. Behavioral Avoidance Test

This measure is typically used with very specific fears such as snake, dog, or water phobias (Bandura, Grusec, & Menlove, 1967; Bandura & Menlove, 1968; Kornhaber & Schroeder, 1975; Lewis, 1974; Ritter, 1968). The child is asked to perform the same graded series of approach behaviors toward the phobic object both pre- and posttreatment. Since the BAT is administered in a standard, carefully controlled fashion, scoring of the child's approach behavior is assumed to be relatively straightforward. Few data are available, however, as to its test-retest or interobserver reliability.

The BAT has successfully discriminated children treated for their fears from no-treatment controls. However, it does not always correlate well with children's self-report measures of fear (Kelley, 1976; Kornhaber & Schroeder, 1975). One study reported the BAT to be highly sensitive to experimental demand characteristics (Kelley, 1976), although the subjects involved were from a nonclinical population. Similar findings have been reported by Bernstein and Neitzel (1974) in adults.

4.2.2. Observational Codes

Several observational codes have been developed to measure behaviors presumably associated with anxiety. The Observer Rating Scale of Anxiety (ORSA) is a 29-category code that includes such behaviors as "crying," "trembling hands," "stuttering," "talking about being afraid." Using a time-sampling procedure, an observer records the presence or absence of each behavior during each observation interval. Interrater agreement has been reported to be as high as 94% (Melamed & Siegel, 1975).

The Behavior Profile Rating Scale (BPRS) is a similar code designed particularly for dental settings. Recording intervals are 3 minutes in length and each behavior on the scale is weighted as to the degree it would disrupt the dentist's examination and treatment of the child. High interrater reliability has been reported (Klorman, Ratner, Arata, King, & Sveen, 1977; Melamed, Hawes, Heiby, & Glick, 1975; Melamed, Weinstein, Hawes, & Katin-Borland, 1975) and dentists' ratings of a child's fear of dentistry have positively correlated with the child's subsequent BPRS scores (Klorman *et al.*, 1977). Both the ORSA and the BPRS have differentiated treated children from untreated children (Melamed, Hawes, Heiby, & Glick, 1975; Melamed & Siegel, 1975; Melamed, Weinstein, Hawes, & Katin-Borland, 1975). However, self-report measures do not always correlate with behavioral measures (Melamed, Weinstein, Hawes, & Katin-Borland, 1975).

Numerous other observational codes have been developed for specific behaviors presumed to be related to anxiety. O'Connor (1969, 1972), for example, has reliably recorded peer interactions in socially withdrawn children. Nordquist and Bradley (1973) observed and recorded cooperative play and speech in a nonverbal isolate child. Such observations are usually highly reliable and reasonably sensitive to various treatment manipulations. However, rarely are they intercorrelated with self-report or peer ratings designed to measure the same thing.

4.2.3. Behavioral Checklists

Behavioral checklists involve a standard set of specific behaviors that are rated by someone who knows the child well (e.g., parent or teacher). Usually each behavior is checked as occurring or not occurring, or it is rated on a scale ranging from low to high frequency. No checklists have been specifically designed to measure children's fearful or anxious behavior. However, the Behavior Problem Checklist (Quay & Peterson, 1975), the Devereux Elementary School Behavior Rating Scale (Spivack & Swift, 1967), and the Connors Teacher Rating Scale (Connors, 1969) all have factor scores specifically related to anxious, withdrawn behavior. Extensive research is available addressing the reliability and validity of these checklists (O'Leary & Johnson, 1979; Quay, 1979).

4.2.4. Global Behavioral Ratings

Global ratings have been used by several investigators as measures of behavior assumed to be related to a child's dental anxieties or fears. Frankl's behavior rating scale (Frankl, Shiere, & Fogels, 1962) has an observer globally rate the child's behavior as either definitely negative, slightly negative, slightly positive, or definitely positive at specific points during the examination and treatment of the child (e.g., separation from mother, initial exposure to the dental environment, administration of medication or anesthesia). Interrater agreement is usually reported to be at least 90% (Johnson, 1971; Johnson & Machen, 1973; Koenigsberg & Johnson, 1972; Wright & Alpern, 1971; Wright et al., 1973). Global ratings of cooperativeness and anxiety have also been used by Melamed, Hawes, Heiby, and Glick (1975) and by Melamed, Weinstein, Hawes, and Katin-Borland, (1975) with intercorrelations between observers of .75 or above.

Global behavioral ratings have positively correlated with measures of maternal anxiety at the young child's first dental visit (Johnson, 1971; Koenigsberg & Johnson, 1972; Wright & Alpern 1971; Wright et al., 1973), and scores on the BPRS (Melamed, 1979). In several studies they have been sensitive to various treatment manipulations (Johnson & Machen, 1973; Melamed, Hawes, Heiby, & Glick, 1975; Melamed, Weinstein, Hawes, & Katin-Borland, 1975). Nevertheless, global ratings should be used cautiously since a number of investigators have found them to be especially susceptible to observer bias (Kent, O'Leary, Diament, & Dietz, 1974; Shuller & McNamara, 1976).

4.3. Physiological Measures

Although the physiological measurement of anxiety is a well-researched area in adults (Borkovec, Weerts, & Bernstein, 1977; Lick & Katkin, 1976), it has received considerably less attention in children. The information that does exist, however, seems to parallel that provided by adults; physiological correlates of anxiety, when they exist, are typically low to moderate in nature and are inconsistently reported from study to study.

One of the earliest works was a verbal conditioning experiment conducted by Patterson, Helper, and Wilcott (1960) with emotionally disturbed children. Both clinical ratings of anxiety and continuous measures of skin conductance were related to the rate of conditioning and correlated $r = .26$ with each other. Stricker and Howitt (1965) reported that apprehensive children in a dental setting had higher heart rates than nonapprehensive children. Heart rate increases have also been reported in children who were asked to imagine their most fearful experiences (Tal & Miklich, 1976) or were given "test" versus "gamelike" instructions (Darley & Katz, 1973). However, it is doubtful that increased heart rate is a physiological change peculiar to fear or anxiety since the same responses occurred in the Tal and Miklich (1976) study when the children were asked to imagine their most angry experience. Similarly, Darley and Katz (1973) found that self-report measures of test-anxiety (TASC) did not correlate with their heart rate data. Consequently, they interpreted increased heart rate subsequent to "test" instructions as the result of increased motivation rather than increased anxiety. Sternbach (1962) continuously recorded a variety of physiological responses (palmar skin resistance, gastric motility, respiration rate, heart rate, eyeblink rate, finger pulse volume) in 10 children as they watched Walt Disney's *Bambi*. Afterwards the children reported to the examiner what had been the "scariest" scene for them in the movie. Although the children had no trouble identifying what was "scary," no correlations were found between what the child reported as scary and the physiological measures obtained at that point in the movie. Similar results have been reported by Kutina and Fischer (1977), who collected heart rate and other nonphysiological measures of anxiety in one neutral and two presumably stressful situations (a dental examination and reading a difficult text in public). No correlations were found involving teacher, observer, or sociometric ratings of anxiety and heart rate. And, in only one of the stressful situations (reading in public) did a child's score on the CMAS significantly correlate with heart rate. However, the correlations obtained ($r = - .25$ and $r = - .28$) were opposite of what was expected.

Although the literature clearly suggests that various measures of anxiety often do not intercorrelate, palmar sweat prints (PSP) have proved useful in several studies as one measure of intervention effects. Lore (1966) detailed a practical procedure for taking PSP in children and reported reasonably good test-retest reliability ($r = .64$ over a 1-day test-retest interval; $r = .60$ over a 15-day interval). He also reported data suggesting that PSP were responsive to experimentally induced environmental stress. Since then several investigators (Johnson & Stockdale, 1975; Melamed, Hawes, Heiby, & Glick, 1975; Melamed & Siegel, 1975; Venham, Bengston, & Cipes, 1977) have reported PSP to be sensitive to situational stresses (e.g., surgery) and to various treatment manipulations (e.g., a modeling film of a child's experience prior to and during surgery).

4.4. Comments

Although a variety of measures have been specifically developed to assess children's fears, reliability and validity data have been only sporadically reported. Different methods designed to measure anxiety are infrequently intercorrelated. Multitrait-multimethod comparisons are even rarer.

Assuming that anxiety is a construct having motor, cognitive, and physiological components, assessment solely in one sphere may be inadequate. Only by measuring in all spheres can we begin to understand how the different components interrelate. The time when measurement occurs must also be taken into consideration. Measures of anxiety taken prior to, during, and subsequent to a stressful experience may all be different and each component may change in different ways and rates over time. Furthermore, we know very little about how change in one sphere influences responses in another sphere.

For example, if a child's behavior toward a phobic object changes due to a particular intervention plan, do cognitive and physiological changes occur as well? If so, do they occur before, concurrent with, or after the elimination of the child's avoidance behavior? Is treating only one component as efficient as treating all three? Does change in more than one sphere lead to better long-term maintenance of treatment gains?

Particularly within self-report measures of anxiety, state-trait distinctions are still made. There are some data to suggest that outcome may be related to how specific is a child's fear, with generalized anxiety having a poorer prognosis (Agras et al., 1972). There are other data suggesting that some children suffer from a cluster of symptoms variously labeled as neurotic, anxious, or withdrawn (Quay, 1979). "Generalized avoidance" seems to be an apt description of these children's behavior. In other words, state-trait distinctions may have some merit but the available measures have yet to demonstrate any real clinical utility. Children high on self-report measures of trait anxiety need to be assessed in terms of their behavior patterns and physiological reactions. Do they show avoidance behavior in more situations than children high in self-reported state anxiety? Are their arousal and habituation patterns different? Longitudinal assessments and follow-up need to be conducted. Is trait anxiety something a child develops early and has throughout his development? If so, is he more likely to suffer from psychological or psychosomatic disturbances as an adolescent or adult? Although current measures of trait versus state anxiety have some heuristic appeal, they tell us little about the child's long-term prognosis, what treatment approach to take, or whether treatment is even necessary. They may serve to guide further research but should be used cautiously (if at all) as a clinical assessment tool. In our view, the specific stimulus conditions associated with a child's fear(s) should be assessed whether his fears are single, multiple, general, or focused in nature. Simply because a child seems to be suffering from "generalized anxiety" does not eliminate the need to define the specific setting events leading to that child's anxiety reactions.

In our desire to treat children, it seems we have often prematurely accepted a particular test or method as an adequate measure for a child's fears, anxieties, or avoidance behavior. Efforts to develop empirically validated assessment measures need to be at least as extensive as the efforts to develop successful treatment procedures. After all, without adequate measurement, we can never be sure whether our treatment really "worked."

5. Treatment

Within the behavior therapy literature, children's fears have usually been treated with either counterconditioning, operant procedures, or modeling techniques. Self-control or self-instructional procedures are a more recent development. Implosive therapy has occasionally been used (Hersen, 1968; Smith & Sharpe, 1970; Ollendick & Gruen, 1972) but is not recommended due to its extremely anxiety-provoking content and the lack of experimental data justifying its use (Graziano, 1975).

5.1. Counterconditioning

In counterconditioning a hierarchy of fear-provoking stimuli is developed and a response incompatible with fear is selected. Beginning with the least fearful item on the hierarchy, the incompatible response is paired with the anxiety-provoking stimulus. Progress up the hierarchy is dependent upon elimination of a fear reaction to items lower on the hierarchy. This procedure is carried out either *in vivo* or by having the child vividly imagine each phobic scene.

Jones (1924) provided one of the earliest examples of this technique. Peter, a 2-year-old, fearful of rats and rabbits, was placed in a high chair and given food he liked. The experimenter then brought a rabbit as close to Peter as she could without arousing so much fear as to interrupt Peter's eating. "Through the presence of the pleasant stimulus (food) whenever the rabbit was shown, the fear was eliminated gradually in favor of a positive response" (p.313). A similar procedure is the basis of Wolpe's (1958) systematic desensitization in which muscle relaxation is used as the positive response to "counter" anxiety.

Individual case studies have described successful use of systematic desensitization for fears of loud noises (Tasto, 1969; Wish, Hasazi & Jurgela, 1973), and water (Weinstein, 1976), as well as for school phobia (Miller, 1972). Since relaxation is not always an easy skill to teach young children, other positive responses such as play behavior (Bentler, 1962; Croghan & Musante, 1975) or feeding (Montenegro, 1968) have been successfully used to counter children's fears. Lazarus and Abramovitz (1962) described the use of "emotive imagery" in which the child imagines phobic scenes designed to include a favorite hero. Others have suggested that the child's positive feelings toward the therapist while in the phobic situation may permit the child to engage in approach behavior (Garvey & Hegrenes, 1966; Kissel, 1972; Lazarus, Davison, & Polefka, 1965; Obler & Terwilliger, 1970).

However, with the exception of test anxiety, few controlled studies have been conducted. Linden (1973) trained third-graders to relax through meditation. A significant reduction in TASC scores occurred for the meditation group compared to children trained in study skills or no-treatment controls. Barabasz (1973) reported significant GSR reductions and improved intelligence test scores after treating high test-anxious fifth- and sixth- graders with systematic desensitization. These changes did not occur in treated low test-anxious children or in no-treatment controls. A second study replicated these findings using a teacher to carry out the treatment procedures (Barabasz, 1975). In a previous controlled investigation, Mann and Rosenthal (1969) reported success using desensitization with somewhat older (12-14 years) test-anxious adolescents.

Miller, Barrett, Hampe, and Noble (1972a) compared counterconditioning techniques to psychotherapy and a waiting list control. Referrals were solicited from a variety of agencies and a total of 67 children, 6-15 years old, were involved. Sixty-nine percent were school-phobic. Both parents and an independent evaluator provided ratings of outcome. No differences were found between groups by the independent evaluator. Parents, however, reported significant improvement in children treated by either form of therapy compared to waiting list controls. Younger children did better than older children. But even no-treatment children showed substantial improvements. Although the study is commendable in its attempt to make controlled treatment comparisons, a number of methodological problems make interpretation of the data difficult: (1) some of the children may not have been clearly phobic (e.g., over 43% of the school-phobic children were attending school; (2) there was a good deal of overlap between treatment procedures (e.g., children in psychotherapy were helped to formulate "behavioral strategies for coping with stress" and their parents were told to remove any secondary gains the child might be receiving at home as a consequence of his phobia); (3) the specific rating procedures of the independent evaluator were not given in detail and the number and results of the *in vivo* tests of outcome were not described. A subsequent follow-up study of these children suggests that children's phobias seem to dissipate over time although treatment may accelerate improvement (Hampe, Noble, Miller, & Barrett, 1973). One and 2 years after termination of treatment or the waiting period, 80% of these children were essentially symptom-free; only 7% still had a severe phobia.

5.2. Operant Approaches

Operant procedures are designed to decrease the child's fears by rewarding appropriate approach behavior. In addition, fearful reactions are usually ignored in order to extinguish avoidance behavior. Very rarely, punishment is also employed concurrent with reward contingencies (e.g., Tobey & Thoresen, 1976; Wulbert, Nyman, Snow, & Owen, 1973).

Numerous case studies attest to the effectiveness of social and material rewards for the treatment of elective mutism (Bauermeister & Jemail, 1975; Conrad, Delk, & Williams, 1974; Nolan & Pence, 1970; Rasbury, 1974), social withdrawal (Patterson & Bradsky, 1966), and school phobia (Ayllon *et al.*, 1970; Lazarus *et al.*, 1965; Neisworth, Madle, & Goeke, 1975). Kennedy (1965) reported outcome and follow-up data on 50 children seen for school phobia over an 8-year period. Treatment involved forced school attendance, ignoring of somatic complaints or other phobic symptoms, and praise for going to and staying at school. All children were suffering from Type I School Phobia and all were considered to be successfully treated. Phobic symptoms continued in remission at yearly follow-up.

Controlled studies using operant procedures typically involve single-subject reversal designs. Baseline observations are made followed by the introduction of social or material rewards contingent upon approach behavior. Rewards are then removed and reintroduced in order to demonstrate a functional relationship between the use of contingent rewards and an increase in approach behavior. Reynolds and Risley (1968) used such a design to increase speech in a nonverbal 4-year-old. Others (Allen, Hart, Buell, Harris, & Wolf, 1964; Hart, Reynolds, Baer, Brawley, & Harris, 1968; Walker & Hops, 1973) have used social and material rewards in a controlled fashion to increase peer interactions in socially isolate children. Occasionally, behaviors other than the target behavior are rewarded, producing subsequent change in the target behavior as well. Kirby and Toler (1970), for example, rewarded a socially withdrawn child for passing out candy to his peers. This led to increased interaction between the child and his classmates, although social interaction *per se* was never directly reinforced. A similar procedure was used by Buell, Stoddard, Harris, and Baer (1968), who increased social and verbal peer interactions by rewarding a child for using the outdoor play equipment. Nordquist and Bradley (1973) increased a child's verbalizations by making teacher attention contingent upon cooperative play.

Other procedures often used concurrent with contingent rewards are shaping, prompting, and stimulus fading. In shaping, the child is reinforced for successive approximations to the desired behavior. Neisworth *et al.* (1975) used such a procedure with a 4-year-old girl suffering from separation anxiety. Whenever she was left at preschool she would cry, scream, and withdraw, never participating in any of the program activities or interacting with the other children. An intervention plan was developed in which the child's mother would leave her for increasing periods of time. Initially, this was for only a few seconds. However, the time increases were so gradual that only 10 minutes of "anxious" behavior (crying, withdrawal) occurred during the intervention program. At the end of treatment the child was able to remain in her preschool setting for the entire 3-hour session without distress and was a willing participant in program activities.

Sometimes a child cannot be rewarded for a desired behavior because he does not engage in that behavior at all. In such cases, the behavior can sometimes be elicited by prompting techniques. Once the behavior is elicited, it is rewarded and then shaped to some criterion level. Nordquist and Bradley (1973), for example, had one child initiate or prompt interaction with a socially isolate child who never talked to or played with any of her peers. The teacher then attended to and socially reinforced any interactions between the two. Over time, the target child's cooperative play and verbalizations steadily increased until the use of a "prompting" child was no longer necessary. Buell *et al.* (1968) wanted to reinforce an isolate child for using outdoor play equipment. However, since the behavior never occurred, they prompted it by initially lifting the child onto a piece of equipment for 30 seconds. As long as the child remained on the equipment, even for very short intervals, she was given positive attention. Gradually the child began to self-initiate play on the equipment and prompting was dropped from the intervention plan.

Stimulus fading is another technique used to elicit behavior in situations where previously it has never occurred. The usual format is to gradually fade out those discriminative stimuli associated with the desired behavior while fading in those stimulus conditions under which the behavior has previously never occurred. Wulbert *et al.* (1973) provide a good example of the effectiveness of this technique. Their subject was a 6-year-old electively mute girl. The child had never spoken in kindergarten, Sunday school, or preschool but readily spoke with her mother. A treatment procedure was developed in which the child and her mother came to a clinic three times a week. There, the mother asked the child to engage in a series of tasks, some ot which required verbal responses. An unfamiliar adult was very gradually faded in until the child was responding to his requests. At this point, the child's mother was faded out and another unfamiliar adult was faded in. Finally, the teacher and some of the child's classmates were faded in. As part of the intervention plan, a time-out procedure was used when the child refused to answer questions asked of her by unfamiliar adults. The experimental procedure clearly demonstrated time-out to be effective only when a fading program was used. When the child was abruptly introduced to an unfamiliar adult, she steadfastly refused to answer his questions despite repeated use of time-out. However, if the adult had been introduced gradually, time-out proved to be a powerful procedure to ensure high levels of verbal response.

Controlled studies of operant approaches using group comparisons are almost nonexistent. Leitenberg and Callahan (1973) treated children who were afraid of the dark by rewarding them for staying in a dark room for increasing periods of time. Compared to no-treatment controls, the treated children were able to remain in an unfamiliar dark room for a significantly greater length of time. This study, however, is best considered an analogue since the children were recruited and had not requested treatment for their problem. Treatment was carried out in a laboratory setting with no attempt to assess the practical significance of the treatment gains produced (e.g., did the treated children show less fear at bedtime at home?).

Obler and Terwilliger (1970) treated emotionally disturbed, neurologically impaired children who had fears of riding on a public bus or fears of dogs. Fifteen children were randomly assigned to a treatment group. Another 15 children served as no-treatment controls. Although the authors describe their treatment program as "a modified version of Wolpe's systematic desensitization therapy," a careful reading of the study suggests that operant procedures seem to be the primary mode of treatment. All children were gradually exposed to the phobic stimulus *in vivo* and were immediately rewarded for increased contact. The children's parents reported significant improvement in the treated children over that of controls. All children in the treatment group were able to ride a bus or touch a dog with the help of another person and half were able to do it alone. This study has been criticized, however, for using no objective outcome measures and for unsystematically using a variety of treatment procedures (Begelman & Hersen, 1971).

5.3. Modeling

There is currently a substantial literature of controlled investigations using peer models to reduce children's fears. The usual procedure is to have a fearful child watch another child successfully cope with the phobic stimulus. This is done either *in vivo* or by having the child observe the model on film. The model is presumed to teach new response patterns to the fearful child or to facilitate the expression of inhibited behaviors that have been previously established (Bandura, 1969).

Jones (1924) provided two early case studies in which children's fears of a white rabbit were both induced and removed by observing other children's reactions to the rabbit. A controlled study was carried out by Bandura *et al.* (1967) with children afraid of dogs. Observing a fearless peer model approach and play with a dog led to less subsequent avoidance behavior in the fearful children than either giving them parties in the presence of a dog or giving them no contact with a dog at all. Subsequent studies demonstrated the effectiveness of filmed modeling in reducing children's animal fears (Bandura & Menlove, 1968; Kornhaber & Schroeder, 1975). Peer models were more effective than adult models (Kornhaber & Schroeder, 1975) and the use of multiple models was slightly more effective than a single model (Bandura & Menlove, 1968).

Having children actually contact the phobic object subsequent to observing a model seems to further enhance approach behavior. Ritter (1968) compared the use of multiple peer models with "contact desensitization" in which the child actually touched a snake with the assistance of an adult model. Both treatment groups were able to subsequently approach snakes better than no-treatment controls but the "contact desensitization" group showed the least avoidance of all. More recently, Lewis (1974) treated water-phobic children at a summer camp. Having the child gradually enter the water subsequent to watching a modeling film produced greater approach behavior than the film alone.

In addition to treating children with fears of animals and water, modeling has also been used to increase peer interactions in social isolates. O'Connor (1969, 1972) observed children identified by their teachers as withdrawn. Those children who were interacting with their peers no more than 15% of the time were shown a modeling film depicting several peer models engaging in a variety of social activities. Subsequent observations of these children done after the film, and approximately 3 weeks later, showed significant increases in social interactions in their nursery school setting. This did not occur for a control group of isolate children who watched a Marineland dolphin film similar in length and interest to the modeling film. In the second study (1972) modeling was also compared to an operant shaping procedure in which trained graduate students systematically attended to any interactions a withdrawn child had with his peers. In addition, a third treatment program involving both modeling and shaping was employed. All three treatments significantly increased peer interactions but the gains made in the operant shaping group were not maintained at follow-up. Further, shaping did not enhance the gains made subsequent to the modeling film alone, a finding replicated by Evers and Schwarz (1973).

In an attempt to assess what specific changes occur in an isolate child in response to film modeling, Keller and Carlson (1974) observed and recorded three categories of behavior: (1) positive reinforcing actions given, (2) positive reinforcing actions received, and (3) total interactions. The modeling film significantly increased all three categories of behavior; this did not occur for a control film. However, the relative frequencies of different types of social reinforcement (e.g., verbal reinforcement, smiling, affection) was not different between isolate and nonisolate children even before viewing the film. Further, the film seemed to increase the most frequent behaviors already in the withdrawn child's repertoire rather than teaching new patterns of behavior.

Keller and Carlson (1974) also report that the behavior changes occurring subsequent to their modeling film were not maintained at follow-up. And, Gottman (1977) completely failed to replicate O'Connor's (1969, 1972) results using a longer follow-up period. Gottman (1977) has cogently argued that children who have low peer interactions are not necessarily suffering from anxiety, social-skills deficits, or peer rejection. Isolate children in his study, for example, were no different from nonisolate children in terms of peer acceptance. Perhaps it is premature to label a child as a social isolate in need of treatment solely on the basis of low frequency of peer interactions. More specific characteristics of a child's relationships need to be assessed. Is he accepted or rejected by other children? Does he relate in qualitatively different ways from those of his more extraverted peers? Or, are the differences only quantitative? The reward value of peers for each individual child should also be taken into consideration. An interesting study by Evers-Pasquale and Sherman (1975) classified socially withdrawn preschoolers as peer-oriented or non-peer-oriented. Classification was determined by the child's response to the description of a series of activities. After each description the child indicated whether he would prefer to do the activity by himself, with an adult, or with a peer. Children who were peer-oriented showed much greater increases in peer interactions subsequent to a modeling film than non-peer-oriented children.

Not all studies focusing on children's fears have been concerned with treating well-established excessive avoidance reactions. Some researchers have attempted to help children cope with normal anxiety-provoking situations. Several studies have used modeling either *in vivo* (White & Davis, 1974) or in films (Johnson & Machen, 1973; Melamed, Hawes, Heiby, & Glick, 1975; Melamed, Weinstein, Hawes & Katin-Borland, 1975) to reduce children's anxious uncooperative behavior while at the dentist. Only Sawtell, Simon, and Simeonsson (1974) failed to report a superior effect for modeling compared to a placebo control. However, this particular study has been criticized on a number of methodological grounds (Melamed, 1979).

Other investigators have worked with children hospitalized for surgery. Johnson and Stockdale (1975) found that a puppet show depicting what was to happen to the child during his operation successfully reduced anxiety as measured by the PSI. However, controls saw no puppet show so it is difficult to assess whether the reduced anxiety shown in the experimental group was due to modeling per se or to the added attention, etc., these children received from simply seeing the show. Furthermore, since the PSI was the only outcome measure, no data were provided as to the children's self-reported feelings of anxiety or their behavior before and after the surgical procedure. A better study was carried out by Melamed and Siegel (1975). Children admitted for surgery saw either a modeling film or a control movie depicting a child on a fishing trip. Self-report, behavioral, and physiological measures were taken before the film, after the film, the evening before the operation, and at a postoperative follow-up visit. In addition, parents filled out a questionnaire and a behavior checklist prior to the child's admission and again at the postoperative follow-up. The children who viewed the modeling film showed significantly less anxiety on all measures. And, by parent report, control children showed significant increases in behavior problems from prehospital to postoperative assessment. This did not occur for the children who had viewed the modeling film.

It is interesting to note that in the late 1960s the models used in the treatment of children's fears were fearless in their handling of the phobic object or situation (e.g., Bandura *et al.*, 1967; Bandura & Menlove, 1968; Ritter, 1968). Currently, models are frequently depicted as initially fearful but subsequently learning to successfully cope with and master their fears (e.g., Melamed and Siegel, 1975). Coping models are assumed to be more similar to the fearful child and thereby enhance imitation. However, there is little published research on this particular issue, although one study with adults did report better results with coping models than with mastery models (Meichenbaum, 1971).

5.4. Self-Control Procedures

Self-control procedures usually involve teaching the client to apply reward or punishment contingencies to his own behavior. Occasionally, the child is taught various self-instructional, cognitive, or problem-solving strategies.

This is a very recent approach to the treatment of children's fears. The one controlled study that is available (Kanfer, Karoly, & Newman, 1975) focused on children who were afraid of the dark. For some of the children their competence was emphasized by teaching them self-intructions such as "I'm a brave boy, I can handle myself in the dark." Others were taught to describe to themselves various nonaversive aspects of being in the dark, such as "the dark is a fun place to be, there are many good things in the dark." A final group of children was taught to repeat a neutral nursery rhyme. Children in the competence group were able to remain longest in the dark, followed by children taught to describe positive characteristics of being in the dark. The neutral rhyme group did the worst of all.

The results of this analogue study must be considered preliminary since the children involved were recruited solely for the purposes of the experiment. Their fears were not so excessive that their parents had requested treatment for them. In fact, children who showed intense discomfort and fears were dropped from the study. The demand characteristics of the two treatment groups are obvious. All aspects of the procedures were carried out in a carefully controlled laboratory setting with no assessment as to whether the reported increases in tolerance of the dark had any practical significance for the children involved.

5.5. Comments

Extensive theoretical discussion of hypothetical mechanisms underlying a particular treatment's success has not been a purpose of this chapter. It is interesting to note, however, that all of the treatments described have one characteristic in common—repeated *exposure* to the phobic situation. Marks (1975) has argued that exposure may be the crucial factor underlying all behavioral approaches to the treatment of fears. Whether desensitization, social reinforcement, modeling, or self-instructions are used, the child remains in contact with the phobic stimulus for increased periods of time. Through such exposure, he learns that no aversive consequences occur, that there is nothing to avoid. Various treatment procedures simply serve to keep the child in the feared situation long enough for extinction to occur.

However, different treatment procedures may be differentially effective at blocking a child's avoidance response depending on the individual child and the nature of his fears. Nevertheless, treatment comparisons have rarely been made. The O'Connor (1972) study is unusual in its comparison of modeling to shaping techniques. Similarly, the characteristics of the child are very infrequently considered in evaluating a treatment's effectiveness. The Evers-Pasquale and Sherman (1975) study is interesting in its assessment of the effects of modeling on peer-oriented versus non-peer-oriented social isolates. Perhaps future work could make treatment comparisons between adult-administered social praise and peer modeling with both peer-oriented and adult-oriented children.

Research to date has focused primarily on treatment versus no-treatment or placebo comparisons. While this is a useful first step, ultimately we need to specify which treatment works best for what fears in what kinds of children. Furthermore, there should be a continued focus on what kinds of procedures help the child comfortably cope with normal stress-provoking situations that he cannot avoid. And, what kinds of procedures best teach the child new responses in addition to extinguishing old ones.

6. Recommendations for Clinical Practice

Since all children experience fear, how does one assess whether a particular fear warrants treatment? And how does one choose which treatment to apply? Conclusive answers to such questions cannot be found from even a careful reading of the available research literature. Consequently, our recommendations to the practicing clinician are necessarily an integration of empirical research and our own clinical experience.

In assessing a child's fears, consideration should be given to the child's age and whether his fears are typical of children at that developmental level. Treatment is probably warranted if his fears are persistent and significantly impair his functioning. Fears that have lasted well beyond the age at which they normally disappear would be appropriate targets for treatment. This would be particularly true if the fears interfered with the child's normal social development, seemed related to psychosomatic complaints, or were the source of sleeping difficulties, nightmares, or obsessive ruminations. The reactions of parents, teachers, and siblings should also be observed. To the extent that significant others in the child's environment are in some way maintaining his fears, treatment must focus on their behavior as well as the child's.

In choosing a treatment approach, the clinician should take a careful look at the extent and nature of the stimulus conditions eliciting the child's fears. Where possible, a graded hierarchy should be developed beginning with the child's least fear-provoking stimulus and progressing to his most feared experience. This is a useful approach regardless of which treatment procedure (e.g., desensitization, operant, modeling) is used. In our view, it results in the least overall discomfort for the child while he is undergoing treatment.

The extent and nature of the child's avoidance reaction also needs to be considered. An electively mute child who talks to no one with the exception of his mother will probably not benefit from modeling, counterconditioning, or simple operant procedures. The child has no doubt observed numerous children model appropriate behavior with no effect. Since he does not speak to anyone outside of the home, a therapist would not be likely to choose a desensitization approach and a teacher could not reward the child for speech. In this case, a stimulus-fading procedure seems essential. If verbal behavior was simply infrequent rather than nonexistent, the therapist could use either modeling or an operant approach. If speech was anxiety-provoking only in particular contexts occurring across settings and individuals (e.g., answering questions in class, giving a class presentation, meeting someone for the first time), desensitization might be the treatment of choice. By teaching the child a particular response to counter his fears (e.g., relaxation), anxiety could be reduced and speech increased in a whole variety of settings without the direct involvement of outside individuals (e.g., teachers, classmates, strangers).

The characteristics and capabilities of the child are also important. Not all children can be taught relaxation. Some may have difficulty imagining scenes in a desensitization hierarchy or are so nonverbal that the therapist would have difficulty assessing or treating the child's fears in the context of office visits. Some children seem very responsive to social praise or adult attention, others to material rewards or peer interactions. Assessment of these variables can help the therapist decide whether to work directly with the child or to focus his efforts on the child's parents or teacher. Similarly, knowing what is of reward value to the child is crucial in determining the specifics of the treatment procedure.

Any intervention plan must also be designed within the confines of available resources. The therapist must assess the willingness and ability of significant others in the child's environment to participate in the therapy program and/or to help maintain any changes in the child after the therapist has withdrawn. Programs that fit easily into daily life activities are the most likely to be successfully carried out.

Finally, some thought should be given to teaching the child new skills in addition to eliminating his fears. Sometimes, the child is phobic partly because he does not know what to do or how to cope with the situation. Or, because he has avoided it so long, he has not learned skills that most nonfearful children would have naturally developed. A child who is test-anxious, for example, may benefit from learning a variety of skills related to testtaking (e.g., learning how to study for a test, approaching the test by answering questions you know first, ignoring what everyone else is doing) as well as training in relaxation. Similarly, the child who has been withdrawn for some time may not have learned how to approach and relate to other children appropriately. Modeling is one of the best ways to teach children new skills, although operant procedures are useful as well. Both self-instruction and relaxation training could be considered ways of teaching children new coping skills that can be applied in a variety of stressful situations.

While the focus of this chapter has been the assessment and treatment of children's fears, maintenance of therapeutic change after treatment has ended and the possible prevention of excessive fears are equally important. The therapist needs to plan for the child's long-term development by teaching him whatever skills will help him maintain or even surpass the gains he has made in treatment. Other persons in the child's environment should also be taught how to support these changes. In many cases, specific recommendations should be given to help the child cope with normally occurring stresses (e.g., going to the doctor or dentist for the first time, going to camp for the first time, learning to swim) so that excessive fears do not develop to other objects or situations in the future.

Although several successful approaches to the treatment of children's fears have been described, the wise clinician will not choose any one procedure to the exclusion of all others. The best treatment program will probably draw from several approaches because it is tailor-made for the individual child; a response to the nature and extent of his particular fears and avoidance reactions, his characteristics, capabilities, and skill-deficits. It will engage parents, teachers, and significant others in a cooperative effort not only to support therapeutic change but to maintain those changes once treatment has ended.

7. References

Agras, W., Chapin, H., & Oliveau, D. The natural history of phobia. *Archives of General Psychiatry*, 1972, 26, 315-317.

Allen, K., Hart, B., Buell, S., Harris, R., & Wolf, M. Effects of social reinforcement on isolate behavior of a nursery school child. *Child Development*, 1964, 35, 511-518.

Ayllon, T., Smith, D., & Rogers, M. Behavioral management of school phobia. *Journal of Behavior Therapy and Experimental Psychiatry*, 1970, *1*, 125-138.

Bandura, A. *Principles of behavior modification*. New York: Holt, Rinehart & Winston, 1969.

Bandura, A., Grusec, J., & Menlove, F. Vicarious extinction of avoidance behavior. *Journal of Personality and Social Psychology*, 1967, *5*, 16-23.

Bandura, A., & Menlove, F. Factors determining vicarious extinction of avoidance behavior through symbolic modeling. *Journal of Personality and Social Psychology*, 1968, *8*, 99-108.

Barabasz, A. Group desensitization of test anxiety in elementary school. *Journal of Psychology*, 1973, *83* (2), 295-301.

Barabasz, A. Classroom teachers as paraprofessional therapists in group systematic desensitization of test anxiety. *Psychiatry*, 1975, *38*, 388-392.

Bauer, D. An exploratory study of developmental changes in children's fears. *Journal of Child Psychology and Psychiatry*, 1976, *17*, 69-74.

Bauermeister, J., & Jemail, J. Modification of "elective mutism" in the classroom setting: A case study. *Behavior Therapy*, 1975, *6*, 246-250.

Bedell, J., & Roitzsch, J. The effects of stress on state and trait anxiety in emotionally disturbed, normal, and delinquent children. *Journal of Abnormal Child Psychology*, 1976, *4*, 173-177.

Begelman, D., & Hersen, M. Critique of Obler and Terwillinger's "Systematic desensitization with neurologically impaired children with phobic disorders." *Journal of Consulting and Clinical Psychology*, 1971, *37*, 10-13.

Bentler, P. An infant's phobia treated with reciprocal inhibition therapy. *Journal of Child Psychology and Psychiatry*, 1962, *3*, 185-189.

Bernstein, D., & Neitzel, M. Behavior avoidance tests: The effects of demand characteristics and repeated measures on two types of subjects. *Behavior Therapy*, 1974, *5*, 183-192.

Borkovec, T. Autonomic reactivity to sensory stimulation in psychopathic, neurotic, and normal juvenile delinquents. *Journal of Consulting and Clinical Psychology*, 1970, *35*(2), 217-222.

Borkovec, T., Weerts, T., & Bernstein, D. Assessment of anxiety. In A. Ciminero, K. Calhoun, & H. Adams (Eds.), *Handbook of behavioral assessment*. New York: Wiley, 1977.

Bregman, E. An attempt to modify the emotional attitudes of infants by the conditioned response technique. *Journal of Genetic Psychology*, 1934, *45*, 169-198.

Brown, R., Copeland, R., & Hall, R. School phobia: Effects of behavior modification treatment applied by an elementary school principal. *Child Study Journal*, 1974, *4*, 125-133.

Buell, J., Stoddard, P., Harris, F., & Baer, D. Collateral social development accompanying reinforcement of outdoor play in a pre-school child. *Journal of Applied Behavior Analysis*, 1968, *1*, 167-173.

Castaneda, A., McCandless, B., & Palermo, D. The children's form of the Manifest Anxiety Scale. *Child Development*, 1956, *27*, 317-326.

Chazan, M. School phobia. *British Journal of Educational Psychology*, 1962, *32*, 209-217.

Coleman, S. Mackay, D., & Fidell, B. English normative data on the Children's Manifest Anxiety Scale. *British Journal of Social and Clinical Psychology*, 1972, *11*, 85-87.

Conners, C. A teacher rating scale for use in drug studies with children. *American Journal of Psychiatry*, 1969, *126*, 884-888.

Conrad, R., Delk, J., & Williams, C. Use of stimulus fading procedures in the treatment of situation specific mutism: A case study. *Journal of Behavior Therapy and Experimental Psychiatry*, 1974, *5*, 99-100.

Coolidge, J., Brodie, R., & Feeney, B. A ten-year follow-up study of sixty-six school-phobic children. *American Journal of Orthopsychiatry*, 1964, *34*, 675-684.

Coolidge, J., Hahn, P., & Peck, A. School phobia: Neurotic crisis or way of life. *American Journal of Orthopsychiatry*, 1957, 27, 296-306.

Cotler, S., & Palmer, R. The effects of test anxiety, sex of subject, and type of verbal reinforcement on maze performance of elementary school children. *Journal of Personality*, 1970, 38, 216-234.

Croghan, L., & Musante, G. The elimination of a boy's high-building phobia by in vivo desensitization and game playing. *Journal of Behavior Therapy and Experimental Psychiatry*, 1975, 6, 87-88.

Darley, S., & Katz, I. Heart rate changes in children as a function of test versus game instructions and test anxiety. *Child Development*, 1973, 44, 784-789.

DeMyer-Gapin, S., & Scott, T. Effect of stimulus novelty on stimulation seeking in antisocial and neurotic children. *Journal of Abnormal Psychology*, 1977, 86(1), 96-98.

Dusek, J., Mergler, N., & Kermis, M. Attention, encoding and information processing in low- and high-test-anxious children. *Child Development*, 1976, 47, 201-207.

Edlund, C. A reinforcement approach to the elimination of a child's school phobia. *Mental Hygiene*, 1971, 55, 433-436.

Eisenberg, L. School phobia: A study of the communication of anxiety. *American Journal of Psychiatry*, 1958, 114, 712-718.

English, H. Three cases of the "conditioned fear response." *Journal of Abnormal and Social Psychology*, 1929, 34, 221-225.

Evers, W., & Schwarz, J. Modifying social withdrawal in preschoolers: The effects of filmed modeling and teacher praise. *Journal of Abnormal Child Psychology*, 1973, 1, 248-256.

Evers-Pasquale, W., & Sherman, M. The reward value of peers: A variable influencing the efficacy of filmed modeling in modifying social isolation in preschoolers. *Journal of Abnormal Child Psychology*, 1975, 3, 179-189.

Finch, A., Jr., Kendall, P., & Montgomery, L. Multidimensionality of anxiety in children: Factor structure of the Children's Manifest Anxiety Scale. *Journal of Abnormal Child Psychology*, 1974, 2, 331-335.

Finch, A., Jr., Kendall, P., & Montgomery, L. Qualitative differences in the experience of state-trait anxiety in emotionally disturbed and normal children. *Journal of Personality Assessment*, 1976, 40, 522-530.

Finch, A., Jr., Kendall, P., Montgomery, L., & Morris, T. Effects of two types of failure on anxiety. *Journal of Abnormal Psychology*, 1975, 84, 583-586.

Finch, A., Jr., Montgomery, L., & Deardorff, P. Children's Manifest Anxiety Scale: Reliability with emotionally disturbed children. *Psychological Reports*, 1974, 34, 658. (a)

Finch, A., Jr., Montgomery, L., & Deardorff, P. Reliability of state-trait anxiety with emotionally disturbed children. *Journal of Abnormal Child Psychology*, 1974, 2, 67-69. (b)

Finch, A., Jr., & Nelson, W. Anxiety and locus of conflict in emotionally disturbed children. *Journal of Abnormal Child Psychology*, 1974, 2, 33-37.

Frankl, S., Shiere, F., & Fogels, H. Should the parent remain with the child in dental operatory? *Journal of Dentistry for Children*, 1962, 29, 150-163.

Frommer, E., Mendelson, W., & Reid, M. Differential diagnosis of psychiatric disturbance in pre-school children. *British Journal of Psychiatry*, 1972, 121, 71-74.

Garvey, W., & Hegrenes, J. Desensitization techniques in the treatment of school phobia. *American Journal of Orthopsychiatry*, 1966, 36, 147-152.

Gaudry, E., & Poole, C. The effects of an experience of success or failure on state anxiety level. *Journal of Experimental Education*, 1972, 41, 18-21.

Gottman, J. The effects of a modeling film on social isolation in pre-school children: A methodological investigation. *Journal of Abnormal Child Psychology*, 1977, 5, 69-78.

Graziano, A. *Behavior therapy with children* (Vol. 2). Chicago: Aldine, 1975.

Hagman, E. A study of fears of children of pre-school age. *Journal of Experimental Education*, 1932, 1, 110-130.

Hampe, E., Noble, H., Miller, L., & Barrett, C. Phobic children one and two years post treatment. *Journal of Abnormal Psychology*, 1973, *82* (3), 446-453.

Hart, B., Reynolds, N., Baer, D., Brawley, E., & Harris, F. Effects of contingent and non-contingent social reinforcement on the cooperative play of a pre-school child. *Journal of Applied Behavior Analysis*, 1968, *1*, 73-76.

Heffernan, M., & Azarnoff, P. Factors in reducing children's anxiety about clinic visits. *HSMHA Health Report*, 1971, *86*, 1131-1135.

Hersen, M. Treatment of a compulsive and phobic disorder through a total behavior therapy program: A case study. *Psychotherapy: Theory, Research and Practice*, 1968, *5*, 220-224.

Hill, K., & Sarason, S. *Monographs*. Chicago: Society for Research in Child Development, 1966, *31* (2).

Holloway, H. Reliability of the Children's Manifest Anxiety Scale at the rural third grade level. *Journal of Educational Psychology*, 1958, *49*, 193-196.

Holloway, H. Normative data on the Children's Manifest Anxiety Scale at the rural third grade level. *Child Development*, 1961, *32*, 129-134.

Jersild, A., & Holmes, F. Children's fears. *Child Development Monographs*, 1935.

Johnson, P., & Stockdale, D. Effects of puppet therapy on palmar sweating of hospitalized children. *Johns Hopkins Medical Journal*, 1975, *137*, 1-5.

Johnson, R. Maternal influence on child behavior in the dental setting. *Psychiatry in Medicine*, 1971, *2*, 221-228.

Johnson, R., & Machen, J. Modification techniques and maternal anxiety. *Journal of Dentistry for Children*, 1973, *40*, 272-276.

Jones, M. The elmination of children's fears. *Journal of Experimental Psychology*, 1924, *7*, 382-390.

Kahn, J., & Nursten, J. School refusal: A comprehensive view of school phobia and other failures of school attendance. *American Journal of Orthopsychiatry*, 1962, *32*, 707-718.

Kanfer, F., Karoly, P., & Newman, A. Reduction of children's fear of the dark by competence-related and situational threat-related verbal cues. *Journal of Consulting and Clinical Psychology*, 1975, *43*, 251-258.

Kaplan, A. & Hafner, A. Manifest anxiety in hospitalized children. *Journal of Clinical Psychology*, 1959, *15*, 301-302.

Keller, M., & Carlson, P. The use of symbolic modeling to promote skills in pre-school children with low levels of social responsiveness. *Child Development*, 1974, *45*, 912-919.

Kelley, C. Play desensitization of fear of darkness in pre-school children. *Behaviour Research and Therapy*, 1976, *14*, 79-81.

Kennedy, W. School phobia: Rapid treatment of fifty cases. *Journal of Abnormal Psychology*, 1965, *70*, 285-289.

Kent, R., O'Leary, K., Diament, C., & Dietz, A. Expectation bias in observational evaluation of therapeutic change. *Journal of Consulting and Clinical Psychology*, 1974, *42*(6), 774-780.

Kestenbaum, J., & Weiner, B. Achievement performance related to achievement motivation and test anxiety. *Journal of Consulting and Clinical Psychology*, 1970, *34*, 343-344.

Kirby, F., & Toler, H. Modification of pre-school isolate behavior: A case study. *Journal of Applied Behavior Analysis*, 1970, *3*, 309-314.

Kissel, S. Systematic desensitization therapy with children: A case study and some suggested modifications. *Professional Psychology*, 1972, *3*, 164-168.

Kitano, H. Validity of the Children's Manifest Anxiety Scale and the modified revised California Inventory. *Child Development*, 1960, *31*, 67-72.

Klorman, R., Ratner, J., Arata, C., King, J., & Sveen, O. Predicting the child's uncooperativeness in dental treatment from maternal treatment, state and specific anxiety. *Journal of Dental Research*, 1977, *56*, 432.

Koenigsberg, S., & Johnson, R. Child behavior during sequential dental visits. *Journal of the American Dental Association*, 1972, 85, 128-132.

Kornhaber, R., & Schroeder, H. Importance of model similarity on extinction of avoidance behavior in children. *Journal of Consulting and Clinical Psychology*, 1975, 43, 601-607.

Kutina, J., & Fischer, J. Anxiety, heart rate and their interrelation at mental stress in school children. *Activitas Nervosa Superior*, 1977, 19, 89-95.

Lang, P. Fear reduction and fear behavior: Problems in treating a construct. In J. M. Schlien (Ed.), *Research in psychotherapy*. Washington, D.C.: American Psychological Association, 1968.

Lapouse, R., & Monk, M. Fears and worries in a representative sample of children. *American Journal of Orthopsychiatry*, 1959, 29, 803-818.

Lazarus, A., & Abramovitz, A. The use of "emotive imagery" in the treatment of children's phobias. *Journal of Mental Science*, 1962, 108, 191-195.

Lazarus, A., Davison, D., & Polefka, B. Classical and operant factors in the treatment of school phobia. *Journal of Abnormal Psychology*, 1965, 70, 225-229.

Leitenberg, H., & Callahan, E. Reinforced practice and reduction of different kinds of fears in adults and children. *Behaviour Research and Therapy*, 1973, 11, 19-30.

Lewis, S. A comparison of behavior therapy techniques in the reduction of fearful avoidance behavior. *Behavior Therapy*, 1974, 5, 648-655.

Lick, J., & Katkin, E. Assessment of anxiety and fear. In M. Hersen & A. Bellack (Eds.), *Behavioral assessment: A practical handbook*. New York: Pergamon Press, 1976.

Linden, W. Practicing of meditation by school children and their levels of field dependence-independence, test anxiety, and reading achievement. *Journal of Consulting and Clinical Psychology*, 1973, 41, 139-143.

Lore, R. Palmar sweating and transitory anxieties in children. *Child Development*, 1966, 37, 115-123.

MacFarlane, J., Allen, L., & Honzik, M. *A developmental study of the behavior problems of normal children*. Berkeley: University of California Press, 1954.

Mann, J., & Rosenthal, T. Vicarious and direct counterconditioning of test anxiety through individual and group desensitization. *Behaviour Research and Therapy*, 1969, 7, 359-367.

Mann, L., Taylor, R., Jr., Proger, B., & Morrell, J. Test anxiety and defensiveness against admission of test anxiety induced by frequent testing. *Psychological Reports*, 1968, 23, 1283-1286.

Marks, I. *Fears and phobias*. New York: Academic Press, 1969.

Marks, I. Behavioral treatments of phobic and obsessive-compulsive disorders: A critical appraisal. In M. Hersen, R. Eisler, & P. Miller (Eds.), *Progress in behavior modification*. New York: Academic Press, 1975.

Meichenbaum, D. Examination of model characteristics in reducing avoidance behavior. *Journal of Personality and Social Psychology*, 1971, 17, 298-307.

Melamed, B. Behavioral approaches to fear in dental settings. In M. Hersen, R. Eisler, & P. Miller (Eds.), *Progress in behavior modification* (Vol. 7). New York: Academic Press, 1979.

Melamed, B., Hawes, R., Heiby, E., & Glick, J. Use of filmed modeling to reduce uncooperative behavior of children during dental treatment. *Journal of Dental Research*, 1975, 54, 797-801.

Melamed, B., & Siegel, L. Reduction of anxiety in children facing hospitalization and surgery by use of filmed modeling. *Journal of Consulting and Clinical Psychology*, 1975, 43, 511-521.

Melamed, B., Weinstein, D., Hawes, R., & Katin-Borland, M. Reduction of fear-related dental management problems with use of filmed modeling. *Journal of the American Dental Association*, 1975, 90, 822-826.

Melamed, B., Yurcheson, R., Fleece, L., Hutcherson, S., & Hawes, R. *Effects of filmed modeling on the reduction of anxiety-related behaviors in individuals varying in level of previous experience in the stress situation.* Unpublished manuscript, Case Western Reserve University, 1978.

Mermis, B., & Ross, D. Rater agreement on the reinforcement and fear survey schedules. *Psychological Reports,* 1971, *28,* 243-246.

Milgram, R., & Milgram, N. The effect of test content and context on the anxiety-intelligence relationship. *Journal of Genetic Psychology,* 1977, *130,* 121-127.

Miller, L., Barrett, C., Hampe, E., & Noble, H. Comparison of reciprocal inhibition, pyschotherapy, and waiting list control for phobic children. *Journal of Abnormal Psychology,* 1972, *79,* 269-279. (a)

Miller, L., Barrett, C., Hampe, E., & Noble, H. Factor structure of childhood fears. *Journal of Consulting and Clinical Psychology,* 1972, *39,* 264-268. (b)

Miller, P. The use of visual imagery and muscle relaxation in the counter-conditioning of a phobic child: A case study. *Journal of Nervous and Mental Disease,* 1972, *154,* 457-460.

Montenegro, H. Severe separation anxiety in two pre-school children successfully treated by reciprocal inhibition. *Journal of Child Psychology and Psychiatry,* 1968, *9,* 93-103.

Montgomery, L., & Finch, A., Jr., Validity of two measures of anxiety in children. *Journal of Abnormal Child Psychology,* 1974, *2,* 293-296.

Mueller, H., & Shamsie, S. *Classification of behavior disorders in adolescents and EEG findings.* Paper presented at the 17th Annual Meeting of the Canadian Psychiatric Association, Québec, June 1967.

Neisworth, J., Madle, R., & Goeke, K. "Errorless" elimination of separation anxiety: A case study. *Journal of Behavior Therapy and Experimental Psychiatry,* 1975, *6,* 79-82.

Newmark, C., Wheeler, D., Newmark, L. & Stabler, B. Test-induced anxiety with children. *Journal of Personality Assessment,* 1975, *39,* 409-413.

Nolan, J., & Pence, C. Operant conditioning principles in the treatment of a selectively mute child. *Journal of Consulting and Clinical Psychology,* 1970, *35,* 265-268.

Nordquist, V., & Bradley, B. Speech acquisition in a nonverbal isolate child. *Journal of Experimental Child Psychology,* 1973, *15,* 149-160.

Nottelmann, E., & Hill, K. Test anxiety and off-task behavior in evaluative situations. *Child Development,* 1977, *48,* 225-231.

Obler, M., & Terwilliger, R. Pilot study on the effectiveness of systematic desensitization with neurologically impaired children with phobic disorders. *Journal of Consulting and Clinical Psychology,* 1970, *34,* 314-318.

O'Connor, R. Modification of social withdrawal through symbolic modeling. *Journal of Applied Behavior Analysis,* 1969, *2,* 15-22.

O'Connor, R. Relative effects of modeling, shaping, and the combined procedures for modification of social withdrawal. *Journal of Abnormal Psychology,* 1972, *79,* 327-334.

O'Leary, K. & Johnson, S. Assessment of psychopathological disorders in children. In H. C. Quay & J. S. Werry (Eds.), *Psychopathological disorders of childhood* (2nd ed.). New York: Wiley, 1979.

Ollendick, T., & Gruen, G. Treatment of a bodily injury phobia with implosive therapy. *Journal of Consulting and Clinical Psychology,* 1972, *38,* 389-393.

Patterson, G. R., & Bradsky, G. A behavior modification program for a child with multiple problem behaviors. *Journal of Child Psychology and Psychiatry,* 1966, *7,* 277-295.

Patterson, G. R., Helper, M., & Wilcott, R. Anxiety and verbal conditioning in children. *Child Development,* 1960, *31,* 101-108.

Poznanski, E. Children with excessive fears. *American Journal of Orthopsychiatry,* 1973, *43,* 428-438.

Pratt, K. A study of the "fears" of rural children. *Journal of Genetic Psychology,* 1945, *67,* 179-194.

Quay, H. Classification. In H. C. Quay & J. S. Werry (Eds.), *Psychopathological disorders of childhood,* (2nd ed.). New York: Wiley, 1979.

Quay, H., & Peterson, D. *Manual for the Behavior Problem Checklist.* Mimeo, 1975.

Rasbury, W. Behavioral treatment of selective mutism: A case report. *Journal of Behavior Therapy and Experimental Psychiatry,* 1974, *5,* 103-104.

Reynolds, N., & Risley, T. The role of social and material reinforcers in increasing talking of a disadvantaged pre-school child. *Journal of Applied Behavior Analysis,* 1968, *1,* 253-262.

Ritter, B. The group desensitization of children's phobias. *Behaviour Research and Therapy,* 1968, *6,* 1-6.

Rodriquez, A., Rodriquez, M., & Eisenberg, L. The outcome of school phobia: A follow-up study based on 41 cases. *American Journal of Psychiatry,* 1959, *116,* 540-544.

Sarason, S., Davidson, K., Lighthall, F., & Waite, R. A test anxiety scale for children. *Child Development,* 1958, *29,* 105-113.

Sarason, S., Davidson, K., Lighthall, F., Waite, R., & Ruebush, B. *Anxiety in elementary school children.* New York: Wiley, 1960.

Sawtell, R., Simon, J., & Simeonsson, R. The effects of five preparatory methods upon child behavior during the first dental visit. *Journal of Dentistry for Children,* 1974, *41,* 37-45.

Scherer, M., & Nakamura, C. A fear survey schedule for children (FSS-FC): A factor analytic comparison with manifest anxiety (CMAS). *Behaviour Research and Therapy,* 1968, *6,* 173-182.

Seligman, M., & Hagar, J. *Biological boundaries of learning.* New York: Appleton-Century-Crofts, 1972.

Shaw, O. Dental anxiety in children. *British Dental Journal,* 1975, *139,* 134-139.

Shuller, D., & McNamara, J. Expectancy factors in behavioral observation. *Behavior Therapy,* 1976, *1,* 519-527.

Sieber, J., Kameya, L., & Paulson, F. Effect of memory support on the problem-solving ability of test-anxious children. *Journal of Abnormal Psychology,* 1970, *61*(2), 159-168.

Simon, A., & Ward, L. Variables influencing the sources, frequency and intensity of worry in secondary school pupils. *British Journal of Social and Clinical Psychology,* 1974, *13,* 391-396.

Smith, R., & Sharpe, T. Treatment of a school phobia with implosive therapy. *Journal of Consulting and Clinical Psychology,* 1970, *35,* 239-243.

Smith, S. School refusal with anxiety: A review of sixty-three cases. *Canadian Psychiatric Association Journal,* 1970, *15,* 257-264.

Solyom, I., Beck, P., Solyom, C., & Hugel, R. Some etiological factors in phobic neurosis. *Canadian Psychiatric Association Journal,* 1974, *19,* 69-78.

Speilberger, C. *Manual for the State-Trait Inventory for Children.* Palo Alto, Cal.: Consulting Psychologists Press, 1973.

Spivack, G., & Swift, M. *Devereux Elementary School Behavior Rating Scale Manual.* Devon, Pa.: Devereux Foundation, 1967.

Stedman, J. Family counseling with a school-phobic child. In J. D. Krumboltz & C. E. Thoresen (Eds.), *Counseling methods.* New York: Holt, Rinehart & Winston, 1976.

Sternbach, R. Assessing differential autonomic patterns in emotions. *Journal of Psychosomatic Research,* 1962, *6,* 87.

Stricker, G., & Howitt, J. Physiological recording during simulated dental appointments. *New York State Dental Journal,* 1965, *31,* 204-213.

Tal, A., & Miklich, D. Emotionally induced decreases in pulmonary flow rates in asthmatic children. *Psychosomatic Medicine,* 1976, *38,* 190-200.

Tasto, D. Systematic desensitization, muscle relaxation and visual imagery in the counter-conditioning of a four-year-old phobic child. *Behaviour Research and Therapy,* 1969, *7,* 409-411.

Thomas, A., Chess, S., Birch, H., Hertzig, M., & Korn, S. *Behavioral individuality in early childhood.* New York: New York University Press, 1963.

Thorndike, E. *The psychology of wants, interests and attitudes.* London: Appleton Century, 1935.

Tobey, T., & Thoresen, C. Helping Bill reduce aggressive behaviors: A nine-year-old makes good. In J. Krumboltz & C. Thoresen (Eds.), *Counseling methods.* New York: Holt, Rinehart & Winston, 1976.

Venham, L., Bengston, D., & Cipes, M. Children's responses to sequential dental visits. *Journal of Dental Research*, 1977, *56*, 454-459.

Waldron, S., Jr. The significance of childhood neurosis for adult mental health: A follow-up study. *American Journal of Psychiatry*, 1976, *133*, 532-538.

Walker, H., & Hops, H. The use of group and individual reinforcement contingencies in the modification of social withdrawal. In L. Hamerlynck, L. Handy, & E. Mash (Eds.), *Behavior change: Methodology, concepts, and practice.* Champaign, Ill.: Research Press, 1973.

Watson, J., & Raynor, R. Conditioned emotional reactions. *Journal of Experimental Psychology*, 1920, *3*, 1-14.

Weinstein, D. Imagery and relaxation with a burn patient. *Behaviour Research and Therapy*, 1976, *14*, 48.

White, W., Jr. Vicarious extinction of phobic behavior in early childhood. *Journal of Abnormal Child Psychology*, 1974, *2*, 25-33.

White, W. & Davis, M. Vicarious extinction of phobic behavior in early childhood. *Journal of Abnormal Child Psychology*, 1974, *2*, 25-32.

Whitehill, M., DeMyer-Gapin, S., & Scott, T. Stimulation seeking in antisocial preadolescent children. *Journal of Abnormal Psychology*, 1976, *85*(1), 101-104.

Wish, P., Hasazi, J., & Jurgela, A. Automated direct deconditioning of a childhood phobia. *Journal of Behavior Therapy and Experimental Psychiatry*, 1973, *4*, 279-283.

Wolff, S. Dimensions and clusters of symptoms in disturbed children. *British Journal of Psychiatry*, 1971, *118*, 421-427.

Wolpe, J. *Psychotherapy by reciprocal inhibition.* Stanford, Cal.: Stanford University Press, 1958.

Wolpe, J., & Lang, P. A fear survey schedule for use in behavior therapy. *Behaviour Research and Therapy*, 1964, *2*, 27-30.

Wright, G., & Alpern, G. Variables influencing children's cooperative behavior at the first dental visit. *Journal of Dentistry for Children*, 1971, *38*, 124-128.

Wright, G., Alpern, G., & Leake, J. The modifiability of maternal anxiety as it relates to children's cooperative dental behavior. *Journal of Dentistry for Children*, 1973, *40*, 265-271.

Wulbert, M., Nyman, B., Snow, D., & Owen, Y. The efficacy of stimulus fading and contingency management in the treatment of elective mutism: A case study. *Journal of Applied Behavior Analysis*, 1973, *6*, 435-441.

Young, F., & Brown, M. Effects of test anxiety and testing conditions on intelligence test scores of elementary school boys and girls. *Psychological Reports*, 1973, *32*, 643-649.

Zabin, M. *Reduction of anxiety in children and its relationship to parental discipline.* Unpublished master's thesis, Case Western Reserve University, 1975.

Ziv, A., & Luz, M. Manifest anxiety in children of different socioeconomic levels. *Human Development*, 1973, *16*, 224-232.

5   *Child Abuse: A Social Interactional Analysis*

Robert L. Burgess

One of the jurors covered her mouth in horror at the sight of 7-year-old Daniel Brownell. Tears dampened the eyes of other jurors and many of the spectators.

The blond-haired boy was curled unresponsive in the fetal position in a crib that was wheeled into the courtroom.

Doctors recited the abuse the child had endured: a beating which caused gangrene and permanent brain damage; and having the words "I cry" burned into his back with a cigarette.

Dr. Wallace Fagan added the postscript to Daniel's case.

"We can get very few demonstrable responses. He is unable to move any finger on command. He has primitive reflexes. He blinks at the sound of a snap in his ear. He is in the 203rd postoperative day. He's not going to get any better."

The jury Wednesday convicted Daniel's stepfather of child abuse and sentenced him to the maximum 20 years in prison. The boy's mother will stand trial later on charges she failed to report the abuse.

Lozier Pickering, a 25-year-old construction worker, showed no emotion at the jury's verdict of guilty but he wept earlier at the appearance of his stepson.

"Only when he lost consciousness did they take the boy to the hospital," Prosecutor Hogan Stripling said. "A surgeon didn't even know what he was looking at because it was a mass of rotten flesh, days old."

Pickering's defense attorneys presented no witnesses and rested their case immediately after the state. Pickering told police he had spanked the boy, but he denied abusing him.

Fagan, who operated on the child when he was hospitalized by his parents October 13, eight days after the beating, testified Daniel suffered a ruptured colon due to insertion of some object in his anus.

An ensuing gangrenous infection led to permanent brain damage.

Fagan said the infection was so advanced by the time he opened the child's abdomen that he was unable to recognize internal organs.

He also found unusual marks on the child's back.

"They looked like an abrasion at first. Later, it took the form of certain letters as scabs forming the letters 'I—C-R-Y-.' "

The doctor said the letters apparently were burned with a cigarette.
[(UPI) 1977]

ROBERT L. BURGESS • College of Human Development, The Pennsylvania State University, University Park, Pennsylvania. Preparation of this document was supported in part by Office of Child Development Grant 90-C-445.

1. Introduction

Child abuse refers to nonaccidental physical and psychological injury to a child under the age of 18 as a result of acts of omission or commission perpetrated by a parent or caretaker. Conceptual problems abound in part because we are clearly dealing with behavior that falls along a continuum of caregiver-child relationships. At one end of the continuum we have seemingly innocuous verbal punishment—disparagement, criticism, threat, and ridicule. Or, we have fairly typical forms of physical punishment such as a slap on the hand or a swat on the bottom. Then there are forms of physical punishment that exceed current community standards—hitting the child with a closed fist or with an object such as a razor strap, belt, cord, or paddle; slamming the child against the wall; kicking the child; burning the child with a cigarette as in the newspaper account above; scalding the child with hot water; torturing or even killing the child. Nor is it always clear where a particular case should be placed on this conceptual continuum. What is more devastating to the development of a child; a single occasion where a parent loses control and slams a child across the room, in the process knocking out a tooth and breaking a child's arm; or the persistent day-by-day, month-by-month, year-by-year use of ridicule, criticism, and sarcasm toward that child? This problem of definition and the establishment of a uniform response class is but one of many problems plaguing the systematic study of child abuse. Other problems, such as the tendency to dramatize the bizarre and extreme use of physical violence or aggression at the expense of more subtle forms of verbal punishment, the tendency to equate child abuse either with psychopathology, on the one hand, or with poverty, on the other, and the tendency to rely upon impressionistic accounts of behavior, also have retarded the accumulation of sound knowledge about the causes, consequences, treatment, and prevention of abusive behavior.

Given the state of our present knowledge, this chapter will largely be suggestive. Rather than describing numerous studies dealing with specific aspects of child abuse, this discussion will try to place the study of child abuse within a framework that it is hoped, can guide future research.

2. Historical Context

A common assumption in research on violence, aggression, and severe punishment is that they are abnormal and pathological forms of behavior. Yet when one looks at the evolution of man as a species, these have been common behaviors throughout our history. Evolutionary biologists such as Alexander (1971) and Bigelow (1969) argue that violent aggressive behavior has played a significant role in our evolutionary development. Indeed, they suggest that aggressive behavior was of primary importance in the evolution of our brain capacity and the development of social organization. Whether they are correct or not, the fact remains that when we examine the evolution of mankind using paleontological and anthropological evidence, it becomes clear that aggressive behavior has been with us since the dawn of history (Dart, 1948; Bigelow, 1969; Blanc, 1962; Freeman, 1964).

So far as the record of maltreating children is concerned, again we find that we are dealing with a phenomenon of ancient proportions. When we look at popular fairy tales such as "Hansel and Gretel," "Little Red Riding Hood," "Snow White," "The Gingerbread Boy," or "The Three Little Pigs," we see children, or their representations, being mistreated, abandoned, or eaten. Even that great repository of Judeo-Christian ethics, the Bible, is filled with examples of the harsh treatment of children from their victimization as objects for ritual sacrifice to a demanding and jealous God, to their outright slaughter. It makes little difference whether we look at Old Testament accounts such as the Pharaoh ordering the slaying of all Hebrew children or the New Testament case of Herod commanding the death of all male children under the age of 2; the pattern is repeated again and again.

Not only are we discussing a behavior pattern that originated in antiquity, it also has been found, in some form, in all known cultures. As Korbin (1977) has pointed out, the harsh treatment of children can be seen in such diverse cultures as the Enga of Papua, New Guinea, and the Hopi of the North American Southwest. Among the Enga, a child may lose a portion of a finger for a transgression as seemingly minor as intruding upon the mother's garden. Sometimes, the child is even forced to eat the cooked digit. Among the Hopi, whippings at initiation rites of children between the ages of 6 and 10 were often of such severity that they left permanent scars.

Nor is mistreatment of the young limited to that diabolical species *homo sapiens*. The sociobiological literature is filled with some rather gruesome accounts of infanticide such as in African lions (Schaller, 1972) and in the Hanuman langurs of India (Hrdy, 1974). The empirical evidence suggest that such behavior is especially likely under conditions of severe stress, scarcity of food resources, or a change in the dominance order. Whatever the precipitant, this behavior, though reprehensible by our standards, seems to represent under those circumstances a highly adaptive evolutionary strategy (see, e.g., Barash, 1977).

3. The Family as a Locus of Violence

Not only does the mistreatment of children have a long diverse history, there may even be certain intrinsic characteristics of families *per se* that more or less assure that conflict will be inevitable and the occurrence of violent and aggressive behavior highly likely (Gelles & Straus, 1977).

3.1. Conflict of Interests

The family is probably seldom the site of parents and children constantly united in the joint pursuit of individual and collective goals, as portrayed in the heartwarming sagas of television. The husband father, having just struggled through a tedious day at the office or through 8 hours working out in the rain, may want nothing more than a cold beer and a period of relaxation with the evening newspaper. His wife may be quietly seething over his obstinate refusal to accompany her to the monthly PTA meeting. Moreover, their eldest son was sent home with a note from the principal and all he could say was that he could understand neither algebra nor why he should be concerned with Julius Caesar's trek through Gaul. He hates his teachers and school and would rather drop out and get a job. On top of all this, he wants to listen to the Top 40 at the same time his father wants peace and quiet and his mother wants to decide finally whether they are going away on their vacation or staying home and painting the house.

Often there is a seemingly zero-sum quality to these familial conflicts. The parents want their young children to go outside and play so they can have some privacy, and the children want to stay in and be entertained. These conflicts of interest are infinite in number and are the grist for escalating disengagement, disaffection, and domestic guerilla warfare.

3.2. Time Together

One of the more elementary features of family life is that the members spend a great deal of time with each other. There are a number of consequences stemming from this fact. For instance, seemingly small annoyances such as one's table manners or how one squeezes a tube of toothpaste may be exaggerated way out of proportion to their true importance. Indeed, the same behaviors observed in a friend would largely go unnoticed. Additionally, the more time spent together, the greater the overlap of common interests and activities. This, in turn, means that there are even more events around which disputes and disagreements might arise.

3.3. High Level of Intimacy

The high level of emotional involvement of their members is another distinguishing characteristic of families. Whether it is the emotional bond linking parent and child that is described as mutual attachment or the attraction between husband and wife that is often described as romantic love, the level of positive emotional affect is usually higher in the family than in any other human group. But such mutual investment in one another generates its own risks and pains. A husband or wife may deceive the other and a child can fail to live up to his or her parents' high expectations.

There seems to be a tendency for students of the family to use a seesaw theory of emotional affect. Thus, the higher the degree of positive affect, or the higher the frequency of positive interactions, the lower the degree of negative affect and the lower the frequency of negative interactions. Actually, these behaviors may be independent of each other and, in some cases, they may even co-vary with each other. At least this is one implication of the high incidence of violence in families. Next to the bedroom, the most dangerous place on earth may very well be the dining room.

There are a number of other features of family living that may combine with the high degree of emotional involvement to increase the likelihood of violence (Gelles & Straus, 1977). One is that in most societies the kinship and household structure insulates the family from the social constraints of others that could, otherwise, mediate their conflicts. Most family fights occur behind closed doors. Second, in contrast to other social groups, membership is largely involuntary and when conflicts do arise, the alternative of resolving them by simply leaving does not exist as a reasonable solution. Finally, membership in a family usually implies the right to influence the behavior of others. Hence, dissatisfaction with the conduct of another family member may be exacerbated by active attempts to change that behavior. This is especially the case since there usually are cultural norms legitimizing the use of violence between family members. This is particularly true so far as the physical punishment of children is concerned.

4. The Frequency of Family Violence

There is a considerable amount of statistical evidence that documents that the family is the most common location of interpersonal violence.

4.1. Homicide

Murder is one feature of family violence for which there are fairly good statistics. Steinmetz and Straus (1974) suggest that one reason for this is because murder is a crime that leaves physical evidence that cannot be ignored. To emphasize the extent of domestic homicide, Gelles and Straus (1977) note that as many people are murdered by their relatives within a normal 6-month period in New York City as have been killed in all of the battles in Northern Ireland to date. Data gathered from a number of societies indicate that domestic quarrels comprise somewhere between 30% and 60% of all homicides (Bohannon, 1960; Curtis, 1974). In 1973, the FBI investigated 17, 123 cases of murder. Of this total, 13.7% were cases of one spouse killing another, 3.3% parent killing child, 8.7% involving other relatives, 7.2% involving romantic triangles and lovers' quarrels, and 42% described as "other arguments" (Kelley, 1973).

4.2. Police Calls

Parnas (1967) has estimated that the number of police calls involving family fights is greater than that for all other criminal incidents combined. He found that 22% of all police calls resulted in the investigation of domestic assaults of one kind or another. Pittman and Handy (1964) found that aggravated assaults between husbands and wives accounted for 11% of all aggravated assaults in St. Louis, Missouri. The figure for Detroit, Michigan, was 52% (Boudouris, 1971). As Gelles and Straus (1977) argue, these are probably conservative estimates since there are a number of factors that operate against the police being called in the first place.

4.3. Physical Punishment

A number of researchers have attempted to estimate the frequency of the use of physical punishment in families. Taking these studies together (Bronfenbrenner, 1958; Erlanger, 1974; Stark & McEvoy, 1970), it appears that 84-97% of all parents employ physical punishment with their children. This pattern is found for children of all ages, even older children. For example Steinmetz (1974) and Straus (1971) found that over 50% of their respondents, as late as their senior year in high school, had experienced physical punishment or its threat as a form of parental discipline.

4.4. Child Abuse

Estimates of the incidence of child abuse in the United States are quite varied, ranging from a low of 6,000 cases per year (Gil, 1970) to 200,000 to 500,000 cases per year (Light, 1973). In 1975 there were approximately 550,000 cases of suspected child abuse and neglect reported in the United States (Helfer & Kempe, 1976).

In an attempt to obtain more accurate statistics on the frequency of all forms of domestic violence, Straus, Gelles, and Steinmetz in 1976 conducted a study employing a national probability sample (Gelles, 1977). Their sample produced data from over 1,000 families. Eligible families consisted of couples who identified themselves as married or being a couple and who had children between the ages of 3 and 17 living at home. For each family, a "referent" child was selected at random and the parents were interviewed concerning their parenting practices during the previous year—i.e., 1975. For the purpose of the study, the researchers assumed that "ordinary" physical punishment and child abuse were but two ends of a single continuum of violence toward children. Sixty-three percent of the respondents mentioned at least one violent act during the survey year. Fifty-eight percent of the parents reported slapping or spanking their child in the previous year while 41% admitted pushing or shoving their child. Thirteen percent of the parents reported hitting their child with an object the previous year. "Approximately 3% of the parents reported kicking, biting, or hitting the referent child with a fist in 1975" (p.16). Extrapolating to the number of children in the United States between the ages of 3 and 17, somewhere between one and two million children had been kicked, bitten, or punched by their parents during 1975. Moreover, again extrapolating to the population at large, approximately 50,000 children had their parents using a knife or gun on them in 1975 (Gelles, 1976).

4.5. Conclusions

Looking at all of the evidence, it is quite clear that when we consider domestic violence, in general, or child abuse, in particular, we are dealing with a phenomenon that has an incredibly long history and that occurs with astonishing frequency—we are, in short, considering a problem of major proportions. Even a casual reading of the papers presented at the First International Congress on Child Abuse and Neglect in Geneva, Switzerland, in 1976 indicates that child abuse is a problem that has neither cultural, societal, nor social class boundaries (Kempe, 1977).

Let us now consider some of the attempts that have been made to explain the occurrence of abusive behavior.

5. Explaining Child Abuse

A number of excellent reviews of the research literature (e.g., Belsky, 1978; Parke & Collmer, 1975) suggest that there have been three major approaches to understanding child abuse.

5.1. The Psychiatric Model

The earliest published research on child abuse was initiated by physicians (e.g., Kempe, Silverman, Steele, Droegemueller, & Silver, 1962); thus it should not be surprising that this early work was strongly influenced by a medical model (Galdston, 1965; Kempe, & Helfer, 1972; Steele & Pollock, 1968/1974). Basically, the chief assumption of the psychiatric approach is that the causes of child abuse are to be found in the parents, who, in turn, possess certain personality characteristics that distinguish them from nonabusing parents. Not only do these adults possess distinctive personality traits but these traits are essentially pathological. Child abuse, like other pathologies, was felt to be indicative of an underlying sickness. After all, who but a sick person would deliberately harm a defenseless child?

There have been a number of difficulties associated with the psychiatric approach from its very inception. Perhaps the most significant problem is that the research upon which it was based consisted largely of small, nonrandom, clinical populations. Moreover, these studies rarely employed nonabusive families as control groups. Consequently, it is often difficult to determine whether the detected characteristics of the abusive parents were unique to them or were characteristics of the population at large.

Undoubtedly, there may be cases of psychopathological assault by parents that reflect psychotic functioning, but these probably involve a very small proportion of abuse cases in general. Indeed, Kempe (1973), a pioneer in the study of child abuse and in the development of the psychiatric model, has recently estimated that less than 10% of child-abusing adults can accurately be labeled mentally ill.

If we consider less severe psychological dysfunctions, some empirical support can be found. For example, in an early follow-up study of 31 children classified as abused, unclassified, or not abused, Elmer (1967) found that emotional difficulties such as frequent crying spells, depression, and disturbances in eating and sleeping occurred significantly more often among the abusive mothers.

One of the more commonly noted characteristics of abusive parents is their tendency to have distorted perceptions of the nature of child-hood. There is said to be a tendency for the abusive parent to expect to be cared for and nurtured by the child (Morris & Gould, 1963). When the child fails to meet parental expectations, the parents presumably strike back in anger at the child (Brown & Daniels, 1968; Johnson & Morse, 1968; Spinetta & Rigler, 1972).

There are a number of other characteristics that are supposed to be commonly found in abusive parents. For example, they are said to have difficulty in dealing with aggressive impulses (Wasserman, 1967), they are rigid and domineering (Johnson & Morse, 1968), and they are impulsive, immature, self-centered and hypersensitive (Kempe *et al.*, 1962). Other characteristics linked to abusive parents include alcoholism (Blumberg, 1974; Johnson & Morse, 1968; Young, 1964), low self-esteem, and a history of having themselves been abused or neglected as children (Curtis, 1963; Kempe *et al.*, 1962; Steele & Pollock, 1968/1974; Spinetta & Rigler, 1972).

In addition to the tendency to base such claims on small unrepresentative clinical populations, another problem with the attempt to locate the causes of child abuse within the psyche of the abusing parents or caretakers is that it has been difficult to replicate the effects of these variables, especially in studies that have planned-comparison or control groups (Gelles, 1973; Parke & Collmer, 1975). These problems led researchers to look for alternative external determinants of abusive patterns.

5.2. The Sociological Model

The psychiatric model was challenged by a number of researchers who argued that the focus should not be on individual psychological differences but on those forces within society that lead adults to abuse their children (Gelles, 1973; Gil, 1970).

There are three major characteristics of this approach. The first is that child abuse can best be understood in terms of "the society's basic social philosophy and value premises" (Gil, 1974, p. 12), especially those values and attitudes toward violence and physical punishment as a means of interpersonal control. As we have seen earlier in this chapter, there certainly seems to be considerable agreement that physical punishment is an acceptable disciplinary tactic—especially with children. So far as the United States is concerned, there seems to be ample evidence that violence is often condoned, justified, and prescribed by social norms (Gil, 1970; Geis & Monahan, 1975; Lystad, 1975; Stark & McEvoy, 1970). Nor is this pattern limited to the United States (Levy, 1969: Sidel, 1972; Stevenson, 1968).

The second key element of the sociological approach is the belief that when families are exposed to stress, violence is likely to erupt. Child abuse is just one form that this violence can take. The third characteristic is that the position of the family within the larger social structure plays an important role in determining the likelihood of domestic violence. Central to the sociological model is the assumption that the degree of stress is inversely related to social status. Thus, lower socioeconomic groups are felt to experience greater social stress and are thereby more likely to display violent aggressive behavior.

The sociological model has been strongly shaped by research based on official statistics collected from various social service agencies. Given the fact that poorer families are more likely to contact these agencies, there may be a tendency for lower socioeconomic groups to be overrepresented. Nonetheless, there is reason to suspect that child abuse, especially physical abuse, may be correlated with social class. Gil's national survey (1970) indicated that child abuse is more likely in lower-class homes. For example, over 48% of the abusive families had an annual income under $5,000, while the percentage of all families at this level was only around 25%. Moreover, less than 1% of the abusive mothers were college graduates and only 17% had graduated from high school. Indeed, 24% had less than 9 years of formal education. In addition to the Gil survey, there is the commonly observed fact that violence, in general, whether it be aggravated assault, armed robbery, or gang fights, tends to be more common in lower socioeconomic areas. Moreover, other studies have documented the contention that child abuse, in particular, is more frequent in poorer families (Garbarino, 1977), though again, there are real problems in interpreting results based on official statistics. Whatever the presumed crime, the lower the socioeconomic level, the greater the likelihood that law enforcement or other social agencies will be called in.

Researchers operating from a sociological perspective have investigated a number of social structural correlates of child abuse. Some of these are more likely to be found in lower socioeconomic groups. For example, unemployment seems to be implicated in child abuse. Gil (1970) in his survey found that nearly 50% of the fathers involved in child abuse were unemployed during the year in which the abusive incident occurred. This finding held up in Light's (1973) subsequent reanalysis of Gil's data.

Another factor found to be associated with the incidence of child abuse is isolation from the larger community (Bennie & Sclar, 1969; Garbarino, 1977; Lenoski, 1974; Young, 1964). A number of things may be operating here. For example, due to their relative social isolation, the abusive parents may simply not be subjected to normal social control pressures that would operate to keep their behavior within socially sanctioned boundaries. Alternatively, or additionally, the abusive parents may simply not have access to others—friends, relatives, neighbors—who could assist them during particularly difficult times.

A number of investigators have found that the structure of the family itself may be related to the incidence of child abuse. For instance, Gil (1970) and Young (1964) have reported data indicating that the proportion of abusing families with four or more children is twice that found in the general population. Light's (1973) data indicate a similar pattern in England and New Zealand. Basically, these researchers have argued that the larger the family, the greater the drain on all the family's resources. In addition to sheer family size, having births too closely spaced may place excessive demands on the family.

Another structural characteristic of families that has been associated with abusive patterns of child care is marital discord (Green, 1976; Spinetta & Rigler, 1972; Young, 1964). Essentially, the assumption here is that conflict between the parents themselves can spill over and affect the parents' treatment of their children.

The basic assumption of the sociological model is that there are a number of stress factors that can impinge upon families, induce frustration, and elicit violent, aggressive behavior. The potential stress factors are many and include such things as poor parental health, drug and alcohol abuse, financial difficulties, unemployment, legal problems, overcrowded or inadequate living conditions, marital instability, too many children, births too closely spaced, and isolation from effective social support systems. While the frequency of these conditions may be correlated with social class, they would undoubtedly be experienced as aversive regardless of one's position in the social structure. Moreover, though the frequency of domestic violence in general, and child abuse in particular, may be correlated with lower socioeconomic status, the fact remains that not all poor faimilies abuse their children. Nor is it clear that if their financial problems were resolved abusive parents would suddenly be transformed into paragons of parental virtue. Such concerns have led to the gradual evolution of a third explanatory perspective.

5.3. The Social Interactional Model

Dissatisfaction with attempts to explain abuse solely as a function of individual psychological characteristics of the abusing parents or as due to social structural stress factors has led to an approach that has alternatively been designated the "social structural" model (Parke & Collmer, 1975), the "effect of the child on his caregiver" model (Belsky, 1978), or the "social psychological" model (Burgess & Conger, 1978a). Whatever it is named, this approach, though still in a stage of conceptual development, has a number of characteristics that set it apart from the two earlier models discussed.

First of all, there is an emphasis upon the fact that abusing parents often lack certain fundamental social and parenting skills. Indeed, the very absence of effective coping skills may not only exacerbate the effects of any stress parents may be experiencing, but it also may create stress in its own right. Thus a child may be difficult to handle and cause stress for a mother precisely because she does not know how to handle the child in the first place.

Second, this approach acknowledges that abused children, themselves, may contribute to the abusive behavior they receive. Efforts to identify the sources of psychological disturbance in the parents may distract the investigator of child abuse from looking at characteristics of the child that may be contributing to the punitive behavior of the parent.

Third, this model for the study of child abuse acknowledges, at least implicitly, that to understand the occurrence of abusive behavior within families, we must look at the patterned forms of interaction that occur within the entire family. In short, we must carefully examine the various dyadic relationships that constitute the family. It is this component of the approach that led Burgess and Conger (1978a) to refer to it as a social-psychological model since social psychologists have, since the turn of the century, emphasized the importance of social interaction.

Fourth, the model is multidimensional in character. That is, emphasis is placed on the potential importance of both psychological and sociological variables. Moreover, this paradigm is vitally concerned with how these variables interact and jointly affect the parent-child relationship. Given all of these considerations, it now seems that the term *social interaction* best captures the model and that is how it shall be labeled here.

The balance of this chapter will consist of a reconceptualization of the social interactional model so that the role of social learning or behavior modification principles can be explicitly brought to bear on the analysis, treatment, and prevention of child abuse.

5.3.1. The Development of Abusive Behavior

When we ask questions about why a particular behavior occurs, we usually overlook the fact that such a question can be approached from four major levels of analysis (Tinbergen, 1951). One, we may want to know how an individual grows up to behave in a particular manner. This is a concern for ontogenetic development. Two, we may want to know why the individual displays that behavior just now. This interpretation of the question represents a concern for the immediate antecedents of the behavior. Three, we may want to know the functions the behavior performs for the person who displays it. In short, this is a concern for the consequences of the behavior for the actor. Four, we may want to know what the evolutionary history of the behavior is. This particular meaning to the question of why a behavior occurs reflects a concern for the phylogeny of behavior and is best represented in the work of sociobiologists (e.g., Barash, 1977). There is reason to believe that by analytically separating these different types of questions, we can move ahead expeditiously and avoid unnecessary theoretical conflict. In this manner, the present section is concerned with the development of abusive behavior.

As we noted earlier in this chapter, a number of studies have documented that many abusive parents were themselves abused or neglected as children (e.g., Curtis, 1963; Kempe *et al.*, 1962; Spinetta & Rigler, 1972). From a behavioral standpoint, there are a number of learning processes that may account for the acquisition of abusive or aggressive behavior. First of all, a child may be directly reinforced for aggressive behavior (Bandura, 1973). This reinforcement can take many forms. A child may win the approval of siblings and peers for behaving in hostile or aggressive ways toward others (Patterson, Littman, & Bricker, 1967). Parents may even directly reinforce aggressive behavior, as when a father proudly exclaims that his son, who just won a fistfight with the boy next door, is "just a chip off the old block." Parents may also unwittingly use a shaping procedure and differentially reinforce successive approximations to aggressive behavior. This may happen when they reinforce increasingly loud or aversive crying and tantrum behaviors.

In addition to direct positive reinforcement, a child may acquire aggressive behavior via modeling and imitation. Indeed, it has been frequently noted that the most important lesson a child may learn when he/she is punished by a parent is that punitive and aggressive behaviors are accepted as effective interpersonal control tactics (Bandura, 1973). The aggressive behavior of siblings, peers, other adults, movies, and television can provide still further occasions for the modeling of coercive behavior.

In a recent paper, Patterson (1977) has suggested that for many settings, such as the home, contingencies of positive reinforcement may actually be of limited value for understanding the performance of aggressive and coercive behavior by children. To the extent that positive reinforcement plays a role in the explanation of aggressive behavior, it may come fairly early in the developmental process. For example, a 3- or 4-year-old child may be positively reinforced for his attacks on his siblings by their complying with his demands. The ultimate effect of these kinds of transactions, however, is that his victims may initiate their own aggressive behavior (Patterson *et al.*, 1967). What then happens is that a cycle of coercion gets established. Once that occurs, subsequent aggressive or coercive behavior serves the function of coping with the other person's aggressive behaviors. The reinforcer for this behavior becomes the termination of the other person's attack. This arrangement, of course, represents a negative reinforcement contingency. Using conditional probability analyses, Patterson (1977) describes some highly suggestive data in support of negative reinforcement as a key mechanism in the maintenance of aggressive behavior. To the extent such behaviors become a part of one's response repertory, the pattern should persist throughout the life-span insofar as those behaviors function accordingly. Thus, abusive parents may exhibit much of their punitive, aggressive behaviors because those behaviors serve to terminate aversive behavior in their children.

An important feature of aggressive behavior, as with punishment *per se* is that it often works—it produces compliance. Especially if there is a large difference in physical size or power, coercive behavior is quickly followed by compliant behavior. Consequently, there is reason to suppose that the more limited a person's social and parenting skills, the more likely he/she is to display punitive, aggressive behavior. At least that is one way to produce a desired response in another. A number of studies of abusive parents have suggested that the adults are lacking in effective care-giving skills (Parke & Collmer, 1975). It would be predicted, then, that abusive parents will exhibit a higher percentage of aggressive and otherwise negative behaviors than nonabusive parents.

Unfortunately, most child-abuse research has not collected the detailed kinds of data necessary to test such a prediction. One investigation, however, does provide information which bears on this prediction. Burgess and Conger (1978a) designed a study to examine patterns of day-to-day interaction in a sample of 17 abuse, 17 neglect, and 19 control two-parent families. The families were observed in their homes over several sessions by highly trained, naive observers. The family members were observed engaging in three kinds of tasks. The first set the stage for cooperative behavior, the second was a competitive game, and the third was a discussion task. Using an observation code designed to explore the type and direction of family interactions, the observers scored approximately 1,500 interactions per family. Interobserver agreement was quite high with the lowest correlation coefficient being .91.

Some of the results can be seen in Tables 1 and 2 and in Figures 1 and 2. From these data, it can be determined that both the abusive and

TABLE 1
Mean Rates of Social Contacts[a]

Family type	Total verbal contacts					Positive verbal and physical contacts					Negative verbal and physical contacts					Total physical contacts			
	Abuse	p^b	Neglect	P	Control	Abuse	P	Neglect	P	Control	Abuse	P	Neglect	P	Control	Abuse	P	Neglect	Control
Total family	19.48		19.61		20.77	.93		.73	.02	1.15	1.11		1.20	.04	.74	4.19		4.52	4.58
Parents	9.26	.03	9.54	.05	10.73	.53		.37	.01	.73	.40	.10	.54	.01	.25	1.34	.04	1.62	1.72
Mothers	4.47	.01	5.42		5.89	.27	.07	.22	.02	.41	.23	.08	.33	.01	.13	.70	.04	.96	.95
Fathers	4.79	.08	4.12	.08	4.84	.26		.14	.01	.31	.17		.21		.12	.64		.66	.77
Children	10.22		10.06		10.03	.40		.37		.43	.71		.66		.49	2.85		2.90	2.86

[a] Rates refer to responses per minute.
[b] Rates in italic are those that are significantly different from rates of the same behavior by control families at $p \leq .10$.

TABLE 2
Mean Rates of Interaction[a]

Family type	Total verbal interaction					Positive verbal and physical interaction					Negative verbal and physical interaction					Total physical interaction				
	Abuse	p[b]	Neglect	p	Control	Abuse	p	Neglect	p	Control	Abuse	p	Neglect	p	Control	Abuse	p	Neglect	p	Control
Mothers to children	2.98	.01	3.90		4.08	.21	.04	.18	.02	.35	.20	.09	.31	.01	.12	.58	.03	.88		.82
Fathers to children	3.36		2.84		3.29	.20		.12	.01	.28	.15		.18	.08	.11	.56		.57		.67
Children to mothers	2.11	.04	2.72		2.80	.09		.11		.11	.10		.14		.09	.73	.02	.92		.98
Children to fathers	2.30		1.65	.04	2.22	.12		.07	.05	.12	.07		.09		.06	.77		.63	.02	.87
Children to children	2.87		2.83		2.39	.08		.11		.09	.44		.35		.29	1.35		1.34		1.00
Mothers to spouses	1.03		.99		1.04	.05		.03		.03	.01		.01		.01	.12		.07	.01	.13
Fathers to spouses	.91		.91		.92	.04		.01		.02	.01		.01		.01	.08		.08		.10

[a] Rates refer to responses per minute.
[b] Rates in italic are those that are significantly different from rates of the same behavior by control families at $p \leq .10$.

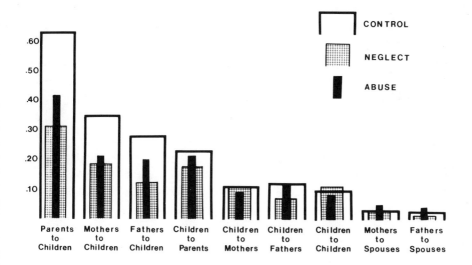

Figure 1. Mean rates of positive verbal and physical interaction.

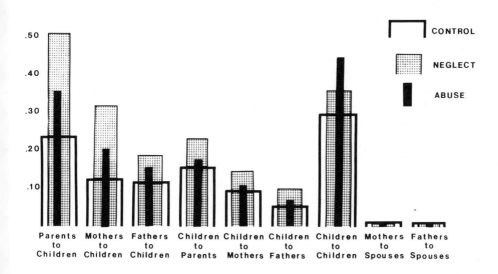

Figure 2. Mean rates of negative verbal and physical interaction.

the neglectful families displayed lower rates of interaction overall. This is especially the case for positive interactions (e.g., affectionate and supportive behavior), where, for example, the mothers in the abuse families displayed rates of positive behavior toward their children 40% lower than the mothers in the matched control families. The neglect mothers and fathers directed positive behavior toward their children approximately 50% lower than the control parents. The pattern was quite different, however, for negative or coercive interactions. The mothers in the abuse families exhibited rates of negative behavior (e.g., threats and complaints) toward their children over 60% higher than the control mothers. The pattern was even clearer in the neglect families, where the mothers displayed rates of negative behavior over twice as high as the control mothers, and the fathers 75% higher than their matched controls.

Admittedly, this is a small sample derived from a largely rural environment, but the families do share many of the characteristics found in typically lower socioeconomic abusive families. These families have low incomes, are poorly educated, and have more children than the norm. However, the matched control families also are poor but while they have enough problems of their own, they do not display patterns of interaction as coercive as those of the abuse and neglect families.

In any event, both the abusive and the neglectful families display the sorts of behavior patterns that Patterson's research (1977) would suggest. And while these specific data failed to reach statistical significance, the children in the abuse families displayed negative behaviors almost 50% more often than did the children in the control families. Thus they seem to be developing the same coercive styles displayed by their parents.

As mentioned earlier in this section, there have not been many attempts to collect detailed observational data of parent-child interaction in abusive and comparison families. Two recent studies do, however, present data consistent with those described by Burgess and Conger (1978a). In one study, Egeland and Brunnquell (1977) followed 275 high-risk mothers and infants through the children's first year of life. In their report, they describe a subsample of 25 mothers who apparently provided good quality care and 26 mothers who abused or mistreated their children. Interestingly, there were no differences between the two groups in the amount of stress they experienced. The major discriminating difference between the groups was that the nonabusing mothers displayed more appropriate caretaking behaviors, more positive affect and, similarly, their infants displayed more social responsiveness.

Reid and Taplin (1977), in a follow-up study of families examined by Patterson and his colleagues at the Oregon Research Institute, presented observational data from 27 nondistressed families, 61 distressed families with no known history of abuse, and 27 abusive families. While they did not present data on positive interactions, they did find that the abusive families displayed significantly higher rates of aversive behavior than did the comparison families. In sum, these studies suggest that abusive parents often fail to exhibit positive behavior-management skills and may never have acquired them in the first place.

5.3.2. Proximal Antecedents of Abusive Behavior

Apart from a concern for the development of abusive behavior, attention must be given to the circumstances surrounding the occurrence of specific abusive incidents. Here we are concerned with situational determinants or antecedents of abusive acts.

From an explicit behavioral standpoint, there is evidence that various kinds of aversive stimulation are capable of eliciting aggressive behavior toward others (Azrin & Holz, 1966). Throughout this chapter, we have seen that there are innumerable features of family life that are potentially aversive. The conflicts of interest that are so much a part of living together under one roof are themselves natural sources of possibly aversive stimulation. The imposition of seemingly unfair rules can be quite painful, indeed, as can threats to one's security and well-being. Whether these conflicts and hurts actually elicit or increase the probability of violent or aggressive behavior will depend to a considerable extent on whether the injured party possesses alternative coping behaviors within his or her behavioral repertoire. It may also depend, in part, on the existence of cultural, social, or familial norms concerning the appropriateness or inappropriateness of aggressive behavior in those circumstances.

There is a growing body of evidence that the abused child, as a stimulus object, may actually function to elicit abusive behavior. Milow and Lourie (1964) were two of the first researchers to suggest that characteristics of the child can influence the probability of an abusive incident. They noted that an abused child is often difficult to manage, is unappealing, and exhibits irritable crying. Similarly, data from Gil's survey (1970) show that 29% of the identified abused children exhibited some deviations in social interaction and general functioning prior to the reported abuse. Finally, Johnson and Morse (1968), reporting on a large clinical sample, found that 70% of their cases showed some form of developmental problem. The problems ranged from poor speech to physical deformities. Even the child welfare workers who dealt with these children found them hard to handle. The children were described as being "whiny, fussy, listless, chronically crying, demanding, stubborn, resistive, negativistic, pallid, sickly, emaciated, fearful, panicky, unsmiling . . ." (p.149). In sum, they noted that "the child most likely to be abused was one who was overly active or one who was most difficult to supervise and care for" (p.147).

The child may contribute to his own abuse in a number of ways. For example, there may be genetic or congenital characteristics that make abuse more likely—the child may be physically malformed or unattractive. Similarly, the child may be retarded and thus display numerous aversive behaviors (Elmer & Gregg, 1967; Martin, Beezley, Conway, & Kempe, 1974). It is, of course, also possible that the child may develop behaviors through interaction with peers or parents that, in turn, make him a target for abuse. As Bakan (1971) notes, "the well taken care of child attracts positive responses. The child who is abused and neglected becomes ugly in appearance and behavior and invites further abuse and neglect" (p. 109). Basically, the message here is that the unattractive unreinforcing child may be a target for abuse. Thus, the child who represents an unwanted pregnancy, or who resembles a disliked or unfaithful spouse, the chronically sick child, the hyperactive child, or the otherwise difficult-to-handle child may incite abusive behavior.

A number of studies have also found the incidence of abuse to be associated with prematurity. Elmer and Gregg (1967) noted that 30% of the sample they studied was below average in weight at birth. Similarly, Fontana (1973) reported that 25% of his sample of abused children were premature. There are two main reasons why prematurity may increase the likelihood of abuse. First, premature infants are more likely to suffer developmental difficulties (Caputo & Mandell, 1970). Second, the typical hospital procedures surrounding prematurity may impede the development of normal social bonding or attachment (Leifer, Leiderman, Barnett, & Williams, 1972; Seashore, Leifer, Barnett, & Leiderman, 1973).

It is important to note, however, that prematurity need not lead to abuse. In the previously cited study by Egeland and Brunnquell (1977) that compared two subgroups of high-risk mothers, one of which was abusing their children while the other was providing good care, it was found that both groups had similar frequencies of prematurity. In each case, 10% of the births were premature. Significant differences between these two groups of mothers included the fact that the well-functioning mothers were better educated and had a better understanding of their child's special needs. Hence, it is possible that the parents' clumsy or aversive actions or their failure to prompt and support appealing positive behaviors in the child may directly affect the extent to which the child develops aversive qualities.

The major conclusion to be drawn from these studies is that in any social relationship each partner possesses characteristics that can interact with those of the other and thereby affect the relationship (Burgess & Huston, 1978). Indeed, in a report by Edmunds and Burgess (1977) it was found that, within abusive families, the abused child and the official perpetrator of that abuse behave differently toward one another from the way they do toward the other family members. For example, the abusers and the victims directed the largest share of both their positive and negative behaviors to each other. Clearly, the pattern of interaction itself has to be carefully assessed.

There is still another class of antecedents to abuse that needs to be considered. As was discussed earlier in this chapter, we can look at child abuse as falling along a continuum of aggressive or punitive behaviors directed toward a child. By doing so, it becomes possible to consider events such as frequent punishment, threats, harsh commands, and other aversive behaviors as correlates and potential precipitants of major abusive incidents.

Patterson (1976) has shown that, within distressed or problem families, aggressive or coercive behaviors tend to occur in bursts. Moreover, parental punishment tends to accelerate ongoing coercive behaviors. The pattern he describes is essentially an escalating cycle of aggression. Two explanations have been mentioned to account for this paradoxical feature of punishment within problem families. One is suggested by the finding of Parke, Deur, and Saivin (1970) that the behavior of children whose conditioning history was marked by intermittent punishment was not as effectively controlled by schedules of consistent punishment as that of children whose history had included consistent punishment. Therefore, parents who punish inconsistently may be contributing to the acceleration of the behavior they are trying to discourage. The second explanation suggests that punishment will be ineffective in suppressing a behavior if it consists of a large number of threats that are seldom backed up (Patterson, 1976). Thus, in desperation, the parent may strike out and physically injure the child. Given the relatively high frequency of negative verbal and physical behaviors that Burgess and Conger (1978a) found in their abuse and neglect families, it certainly seems that the stage is set in those families for escalating violence. In another analysis of those data, Anderson and Burgess (1977) found that the children in abuse families are significantly more likely to reciprocate their parents' negative behaviors than are the children in matched control families.

Clearly, the generally high rates of negative interaction found by Burgess and Conger (1978a), when combined with the other stress factors commonly found in abusive families such as poor health, unemployment, marital instability, and legal problems, are sufficient to produce levels of aversive stimulation conducive to outbreaks of domestic violence.

5.3.3. The Consequences of Abusive Behavior

An assumption underlying our discussion of the social-interactional model is that most cases of abusive behaviors are operants. That is, these behaviors are proximally maintained by their immediate environmental consequences. The only exceptions to this are likely to be the rare occurrences of psychotic attack. But even here, the situation is unclear and we might be better off assuming that the behavior is operant.

Our concern in this section is with the functional consequences of abusive behavior—i.e., the consequences for the abuser. Aggressive behavior, in general, often produces at least short-run benefits for the aggressor and these consequences may functionally control future occurrences of similar behaviors. Such potentially reinforcing consequences include such diverse events as simply seeing the victim in pain, access to scarce resources, the restoration of equity, the gaining of compliance, the acclaim of others, and the termination of ongoing aversive behavior (Burgess & Conger, 1978b).

As we have seen in our discussion of the development of abusive behavior, there are ample circumstances in families where conflicts of interest can be decided by the successful aggressor—to his benefit. Unfortunately, this is a dimension of child abuse that has not received direct or sustained attention. Nonetheless, any successful attempt to treat child abuse will require careful examination of the reinforcing consequences of the abusive and coercive behavior.

It is axiomatic within a behavioral framework that behaviors are often maintained by their immediately reinforcing consequences even though the long range effects are detrimental to the actor. This may help explain the data cited by Patterson (1976) indicating that the frequency of aversive behaviors can actually be increased by the parents' punitive actions. In the short run, coercive acts are negatively reinforced by the termination of the target person's aversive behavior. The long-run consequence, however, is an acceleration of coercive behaviors throughout the family. Obviously, this pattern needs to be investigated carefully in abusive families.

5.4. Conclusions

In this section we have reviewed the attempts that have been made to understand the dynamics of child abuse. Some investigators have focused their research on trying to isolate the distinctive personality characteristics of the abusing parents. Others have concentrated on the social structural determinants of abusive patterns. The third approach we considered—the social-interactional model—has focused on the combined effects of psychological and sociological variables. The principal characteristic of this approach, however, is the emphasis that is placed on the reciprocal effects family members have on one another. From this perspective, even the abused child is considered as a potential causal locus for the abusive behavior. In our analysis of the social-interactional model from a behavioral standpoint, we have seen that the way in which the child is reared may influence whether he/she is abusive as an adult. We have also seen that there are a variety of situational, individual, and behavioral stimuli of an aversive nature that can prompt aggressive interchanges of increasing intensity that may eventually culminate in violent physical attack. We have considered, finally, that such coercive patterns are especially likely, given the absence of alternative disciplinary tactics, in particular, and social skills, in general.

6. Intervention

In this section, we shall consider briefly some of the efforts that have been made to modify abusive behavior.

6.1. The Psychiatric Model

The conventional approach to the treating of child abuse takes the form of psychotherapy. Accordingly, efforts are made to uncover the deep-seated emotional problems responsible for the abusive behavior. It is commonly assumed that the deviant behavior will disappear once insight into its etiology is acquired. The most systematic attempt at the psychiatric treatment of abusive parents has been by Steele and his associates in Denver, Colorado (Steele & Pollock, 1968/1974). Even though their treatment program developed from a traditional psychiatric model, it gradually became increasingly multidimensional. Their efforts eventually included home visits by social workers with considerable emphasis being placed on restructuring the parent-child relationship. Although they present data suggesting that their program has been successful in suppressing abusive behavior, a number of problems remain. First, the generalizability of their treatment effects has not been established. Second, the costs in time and money required by their program seem considerable, especially in light of the fact that some of their clients are treated for as long as 3-5 years. Consequently, this type of intervention may not be applicable to the large number of lower-class abusers. Third, their assessment procedures are not sufficiently detailed to allow us to determine which components are vital to successful treatment.

In spite of these problems, programs have spread across the country using multiple treatment services, including casework services, individual psychotherapy, marital treatment, lay therapists, group psychotherapy, Parents Anonymous groups, crisis nurseries, homemaker services, day care services, family therapy, and parent education (Helfer & Kempe, 1976). Unfortunately, these programs, as a rule, do not collect the kinds of data that are needed for appropriate assessment.

6.2. The Sociological Model

As we have seen, the basic premise of this paradigm is that social structural conditions within society cause abuse. Working from this perspective, Gil (1970) has argued that the successful treatment of child abuse will ultimately require radical restructuring of society, including the resource-distribution system. Poverty and its correlates must be eliminated. Thus, education, comprehensive health care, social services, and adequate housing must be provided to every citizen. Despite the merits of such a proposal, it is unclear whether such radical social change would by itself eliminate domestic violence.

At a more modest level, some of the intervention tactics noted in the previous section have been influenced by the sociological model, e.g., the use of crisis nurseries, and homemaker services, and the establishment of child-care networks. Each of these procedures is designed to lower the level of stress within the home and thereby reduce the incidence of child abuse (Gil, 1970). But, again, such programs do not usually have the kind of evaluation procedures that are necessary to assess their relative effectiveness.

In addition, there remains the tendency to place most of the emphasis on physical abuse at the expense of the more subtle forms of psychological abuse. Hence, success may be claimed simply because there has been no further instance of excessive physical abuse. Meanwhile, the typical pattern of interaction within the home may remain one of accentuating the negative. This issue aside, a recent report by Herrenkohl, Herrenkohl, Seech, and Egolf (1977) persuasively argues that the study of recidivism in child-abuse families is complicated by the fact that there is more abuse in subject families than there are corresponding official citations.

6.3. The Interactional Model

Issues such as these point out again the importance of carefully observing the interaction patterns among family members, Burgess (1978b) recently classified a number of problems commonly found in research and therapy in the area of child abuse, noting that a considerable amount of our uncertainty as to the principal determinants of abuse may be attributed to the research methodology employed in most studies. The majority of this research has placed much greater emphasis upon what people say about themselves than on what they do. Most of this research has relied upon secondhand information, clinical assessments, rating scales, survey questionnaires, and the secondary analysis of official statistics.

Undoubtedly, these indirect assessment procedures have their place but, by themselves, they may not be capable of providing the kinds of unbiased, highly detailed accounts of behavior that are necessary for the design of effective treatment programs and for the evaluation of those programs (Jones, Reid, & Patterson, 1975). For these reasons, there is a need to restore some balance to our research efforts by encouraging studies that employ direct observations of behavior and that make those observations in ecologically valid settings at the time those behaviors occur, rather than retrospectively.

A second problem centers around the emphasis on dramatic, sensational behaviors—behaviors that typically are low-frequency events. Low-frequency behaviors are difficult to study for a number of reasons, such as our inability to be present when they occur and to predict their occurrence with any accuracy. Basically, there is a need to address ourselves to higher-frequency behaviors—behaviors that can be specified precisely, that occur on a day-by-day basis, that are clearly correlates of abuse, and that are capable of being modified. Family interaction patterns, physical and verbal, meet these requirements. Family members interact daily and the quality of those interactions as they occur day by day, week by week, indeed year by year, may be far more significant for a child's and family's development than the drastic but seldom-occurring physical assault leading to severe injury.

The third problem with much of the intervention research on child abuse has centered around the failure to assess carefully the components of the various procedures used. This especially applies to large-scale demonstration studies. Indeed, the larger the scale, the more difficult this problem becomes. While the "shotgun" approach may be defensible at an early stage of research, we eventually must determine the necessary and sufficient procedures for effecting behavior change.

Component analyses not only require precise specification of procedures and behavioral events but, to be effective, they require carefully-designed longitudinal studies to assess the effectiveness of the procedures over time. Recent developments in sequential-longitudinal strategies (Nesselroade & Baltes, 1974) make this strategy even more possible. In any event, we would probably be much better off, over the long run, by designing a large number of fairly small studies than a small number of gigantic studies (Campbell & Stanley, 1963/1966; Scott & Wertheimer, 1962).

There are some promising efforts being made in these directions. For example, Patterson (1976) and his associates have been investigating the extent to which social learning principles can be utilized to teach and maintain noncoercive interactions among family members. Reid and Taplin (1977) have applied Patterson's model to the treatment of abusive families.

Their program has the following five components. One, all family members are systematically observed in the home at several stages, including a baseline period, at specific points during intervention, at the conclusion of treatment, and at several points during a 12-month follow-up period. Two, using a variety of educational materials, including programmed texts on child management, films, and videotapes, discussion between parents and therapists, and the modeling of treatment techniques, the parents are instructed in social learning theory and its application to child management. Three, the parents are taught to pinpoint, observe, and record specific behaviors of their children. Four, parents and children are involved in negotiation sessions that result in the development of family programs designed to alter the reinforcement and punishment contingencies operating in the family. Five, the parents are taught to use positive reinforcing consequences for appropriate child behavior and time-out procedures for inappropriate behavior.

Their preliminary outcome data "*suggest* that intensive training in parenting skills can be highly effective in reducing the level of parent-child conflict in abusive homes" (p. 19). They caution, however, that their therapeutic strategy must be expanded such that aggressive behaviors by parents are pinpointed for specific intervention. They also recommend that longitudinal follow-up studies of these families be implemented.

A similar program has been described by Christophersen, Kuehn, Grinstead, Barnard, Rainey, and Kuehn (1976). Using a two-therapist team approach in the home, the parents are trained to give frequent amounts of attention and love and praise throughout the day whenever the child is behaving appropriately. The parents are also taught to establish reasonable rules and to apply them consistently. They are encouraged to spend time teaching and having their children practice new appropriate behaviors. They are taught to avoid hugging, picking up, or physically loving the child when he misbehaves. While the parents are encouraged to be as pleasant and calm as possible, they are also instructed in the use of time-out for the child's inappropriate behaviors. Regrettably, this program has been in effect for only a few months, thus it is not possible as yet to report on its effectiveness. A third program based on similar procedures has been described by Jensen (1976). Unfortunately, it, too, is of such recent origin that no published accounts of its effectiveness are available.

A fourth program is under way by Burgess and his colleagues (Burgess, 1978a). This program has two basic phases. The first phase was designed to collect detailed observational data on the patterns of interaction in a number of abusive, neglectful, and matched control families. To date, over 100 families have been systematically observed. Some of the findings have been described earlier in this chapter (Anderson & Burgess, 1977; Burgess & Conger, 1977, 1977a; Edmunds & Burgess, 1977). This particular phase required 2 years of concerted effort.

The second phase was designed to develop, implement, and test an intervention program based on the observational findings collected during the first 2 years. This stage is still under way and consists of the following steps. First, detailed observations of family interaction are collected over several sessions to provide baseline data. Second, based on these data, as well as on conferences with the parents, a list of target behaviors is compiled. Third, an instructional program is instituted. The parents are taught basic social learning principles such as reinforcement, extinction, time-out, and overcorrection. They are also taught how to pinpoint behavior and observe its daily occurrence. And, finally, they are taught to apply contingency-management principles. Fourth, the effects of the intervention tactics are regularly assessed through reversal and multiple-baseline experimental designs. Fifth, further observational sessions are scheduled to assess the generalization of the intervention tactics to the general patterns of family interaction that were recorded during the initial baseline period.

7. Conclusions

We have seen in this chapter that domestic violence, in general, and the maltreatment of children, in particular, have a long and inglorious past. Aggressive behavior within families cannot be restricted to any one historical period or to any single culture or society. We have considered statistical evidence documenting that the family is apparently the most common locus of interpersonal violence. We have also seen that there are certain natural characteristics of family life that contribute to the incidence of violence. These characteristics include the conflicts of interest that are intrinsic to group living, and the intensity of emotional involvement that is found in kinship groups.

Finally, we have examined a variety of attempts to understand the causes of child abuse. This review has substantiated the idea that we have come a long way since Kempe and his colleagues first brought the problem of child abuse to international attention with their paper on "the battered-child syndrome" (Kempe *et al.*, 1962). But we have a long way to go.

It has been a central thesis of this chapter that an accurate understanding of the causes of child abuse and its successful treatment require an examination of abuse within its social context. Abuse does not occur in a vacuum. It happens within a social matrix and that matrix consists largely of the recurring transactions taking place between various members of the family. While it is certainly true that child abuse occurs within a larger historical and cultural context tolerant of aggressive behavior, these abusive behavior patterns are more immediately traceable to contingency histories located within the family itself. Given this, we need to place special emphasis on isolating the causes or determinants of coercive styles of family interaction. We need to learn more about how these behaviors are acquired in the first place, what their situational antecedents are, and the kinds of environmental consequences that sustain them. If we are to answer these questions effectively, it is imperative that we design studies that have experimental and longitudinal components. A concern for service delivery systems, preventive programs, even massive social change, independent of the search for causality, will be a futile endeavor, costly in human as well as economic terms.

8. References

Alexander, R. D. The search for an evolutionary philosophy of man. *Proceedings of the Royal Society of Victoria*, 1971, *84*, 99-120.

Anderson, E. A., & Burgess, R. L. *Interaction patterns between same-and-opposite gender parents and children in abusive and nonabusive families.* Paper presented at the annual meeting of the Association for the Advancement of Behavior Therapy, 1977.

Azrin, N. H., & Holz, W. C. Punishment. In W. K. Honig (Ed.), *Operant behavior: Areas of research and application.* New York: Appleton-Century-Crofts, 1966.

Bakan, D. *Slaughter of the innocents.* San Francisco: Jossey-Bass, 1971.

Bandura, A. *Aggression.* New York: Holt, Rinehart & Winston, 1973.

Barash, D. P. *Sociobiology and behavior.* New York: Elsevier, 1977.

Belsky, J. Three theoretical models of child abuse: A critical review. *Child Abuse and Neglect*, 1978, *2*, 37-49.

Bennie, E., & Sclar, A. The battered child syndrome. *American Journal of Psychiatry*, 1969, *125*, 975-979.

Bigelow, R. *The dawn warriors*. Boston: Little, Brown, 1969.

Blanc, A. C. *Some evidence for the ideologies of early man*. London: Methuen, 1962.

Blumberg, M. L. Psychopathology of the abusing parent. *American Journal of Psychotherapy*, 1974, *28*, 21-29.

Bohannan, P. Patterns of murder and suicide. In P. Bohannan (Ed.), *African Homicide and Suicide*. New York: Atheneum, 1960.

Boudouris, J. Homicide and the family. *Journal of Marriage and the Family*, 1971, *33*, 667-676.

Bronfenbrenner, U. Socialization and social class through time and space. In E. E. Maccoby, T. M. Newcomb, & E. L. Hartley (Eds.), *Readings in social psychology*. New York: Holt, 1958.

Brown, Jr., & Daniels, R. Some observations on abusive parents. *Child Welfare*, 1968, *47*, 89-94.

Burgess, R. L. *Project interact*. Final report to National Center on Child Abuse and Neglect, Department of Health, Education and Welfare, 1978a.

Burgess, R. L. Research: Too much or too little? *Proceedings of the Second National Conference on Child Abuse and Neglect*, 1978b.

Burgess, R. L., & Conger, R. D. Family interaction patterns related to child abuse and neglect: Some preliminary findings. *Child Abuse and Neglect: The International Journal*, 1977, *1*, 269-277.

Burgess, R. L., & Conger, R. D. Family interaction in abusive, neglectful and normal families. *Child Development*, 1978a, *49*.

Burgess, R. L., & Conger R. D. *Aggressive behavior*. *Paper presented at the annual meeting of the* Midwestern Association of Behavior Analysis, 1978b.

Burgess, R. L., & Huston, T. (Eds.). *Social exchange and developing relations*. New York: Academic Press, 1978.

Campbell, D. T., & Stanley, J. C. *Experimental and quasi-experimental designs for research*. Chicago: Rand McNally, 1966. (Originally published, 1963.)

Caputo, D., & Mandell, W. Consequences of low birth weight. *Developmental Psychology*, 1970, *3*, 363-383.

Christophersen, E. R., Kuehn, B. S., Grinstead, J. D., Barnard, J. D., Rainey, S. K., & Kuehn, F. E. A family training program for abuse and neglect families. *Journal of Pediatric Psychology*, 1976, *Spring*, 90-94.

Curtis, G. Violence breeds violence. *American Journal of Psychiatry*, 1963, *120*, 386-387.

Curtis, L. A. *Criminal Violence: National Patterns and Behavior*. Lexington, Mass.: Lexington Books, 1974.

Dart, R. A. The Makapansgat proto-human *Australopithecus promethus*. *American Journal of Physical Anthropology*, 1948, *6*, 259-281.

Edmunds, M., & Burgess, R. L. *Selectivity of child abuse: A comparison of interactions between abused children and other family members*. Paper presented at the annual meeting of the Association for the Advancement of Behavior Therapy, 1977.

Egeland, B., & Brunnquell, D. *An at-risk approach to the study of child abuse: Some preliminary findings*. Unpublished manuscript, University of Minnesota, 1977.

Elmer, E. *Children in jeopardy: A study of abused minors and their families*. Pittsburgh: University of Pittsburgh Press, 1967.

Elmer, E., & Gregg, G. S. Developmental characteristics of abused children. *Pediatrics*, 1967, *40*, 596-602.

Erlanger, H. S. Social class differences in parents' use of physical punishment. In S. K. Steinmetz & M. A Straus (Eds.), *Violence in the family*. New York: Harper & Row, 1974.

Fontana, V. J. Further reflections on maltreatment of children. *Pediatrics*, 1973, *51*, 780-782.

Freeman, D. Human aggression in anthropological perspective. In J. Carthy & F. J. Ebbing (Eds.), *The natural history of aggression*. London: Academic Press, 1964.

Galdston, R. Observations on children who have been physically abused and their parents. *American Journal of Psychiatry*, 1965, *122*, 440-443.

Garbarino, J. The human ecology of child maltreatment: A conceptual model for research. *Journal of Marriage and the Family*, 1977, *November*, 721-735.

Geis, G., & Monahan, J. The social ecology of violence. In T. Likona (Ed.), *Man and morality*. New York: Holt, Rinehart & Winston, 1975.

Gelles, R. J. Child abuse as psychopathology: A sociological critique and reformulation. *American Journal of Orthopsychiatry*, 1973, *43*, 611-621.

Gelles, R. J. *Methods for studying sensitive family topics*. Paper presented at the annual meeting of the National Council on Family Relations, 1976.

Gelles, R. J. *Violence towards children in the United States*. Paper presented at the annual meeting of the American Association for the Advancement of Science, 1977.

Gelles, R. J., & Straus, M. A. Determinants of violence in the family: Toward a theoretical integration. In W. R. Burr, R. Hill, F. I. Nye, & I. L. Reiss (Eds.), *Contemporary theories about the family*. New York: Free Press, 1977.

Gil, D. G. *Violence against children: Physical child abuse in the United States*. Cambridge, Mass.: Harvard University Press, 1970.

Gil, D. G. *A holistic perspective on child abuse and its prevention*. Paper presented at a conference on child abuse and neglect at the National Institute of Child Health and Human Development, Washington, D. C., 1974.

Green, A. A psychodynamic approach to the study and treatment of child abusing parents. *Journal of Child Psychiatry*, 1976, *15*, 414-429.

Helfer, R. E., & Kempe, C. H. (Eds.), *Child abuse and neglect: The family and the community*. Cambridge, Mass.: Ballinger, 1976.

Herrenkohl, R. C., Herrenkohl, E. C., Seech, M., & Egolf, B. An investigation of the effects of a multidimensional service program on recidivism/discontinuation of child abuse and neglect. Center for Social Research, Lehigh University, 1977.

Hrdy, S. B. Male-male competition and infanticide among the langurs (*Presbytis entellus*) of Abu Rajasthan. *Folia Primatologica*, 1974, *22*, 19-58.

Jensen, R.E. A behavior modification program to remediate child abuse. *Journal of Clinical Child Psychology*, 1976, *5*, 30-32.

Johnson, B., & Morse, H. A. Injured children and their parents. *Children*, 1968, *15*, 147-152.

Jones, R. R., Reid, J. B., & Patterson, G. R. Naturalistic observations in clinical assessment. In P. McReynolds (Ed.), *Advances in psychological assessment (Vol. 3)*. San Francisco: Jossey-Bass, 1975.

Kelley, C. M. *Uniform crime reports for the United States*. Washington, D. C.: U. S. Government Printing Office, 1973.

Kempe, C. H. A practical approach to the protection of the abused child and rehabilitation of the abusing parent. *Pediatrics*, 1973, *51*, 804-812.

Kempe, C. H. *Child Abuse and Neglect: The International Journal*, 1977, *1*.

Kempe, C. H., & Helfer, R. E. (Eds.). *Helping the battered child and his family*. Philadelphia: Lippincott, 1972.

Kempe, C. H., Silverman, F. N., Steele, B. B., Droegemueller, N., & Silver, H. K. The battered-child syndrome. *Journal of the American Medical Association*, 1962, *181*, 17-24.

Korbin, J. Anthropological contributions to the study of child abuse. *Child Abuse and Neglect: The International Journal*, 1977, *1*, 7-24.

Leifer, A. D., Leiderman, P. H., Barnett, C. R., & Williams, J. A. Effects of mother-infant separation on maternal attachment behavior. *Child Development*, 1972, *43*, 1203-1218.

Lenoski, E. F. *Translating injury data into preventive and health care services–physical child abuse.* Unpublished manuscript, University of Southern California School of Medicine, 1974.

Levy, R. I. On getting angry in the Society Islands. In W. Candell & T. Y. Lin (Eds.), *Mental health research in Asia and the Pacific.* Honolulu: East-West Center Press, 1969.

Light, R. J. Abused and neglected children in America: A study of alternative policies. *Harvard Educational Review,* 1973, *43,* 556-598.

Lystad, M. H. Violence at home: A review of the literature. *American Journal of Orthopsychiatry,* 1975, *45,* 328-345.

Martin, H. P., Beezley, P., Conway, E. F., & Kempe, C. H. The development of abused children. *Advances in Pediatrics,* 1974, *21,* 25-73.

Milow, I., & Lourie, R. The child's role in the battered child syndrome. *Society for Pediatric Research,* 1964, *65,* 1079-1081.

Morris, M. G., & Gould, R. W. Role reversal: A necessary concept in dealing with the "battered child syndrome." In *The neglected/battered child syndrome.* New York: Child Welfare League of America, 1963.

Nesselroade, J. R., & Baltes, P. B. Adolescent personality development and historical change: 1970-1972. In R. R. Sears (Ed.), *Monographs of the Society for Research in Child Development* (Vol. 39), 1974.

Parke, R., & Collmer, C. Child abuse: An interdisciplinary analysis. In M. Hetherington (Ed.), *Review of child development research* (Vol. 5). Chicago: University of Chicago Press, 1975.

Parke, R. D., Deur, J. L., & Saivin, M. The intermittent punishment effect in humans: Conditioning or adaptation. *Psychonomic Science,* 1970, *18,* 193-194.

Parnas, R. I. The judicial response to intra-family violence. *Minnesota Law Review,* 1967, *54,* 585-644.

Patterson, G. R. The aggressive child: Victim and architect of a coercive system. In L. A. Hamerlynck, L. C. Handy, & E. J. Mash (Eds.), *Behavior modification and families. I. Theory and research.* New York: Brunner/Mazel, 1976.

Patterson, G. R. A performance theory for coercive family interaction. In L. G. Cairns (Ed.), *Social interaction: Methods, analysis, and illustration.* Chicago: University of Chicago Press, 1977.

Patterson, G. R., Littman, R. A., & Bricker, W. Assertive behavior in children: A step toward a theory of aggression. *Monographs of the Society for Reseach in Child Development* (Vol. 32), 1967.

Pittman, D. J., & Handy, W. Patterns in criminal aggravated assault. *Journal of Criminal Law, Criminology and Police Science,* 1964, *55,* 462-470.

Reid, J. B., & Taplin, P. S. *A social interactional approach to the treatment of abusive children.* Unpublished manuscript, 1977.

Schaller, G. B. *The Serengeti lion: A study of predator-prey relations.* Chicago: University of Chicago Press, 1972.

Scott, W. A., & Wertheimer, M. *Introduction to psychological research.* New York: Wiley, 1962.

Seashore, M. J., Leifer, A. D., Barnett, C. R., & Leiderman, P. H. The effects of denial of early mother-infant interaction on maternal self-confidence. *Journal of Personality and Social Psychology,* 1973, *26,* 369-378.

Sidel, R. *Women and child care in China.* New York: Hill & Wang, 1972.

Spinetta, J. J., & Rigler, D. The child-abusing parent: A psychological review, *Psychological Bulletin,* 1972, *77,* 296-304.

Stark, R., & McEvoy III, J. Middle class violence. *Psychology Today,* 1970, *4,* 52-65.

Steele, B. F., & Pollock, C. B. A psychiatric study of parents who abuse infants and small children. In R. E. Helfer & C. H. Kempe (Eds.), *The battered child.* Chicago: University of Chicago Press, 1974. (Originally published, 1968.)

Steinmetz, S. K. Occupational environment and its relationship to physical punishment In S. K. Steinmetz & M. A. Straus (Eds.), *Violence in the family.* New York: Harper & Row, 1974.

Steinmetz, S. K., & Straus, M. A. (Eds.), *Violence in the family.* New York: Harper & Row, 1974.

Stevenson, H. W. Developmental psychology. In Sills D. (Ed.), *International encyclopedia of the social sciences.* New York: Macmillan, 1968.

Straus, M. A. Some social antecedents of physical punishment: A linkage theory interpretation. *Journal of Marriage and the Family,* 1971, *33,* 658-663.

Tinbergen, N. *The study of instinct.* London: Oxford University Press, 1951.

Wasserman, S. The abused parent of the abused child. *Children,* 1967, *14,* 175-179.

Young, L. *Wednesday's children: A study of child neglect and abuse.* New York: McGraw-Hill, 1964.

6 Clinical and Community Interventions with Children:

A Comparison of Treatment Strategies

Thomas Sajwaj,
M. Patrick McNees,
and John F. Schnelle

Applied child psychology has evolved to a state where a variety of specific therapeutic techniques are available for a long list of behavior disorders of children. The development of effective treatment techniques has brought great hope to the parents of children with behavior disorders and has given more confidence to therapists responsible for treating these children. Child therapists can now choose from an array of behavior procedures of demonstrated effectiveness. In many respects, then, clinical child psychology has taken a great step toward maturity.

This progress has, paradoxically, raised a new issue. It is one thing to have a set of procedures that will change children's behavior, but it is another issue for these procedures to be used appropriately, consistently, and reliably with the children in need. It is abundantly clear that successful treatment of behavior disorders will not flow simply from the existence of effective behavior change methods. There must, also, be strategies for using the methods, strategies that specify the place, the timing and manner of intervention, the identity and role of the implementers of the behavior-change techniques, and the goals and constraints of intervention, among other issues.

An example will illustrate the distinction between a behavior change technology and an intervention strategy. Differential positive reinforcement is a specific behavior change technique and refers to a procedure in which certain consequences follow a specified behavior. Desired behaviors are followed by a consequence that, ideally, will in-

Thomas Sajwaj, M. Patrick McNees, and John F. Schnelle • Luton Community Mental Health Center and Middle Tennessee State University, Murfreesboro, Tennessee.

crease the frequency of the desired behaviors. Undesired behaviors, incompatible with the desired ones, are ignored. The use of differential positive reinforcement has been repeatedly demonstrated to be successful in replacing inappropriate problematic behaviors with more socially acceptable ones in a wide range of children. The use of differential positive reinforcement to eliminate a problem behavior necessitates more than an awareness of its potential effectiveness of the specific nature of the consequences used. A strategy for using it must be devised so that intervention results in the most socially significant remediation of the problem behavior. A considerable number of concerns need to be addressed before, during, and after differential reinforcement for it to be used. These concerns include a specification of the practical limits and social impact of the child's behavior problems, the nature of the person who will actually administer the consequences to the child, the place and circumstances of administering the consequences, the exact nature of the consequences, the specific behaviors and their precipitating circumstances for which the consequences will be used, a system for monitoring and providing feedback for the person using the procedure, the practical and ethical limits of the use of the procedure, and so on. All of these specific concerns will have some bearing on the use and effectiveness of differential positive reinforcement. Yet it is clear that these concerns can be decided in different ways, yielding different patterns of intervention with the child. A highly trained professional could sit the child in an outpatient clinic office, diagnose the child as having a behavior disorder of childhood (e.g., unsocialized aggressive reaction, DSM II: 308.4), and then praise the child for socially appropriate statements and ignore aggressive statements. Alternatively, the professional might give the child's parents a copy of Gerald Patterson's book *Families: Application of Social Learning to Family Life*, (1975) instructing them to read Chapter One on social reinforcers, discuss it in the next week with them, and then have them try to use differential social reinforcement with their child. In still other cases, the professional might decide that the impact of the child's problem behavior is intolerable for the family and the community or that the parents or the professional cannot effectively use differential reinforcement. Accordingly, the child would be placed in a residential treatment program where the impact of the child's problem behavior is minimized and where highly trained staff can use differential reinforcement most effectively.

Each of these approaches defines a different intervention strategy. Each utilizes the technique of differential positive reinforcement, but the usage occurs in different circumstances, with differing impacts on the child, his/her family, and society. Obviously there are a variety of logically possible intervention strategies. Thus, perhaps one of the most important problems confronting clinical child psychology today is the issue of developing coherent and socially acceptable strategies for intervention where the available behavior change technology can be effectively used.

Intervention strategies, such as therapy in the therapist's office, have been developed to accommodate the dynamic psychotherapies. And, most service systems, as, for example, the typical community mental health center, have been designed to accommodate these intervention strategies. Forcing behavior technologies, however, into these dynamically derived intervention strategies has been only marginally successful, and one result has been explorations into other intervention strategies, better suited, one hopes, for behavioral technology. Most relevant to newer strategies has been the utilization of parents as the primary agent of intervention, a direction pioneered by Robert Wahler, Gerald Patterson, and others. Also, the explicitness of behavioral technology has suggested the possibility of an increased therapeutic efficiency of residential care. More recently, there has been a greater utilization of day-treatment programs where intervention via parents has not been feasible.

Fifteen years, more or less, have been spent exploring behaviorally oriented intervention strategies, and their advantages have been demonstrated. Their limitations, however, are also becoming apparent, and it is clear that these intervention strategies will not be sufficient to eliminate the bulk of behavior disorders in children. Other types of intervention strategies, probably at the broad community level, will be necessary to complement the existing strategies, if child behavior disorders are to be most effectively addressed.

It is appropriate to review the various intervention strategies. This chapter will begin with a review of the office therapy intervention mode as it developed from dynamic play therapy. The role of intervention via residential care will be noted. The changes in these two strategies as a result of the introduction of behavioral technology will be discussed, as well as the advantages and limitations of the behaviorally oriented strategies. Last, a community-based intervention strategy will be presented in the context of its successful utilization. The chapter will thus define five intervention strategies, cite their advantages and limitations, and illustrate their use. First, though, the criteria for evaluating the strategies will be presented.

1. Criteria for Evaluating Intervention Strategies

A thorough quantitative scheme for evaluating intervention strategies is beyond the scope of this chapter. Instead, 13 simple criteria will be used. Four criteria are related to those features of intervention strategies that bear on their potential effectiveness: (1) the proportion of time that the child is exposed to therapeutic intervention; (2) the utilization of the natural environment for behavior change procedures; (3) the dependency of intervention on parental or paraprofessional staff cooperation in executing therapy; and (4) the size of the potential population of children that the strategy will eventually impact.

A second set of four criteria involve the implementation or the mechanics of using the intervention strategy. They are (5) the number of service delivery systems—e.g., community mental health centers and private clinics, that can readily accommodate the intervention strategy; (6) the extent to which the intervention strategy can generate objective data for the assessment of the need and progress of therapy; (7) the extent to which the strategy depends on auxiliary systems to provide life necessities; and (8) the extent of the administrative structure and degree of professional coordination needed for intervention.

The final five criteria are cost-related. Of these, (9) financial expense is critical. Also included are (10) the staff-to-child ratio; (11) the extent to which paraprofessionally trained individuals can be utilized; (12) the degree to which the child is stigmatized as deviant; and (13) the degree of the restrictive impact of the intervention strategy on the child's life.

Table 1 summarizes the ratings of each criterion for five intervention strategies. A plus (+) is used to indicate that the authors consider a given criterion as an advantage for a specific intervention strategy. A minus (−) indicates a disadvantage or a liability. A plus/minus (+/−) indicates a mixture of advantages and disadvantages or an intermediate value between plus and minus. A double plus or minus is used to indicate a highly significant advantage or limitation.

2. Strategies Associated with Dynamic Therapies

Until the advent of behavioral techniques, the only available treatment technology for eliminating behavior disorders in children involved variations of dynamic psychotherapies. Predominant among these variations, especially for young children, was play therapy. It was introduced in the 1920s (Klein, 1932) and later popularized by Virginia Axline (1947). Although critics have noted the lack of compelling evidence of its effectiveness (Levitt, 1957, 1963), it must be stressed that play therapy was the only respectable treatment technology available for children until the early 1960s. Thus, an intervention strategy had to be evolved to accommodate and facilitate the implementation of play therapy. The term *office therapy* will be used to describe the model that evolved or, more accurately, was borrowed from adult psychotherapy.

TABLE 1

Advantages (+), Limitations (−), and Mixed Blessings (+/−) of 5 Intervention Strategies Relative to 13 Criteria of the Effectiveness, Mechanics, and Cost of Eliminating Behavior Problems[a]

	Office therapy	Office training of parents	Day treatment	Residential treatment	Community
Effectiveness					
1. Waking time in therapy	−	+	+/−	+	+
2. Utilization of natural environment	−	+	+/−	−	+
3. Dependency on parent/staff cooperation	+	−	+	+/−	−
4. Size of affected population	−	−	+	+	++
Mechanics					
5. Existing service systems	+	+	+/−	−	+/−
6. Ability to use objective indices for assessment	−	+/−	+	+	+/−
7. Dependence on systems providing life necessities	+	+	+/−	−	+
8. Administrative dependence and professional coordination	+	+	+/−	−	−
Cost					
9. Financial	+	+	−	−	+/−
10. Staff-child ratio	−	−	+	−	+
11. Use of paraprofessionals	−	+	+/−	+/−	+
12. Stigmatization of child	−	−	−	− −	+
13. Restriction of child's life	+	+	−	− −	+

[a] Two pluses (++) or two minuses (− −) are used to denote especially critical criteria in a given strategy.

2.1. Office Therapy

The issues related to the nature of the intervention strategy involving play therapy were straightforward. Therapy was conducted by a highly trained professional, usually a psychologist or a psychiatrist, in a setting conducive to the development and evolution of the relationship between the child and the therapist and to the expression and interpretation of the child's feelings. The natural environment with its competing demands and distractions was inappropriate. The child's parents would bring the child to the clinic, where the therapist and the child could interact—without the parents—in a setting designed to put the child at ease, usually a modestly furnished playroom. Thus, therapy occurred in a playroom of a clinic, an essentially artificial environment, conducted by an individual unlike other individuals in the child's life.

Leaving aside the issues of the effectiveness of play therapy, the office therapy mode of intervention does have significant advantages. One, since the child-therapist relationship is critical, the role of the parent is clearly secondary. Parents are often given a supportive role, but the only essential demand on the parent is to get the child reliably to the therapist's office. Therefore, the therapy does not depend heavily on the extent of the parents' cooperation. Two, many existing medical and mental health facilities can readily accommodate play therapy, since it requires only a room and a few toys. Three, again since the therapy revolves about the child's relationship with a single therapist, there is little need for expensive administrative or support systems providing life necessities or difficult interdisciplinary coordination. Four, the financial expense of therapy is essentially limited to the salary of the therapist. If therapy is conducted by a doctoral-level individual over many sessions, cost can be extreme. If master's-degree-level therapists, however, are utilized for a reasonable number of sessions, cost will be low to moderate. Last, since therapy occurs for only a few hours per week, usually 1 hour, the restriction of the child's life activities is minimal. This advantage is of considerable significance, given current trends toward the utilization of the least restrictive treatment alternatives.

Offsetting these advantages are serious limitations. One, since therapy occurs typically for 1 hour per week, only about 1% of the child's weekly waking time is utilized. Progress is then necessarily slow, consuming many weeks. Even if the child is seen daily for a 1-hour session, less than 10% of the child's waking time is utilized. Two, since therapy is conducted in the therapist's office, generalization of behavior changes to the natural environment is poor. Three, given the one-to-one nature of therapy, the potential number of children treated over a period of time will be limited. Four, since the child is observed only in the therapist's office, the extent of his/her behavioral changes in the more typical and frequent living situations is available to the therapist only via the reports of other adults. Five, the therapy is inefficient use of the therapist's time, since a one-to-one therapist-child ratio is typical. Six, the efficiency of the therapist's time is further reduced, since paraprofessional individuals (i.e., those trained at less than the master's degree level) can only infrequently be utilized. Seven and last, since the child is typically taken to an outpatient clinic, he/she is stigmatized to some significant degrees as deviant.

It is obvious that the office therapy mode of intervention is less than ideal. Its significant advantages are offset by its serious liabilities. If the dubious effectiveness of play therapy is also considered, the reasons for the rapidly waning popularity of play therapy are clear.

This discussion is relevant for behavior therapy for two reasons: Intervention via office therapy was the strategy utilized in some pioneering behavior therapy efforts. And, this strategy still has some utility for the child behavior therapist.

2.2. Residential Care

Within the context of dynamic play therapies, residential care is not a primary intervention. Since the essential focus of therapy is the child-therapist relationship, residential care is utilized to remove the child from environmental stresses that would interfere with the therapeutic relationship and/or to provide the necessities of life where the child's difficulties have exceeded the parents' ability to provide for them. With the child's basic needs assured, play therapy or related forms of group or individual psychotherapy would be employed using the office therapy mode of intervention. Thus, residential care was not an intervention strategy itself but only was undertaken to facilitate or make possible the office therapy intervention.

3. Strategies Associated with Behavior Therapies

When behavior therapy burst upon the scene in the early 1960s, it was obvious that a revolution of considerable magnitude was under way with numerous implications and consequences for clinical child psychology. For the first time, a variety of techniques of significant effectiveness were unequivocally demonstrated. Initially, though, some of these early demonstrations were executed using the office therapy mode of intervention borrowed from dynamic therapies. An example is an early case presented by Gerald Patterson (1965). The child presented school-phobic behavior. Initially, behavioral procedures were mainly applied to the child by highly trained individuals in one-to-one situations in the clinic. After substantial progress was made, the locus of treatment was slowly shifted to school. Even there, a clinic therapist still implemented the behavior change procedures. Parents were involved to supplement and support therapeutic progress.

Since effective behavioral techniques were so explicit, it was obvious that paraprofessional-level individuals could be trained to utilize the technology to an effectiveness equal to that of doctoral-level staff (e.g., Wolf, Risley, & Mees, 1964). Not only could the expense of highly trained staff be substantially reduced but also it became possible to have the child in therapy for 100% of every day, if his/her parents or caregivers could be trained to use behavioral techniques appropriately. Thus, a fantastically improved cost-effectiveness ratio became potentially obtainable if behavioral procedures replaced the dynamic treatment technology. Obtaining the maximum potential of behavioral procedures would, however, require intervention strategies beyond office therapy.

The development of behaviorally oriented intervention strategies took as its starting point the identification of a specific child as needing specialized assistance. Typically, parents, teachers, or some other societal figure (e.g., police) would recognize difficulties in a given child and refer that child for professional assistance. Hence, behavior therapy is modeled on its dynamic predecessors in initially accepting the starting point of a specific child. The nature of the starting point of intervention is crucial, since it dictates the general nature of the subsequent intervention strategies. Another starting point is possible; it will be discussed later in this chapter.

Four general modes of intervention have evolved to accommodate behavioral technology, given the identification of a specific child in need. The differences involved in these strategies are primarily based on the nature of the individual who will actually implement therapy for the child. It should be noted that therapy with a given child may utilize only one of these intervention strategies. In practice, though, therapists will utilize several strategies in many cases, depending on the unique behaviors of the child, the parents' capabilities, and the resources available to the therapist.

3.1. Office Training of Parents

Parents are the most obvious candidates for training as the primary therapist. They are usually with their child nearly 100% of the time; they are ideally the individuals most committed to his/her welfare; and they have the most detailed awareness of the specific expressions of the child's difficulties. Behavior therapists, accordingly, readily substituted parents for children in their offices. The child's behaviors are discussed there, and the behavior therapist will suggest general principles to change these behaviors, tailoring specific procedures for specific behaviors. Parents are often asked to record occurrences of the behaviors, with return visits to the therapist's office to assess progress (or nonprogress) and to revise the specific procedures. Thus, this intervention strategy is similar to the office therapy mode, except that the therapist's office is used to train the parents so that they can conduct the actual therapy of the children in their own home. A minor variation of this intervention strategy involves training the parents in their home. Here, the therapist travels to the home of the parents, instead of the parents coming to the therapist's office. The therapist is allowed the opportunity to observe the child in his/her natural environment, and the parent-training tends to be more realistic. On the negative side, the therapist's time per case is increased due to the addition of the travel time.

A major variation of office training of parents has been developed to increase the reality of office training without the expense and time of traveling to the parents' home. This variant consists of training parents in a specially contrived situation in the therapist's clinic or office. The contrived situation is designed to approximate circumstances found in the home. A highly successful example of this approach is the Regional Intervention Project for Preschoolers and Parents in Nashville, Tennessee (Eller, Jordan, Parish, & Elder, in press).

The utilization of teachers as therapists is considered as part of this intervention strategy, since they are parent surrogates for a portion of the day. Further, the approach used by the behavior therapist, with similar advantages and disadvantages, is virtually identical to that taken for parents.

Office training of parents and its variants have several significant positive features as an intervention strategy. Like office therapy intervention, parent training can be incorporated readily into existing systems, such as community mental health centers, and is minimally dependent on support and administrative systems. Financial cost and the restriction of the child's life are relatively minimal. Unlike office therapy, however, office parent training and its variants potentially have the child in therapy for 100% of his/her waking day in the naturally occurring environment. Since the parents are the primary therapists, the involvement of the doctoral-level behavior therapists is minimal and in many cases can be eliminated if subdoctoral individuals or other parents are used as the trainers. Last, the possibility of using objective data is greater than in office therapy, since the parents are directly involved in the therapeutic process. Actually obtaining reliable data from parents can, of course, be difficult.

There are significant limitations of this intervention strategy. Most serious is the virtually complete dependence of the success of the strategy on the cooperation of the parents. Typically, many demands are made on them in terms of time, alterations of their own habits and lifestyle, and, occasionally, modification of the home itself. Without their full and complete cooperation, this intervention strategy is useless. Unfortunately for many of the children in greatest need (e.g., abused children), the parents either cannot or will not provide the necessary degree of cooperation. Other disadvantages include a relatively small number of behavior-disordered children actually treated compared to the total number needing services, a typically one-to-one therapist-parent ratio, and some stigmatization of the child following from bringing him/her to a treatment program.

Compared to office therapy, office training of parents is a more efficient and realistic intervention strategy. After all, the child's problems usually exist in the home. It only makes good sense to utilize the parents as therapists in the home where the child's problems occur. Unfortunately, the strategy succeeds or fails according to the extent of the parents' willingness and ability to cooperate in the training program.

3.2. Day Treatment

For children whose behavior problems are severe to the point of exclusion from normal school and day-care situations or where parental cooperation is chronically lacking, specialized day-treatment programs have been developed. These specialized programs feature a carefully designed quasi-natural environment, routine and efficient usage of behavioral procedures, and specially trained "teaching" staff. The settings of the program approximate many of the normal settings where the children's social and conduct difficulties occur. More accurate assessment is possible, as is a quick tailoring of behavioral techniques to the individual child. A reliance on parental data systems and retrospective reports is avoided. Risley, Sajwaj, Doke, and Agras (1975) present an example of such a specialized program for use in a psychiatric setting and discuss its advantages.

As an intervention strategy, day treatment has the major advantage of being considerably less dependent on parental cooperation than the office training of parents intervention. Parents need only to get the child to the program. Since a day-treatment program will typically have a minimum of 6 to a maximum of 15 children involved at any one time, a substantial number of children will be affected over a period of time, and the staff-child ratio will be efficient. Accurate assessment is also a major strength, since the child will be observed by trained staff in situations approximating real-life ones.

Some of these advantages also imply limitations. Since the parents are replaced as therapists by a professionally trained staff, the potential time in therapy is reduced to 5-35% of the child's waking day, depending on the hours of the program. Also, therapy does not occur in the natural environment, even though the day-treatment program will have some similarities to the natural environment. Further, although paraprofessional staff are used, they are often trained and closely supervised by doctoral-level staff.

Clear disadvantages of the day-treatment intervention strategy include the existence of few such programs nationally, the high cost of operation, and the significant stigmatization of the child by participation in the program. Further, the child spends a considerable portion of his/her waking time in the program, thus restricting his/her life experiences significantly. Last, specialized day-treatment programs require support systems (such as food, safety, and perhaps transportation), administrative support, and coordination of its staff. Although these requirements are substantial, they are not as burdensome as in residential intervention.

In sum, the day-treatment intervention has significantly more disadvantages and fewer advantages than the office training of parents approach. It is, though, probably the only viable intervention if parental cooperation is poor or nonexistent.

3.3. Residential Treatment

The development of explicit behavioral techniques allowed residential programs to move from the role of a care provider to a therapeutic one. It was obvious early that all staff, not only doctoral-trained individuals, could have a therapeutic role to play in the treatment of the behavior-disordered child. In fact, aide-level staff became paramount, since the child spends most of his/her time with them. Ideally, children could be exposed to therapeutic techniques for 100% of the day by well-trained and continuously supervised staff. Thus, residential treatment became a viable intervention strategy for the behavior therapist.

Besides having the child potentially in therapy for 100% of the time, two other major advantages exist: One is that a most accurate assessment of the child's behavior is possible in this strategy. In no other strategy can the child's behavior before, during, and after treatment be observed as objectively by trained staff. Second, since residential programs tend to be short-term in nature and serve a fair number of children, a sizable number of children will be served by the program over a period of time. A mixed blessing is that parental cooperation is not necessary for successful therapy. However, the cooperation of aide staff is needed, a cooperation not always obtained. Similarly, most residential staff will be paraprofessionals. Again, however, the direction and supervision of the staff usually remains in professional hands.

Unfortunately, many serious disadvantages hamper the residential intervention approach. One, treatment occurs in a near-artificial environment. Generalization to the child's home or school is doubtful. Two, although many residential programs exist for children, access to them is becoming increasingly restricted because of court decisions. Three, because the child lives full-time in the program, the support systems involving the necessities of life must be functioning continually. Four, administrative overhead is great, and the coordination of the residential program's disparate professional and nonprofessional staff is a chronic headache. Five, financial cost is excessive to the point of being prohibitive. Six, the number of staff in accredited programs often exceeds the number of children in residence at any given time. Seven, residential placement stigmatizes the child more severely than any other intervention strategy, and eight, it is the most restrictive treatment alternative.

The disadvantages plaguing the residential treatment strategy outweigh the advantages. It appears that residential treatment intervention will be used only for those children whose difficulties are extreme.

3.4. Office Therapy

It may appear strange to list office therapy as an intervention strategy for use with behavioral techniques. Certainly, the many disadvantages noted for it in the context of play therapy hold for its use by behavior therapists. The advantages of the intervention can, however, be put to good use occasionally by the child behavior therapist. The cast study previously cited by Patterson (1965) and those presented by Lazarus and Abramovitz (1962) are examples of the successful use of this strategy.

A simple case study illustrates the strategy. A 7-year-old child was referred to the first author with the complaint of soiling. The mother's description of the soiling suggested encopresis—i.e., the boy withheld bowel movements to the extent that a small amount of fecal material would be forced out. Since the boy appeared and was reported to be normal in all other respects, a composite of suggestion and positive reinforcement was initiated by the therapist in his office. The mother was not initially used as the therapist, because the therapist felt that his suggestion and praise would be more effective. The parents' interactions with the boy over soiling and toileting were primarily negative. On the first session, the boy was told that he was to drink a glass of orange juice at breakfast, as an after-school snack, and at supper. Since the juice would facilitate a bowel movement, he was to sit on the commode for 15 minutes after these times. He was also told to return in 3 days and tell the therapist the number of bowel movements he managed in the commode. For each one, he would receive $.50 from the therapist. The mother was asked to provide the juice, prompt commode sitting, and check the occurrence of commode bowel movements.

At the second appointment, he reported four successful bowel movements (the largest number in a long time) and received $2.00 and a great deal of praise from the therapist. A $.25 penalty for each soiling episode was added to the program. A third appointment in 1 week found an average of one commode bowel movement per day and only one soiling episode. Money and praise were again provided, and the program was successfully turned over to the mother.

This case and those of Patterson (1965) and Lazarus and Abramovitz (1962) suggest that an office therapy intervention using behavior techniques may be a viable strategy in cases of discrete, uncomplicated, and easily manipulable behaviors for which parental involvement may be counterproductive or unavailable.

4. Evaluation of Strategies for Individual Children

Considering the three intervention strategies uniquely oriented to behavioral technology (middle portion of Table 1), the evaluative criteria shared similarly by each strategy are few. Waking time in therapy is generally high, as is the ability to obtain objective assessment data and effectively use paraprofessional individuals. The only negative criterion in common is the stigmatization of the child as deviant.

The other nine criteria vary sharply across the three strategies. The utilization of behavioral technology does not affect the strategies in the same ways. For example, behavior technology allows the child to be treated by the child's parents with virtually no restriction of his/her life. Yet it does not relieve the severe restrictiveness of residential intervention. Similarly, day-treatment intervention can be used for a given child, even though parent training is impossible or impractical, regardless of the extent that behavioral techniques are used.

On the positive side, the disparate advantages and limitations of these three intervention strategies allow the child behavior therapist some latitude in choosing an intervention approach. In contrast, the play therapist is virtually limited to office therapy. On the negative side, the disparate advantages and limitations may suggest that none of the three behaviorally oriented intervention strategies utilize behavioral technology to its maximum potential.

5. Community Intervention Strategies

The starting point for the aforementioned interventions for the problems of children and youth is an identified "problem child." Indeed, it was the identification and referral of these individuals almost two decades ago that set the occasion for building the foundations of child behavior therapy. Consider part of the original working title that the present authors were assigned by the editors of this book: ". . . problems of children and youth." The terms *problems* and *children and youth* exemplify what our work is all about: an identifiable child(ren) with an identifiable "problems"(s).

Using the same set of terms, we can also characterize another starting point for intervention. Rather than directly treating *children* who have identifiable *problems*, the separation of (1) problems from (2) specific children suggests a different point of intervention: the *problem* itself. Community intervention could, tentatively, be defined as the integration of behavioral methodology and technology into existing community organizations and institutions, with relatively minor modifications so that a specific problematic behavior can be affected without the identification of specific individuals. This distinction between specific problem behavior and specific children is necessary because there are many problems of childhood that will not be substantially affected by working with the individual as the starting point for intervention. One primary reason for this limitation is the existence of wide-scale problems where the detection of deviant individuals is currently impractical and/or unlikely, resulting in an undermining of interventions using psychodynamic or behavior-therapeutic approaches.

If an example is considered, perhaps the difference in these two starting points will become more apparent. Stealing is a problem that has been dealt with by behavior therapists. Institutionalized retardates who were identified as having stolen articles of other retardates have been successfully treated by using overcorrection (Azrin & Wesolowski, 1974). Thus, by targeting *individuals* for treatment, the problem was reduced.

However, applying individualized overcorrection or any other therapeutic procedure on a wide-scale societal basis is currently unrealistic since most people who steal are, in fact, not detected. The problem is simply that an individual cannot be treated until the individual is identified. Thus, the individual is considered the starting point for intervention.

Community intervention has been used to describe just about anything, including the intervention strategies previously mentioned in this chapter. In a broad sense, almost all child therapy occurs in the community: Institutes are often in communities; community mental health centers are community agencies; schools are community educational resources; and families are the basic living units of any community. However, we are defining community interventions as those interventions that, in some way, go beyond institution wards, classrooms, mental health center offices, and to a lesser extent, the home. We are also considering community interventions as those that address problems for which individualized or traditional group treatment is impractical or impossible.

5.1. Interventions to Reduce Theft

A community-wide intervention strategy can be illustrated by the problem of theft. Stealing, a specific problem area involving many children, was utilized as the starting point for intervention. McNees, Egli, Marshall, Schnelle, and Risley (1976) reduced theft in a "teen clothing department" by about 90%. No individuals were identified as shoplifters. Instead, the authors identified merchandise that was frequently stolen by utilizing a daily sample of merchandise and controlling internal movement of merchandise. Hence, merchandise that could not be accounted for was considered, by exclusion, stolen. After determining base rates of stolen merchandise for frequently stolen items by utilizing the same sampling system and increasing the sample size, the types of merchandise that were frequently stolen were sequentially identified by placing large stars over the target merchandise. Signs placed in the entrances to the department notified shoppers that the merchandise designated by stars was frequently stolen merchandise. Thus, because direct observation of shoplifters was found to be unreliable and extremely costly, the authors developed an alternative assessment technology, one focusing on the problem. Additionally, since response-contingent procedures could not be utilized, another type of technique, the use of signs, to publicly identify frequently stolen merchandise was developed.

In a more recent theft-prevention effort directed at younger children, stealing popular child merchandise in a convenience food market was substantially reduced with the utilization of a special program (McNees, Schnelle, & Kennon, unpublished). Children who frequented the market were asked by the cashier if they had remembered to pay for everything. Those children who indicated that all merchandise had been paid for and those children who "remembered" and paid for merchandise that they had forgotten were given a shark's tooth. No effort was made to check the accuracy of the children's report. When a child had collected five shark's teeth, he/she could redeem them at the market for a prize. A large poster was secured above the check-out counter that represented the theft rate of popular child merchandise. A 20% reduction in theft was set and depicted on the poster as a criterion. If a child redeemed his/her tokens on a day in which theft had been reduced to the criterion level, the child was given a special small prize. When the 20% reduction criterion was met, the criterion was readjusted to reflect an additional 20% reduction.

In both examples, behavioral methodology was utilized extensively in developing a youth shoplifting prevention program. However, strategically, the programs differed substantially from typical therapeutic efforts. Not a single child had to be identified to reduce youthful stealing in either the department store or the convenience market. Whether such programs are educational or therapeutic for individual children is a question that could be addressed as more such examples are developed. To dwell on this latter point at present would be reminiscent of the early criticisms of behavior therapy as being a simplistic treatment of symptoms with no thought or attention given to the individual's underlying psychic pathology. Regardless of these interpretations, the major point is that a problem behavior of children and youth was substantially reduced, even though no individual child was identified as "troubled," disturbed, behavior-disordered, or delinquent.

5.2. Interventions to Reduce Litter

Another example of a community intervention with the exclusion of specific child identification is provided by Schnelle, McNees, and Gendrich (in press). High levels of litter plagued three areas of a city. Baseline litter levels were established for the three areas by counting litter pieces in a manner similar to that of other investigators (Chapman & Risley, 1974). Subsequently, an article with pictures was placed in the local newspaper describing the litter problem in one of the three target areas. On days following the article, a simple graph and interpretation was placed in the newspaper depicting and describing both baseline and current litter levels. The second and the third areas were identified sequentially in a similar fashion. Litter across the three areas was substantially reduced when each was targeted.

In a more comprehensive community litter-control program, McNees, Schnelle, Gendrich, Hannah, and Thomas (unpublished) reduced litter by over 33% across an entire city of 30,000 people. The program, sponsored by a local McDonald's restaurant, included the random placement of adhesive code stickers on pieces of litter throughout the city. A group of children comprised of one representative from each of the city schools formed a "litter patrol." The function of the patrol was to give a litter merit (adhesive sticker similar to those placed on litter) to any child found picking up litter. Local radio stations, newspaper, and businesses advertised the program. McDonald's provided schools with descriptions of the program for each student and their parents. While each child who participated in the program was given small prizes by McDonald's, children who had litter merits (adhesive stickers) were given special prizes through a special drawing held at McDonald's on Saturdays.

In both of these litter programs, individual children were not selected for special training in environmental preservation. Any child in the city was a potential participant, and no culprits were identified.

6. Community Intervention versus Individual Child Intervention Strategies

From the two previous examples, it is clear the problems, as well as individuals, can provide starting points for intervention. Other differences arise when community intervention is contrasted with office, parent, day-treatment, and residential intervention strategies.

When compared with other treatment strategies, community intervention gains its greatest strength from the size of the population that can be potentially affected by effective procedures. Since the procedures are in effect on a community-wide basis, individuals can be in almost constant contact with the behavior-change procedures. Additionally, community intervention typically maximizes the utilization of the natural environment. In terms of effectiveness, perhaps the greatest limitation of community interventions lies in the high level of dependency on other community adults. Since the success of such interventions is typically dependent on cooperation of official community agents (e.g., storekeepers, parents, local officials), noncooperation can be directly analogued to noneffectiveness.

While there is dependence on other community individuals, there is virtually no dependence on life-necessity systems since there are few interruptions in children's normal daily routines, and there is no obligatory participation. Less positive circumstances, however, exist for the mechanics of service delivery in at least three other areas. First, service systems that would be the official service delivery mechanisms for community interventions do not currently exist on a wide-scale basis. Second, objective indices for assessment are only sporadically available. Perhaps the most criticial variable when considering the limitations of service delivery is that of professional administrative dependency. Since few models exist for solving community-wide problem behaviors, high levels of professional coordination are essential.

In terms of the cost of community interventions, four of the five categorial considerations appear to be positive. Because problem behaviors are the intervention focus rather than a child with a problem, stigmatization and restrictions of children's lives are minimized. Also, the utilization of paraprofessionals has greater potential than any other therapeutic strategy. Thus the professional-child ratio is extremely favorable. The greatest variability in cost considerations is actual dollars spent. Programs can range from tremendously costly to almost no cost at all, other than professional coordination.

In summary, while many of the considerations in utilizing community strategies as therapeutic interventions indicate specific strengths and weaknesses, two considerations are particularly noteworthy. Community interventions are often heavily reliant on professional coordination and orchestration. However, if this condition is met, the number of people's lives that can be positively affected is tremendous.

7. Summary and Conclusions

This chapter has identified five intervention strategies for utilizing behavioral techniques in coping with the behavior problems of children and youth. Intervention strategies were distinguished from behavioral procedures *per se* and were defined as distinctive patterns of circumstances surrounding the use of behavioral techniques. Circumstances included the location, timing, and agent(s) of intervention and the goals, manner of execution, and limits of the use of the behavioral procedures, among other issues. The five intervention strategies were compared and discussed in terms of 13 simple criteria related to the three broad categories of effectiveness, mechanics, and cost of intervention.

A critical determinant in the development of intervention strategies was noted to be the starting point of intervention. Behavior therapy, like its dynamic predecessors, has most commonly utilized the identification of specific children and youth as behavior-disordered. Four intervention strategies have evolved to accommodate the use of behavioral techniques, given the starting point of individually identified problem children. These strategies were (1) therapy conducted by the professional in his/her office or clinic; (2) utilization of the child's caregivers, usually the parents, as the primary therapist; (3) treatment via professional and/or paraprofessional staff in day programs that approximate portions of the child's natural environment to some extent; and (4) treatment in residential facilities. Although each of these four intervention strategies was found to have unique and important advantages, the extent of their disadvantages suggested that they have reached their limits in the efficient use of behavioral procedures.

A second starting point for intervention was suggested, that being problem behavior itself. Intervention starting with a specific problem behavior was seen to involve the community at large and was defined as the insertion of behavioral methodology and techniques into existing community organizations and institutions so that specific problem behaviors are affected without the identification of individual children. This community intervention was illustrated in the context of shoplifting and littering. Although such a community intervention strategy had liabilities, it appeared to promise an efficiency far beyond strategies that start with individual problem children.

8. References

Axline, V. *Play therapy*. Boston: Houghton Mifflin, 1947.

Azrin, N. H., & Wesolowski, M. D. Theft reversal: An overcorrection procedure for eliminating stealing by retarded person. *Journal of Applied Behavior Analysis*, 1974, 7, 577-582.

Chapman, C., & Risley, T. R. Anti-litter procedures in an urban high-density area. *Journal of Applied Behavior Analysis*, 1974, 1, 377-383.

Eller, P., Jordan, H., Parish, A., & Elder, P. Professional qualification: Mother. In R. York & E. Edgar (Eds.), *Teaching the severely handicapped*, (Vol. 4). Seattle: American Association for the Education of the Severely/Profoundly Handicapped, in press.

Klein, M. *The psycho-analysis of children*. London: Hogarth Press, 1932.

Lazarus, A. A., & Abramovitz, A. The use of "emotive imagery" in the treatment of children's phobias. *Journal of Mental Science*, 1962, 108, 191-195.

Levitt, E. E. The results of psychotherapy with children: An evaluation. *Journal of Counsulting Psychology*, 1957, 21, 189-196.

Levitt, E. E. Psychotherapy with children: A further evaluation. *Behaviour Research and Therapy*, 1963, 1, 45-51.

McNees, P., Egli, D., Marshall, R., Schnelle, J., & Risley, T. R. Shoplifting prevention: Providing information through signs. *Journal of Applied Behavior Analysis*, 1976, 9, 399-406.

McNees, P., Schnelle, J., & Kennon, M. *A program for reducing youth shoplifting*. Unpublished manuscript.

McNees, P., Schnelle, J., Gendrich, J., Hannah, J., & Thomas, M. *McDonald's litter hunt: A community litter control system for youth*. Unpublished manuscript.

Patterson, G. R. A learning theory approach to the treatment of the school phobic child. In L. P. Ullmann & L. Krasner (Eds.), *Case studies in behavior modification*. New York: Holt, Rinehart & Winston, 1965, Pp. 279-285.

Patterson, G. R. *Families: Applications of social learning to family life*. Champaign, Ill.: Research Press, 1975.

Risley, T., Sajwaj, T., Doke, L., & Agras, S. Specialized daycare as a psychiatric outpatient service. In E. Ramp & G. Semb (Eds.), *Behavior analysis: Areas of research and application*, Englewood Cliffs, N.J.: Prentice-Hall, 1975, pp. 97-123.

Schnelle, J., McNees, P., & Gendrich, J. Producing community behavior change through the mass media. *Environment and Behavior*, in press.

Wolf, M., Risley, T., & Mees, H. Application of operant conditioning procedures to the behaviour problems of an autistic child. *Behaviour Research and Therapy*, 1964, 1, 305-312.

7 Elective Mutism in Children*

Thomas R. Kratochwill, Gene H. Brody, and Wayne C. Piersel

Over the past 100 years mental health professionals have been involved in treatment and research on a childhood behavior problem that has come to be labeled "elective mutism." Although Tramer (1934) is commonly attributed with launching this descriptive label in the clinical treatment literature, it was the German physician Kussmaul who in 1877 described "voluntary mutism" (cf. Von Misch, 1952). Subsequently, a number of other terms have been introduced to describe this behavioral pattern, such as *speech inhibition* (Truper, 1897), *speech shyness* (Nadoleczng, 1926; Rothe, 1928; Spieler, 1941), *speech phobia* (Mora, DeVault, & Schopler, 1962), *thymogenic mutism* (Waterink & Vedder, 1936), *functional mutism* (Amman, 1958), *selective mutism* (Kass, Gillman, Mattis, Klugman, & Jacobson, 1967), *reluctant speech* (Williamson, Sewell, Sanders, Haney, & White, 1977), and *speech avoidance* (Lerea & Ward, 1965).[1] Following Tramer's (1934) portrayal, these children are typically described as exhibiting abnormally silent behavior outside all but a small group of intimate relatives and certain peers.

A considerable body of literature has now accumulated which reflects the concern of educators, psychologists, physicians, speech therapists, and other mental health professionals over management and treatment of elective mutism. However, aside from the brief reviews provided in various research- and treatment-oriented articles, there is no comprehensive review and methodological critique of research on

* Portions of this chapter were presented at the annual meeting of the American Educational Research Association, New York, April 1977.

[1] The study of elective mutism is replete with definitional problems, but unfortunately no writers have adequately dealt with the issue. An attempt to sort out issues involved in this area are provided in this chapter.

Thomas R. Kratochwill • Department of Educational Psychology, The University of Arizona, Tucson, Arizona. Gene H. Brody • Department of Child and Family Development, The University of Georgia, Athens, Georgia. Wayne C. Piersel • Department of Educational Psychology, The University of Arizona, Tucson, Arizona.

this behavior pattern. Only two brief reviews of select portions of this relatively large literature exist (cf. Friedman & Karagan, 1973; Yates, 1970). After reviewing several reports, Yates (1970) concluded that these children are highly resistant to treatment. In a somewhat more extensive discussion, Friedman and Karagan (1973) presented characteristics of mute children from their experience with 13 cases seen in the psychological diagnostic clinic at the University of Iowa, and offered seven non-empirical suggestions for management of these children.

This chapter reviews the published literature from 1877 to the present, with our focus being a careful examination of the various therapeutic methods and research procedures used in the treatment of elective mutism. The published literature generally includes two theoretical approaches to explanation and treatment: namely, an intrapsychic orientation, which explains childhood mutism based on internal dynamics, and a behavioral psychology orientation, which advances a learning-theory explanation. Since each of the orientations has had an impact on treatment approaches across a diverse number of professional fields (e.g., psychology, psychiatry, speech), the review is organized according to an intrapsychic (or psychodynamic) and behavioral orientation. Several other reports from different orientations that employed relatively unique treatment procedures are discussed separately. Thereafter, a methodological evaluation and critique is provided of the published English literature.[2]

1. Elective Mutism: A Review

1.1. Intrapsychic Perspectives

This section reviews research and treatment strategies affiliated with an intrapsychic or psychodynamic approach. In this context, writers have viewed personality as an assortment of psychic forces inside the child, including drives, impulses, needs, motives, and personality traits. Thus, abnormal behavior reflects a dysfunction or "disease" process in personality which eventuates in the development of maladaptive traits (see Bandura, 1969, 1977; Kazdin, 1975; Ullman & Krasner, 1965).

1.1.1. Psychodynamic Case Studies

All research and treatment programs for the elective mute child established from the intrapsychic orientation have been in the form of descriptive and/or treatment case studies. Some authors have simply described characteristics of the child referred for mute behavior, while

---

[2] The research and treatment literature on elective mutism includes numerous reports in foreign journals, particularly in the German literature. Although many of these reports are discussed here, in many cases they were unavailable for translation.

other authors have typically reported a combination of descriptive information and planned intervention procedures.

The psychodynamic literature on elective mutism included writings from Germany, Switzerland, Great Britain, and the United States. The earliest and most extensive number of clinical reports appeared in the German literature (Amman, 1958; Arnold & Luchsinger, 1949; Bally, 1936; Bleckmann, 1953; Ehrsam & Heese, 1954; Furster, 1956; Geiger-Martz, 1951; Gutzman, 1893, 1912; Heuyer & Morgenstern, 1932; Heinze, 1932; Kistler, 1927; Kummer, 1953; Kussmaul, 1885; Lesch, 1934; Liebmann, 1898; Mitscherlich, 1952; Nadoleczng, 1926; Pangalila-Ratulangie, 1959; Rothe, 1928; Schepank, 1960; Spieler, 1941, 1944; Stern, 1910; Tramer, 1934, 1949; Tramer & Geiger-Marde, 1952; Treidel, 1894; Truper, 1926; Wallis, 1957; Waterink & Vedder, 1936).

While Tramer (1934) is attributed with coining the term *elective mutism*, a number of German writers published earlier papers that descriptively reported cases of "voluntary" mute behavior in children (cf. Gutzman, 1893; Liebmann, 1898; Stern, 1910; Truper, 1897). Other early German papers described therapeutic interventions (e.g., hypnosis, suggestion, persuasion) for the elective mute child (cf. Froschels, 1926; Heuyer & Morgenstern, 1927; Kistler, 1927; Lesch, 1934).

German clinicians offered a variety of causes to account for elective mutism in children. Nadoleczng (1926) indicated that the elective mute child may have a "weak speech impulse," while Treidel (1894) noted that the cause of mutism was the inability of these children to comprehend the symbolic content of language. In contrast, Gutzman (1912) suggested that mutism often occurred after a child was teased by peers. Heuyer and Morgenstern (1932) attributed the cause of a 9 ½-year-old boy's elective mutism to castration anxiety. Weber (1950), on the other hand, related elective mutism to excessive oral dependency needs that were manifested by an abnormal dependence on the mother. Finally, Spieler (1944) referred to four varieties or types of mutism resulting from psychogenic causes: hysterical, elective, thymogenic, and ideogenic. In the hysterical variety the child was said to speak in an emergency, thereby stimulating partial "elective mutism." Spieler (1944) also reviewed 50 cases of mutism, noting that the outstanding feature of the elective mute child was a neurotic personality.

During the early 1950s, reports of elective mutism began to appear in the Swiss, British, and American literature. Two swiss writers, Von Misch (1952) and Weber (1950), reported cases of children diagnosed as elective mutism who presented similar histories and etiologies. These writers reported the families of elective mute children to be withdrawn, social isolates in their communities, and to evidence neurotic and psychotic disorders. The children were further described as low in intellectual ability and poorly adjusted when in the presence of strangers. Von Misch (1952) described four cases of elective mutism and compared them with Weber's (1950), emphasizing that the milieu was important in influencing therapy. Von Misch concluded that (a) environmental factors may precipitate mutism; (b) mutism often occurred upon the child's separation from the family, especially at the time of entry into school; (c) the disorder was primarily psychogenic, although heredity and intelligence have a role; (d) all cases demonstrated excessive ties to the mother; and (e) neurosis was possibly related to a traumatic experience at the time the child was developing speech. In concert with a milieu orientation, Von Misch (1952) recommended changing the child's environment through placement, providing instructions of a therapeutic nature to caretakers in the home environment, treatment of the neurosis itself, and speech exercises. These suggestions were later to reflect those offered by more behaviorally oriented therapists.

Salfield, Lond, and Dusseldorf (1950) reported one case and reviewed other cases from their own clinical work as well as from the work of Tramer (1934, 1949). They neglected to report a specific description of their treatment procedures. The report did indicate that their client began to talk freely at home and to strangers, but continued to be mute in school. After reviewing their own and other cases, Salfield *et al.* (1950) provided the following observations: (a) Elective mutism occurs between 3 and 5 years of age, (b) there appears to be no mental defect, (c) there frequently appears to be a familial factor, (d) a great resistance to treatment appears, and (e) there may be an early somatic, psychological, or compound trauma. The authors concluded that mutism "can be understood as a fixation at an early infantile level on which an apprehended danger situation is met by refusal to speak" (p. 1031).

Morris (1953) described six cases of elective mutism, diagnosed through exclusion of hysteria, childhood schizophrenia, hyperkinetic disease, and dementia praecox. The reports are mainly case history descriptions with common factors including a traumatic situation and a degree of constitutional shyness and timidity. Success of "psychiatric" intervention was limited, with two cases demonstrating spontaneous recoveries. In two other cases, removal from an environment that was considered to be the cause of their condition was met with a restoration of speech.

Turning to the American literature, Adams and Glasner (1954) described four cases of children between the ages of 4 and 9 referred to Johns Hopkins Hospital. In one case, after 2 months of play therapy, the child started to say a few short sentences, but follow-up indicated no progress after leaving the clinic. In another case, speech therapy was the primary mode of intervention, with some unspecified concomitant "psychotherapy" offered. The case generally could be considered a failure since after several months of therapy only several simple words were spoken and no follow-up measures were specified. In the last case, two siblings, aged 9 and 6, received speech therapy that was unsuccessful due to what they termed "resistance" and "hostility." Again, no follow-up measures were reported. Adams and Glasner (1954) stressed the home situation as a primary cause of mutism, noting that children were fearful of fathers who were alcoholic and abusive. They further noted that the outstanding difference between their cases and those previously discussed was a strong hostility and resistance to therapy.

Parker, Olsen, and Throckmorton (1960) reviewed the social work files from the Tacoma Public Schools and found 27 children referred for service over a 12-year period who did not talk in school. This constituted approximately .7% of the total population served during that time. Parker et al. (1960) noted that the children were given a neurotically based symptom diagnosis with therapy focusing on teacher, parent, and child. Thus, in contrast to most previous psychodynamic therapists, these authors stressed some treatment in the school setting where the initial problem behaviors occurred.

In describing their work with mute children, Browne, Wilson, and Laybourne (1963) indicated that following 1½ years of disappointing results, one child was given an injection of Desoxy ephedine and Amytal in an attempt to alleviate the mutism. This tactic also resulted in failure. In another case, therapy focused on the entire family. The authors noted that an improvement in the father correlated with an improvement in the child. In discussing the cases, Browne et al. (1963) noted that mute children appear to be either fixated or regressed to the anal stage of development, have urinary or bowel difficulty, are shy, negativistic, withdrawn, regard other people as strange or frightening, develop a sadistic relationship toward most adults, and utilize mutism as a weapon to punish people who offend them (possibly therapists). The pathology was observed to extend to the parents, with successful treatment of the child dependent on the parents' response to treatment.

In one of the few studies to include a reasonably clear description of follow-up procedures, Elson, Pearson, Jones, and Schumacher (1965) reported interventions with four girls aged 7 to 10 and followed them from 6 months to 5 years, depending on the case. Treatment was primarily family-oriented. The authors were able to document marked improvement and school attendance was 90% to 100% during the time of each follow-up. No child was hospitalized during the follow-up period and none required psychiatric treatment. Further, there was no evidence of depression, excessive anxiety, sleep disturbance, orientation defects, hallucination, or sociopathic behavior. Interpersonal relations were improved in the home and at school, although they remained impaired. In the psychodynamic formulation of the mutism disorder, Elson et al.

(1965) saw these children as possessing passive-aggressive personality trait disturbances.

In one of the more carefully documented reports of the characteristics of elective mutism, Wright (1968) evaluated 24 cases of children between the ages of 5 and 9 years who were referred to a psychiatric clinic because they failed to talk in school. The children were treated for periods varying from a few weeks to 2 years, the majority being treated for 3 to 4 months. All children were treated initially in an outpatient clinic and 3 of the 24 cases were subsequently admitted to the inpatient service for periods of 3 to 6 months. Interventions consisted of individual psychotherapy with rewards occasionally offered for speaking. Wright (1968) noted that the children responded well to short-term treatment, particularly when they were referred at an early age. Interestingly, there was great diversity in terms of sex, age of onset, age at time of referral, grade level, intelligence, and other conditions. Where there were concomitant problems such as low intelligence, organic factors, or thought disorders, the prognosis was poorer, even though many responded well to treatment. In the 19 cases available for follow-up evaluation (6 months to 7 years), talking was documented and 21% had excellent adjustment, 58% good, 16% fair, and only 5% poor adjustment. Wright (1968) observed that the most common dynamic finding was a controlling, ambivalent, and dependent relationship between child and mother, which carried over into the child's relationship with others in the environment.

Some authors have reported marginal success with the mute child in the natural environment but failed to establish speech with the therapist (e.g., Chetnik, 1973; Mora et al., 1962; Pustrom & Speers, 1964). Pustrom and Speers (1964) presented three case studies of elective mutism with clinic-based psychotherapy for child and parents. The authors noted that the focus of therapy was on the family unit, in which mutism was viewed as the symptomatic expression of family conflict. It is unclear exactly how long therapy lasted, but it was noted that it did continue after 4 years. The authors generally were encouraged with the therapeutic results, noting that over the treatment period children did begin to speak to others. However, there were problems in eliciting speech with the therapist:

> We are concerned that none of these children was able to talk to his therapist even though all were able to talk to others. It is our impression that the child's failure to speak to his therapist represents a last ditch stand against giving up his omnipotent control of others. One can speculate that as long as this remains, the child, in future stresses, might revert to stubborn silence in dealing with the stress. (p. 296)

Chetnik (1973) presented an extensive description of one case of a 6½-year-old female who had refused to speak to schoolteachers and peers for a full year. Therapeutic intervention consisted of working on conflicts related to oral, anal, and phallic strivings. Despite the fact that the child was totally silent throughout the 2-year period of treatment, some forms of communication were noted (e.g., drawing, writing, intense play, body gestures, and some sounds).

Kass, Gillman, Mattis, Klugman, and Jacobson (1967) reported the case of a 6½-year-old blind girl who was silent throughout both nursery school and kindergarten. The intervention consisted of individual psychotherapy (unspecified) and integration into a regular first grade, with cooperation and participation from school personnel. The authors demonstrated success by documenting speech in individual sessions, alone with a Braille teacher, and then dramatically during telephone play in the school class. Follow-up indicated that the subject became a fully integrated class member, and academic achievement was noted as being equal to or excelling those of her classmates. The cause of mutism was related to a retentive reaction to trauma, experienced during the anal phase of development, displaced to the oral sphere.

Some investigators have reported mutism in twins (e.g., Halpern, Hammond, & Cohen, 1971; Mora et al., 1962). Mora et al. (1962) reported the case of twin girls referred by the school for elective mutism. Their mutism was first noted in school when the girls began kindergarten at age 5. Apparently, all attempts by teachers, a counselor, and the guidance department failed to elicit any verbal response for 7 years. Mora et al. (1962) emphasized that the mutism was maintained by the "twinship society" and the expectations of school and peers.[3] Treatment involved breaking the tie of the "twinship" and then encouraging differentiation through talk therapy, drawing, and play therapy. Casework with a resistant mother helped resolve the ambivalent relationship between the twins and their mother. The twins apparently developed more normalized social patterns during adolescence, with both taking boyfriends and talking freely with other people. Interestingly, neither child would communicate verbally with the therapists, so all communication occurred only in writing. The twins' continued refusal to talk to the therapists was viewed as an intrinsic part of their improvement; "it provided them with a means of expressing hostility while maintaining their freedom of self-expression and verbal communication with the rest of the world. . ." (p. 51).

In quite a different vein, Halpern et al. (1971) proposed that mutism is a speech phobia arising out of an evaluation by the child of his/her power. These authors report three cases in which the focus of therapy was on eliciting the cooperation of school personnel, who in turn en-

---

[3] The "twinship society" refers to a confusion in self-identification of identical twins that causes a delay in normal personality development. It is hypothesized that the "mirror image of the self" serves as a means of mastering their rivalry and reinforces the twinship society sometimes to the point of fantasies of omnipotence.

couraged the children to talk in school. Although no follow-up measures were taken, the authors reported a successful therapeutic intervention.

In the longest documented follow-up investigation, Koch and Goodlund (1973) reexamined the files of 17 children who were considered electively mute while hospitalized at the child psychiatry service at the University of Minnesota. Most of the children were seen individually in psychotherapy (unspecified) and parental counseling (unspecified) sessions. The average length of hospital stay was 14 weeks. At discharge 3 of the children still demonstrated elective mutism with their physician or some of the hospital staff, but only 1 refused to talk to anyone outside of family members.

In contrast to the individual therapy approach, three of the children in the Koch and Goodlund (1973) report had reward systems established for speaking and a withdrawal of privileges unless they were verbally requested by the child. While a stragegy that consisted of ignoring the mutism had failed, this strategy appeared effective with these three children.

The authors were able to obtain follow-up data on 13 children. At the time of the follow-up, all subjects were living at home. The youngest, aged 8 years, had a 4-year follow-up. The remainder ranged from 14 to 21 years of age and the average follow-up was 9 years. Both subjects and parents were interviewed in private and conjointly. The follow-up data consisted of an MMPI profile, intelligence test results, school reports, and data from social and mental health facilities.

Based on the follow-up data, the authors concluded that elective mute children are a heterogeneous group. Academic performance of the subjects was below grade level. School performance was good in only one case and in two cases the children had problems and one was still mute. As a group the children did not present a picture of good adjustment, academically or socially.

1.1.2. Summary of Psychodynamic Interventions

Quite diverse therapeutic interventions have been employed with mute children within the psychodynamic orientation, but unfortunately, virtually all are unspecified with respect to therapeutic content. Different classifications of elective mutism have developed with some authors considering it a neurotic reaction (e.g., Elson et al., 1965) and others labeling it a personality trait disturbance (e.g., Pustrom & Speers, 1964). Some authors who have examined the etiology stress its overdetermined nature (e.g., Amman, 1958; Geiger-Martz, 1951; Von Misch, 1952; Morris, 1953; Salfield, Lond, & Dusseldorf (1950). Actually, a combination of conditions has been observed (cf. Halpern et al., 1971). Some common features of these children include (a) a predisposing constitutional hypersensitivity to instinctual drives, which is manifested by social reticence; (b) a traumatically experienced event during critical periods of language development (e.g., punishing speech attempts); (c) an insecure environment (e.g., disturbed parents); (d) a psychological fixation (e.g., utilizing mutism as a fear-reduction mechanism; (e) a neurotic symptom (e.g., dependency); (f) heredity not being typically a significant factor; (g) mutism being a speech-motivation problem rather than a speech inability *per se*; (h) a fear of unknown people and situations; (i) an onset at any age, but frequently identified in school, long after speech is fully developed; (j) a relationship to separation anxiety, especially when school entrance occurs; (k) a strong dependence on the mother, with fixation at the oral level; (l) aggressive and destructive fantasies of an oral nature; (m) a wide range of intellectual ability; (n) persistence of the mutism for several months to several years; (o) intervention having consisted of individual therapy, (e.g., talk therapy, play therapy), family therapy, and a variety of unspecified procedures.

A generally consistent theme running throughout the psychodynamic literature is that this childhood problem is difficult to treat. This is reflected in the length of time reported for treatment (several months to several years), lack of consistent generalization from the treatment setting to other problem areas in the natural environment (e.g., school), and some poor results when follow-up measures were taken.

1.2. Behavioral Perspectives

It is only within the last 15 years that the methods of behavioral psychology, particularly applied behavior analysis, based on principles of operant conditioning have been used in the modification of elective mutism. Although it has been commonly assumed by some writers that elective mutism has not received the attention of behavioral therapists (e.g., Franks & Wilson, 1976), there is indeed a sizable literature in this area. The behavioral literature can be segmented into two subareas with respect to methodology: namely, those reports employing case study and/or descriptive formats and those using some more formal design that includes continuous measurement and reporting.

1.2.1. Behavioral Case Studies

Behavior therapists have intervened with elective mutism in clinics (Reed, 1963; Reid, Hawkins, Keutzer, McNeal, Phelps, Reid, & Mees, 1967), schools (Brison, 1966; Bauermeister & Jemail, 1975; Bednar, 1974; Colligan, Colligan, & Dilliard, 1977; Conrad, Delk, & Williams, 1974; Dmitrieve & Hawkins, 1973; Rosenbaum & Kellman, 1973), home (Sluckin & Jehu, 1969), and other natural settings (Nolan & Pence, 1970). Like many of their psychodynamic predecessors, some authors conducted a retrospective evaluation of clinic cases and offered classification and treatment strategies (cf. Friedman & Karagan, 1973; Reed, 1963). In one of the first quasi-behavioral reports in the literature, Reed (1963) found only four cases of elective mutism in 2,000 referrals to a child guidance clinic and these did not conform to the patterns reported by Salfield *et al.* (1950) and Morris (1953). On the basis of only four cases, Reed suggested that the cases fell into two distinct "groups." One group showed relaxed and unresponsive behavior and appeared to be immature. The second group demonstrated tenseness and was overreactive to fear with concomitant anxiety. While the first group was purported to have "learned" mutism as an attention-gaining and evasive form of behavior, the latter group used mutism as a fear-reducing mechanism. Reed (1963) was apparently influenced by Dollard and Miller (1950) in their discussion of how speech terminates in cases of combat anxiety. While he suggested that operant conditioning procedures might be used to eliminate mutism that was attention getting, he presented no experimental procedure to document this claim.

Experience with 13 electively mute children in the psychological diagnostic clinics at the University of Iowa also led Friedman and Karagan (1973) to divide electively mute children into groups. The first group used refusal to speak as a means of manipulating the environment. In the other group, speaking was purported to be sufficiently anxiety producing so that the child chose to remain mute. In this analysis, anxiety reduction that results from mute behavior served as a reward and reinforced remaining mute. Similar to Reed's (1963) second "group," such children were shy, withdrawn, and socially inept. Friedman and Karagan (1973) perceived both groups to have learned mutism. Drawing on the work of Dollard and Miller (1950), the authors offered seven management programs for mute children (see pp. 250-252). Management of these children is hypothesized to be most successful when (a) no coercive practices or pressures are used to obtain speech (e.g., the child should not be "bribed"); (b) the child is included in all peer group activities; (c) emphasis is placed on reading and story telling and other verbal activities, especially in situations where the child feels comfortable (e.g., the home); (d) the parents encourage visits within their own home by relatives and peers so that the child may come to speak in their presence; (e) the child is encouraged in nonverbal, nonthreatening, interpersonal relationships with adults in the classroom; (f) a gradual shaping sequence is employed by a teacher, first by eliciting speech in a one-to-one situation, and gradually extending it in the classroom; and (g) the child and his/her parents, and all those individuals in whose presence the child will speak, are encouraged to participate in many activities outside the home. Unfortunately, Friedman and Karagan (1973) offered no empirical validation of these management procedures specifically for mute children.

In dramatic contrast to the length of some of the psychodynamically oriented interventions, Reid et al. (1967) eliminated a child's mutism through use of SD-R in one day. In the first step, the mother was alone with the child in the clinic and fed her breakfast in small portions, with receipt of each portion being dependent on the child's asking for it. The first experimenter (E_1) was substituted for the mother in feeding the child. Gradually the situation was turned into a social occasion, with E_2 and E_3 taking part, as well as other children. Less than seven stages were introduced during the single day. Three follow-up visits to the clinic on successive weeks demonstrated continuation of speech. The mother reported that the child began to talk to people outside the family (e.g., Sunday school teacher, friends of family).

Also operating from a clinic-hospital base, Shaw (1971) reported a 7-month treatment of a 12-year-old girl who refused to speak. At one point in her hospital stay, the girl was started on a series of twice-weekly intravenous injections of amobarbital sodium (7½ g) and methamphetamine hydrochloride (30 mg), aimed at helping her overcome speech inhibitions. After 4 weeks, the amobarbital sodium was stopped, but she continued to receive twice-weekly injections of methamphetamine hydrochloride (20 mg), which she intensely disliked. Thereafter, a specific conditioning program was set up which involved progressive expansions in her use of speech, with failure to meet specific daily requirements resulting in an aversive injection the following morning. The author argued that the daily renewed threat situation became a conditioned aversive stimulus, which her speech automatically terminated, resulting in operant conditioning of speech. A follow-up 1 year after discharge found the child maintaining normal adjustment, with appropriate speech occurring in all situations.

As behavioral procedures became increasingly employed, several authors reported successful treatment of elective mute children in school settings. Brison (1966) succeeded in eliminating mutism in a kindergarten child by moving him to a new class and arranging for the mutism to be ignored. Nonverbal behavior that achieved results normally achieved by talking was also ignored. The child soon began talking in a whisper (which was reinforced with social approval) and was within a short period of time talking normally. Follow-up measures 3 years after the intervention indicated good adjustment and no mutism in the school setting.

Likewise, Dmitrieve and Hawkins (1973) report a similar treatment of a "selectively mute" girl who had remained silent for 2 years despite protracted and concentrated efforts on the part of her parents, teachers, and other professionals to get her to talk. The treatment plan consisted of eliminating all social reinforcement for silence and providing specific cues for verbal responses. After 5 days the child began to verbally respond to the teacher cues. Increased rate of verbalizations occurred with fewer cues. On the 22nd day of the procedures, the girl spoke 421 words, averaging 4 words per each teacher cue. The authors reported generalized talking and maintenance over a period of 4 years. Normal academic and social adjustment were also obtained.

Rosenbaum and Kellman (1973) reported the case of a third-grade girl who did not speak in school and who was treated by school personnel using behavioral principles. The treatment program consisted of three phases. In Phase I, speech with an adult in a one-to-one setting was reestablished. A shaping procedure was used in two 20-minute sessions each week in which she had to speak to receive M&Ms and social approval. Phase II consisted of a transfer of speech to the classroom through successive approximations to the actual classroom situation (cf. Bandura, 1969). Gradually, the teacher and peers entered a room in the presence of the girl's speech. Phase III involved expansion of the group by having the girl invite some other children from her class to the speech sessions. After all children in the class had been invited, and with the teacher providing social approval for the girl's verbal behavior in the classroom, the girl was finally able to respond aloud when asked a question in front of the entire class. Follow-up at 2½ months suggested that the child continued to interact verbally.

Conrad et al. (1974) reported the case of an 11-year-old American Indian child who had never spoken a word in a reservation classroom during the entire 5 years of her schooling. The behavior therapy strategy involved stimulus-fading procedures in the home with the mother and an indigenous mental health worker, as the child would verbally respond in this situation. Gradually situations were changed through successive approximations until finally the child responded verbally to the teacher in the classroom when directly spoken to but rarely spontaneously verbalized or initiated conversation with the teacher. However, school staff no longer considered her verbal behavior a problem.

In one of the longer behaviorally-based intervention programs, Bednar (1974) reported successful treatment of a 10-year-old Mexican-American child attending public school. It was reported that he had never, to anyone's knowledge, spoken a word either in school or outside his home. The treatment program consisted of individual sessions over a 15-month period in which the therapist systematically shaped verbal responses through the use of contingent tangible reinforcement (i.e., a penny). It took 17 sessions for the therapist to elicit a clear audible word, which was spoken in response to a letter-naming task. At termination, the child was talking to some children and whispering to his teacher. In a follow-up investigation 2 years after therapy, the child was described as verbally responsive to individuals around the school.

An 11-year-old boy with a 6-year history of mutism in school was successfully treated with operant reinforcement and contingency management techniques by Colligan et al. (1977). A three-phase plan was carried out by the classroom teacher with only a minimal amount of consultation from the school psychologist. In Phase I the objective was to develop the teacher into a potent social reinforcer, a goal successfully accomplished, but the child's rate of speech did not change. During Phase II the child was taught to use the teacher's tape recorder, record speech at home, and then have it played in front of the teacher (home speaking was evident, although at a low frequency). The child was then requested to record some academic tasks at school with the teacher gradually fading into the individual session. However, no generalization to the classroom occurred. Thereafter a speech contingency was established wherein the child had to speak (i.e., say "book") in order to obtain a desk in the classroom. This strategy was effective in eliciting speech and the child gradually began to speak in class "in a manner satisfactory for fifth-grade youngsters." Phase III was designed to produce generalization. School staff engaged the child in short verbal responses and by the end of the school year, the child was speaking normally. A 12-month follow-up with the sixth-grade teacher suggested excellent verbal and social skills.

Some authors employing behavioral procedures established the intervention across several different situations. Sluckin and Jehu (1969) report the case of a 4-year-11-month-old girl who was initially referred to a child guidance clinic for her restricted speech in various situations. Because the child appeared extremely fearful of strangers, it was decided not to see her at a clinic. Initially, a psychiatric social worker consulted with the mother on what type of intervention to employ. It became necessary for the social worker to meet with the child directly in the home. A systematic shaping procedure with contingent tangible reinforcement was employed. Gradually the mother was faded out of the home while talking was reinforced. Eventually the child began to speak to adults and children. A 1-year follow-up suggested normal speech behavior patterns.

Nolan and Pence (1970) report the treatment of a 10-year-old girl in the natural environment. Over an 8-month period the child was involved in a series of behavioral strategies, some of which occurred simultaneously. In the first attempt to manipulate the girl's speech, the mother was told to inform the child that all nonvocal behavior could no longer occur in the car. The mother enforced this contingency by ignoring all attempts at nonvocal communication while going to and from school. After 3 days of this program the girl began to whisper. In an ingenious plan, the mother was directed to turn up the volume on the radio a little bit louder each day as a systematic fading procedure. On occasion, the child emitted normal speech. Thereafter, a series of management programs was established across a variety of situations and individuals. In the school, a teacher was able to employ a standard token economy and reward all speaking behaviors. Subsequently, the girl began to speak in a normal fashion. The authors reported that a 1-year follow-up indicated normal speech and no new problems.

Rasbury (1974) reports the case of an 11-year-old girl who had a 6-year history of unwillingness to speak with anyone outside her immediate family. The selective mutism had developed shortly after an aversive incident (never identified) that occurred on a school bus. Eight months prior to implementing an operant desensitization program, the girl was involved in two different therapeutic programs. The first procedure was a traditional play therapy approach (cf. Axline, 1947), and the second was a behavior therapy technique that emphasized contingent positive reinforcement for language imitation. However, neither program was successful with respect to reinstatement of the child's verbal behavior. A desensitization procedure was then implemented in the family car on the way to school (it was noted that speech became increasingly inhibited the closer she came to the school setting). Each school morning the child was asked to read aloud a set of sentences that were printed on index cards. The sentences described activities that the child could become involved in at school (e.g., recess, art class). If she read all the cards she was allowed access to a school activity that day. Movement up a hierarchy was based on speaking in a normal tone of voice and speaking for 3 successive days. The hierarchical steps included speaking in the presence of the father in close proximity to the school, speaking to other people, and speaking to people outside the family without the father present. The complete program involved 140 sessions (1 per day) of 10 minutes' duration each, and there were 15 steps in the hierarchy. The author reports success from the program and stability of the verbal behavior, until the child's untimely death a year later.

In a somewhat formal measurement strategy, Norman and Broman (1970), using a positive reinforcement procedure, successfully treated a 12-year-old elective mute boy who had not said a word in more than 8 years outside of his immediate home. Visual feedback from a volume-level meter was used to induce sounds and to raise speech volume. Reinforcement (e.g., a soft drink) was also employed to increase rate of speech and generalize it to other situations. The sound meter contained a background divided into red (loudest sounds) and black (low- or no-sound regions). Intervention procedures consisted of 44 sessions and anywhere from 40 to 400 trials per session (range 30-60 minutes per session). The target variables consisted of three measures: Either the child's voice moved the meter needle into a black or red region or no response was made. The authors increased responses in the red and decreased the percentage of no responses. Black-region responses also gradually decreased over sessions. During the last session the child responded to 80% of the questions from one adult and 54% from a new person. An 18-month follow-up indicated that the boy was still speaking, although the authors do report that school personnel trained in behavior modification techniques took over the treatment program in the school.

The case studies of behavioral interventions focusing on elective mutism have shown a positive pattern of results. However, some reports have focused on the target behavior in one setting (e.g., clinic) and have not carefully documented change in other settings. In contrast to the case studies reported in the psychodynamic literature, a large number of behavioral interventions were focused on treating mutism directly in the school setting. Finally, the reported stability of the behavioral treatment programs appeared quite positive.

1.2.2. Single-Case AB Designs

Some authors have provided a more formalized design with baseline measures from which to evaluate treatment programs with elective mute children. Straughan and his associates (Straughan, 1968; Straughan, Potter, & Hamilton, 1965) document several cases of successful treatment using behavioral procedures. In a report aimed at extending the application of a technique originally designed for modifying hyperactive behavior in the classroom (cf. Patterson, 1965), Straughan *et al.* (1965) employed a reinforcement procedure to treat a 14-year-old boy in a school for the mentally retarded. The procedure consisted of a flashing light, which served as a signal that a reward such as candy or points toward a party had been earned. In contrast to many previous cases, the youth was observed making vocal responses to peers on the playground, although there was no speech in the classroom. The treatment program was divided into four phases: (a) preliminary observation, (b) systematic observation (A_1), (c) treatment (B_1), and (d) posttreatment observation. During baseline, the boy's behavior was carefully recorded for 21 days, 20 minutes a day. Variables recorded during this period included looking at another person, smiling, motor responses, no responses, and talking. During baseline there was a 2.31 frequency of verbal responses per 10 minutes of recording (11%). Duirng 18 days, for 20 minutes per day, reinforcement was provided in the classroom through the apparatus described by Patterson (1965). A reinforcer was given each time the boy responded vocally to some appropriate instigation of another individual (e.g., the teacher). The boy earned a classroom party after 9 days. The treatment period was quite successful as reflected in a 27.39 frequency of verbalization per 10 minutes (54%). Furthermore, talking in response to the teacher and peer vocal responses to the boy also increased. A posttreatment phase in which the boy was observed for nine consecutive days demonstrated continued frequency of talking (61%). A 1-year follow-up suggested that the boy was still talking, although his responsiveness was not as high as observed immediately following the treatment. Straughan (1968) also reports another intervention with a 15-year-old girl whose behavior disorder was labeled "delayed speech" or "schizophrenic mutism" rather than elective mutism (i.e., speech loss occurred at a very early age and speech continued to be limited to that with close friends and relatives). After employing a procedure very similar to the aforementioned intervention with the 14-year-old boy, some success was noted. Although frequency of talking increased, indirect evidence suggested that she remained mute. Straughan (1968) emphasized that peer behavior must be changed if treatment of the mute child is to be effective.

Blake and Moss (1967) also stress the development of socialization skills in mute children, although their definition of elective mutism is quite different from the majority of writers in this area. Their procedure is described here because of its potential usefulness in the treatment of mute children. In a booth designed especially for work with "autistic" and "electively mute" children, a 4-year-old girl who had no communicative speech or imitative skills was given a preliminary session in which her verbal output was assessed. To elicit sounds from the girl, an instrument called a "color organ" was used as a positive reinforcer. The instrument (described by Fineman, 1966) translates sounds into an array of fusing colors on a screen. Intensities of the colors vary in proportion with the intensities of sounds emitted into the microphone. After baseline assessment, in 40 half-hour sessions, the girl was taught to make eye contact with the clinician and to obey instructions. It was also necessary to extinguish disruptive behavior, particularly operant cyring. During the intervention, the child learned nonverbal imitative behavior, such as hand clapping, and verbal imitative behavior, such as saying "hi." During session 21 and thereafter, play periods were begun (e.g., singing songs) in which some of the verbal behavior was generalized beyond the booth. Although the authors consider the program a success, the two sounds "hi" and "ee" were the only discriminable responses within the subject's repertoire upon completion of the treatment program. No follow-up measures were reported.

In the only investigation in which a group of school children ($N = 8$) were involved in an intervention to modify elective mutism, Calhoun and Koenig (1973) were able to document a successful operant treatment program that consisted of dispensing rewards contingent on verbal interaction in the classroom. Four children were untreated and four experienced the modification procedures suited to the individual child's problem and level of social development. A change in verbal behavior occurred from approximately 17 words per 30 minutes of observation to approximately 60 per minute for the treated group. A 1-year follow-up suggested relatively high rates of verbalization. No data were reported on the generalizability of talking.

Also operating in a classroom setting, Bauermeister and Jemail (1975) employed operant conditioning techniques with an 8-year-old Puerto Rican boy who refused to participate in classroom activities that required verbal communication. It was observed that outside the classroom setting the boy communicated freely and without difficulty. In contrast to many previous interventions in the behavioral literature, the total program was administered by classroom teachers. The four target behaviors selected for modification in the classroom setting included hand raising, answering questions from teachers, reading aloud, and completing classroom assignments. Contingent social and tangible reinforcers improved all target behaviors. Answering questions improved from 18.25% during baseline to 100% during the final treatment phase, and reading aloud increased from 0% to 100% during baseline and the final treatment phase, respectively. The authors noted a concomitant grade improvement that resulted in promotion to fourth grade. Follow-up observation a year later indicated that treatment gains were maintained. This study is distinguished from previous studies in which operant conditioning techniques were employed in classroom settings to modify elective mutism (cf. Brison, 1966; Nolan & Pence, 1970; Straughan et al., 1965), as the procedure did not interfere with normal classroom activities and was briefer than previous treatment programs (the program ran over 20 school days).

In one of the better designed behavioral interventions, Wulbert, Nyman, Snow, and Owen (1973) compared stimulus-fading techniques to those of contingency management in the treatment of a 6-year-old electively mute girl. The child had not spoken in kindergarten, in years of Sunday school, or in 1 year of preschool. In a procedure similar to that reported by Reid et al. (1967), intervention procedures consisted of the mother rewarding the child for verbal and motor responses to scheduled tasks, while a stranger slowly entered the room and then gradually administered the task items as the mother left the room. In addition, a time-out contingency for nonresponse to task items was employed. Control periods consisted of a stranger administering the same tasks to the child under the same contingencies but without the presence of the mother or the use of stimulus fading. Experimental and control periods were alternated during each treatment hour. The stimulus-fading procedure was found to be a necessary component of the treatment program. While the time-out contingency for nonresponse was found to facilitate the treatment if combined with stimulus fading, it was completely ineffective without the stimulus fading. Although the program was successful, no attempt was made to ensure generalization to other settings, and no follow-up results were reported. However, the authors did report that the teacher and several peers were faded into the program.

Using a variety of combined behavioral techniques, Van der Kooy and Webster (1975) reported a successful intervention on a 6-year-old child who had not spoken in most social situations outside the home, including school, for nearly 2 years. The treatment program, conducted at a summer camp, involved an initial avoidance-conditioning component, positive social reinforcement, generalization procedures, and the fading of extra attention. The initial procedures were somewhat severe and can be questioned ethically. Nevertheless, they appeared successful in eliciting speech:

> The procedures used by first author during the first two days of the fourth week were simple: After being dunked deliberately in the camp swimming pool he was told that further dunkings could be averted by his saying "no." When asked whether he wanted to go under the water, Jimmy began to respond with the appropriate spoken word. (p. 150)

In concert with Straughan's (1968) observation, the authors noted that the fading program was greatly assisted by peers who reinforced the child by verbally responding to him and by complying with his verbal requests. However, this did not appear to be programmed as part of the treatment procedure. Six months later it appeared that speaking had generalized and the child was reported to be speaking appropriately in school.

Williamson, Sanders, Sewell, Haney, and White (1977) described the treatment of two electively mute children with several behavior therapy procedures. Following a baseline assessment, subject 1 was exposed to the following chronology of treatment combinations: shaping with modeling, escape and positive reinforcement, and shaping with fading. This treatment package was successful in completely eliminating elective mute behavior. The investigators obtained follow-up information from the subject's teacher 2 weeks and 1 year after treatment was terminated. According to the teacher's report, the treatment effects were still evident at both follow-up periods.

Subject 2 in the above report received an intervention similar to the one that was successful with subject 1. The components of this intervention included reinforcement and reinforcement sampling with stimulus fading, reinforcement and reinforcement fading, and a 1-month follow-up. This program was successful in eliminating elective mute behavior based upon both the termination of treatment and 1-month follow-up assessments.

Williamson and his colleagues (Williamson, Sewell, Sanders, Haney, & White, 1977) reported the treatment of two children who manifested "reluctant speech." They distinguished elective mutism from reluctant speech by arguing, "It differs from elective mutism for though there is a normal frequency of speech under one set of stimulus conditions, there is a very low frequency of speech in others" (p. 151). In this report these authors were able to successfully treat two cases of "reluctant speech" by employing only token economy strategies. Observations of the children's speech 1 year after intervention was terminated revealed that the behavioral changes were maintained.

1.2.3. Changing Criterion Designs

Munford, Reardon, Liberman, and Allen (1976) report the case of a 17-year-old adolescent girl, diagnosed as having a "hysterical neurosis," who demonstrated incessant coughing at the rate of 40 to 50 coughs per minute over a 4-year period, and mutism for 2 of those last 4 years. The mutism was treated through shaping procedures using home visits requested by the child as a reinforcer. The shaping procedure included several major behavioral components. The first behaviors to be shaped were those muscles requiring control over shoulder, head, and neck areas. Thus, to reduce rigidity in these areas, she was instructed to perform progressively ordered exercises that resulted in accomplishing neck rolls, tongue extensions, parting her teeth, and so forth. Thereafter, the major target was to increase her control over inhalation and exhalation, which in turn led to sound production beginning with plosives, then moving to consonant and vowel combinations. The final cluster of behaviors focused on the pronunciation of words, followed by phrases and sentences.

This early version of the changing criterion design with a treatment reversal was employed to assess the effects of instructions, feedback, and the reinforcing properties of home visits contingent on the resumption of speech-related behaviors. The shaping procedure was slow due to the nature of the target behaviors. The treatment program extended over 24 weeks. However, within 6 weeks following treatment, the client was discharged from the hospital speaking fluently and appropriately. Interestingly, at this point the cough frequency and volume were reduced by about half the baseline rate. Apparently, the lessened frequency was partly attributable to the resumption of speech, a behavior that was incompatible with coughing. The client was symptom-free 41 months after discharge. Also noteworthy was the fact that the client completed two quarters of college where she majored in biology and earned a 4.0 grade-point average.

Although one can generally attribute the elimination of mutism to the shaping program, concurrent individual, family, and ancillary therapies were employed. For example, throughout the client's hospitalization, daily individual therapy sessions were held to maintain motivation to continue in the treatment program. She was reinforced by means of social praise for her almost daily successful achievements and assured that a positive outcome would likely be a result. Also, weekly family therapy sessions were held to provide a common forum for each member's reacting to the events of hospitalization and to help generalize the client's success to the home.

1.2.4. Summary of Behavioral Interventions

Again, the effectiveness of behavioral principles has been demonstrated, yet a number of authors stress the importance of natural reinforcers in the environment as important for maintaining treatment gains (e.g., Munford et al., 1976; Straughan, 1968; Van der Kooy & Webster, 1975). Most studies have focused only on the mutism behavior, with the focus on other "social skills" being stressed by only a few authors (e.g., Blake & Moss, 1967; Bauermeister & Jemail, 1975; Munford et al., 1976). Finally, the actual characteristics of these children have ranged from total mutism in some situations (Williamson, Sanders, Sewell, Haney, & White, 1977) to a low incidence of speaking (cf. Calhoun & Koenig, 1973; Straughan et al., 1965; Williamson, Sewell, Sanders, Haney, & White, 1977) and near lack of speech capability in others (e.g., Blake & Moss, 1967).

1.3. Other Perspectives and Interventions

In addition to the two aforementioned classifications of treatment approaches, there are two others that deserve separate discussion since they represent unique interventions with the elective mute child. These interventions include speech (cf. Smagling, 1959; Strait, 1958) and art therapy (cf. Chetnik, 1972; Heuyer & Morgenstern, 1927; Howard, 1963; Mora et al., 1962). It should be noted that many of the aforementioned cases used these procedures in combination with other forms of intervention, but only the more "pure" forms are described in this section.

Some writers have employed speech therapy procedures for the child with delayed speech (e.g., Werner, 1945) or the child with speech inhibitions (Chapin & Corcoran, 1947). Some procedures employed by these authors were used with children "diagnosed" as elective mutism. It is no surprise that some mute children would logically be referred for speech therapy. Strait (1958) did not label her case "elective mutism." Rather, she described a child who was "speechless in school and social life," but who exhibited normal speech in the family unit. Therapy consisted of a series of "speech sessions" in which the therapist talked to the child, encouraged reading, and involved him in social situations. The involvement continued for several months and success was reported.

Smagling (1959) reported the analysis of six cases of "voluntary mutism" in children ranging in age from 5½ to 10 years who were referred to a clinic facility. All cases were seen for two or three individual half-hour speech therapy periods weekly. In each case the child's mother observed a minimum of one training period each month and was usually present in the training room for each period. Speech therapy focused on correction of speech and language behavior, utilizing conventional speech training methods. Although Smagling (1959) noted that speech therapy was the primary therapeutic variable accounting for success in some cases, considerable confounding occurred due to unspecified psychiatric intervention either prior to or during the speech intervention. Furthermore, it seems apparent that various operant reinforcement procedures were employed. In Case A, speech stimulation on common phrases and training on reinforcement and modification of vegetative and respiratory reflexes subserving speech were employed. Case A began speaking in the classroom and in all other situations immediately after her sixth speech session and no reversion to mutism occurred. Cases B and C (twin girls) were observed to have no mutism at the end of 3 months of therapy. Case D was reported to show signs of "psychological disturbances" and was engaged in both speech therapy and some unspecified psychiatric treatment carried out twice a week. Although the author reported that within 2 months the mutism in all situations was absent, the contribution of the psychiatric intervention is unknown. Case E, who also experienced an articulation problem, did not improve despite concomitant psychiatric intervention (unspecified). The child who had completed her kindergarten year at the initiation of therapy remained mute through the fourth grade. Case F was involved in psychiatric treatment (unspecified) for over a 2-year period with no apparent results and was then terminated. After initiation of speech therapy the child responded consistently to all stimuli, but all responses were whispered and no voicing occurred. Subsequently, after a 21-month period, normal speech patterns developed in the speech sessions and were reported to have generalized to the school.

There have been relatively few reported cases where art therapy has been the primary mode of treatment for the elective mute (cf. Howard, 1963; Landgarten, 1975), although it has been used as a supplement to other conventional forms of psychotherapy (cf. Chetnik, 1972; Heuyer & Morgenstern, 1932; Mora et al., 1962). Landgarten (1975) presented a case of a 7-year-old female child referred to an outpatient clinic because she refused to talk. Art sessions were scheduled wherein the child and occasionally her siblings were required to paint. The author reported that initially the children were given cookies and candy somewhat randomly, while, later, candy was given contingently on painting. The author reports that the 7-month art therapy treatment was generally successful. However, a follow-up after 4 months indicated a regression to nonspeaking.

Howard (1963) reported the case of an 8-year-old child who was referred to a hospital for not talking in school, but who was quite talkative at home. The child was diagnosed as psychoneurotic, anxiety reaction. During the first 6 months his daily art therapy progressed through five phases: passive, fantasy, Oedipal anxiety, aggressive, and again a passive stage. Nevertheless, the child was eventually withdrawn from therapy and still remained mute at school.

1.3.1. Summary of Other Approaches

Interventions using "speech therapy" generally show a positive pattern of results, but it remains questionable as to what specific therapeutic mechanisms were operating. Furthermore, follow-up on such therapy provided mixed results. More careful examination is needed of the generalizability of the changes produced. Although very few cases are reported in which art therapy was used as the primary intervention, Landgarten (1975) reported a successful intervention, but regression on follow-up. Howard (1963) also reported disappointing results.

2. Methodological Evaluation and Critique

The results of the research reviewed here generally present a positive pattern of treatment outcomes for elective mutism with some durability noted in many reports. Our perusal of the research strategies that researchers choose to employ across all theoretical treatment approaches occasioned a number of concerns and suggestions that will be elaborated in the following sections. While many of the comments will appear to be criticisms of single-subject clinical research strategies, such is not the intention. Indeed, the $N = 1$ research strategy would appear to be the major option in conducting investigations in this area. However, a significant number of questions remain unanswered, particularly in the research designs and follow-up results, which require careful examination if recommendations about the future research and treatment strategies for children labeled elective mutism are to be put forth.

In this regard, the crucial question to which we address ourselves is: How methodologically sound are our grounds for belief in the efficacy of intervention programs with elective mutism? In other words, have the important questions related to interventions with mute children been adequately answered and to what extent have alternative plausible explanations for findings been considered or ruled out?

In the following section we present our perspective on the above questions. Since virtually all the reported cases of elective mutism have been "researched" through single-case methodology, we present issues relevant to this methodology across the various theoretical paradigms, remaining as unbiased as possible in describing the efficacy of an intervention with respect to theoretical approach.

2.1. Single-Subject Methodology

Considerable refinement has taken place in single-subject or time-series research since Sidman (1960) published his major work on research methodology, as is reflected in major works recently devoted to $N = 1$ methodology (e.g., Glass, Willson, & Gottman, 1975; Hersen & Barlow, 1976; Kratochwill, 1978; Thoresen, in press). Methodologists in applied behavioral psychology have expanded the use of conventional behavioral designs (e.g., ABAB, multiple baseline) and have developed new design formats (e.g., multiple schedule, concurrent schedule, changing criterion, multiple probe). While a large percentage of experiments conducted in applied behavioral psychology involve one subject (cf. Kazdin, 1975), designs in this area are by no means limited to one subject (cf. Kratochwill, 1978). An example of the latter procedure was reported in the Calhoun and Koenig (1973) study in which a group composed the experimental unit.

An important methodological concern in the elective mutism literature is whether the observed changes in behavior would have occurred without the experimental manipulations under investigation. This seems to be of particular importance in research with mute children since it can be observed from most published reports that they are at a point in their lives when maturational influences (e.g., rapid body growth), social changes (e.g., entry into school), and so forth, would produce gradual behavioral changes irrespective of an intervention program. This is compounded by the fact that the vast majority of intervention programs extended over a relatively long period of time. Unfortunately, in the literature reviewed here, only one study reported use of a research design that allowed some demonstration of a functional relationship (cf. Munford *et al*. 1976), and this study was confounded because the subject was also in the midst of psychotherapy. Approximately 21% of the reported research studies did employ a basic time-series (or AB) design and one used an early version of the changing criterion design (Munford *et al*., 1976) (see Table 1). All of these reports were affiliated with the behavioral paradigm. The remaining 77% of the studies employed a conventional case study format, a procedure characteristic of psychotherapy research over the past 50 years which has severely curtailed its credibility (cf. Hersen & Barlow, 1976). This does not mean that the case study format employed by researchers cannot make a contribution to an experimental effort (cf. Lazarus & Davidson, 1971). In psychotherapeutic interventions, Hersen and Barlow (1976) suggest that case studies can (a) foster clinical innovation, (b) cast doubt on certain theoretical assumptions, (c) permit study of rare phenomena, (d) develop new technical skills, (e) buttress theoretical views, (f) promote refinement in technique, and (g) provide clinical data that can be used to design more highly controlled research. Although a case study can be used to generate hypotheses for subsequent research (cf. Bolgar, 1965; Lazarus & Davidson, 1971), such research typically involves "misplaced precision" in that while considerable effort goes into a case study, time would be better spent on a well-controlled experiment wherein appropriate comparison techniques are involved (cf. Kratochwill, 1978). Finally, case study methodology is subject to all major threats to establishing internal validity. Subjective dependent variables are frequently employed, making it unclear if bias or "placebo" effects were responsible for change (cf. Hersen & Barlow, 1976).

All the research reports affiliated with the psychodynamic orientation to treatment involved case studies. Even though two methodologists affiliated with psychodynamic therapy went beyond noting the advantages of applied research with single cases and began to construct an adequate methodology (cf. Chassan, 1967; Shapiro, 1961, 1966), research on elective mutism has apparently not been influenced by their work.

Some investigations of elective mutism employed a basic or AB design (e.g., Blake & Moss, 1967; Calhoun & Koenig, 1973; Straughan, 1968; Straughan *et al*., 1965; Wulbert *et al*., 1973). In this research strategy, controlled observations were taken repeatedly over time and at some point in the data series an intervention was introduced and changes in the dependent variables were noted. The design differs from case study formats in that a baseline or a pretest data series is taken. The design can further be conceptualized as an improved form of the pretest-posttest design in that more frequent measurement of the dependent variable occurs. The AB design has been used to some advantage in psychotherapeutic research and appears useful with (a) a single target measure and extended follow-up, (b) multiple target measures, and (c) follow-up and booster treatment (Hersen & Barlow, 1976). Although use of the design in the elective mutism literature has generated fruitful areas for future research, investigators using the AB design are unable to rule out historical (and other) invalidity influences. Another major problem is that there is great difficulty in interpreting an intervention effect with a baseline trend. The baseline series must either be stable, exhibit a significant shift in the series, or be in the opposite direction from the baseline trend. Although the establishment of a stable baseline is generally considered a necessary condition for initiating various manipulations, other more credible designs also require this feature (e.g., multiple baseline). The issue of establishing a stable baseline has been of some concern in the research methodology literature. The concerns for establishing stable criteria are amplified when low-frequency behaviors are targeted, as is typical in treatment of elective mutism. Fortunately, these issues have received increased attention by methodologists who have provided recommendations for data analysis procedures (cf. Kratochwill, 1978).

Given that there are problems in the case study and AB format, what options might be pursued? The investigator who designs an intervention program should structure the situation to demonstrate the specific contribution of the intervention, a plan that includes a more credible experimental design. Although a variety of different behavior analyses or time-series designs can be used to determine whether the intervention rather than the extraneous events account for an effect (see Hersen & Barlow, 1976; Kazdin, 1977c; Kratochwill, 1978, for an overview), the conventional ABAB intrasubject replication design will typically be inappropriate, with respect to both its assumptions for a treatment reversal (and for withdrawal) and ethical considerations in returning mute behavior to baseline. The reversal variation possibly has more utility (e.g., Munford et al., 1976) than the withdrawal variation since it circumvents the complete withdrawal. However, the multiple-baseline design and two relatively new designs appear to be especially useful in the evaluation of treatment of elective mutism: namely, the concurrent-schedule design and the changing-criterion design.

The multiple-baseline design has application across responses, situations, and individuals (Kazdin, 1977c). Its use across situations (settings or time) would be quite useful in research on treatment programs for elective mute children since the mutism appears to be specific with

TABLE 1
Overview of Treatment Studies on Elective Mutism

Author(s)	N	Setting(s)	Theoretical orientation of treatment	Sex of subjects
Adams & Glasner (1954)	1	Clinic	(Speech therapy) Psychodynamic	Female
	1	Clinic	Psychodynamic	Male
	1	Clinic	Psychodynamic	Female
	1	Clinic	Psychodynamic	
Bauermeister & Jemail (1975)	1	School	Behavioral	Male
Bednar (1974)	1	School	Behavioral	Male
Blake & Moss (1967)	1	Clinic	Behavioral	Female
Brison (1966)	1	School	Behavioral	Male
Browne, Wilson, & Laybourne (1963)	1	Home, school	Psychodynamic	Male
Calhoun & Koenig (1973)	8	School	Behavioral	Unspecified
Chetnik (1973)	1	Clinic	Psychodynamic	Female
Colligan, Colligan, & Dilliard (1977)	1	School	Behavioral	Male
Conrad, Delk, & Williams (1974)	1	Home, school	Behavioral	Female
Dmitrieve & Hawkins (1973)	1	School	Behavioral	Female
Elson, Pearson, Jones, & Schumacher (1965)	1	Clinic	Psychodynamic	Female
	3	Clinic	Psychodynamic	3 Females
Friedman & Karagan (1973)	13 Single-case studies	Clinic	Behavioral	
Halpern, Hammond, & Cohen (1971)	1	Clinic, natural environment	(Quasi) behavioral	Male
	2	Clinic, natural environment	(Quasi) behavioral	Females
Howard (1963)	1	Hospital	Art therapy	Male
Kass, Gillman, Mattis, Klugman, & Jacobson (1967)	1	Clinic	Psychodynamic	Female
Koch & Goodlund (1973)	13	Hospital	Psychodynamic	9 Males, 4 females

Subjects (ages)	Design	Systematic variation of treatment	Multiple measures	Observer agreement assessed	General-ization measures	Follow-up
4-4	Case study	No	No	No	No	Yes
4-6	Case study	No	No	No	No	No
9-0	Case study	No	No	No	No	No
6-0		No	No	No	No	No
8-0	Case study	Yes	Yes	Yes	Yes	Yes (1 yr)
10	Case study	No	No	No	Yes	Yes (2 yrs)
4	AB	Yes	Yes	No	Yes	No
kinder-garten	Case study	No	No	No	No	Yes (3 yr)
6	Case study	No	No	No	No	No
5-8 yrs	AB	Yes	No	Yes	No	Yes (1 yr)
6-5	Case study	No	No	No	No	No
11	Case study	No	No	No	Yes	Yes (1 yr)
11	Case study	Yes	No	No	Yes	Yes (1 yr)
9	Case study	Yes	No	No	Yes	Yes (4 yrs)
7-6	Case study	No	No	No	Yes	Yes (6 mos
7-10 yrs	Case study	No	No	No	No	Yes to 5 yrs)
	Case studies	No	No	No	No	No
7	Case study	No	No	No	No	No
6-6	Case study	No	No	No	No	No
6-6						No
8	Case study	No	No	No	No	No
6-5	Case study	No	No	No	No	Yes
3-6 yrs	Case study	No	Yes	No	No	Yes ($\bar{X} = 9$ yrs)

Continued

Table 1 *(Continued)*

Author(s)	N	Setting(s)	Theoretical orientation of treatment	Sex of subjects
Landgarten (1975)	1	Clinic	(Art therapy) psychodynamic	Female
Mora, DeVault, & Schopler (1962)	2 (twins)	Clinic	Psychodynamic	Females
Morris (1953)	1	Clinic	Psychodynamic	Female
	1	Clinic	Psychodynamic	Male
	1	Clinic	Psychodynamic	Female
	1	Clinic	Psychodynamic	Male
	1	Clinic	Psychodynamic	Female
	1	Clinic	Psychodynamic	Male
Munford, Reardon, Liberman, & Allen (1976)	1	Clinic, home	Behavioral	Female
Nolan & Pence (1970)	1	Home, school	Behavioral	Female
Norman & Broman (1970)	1	Clinic	Behavioral	Male
Parker, Olsen, & Throckmorton (1960)	27 Ex post facto (single-case studies)	School	Psychodynamic	13 Females, 14 males
Pustrom & Speers (1964)	1	Hospital	Psychodynamic	Male
	1	Hospital	Psychodynamic	Male
	1	Hospital	Psychodynamic	Female
Rasbury (1974)	1	Clinic	Behavioral	Female
Reed (1963)	1	Clinic	(Quasi) behavioral	Female
	1	Clinic	(Quasi) behavioral	Female
	1	Clinic	(Quasi) behavioral	Female
	1	Clinic	(Quasi) behavioral	Male
Reid, Hawkins, Keutzer, McNeal, Phelps, Reid, & Mees (1967)	1	Clinic	Behavioral	Female
Rosenbaum & Kellman (1973)	1	School	Behavioral	Female

Subjects (ages)	Design	Systematic variation of treatment	Multiple measures	Observer agreement assessed	Generalization measures	Follow-up
7	Case study	No	No	No	No	Yes (4 mos)
13	Case study	No	No	No	No	Yes
10	Case study	No	No	No	No	Yes
6	Case study	No	No	No	No	No
4	Case study	No	No	No	No	Yes
4	Case study	No	No	No	No	Yes
9	Case study	No	No	No	No	No
Unspecified	Case study	No	No	No	No	No
17 yrs	Combination changing criterion and ABCA	Yes	Yes	No	Yes	Yes (41 mos)
10	Case study	No	No	No	Yes	Yes (1 yr)
10	Case study (B design)	Yes	Yes	No	Yes	Yes (18 mos)
Unspecified elementary	Case study	No	No	No	No	No
8	Case study	No	No	No	No	No[a]
8	Case study	No	No	No	No	No[a]
8	Case study	No	No	No	No	No[a]
6	Case study	Yes	No	No	Yes	Yes (1 yr)
14	Case study	No	No	No	No	Yes
13	Case study	No	No	No	No	Yes
12	Case study	No	No	No	No	Yes
12	Case study	No	No	No	No	Yes
6	Case study	Yes	No	No	Yes	Yes
8	Case study	Yes	Yes	No	Yes	Yes (2½ mos)

Continued

TABLE 1 (*Continued*)

Author(s)	N	Setting(s)	Theoretical orientation of treatment	Sex of subjects
Salfield, Lond, & Dusseldorf (1959)	1	Clinic	Psychodynamic	Male
Shaw (1971)	1	Clinic, hospital	Behavioral (drug)	Female
Sluckin & Jehu (1969)	1	Home	Behavioral	Female
Smagling (1958)	1	Clinic	Speech	Male
	1	Clinic	(psychodynamic)	Female
	1	Clinic		Female
	1	Clinic		Female
	1	Clinic		Female
	1	Clinic		Male
Strait (1958)	1	School	Speech	Male
Straughan (1968)	1	School	Behavioral	Male
	1	School	Behavioral	Female
Straughan, Potter, & Hamilton (1965)	1	Special school	Behavioral	Male
Werner (1945)	1	School	Speech (psychodynamic)	Female
Wright (1968)	24 single cases	Clinic	Psychodynamic	7 Males, 17 females
Wulbert, Nyman, Snow, & Owen (1973)	1	Public school, kinder-garten psychology clinic	Behavioral	Female
Van der Kooy & Webster (1975)	1	Summer camp	Behavioral	Male
Williamson, Sanders, Sewell, Haney, & White (1977)	1	School	Behavioral	Male
	1	School	Behavioral	Female
Williamson, Sewell, Sanders, Haney, & White (1977)	1	Clinic, school, home	Behavioral	Male
	1	Clinic, school, home	Behavioral	Male

[a]Therapy was continuing with these children at the time of publication.

Subjects (ages)	Design	Systematic variation of treatment	Multiple measures	Observer agreement assessed	General- ization measures	Follow-up
7	Case study	No	No	No	No	No
10-6	Case study	No	No	No	No	Yes (1 yr)
4-11	Case study	No	No	No	Yes	Yes (1 yr)
6	Case study	No	No	No	No	No
5-6	Case study	No	No	No	No	No
5-6	Case study	No	No	No	No	No
6	Case study	No	No	No	No	No
6	Case study	No	No	No	No	No
10	Case study	No	No	No	No	No
6	Case study	No	No	No	No	No
14 (re-tarded)	AB	Yes	Yes	No	Yes	Yes (1 yr)
	AB	Yes	Yes	No	Yes	Yes (1 yr)
14 (re-tarded	AB	Yes	Yes	No	No	Yes (1 yr)
5	Case study	No	No	No	No	No
5-25%, 6-25% 6-25%, 7-34%, 8-8%, 9-8%	Case study	No	No	No	No	Yes (6 mos to 7 yrs)
6	AB	Yes	Yes	Yes	Yes	No
6	AB	Yes	Yes	No	Yes	Yes (6 mos)
8	AB	Yes	No	No	No	Yes (2 wks & 1 yr)
7	AB	Yes	No	No	No	Yes (1 mo)
8	AB	Yes	No	No	No	Yes (1 yr)
7	AB	Yes	Yes	Yes	Yes	Yes (2 wks, 1 yr)

respect to situations. For example, baseline data for a given response (i.e., talking) could be collected across two or more situations or settings such as in the classroom, on the playground, and in other settings where talking does not occur. After behavior has stabilized in each situation, the intervention is applied sequentially to each situation. The specific effect of the intervention would be shown if talking changes in a particular situation only when the intervention is introduced. Such a procedure would be similar to that employed by Allen (1973), who eliminated bizarre verbalizations in a brain-damaged boy across a number of situations. In the multiple-baseline design across situations, an unambiguous demonstration of the intervention depends upon changes in behavior only in those situations in which the intervention is in effect. Although the multiple-baseline design could be employed to assess response generalization, this will militate against a functional relationship. For example, in some cases changing behavior in one situation has changed behavior in other situations in which the intervention was not introduced (e.g., Bennett & Maley, 1973; Hunt & Zimmerman, 1969; Kazdin, 1973b). Thus this version of the multiple-baseline design may not unambiguously demonstrate a functional relationship if situations are so similar that altering behavior in one situation changes behavior in another. Generalized effects across different baselines appear to be an exception rather than the rule (Kazdin, 1977c).

Another design that could be useful in treatment research on elective mutism is the concurrent-schedule or the "simultaneous-treatment" design (Hersen & Barlow, 1976; Kazdin, 1977c; Kratochwill, 1978). This design examines the effect of different interventions, each of which is implemented in the same phase of the program. The design is especially useful when the investigator is interested in determining the efficacy of two or more procedures. The design is characterized as follows: After a baseline observation on a single talking response is completed, two or more interventions are implemented to alter the response. The interventions are implemented in the same phase but under varied stimulus conditions. Thus, two interventions could be compared by implementing both of them on a given day in the intervention phase, with one in the morning and the other in the afternoon. The interventions are varied across periods of the day (e.g., morning and afternoon) and across two staff members (e.g., teachers in a school). The different interventions are balanced across all conditions so that their effects can be separated from these conditions. The intervention phase is continued, varying the conditions of administration, until responses stabilize under separate interventions. The design is limited in that (a) a large number of sessions are required so that each intervention can be administered by a given individual and across time periods an equal number of times, (b) a client may not discriminate different contingencies correlated with a particular intervention, and (c) the effects of administering each intervention in the same phase may differ from what they would be if the intervention were administered in separate phases (cf. Kazdin, 1977c).

Finally, the changing criterion design (cf. Hall & Fox, 1977; Hartmann & Hall, 1976) would be especially useful for evaluating interventions with elective mutism, particularly where gradual shaping procedures are used as part of the treatment program (as for example in the Munford *et al.*, 1976, report). The changing-criterion design requires initial baseline observations on a single target behavior. Subsequent to baseline, an intervention program is implemented in each of a series of intervention phases. A stepwise change in criterion rate for a target behavior is applied during each intervention phase. Thus, each phase of the design can be conceptualized as a baseline for each subsequent phase. Functional control is demonstrated through correlated changes in the target behavior with each stepwise change in the criterion. Criteria changes function analogously to the sequential changes in behavior, situation, or individual to which an intervention is applied in variants of the multiple-baseline design. The reader is referred to Kazdin (1977c) and Kratochwill (1978) for a thorough discussion of its application. It should be noted that Munford et al. (1976) employed an early variant of the design, although refinements of baseline and systematic criterion shifts were not specified. While their procedure came close to a credible research design, considerable refinement would be necessary to argue for a functional relationship.

2.2. Systematic Treatment Variation

A second methodological issue concerns the systematic variation of one treatment at a time. In the absence of a systematic introduction of each treatment it is impossible to determine the mechanisms responsible for any observed therapeutic change. For example, Kazdin (1973a) noted that in attempting to tease out the efficacy of a particular treatment, it is important to separate the instructions from the varying amounts of reinforcement. While appropriate single-case "interaction-type" designs are available (cf. Hersen & Barlow, 1976; Kratochwill, 1978), these procedures require either variations on the ABAB withdrawal-type design or multiple independent subjects. Of the studies reviewed here, only approximately 40% included such a systematic manipulation. Furthermore, while some researchers (typically the behavioral researchers) described various components of their treatment manipulations, rarely, if ever, were the operative processes systematically monitored. As noted in the review, a large majority of studies involved the client in concomitant therapies during the major intervention program.

Because the research on elective mutism is still quite primitive with respect to methodology, it is particularly important to critically assess each variable. Three recommendations advanced by Callner (1975) in a different context can help generate research that leads to our knowledge of variables affecting mutism treatment effectiveness. First, journal editors should encourage researchers to report *controlled* treatment studies that obtain unsuccessful results. Thus, it may indeed be more important to isolate and discuss the conditions surrounding an ineffective treatment in the context of a well-controlled study than to demonstrate treatment success in a poorly controlled study (like the vast majority of studies reviewed herein). This departs from convention but can be useful within the context of $N = 1$ research strategies, especially in increasing the generalizability of experimental results. Replication research should also be encouraged in this context. Systematic, direct, and clinical replication strategies would be useful (cf. Hersen & Barlow, 1976). Second, researchers should design and appraise their studies on variables, similar to those presented in Table 1. Although these variables do not exhaust the list of important criteria necessary to critique mutism treatment research, they may provide a list of minimum standards to include and discuss within the study. Finally, researchers should suggest future research ideas based upon refinement, elaboration, or replication of their own work in the area. Noteworthy is the fact that Straughan (Straughan, 1968; Straughan *et al.*, 1965) and Williamson and his associates (Williamson, Sanders, Sewell, Haney, & White, 1977; Williamson, Sewell, Sanders, Haney, & White, 1977) were the only researchers to extend their own work in the mutism area. As Callner (1975) has observed in reviewing behavioral treatment of drug abuse, ideas for extended study will help to produce a more homogeneous body of literature developing out of past shortcomings and progress rather than a heterogeneous body of literature replicating repeated difficulties (e.g., weak designs, confounded variables, no follow-up).

2.3. Multiple Measures

The third methodological issue concerns the use of multiple measures for the assessment of both the outcome and process of the intervention procedures. Davidson and Seidman (1974) have observed that no single measurement operation is inherently valid (cf. Campbell & Fiske, 1959, for a conventional psychological measurement perspective). While the same concerns are applicable to examining the efficacy of treatment strategies with elective mutism, it seems that multiple measures of experimental effects and their degree of agreement are necessary. Snow (1974) introduced "referent generality" to designate the range or pervasiveness of possible experimental outcomes measured in a given study and suggested that outcomes should be conceptualized on many dimensions (i.e., multivariate). In addition to understanding mute behavior *per se*, such measures would increase the external validity of the experiment (Kratochwill & Levin, 1978). Kazdin (1973a) also observed that although many behavioral programs have been restricted to a single target behavior, there are distinct advantages in using measures of nontarget behaviors as well (e.g., such assessment would allow examination of response generalization and discrimination). For example, an investigator studying the effects of a reinforcement program on elective mutism could employ multiple dependent variables to explore how other social behaviors are influenced by reinstatement of talking. Thus, for adequate assessment of effects, the evaluation of parents, peers, and so forth, must all be considered in addition to usual assessment by experimenters, observers, and standardized tests. In concert with Davidson and Seidman (1974), we believe that the multitrait multimethod paradigm is applicable in future research. In the present research, 26% of the reports included multiple measures.

2.4. Observer Agreement

A fourth issue relates to the observer agreement (also referred to here as "reliability") of data collected, a methodological consideration that has recently received a great deal of attention in the applied behavioral therapeutic literature (e.g., Baer, 1977; Cone, 1977; Hersen & Barlow, 1976; Jones, 1977; Kazdin, 1977a; Kelly, 1977; Kent & Foster, 1977; Kratochwill & Wetzel, 1977; Nelson, Rudin-Hay, & Hay, 1977). Aside from the fact that reliability should be assessed (only 9% of the studies reported here did so), and assessed correctly (impossible to determine from those that did), various sources of artifact and bias as well as characteristics of assessment influence interpretation of observer agreement. These include reactivity of reliability assessment, observer drift, complexity of response codes and behavioral observations, observer expectancies, and feedback, among others (Kazdin, 1977a; Kent & Foster, 1977). Although it is impossible to discuss all of these considerations in this chapter, no study on elective mutism provided adequate controls of these issues. While future research must focus on these factors, they represent only some of the major conditions that may influence the interpretation of reliability. Indeed, interobserver agreement and accuracy can be viewed as target behaviors in their own right that are a function of numerous variables (cf. Kazdin, 1977a). Such factors include the observational system, characteristics of the experimenter, observer, and client, methods of scoring behavior, the nature and duration of observer training, situational and instructional variables during assessment of reliability, the pattern of client behavior, and concurrent observation of stimulus and consequent events. Thus, it appears that observer agreement is complex and multiply determined. Because it is so complex, generalizability theory (Cronbach, Gleser, Nada, & Rajaratmam, 1972) may provide a useful way to conceptualize behavioral observations (cf. Coates & Thoresen, in press; Jones, Reid, & Patterson, 1975; Kazdin, 1977a; Mash & McElwee, 1974; Strossen, Coates, Thoresen, & Wilbur, 1977). Generalizability theory allows conceptualization of reliability for assessment across different conditions within an experiment. For example, it provides a comprehensive method for assessing simultaneously the independent and interactive effects of several factors on an observed score and it can assist the investigator in the design of assessment procedures so that information-gathering efforts can be distributed to yield as much accuracy as needed and afforded (cf. Coates & Thoresen, in press). Thus, the extent to which observations in a study vary across certain dimensions, such as observers and occasions, can be examined and the generalizability of the data across different levels of these facets can be evaluated directly. Future research on elective mutism must consider that an advantage of generalizability theory is that it simultaneously examines the contribution of diverse characteristics of data assessment.

2.5. Generalization

A fifth methodological issue relates to the generalizability of results. The notion of generalization presented here follows that advanced by Stokes and Baer (1977, p. 350), i.e., generalization is the occurrence of relevant behavior under different, nontraining conditions without the scheduling of the same events in those conditions as had been scheduled in the training conditions.[4] A useful way to conceptualize the generalizability dimension in the mutism literature is in terms of the 10 categories presented by Stokes and Baer (1977). Because they provide potentially useful treatment strategies for dealing with mutism the categories are briefly described here. They include (a) train and hope (i.e., the potential for generalization is recognized, its presence or absence is noted, but no particular effort is expended to accomplish it); (b) sequential modification (i.e., given the absence of generalization, procedures to effect changes are instituted to achieve it); (c) natural maintaining contingencies (i.e., generalization is programmed by "trap-

---

[4] It should be observed that this conception of generalization differs from that of conventional notions (e.g., Keller & Schoenfeld, 1950; Skinner, 1953).

ping manipulations," where responses are introduced to natural reinforcement that maintain the skills without further intervention); (e)
training sufficient exemplars (i.e., generalization to untrained stimulus
conditions and to untrained responses is programmed by the training of
sufficient exemplars of those stimulus conditions or responses); (f) train
loosely (i.e., training is conducted with little control over the stimuli and
responses); (g) indiscriminable contingencies (i.e., contingencies of reinforcement or punishment, or setting events thereof, are deliberately
made less predictable, thereby making it difficult to discriminate reinforcement from nonreinforcement occasions); (h) common stimuli (i.e.,
incorporating into training settings social and physical stimuli that are
salient in generalization settings and that can be made to assume
functional roles in the training setting); (i) mediated generalization (i.e.,
establishing a response as part of new learning that is likely to be utilized
in other problems as well); and (j) train "to generalize" (i.e., reinforcing
generalization itself as if it were an explicit behavior).

While a major concern must be with the generalization of the treatment, nearly all mutism researchers considered generalization a passive
phenomenon. For example, 58% of the studies reviewed reported no
generalization measures. Of the 42% that reported generalization, the
majority fall within the "train and hope" category. Even then, such reports are suspect since very informal measures were employed. In the
elective mutism literature the transition of speech in one setting to verbal
performance under wide-ranging conditions has received far less attention than it deserves.

The paucity of research reports that actively promoted generalization possibly reflect the heretofore lack of technology for such intervention. However, as Stokes and Baer (1977) and others (e.g., Davidson &
Seidman, 1974; Harris, 1975; Kazdin, 1975; Willems, 1974) have noted,
an embryonic technology is evolving. Although evidence for many of
the procedures is not sufficiently clear so that unequivocal statements
can be made about their utility, the seven procedures presented by
Stokes and Baer (1977) appear quite useful in ensuring response maintenance and transfer of training in treatment of elective mutism. Not only
do these specific tactics offer a set of what-to-do treatment possibilities
but they also could be employed in future mutism research to advance
the generalization technology (see also Wildman & Wildman, 1975).

2.6. Definition

A sixth methodological issue relates to the definition of elective
mutism. While many psychodynamic researchers characterized mutism
as part of a more global neurotic personality disorder, those researchers
operating from the behavioral orientation tended to define it as a de-

creased frequency of speech in specific situations. Over all research studies there appear to be some definitional problems. First, different types of "populations" have been subsumed under the umbrella term *mutism*. Some subjects have limited functional speech (e.g., Blake & Moss, 1967) and should not have been categorized as elective mutes since they did not demonstrate speech in any situation. Thus, those subjects who have never talked, or who have failed to develop relatively normal speech, should not be put into an elective mutism classification but could be categorized as nonverbal in the context of research reviewed by Harris (1975). In those cases where there is a history of language, the issues are somewhat blurred. Even then a researcher can carefully evaluate the subject's language over a variety of situations to determine if the mutism is select or if a more pervasive language disorder exists (cf. Harris, 1975).

Some researchers have included as elective mutism children who exhibit a low frequency of talking in some situation (e.g., Calhoun & Koenig, 1973). The strategy of taking the relatively nonverbal or withdrawn children from a classroom and labeling them electively mute would likewise seem inappropriate, since these subjects do exhibit speech to some degree in all situations.

Recently, Williamson, Sewell, Sanders, Haney, and White (1977) suggested that the term *reluctant speech* should be employed in situations where there is a normal frequency of speech under one set of stimulus conditions, but a very low frequency of speech in others. *Elective mutism* is employed for cases in which there is a zero frequency of speech in certain situations. From our perspective, use of the term *reluctant* conveys (as does *elective*) a connotation of subject-mediated behavior control and adds little information to a careful behavior analysis of the problem. Therefore, by whatever name, it may be useful in conducting a behavior analysis to know if speech is of zero or low frequency in terms of various treatment components to employ (e.g., shaping, modeling, etc.).

What, then, might be some useful parameters for constructing an operational definition for elective mutism. First, the researcher should gather data on the frequency of talking across a number of different situations and individuals (e.g., home, school, community). The mutism could then be defined as a lack of speech in certain situations or with certain individuals, or speech that has a zero or extremely low occurrence. It follows that speech will be select with respect to certain situations or individuals and that the term *selective mutism* is a more useful term, vis-à-vis the select nature of speech.

The term *selective mutism* covers the vast majority of cases reviewed in this chapter. Even though subjects involved in the research reviewed herein vary in diagnostic category and individual characteristics (e.g.,

IQ), they would still share the characteristic of zero or near-zero frequency of talking in certain select situations.

2.7. Social Validation

A seventh methodological consideration in the elective mutism literature refers to criteria employed for documentation of a treatment effect. Recent developments in applied behavior analysis suggest that experimental and therapeutic criteria be employed (cf. Kazdin, 1977c; Risley, 1970). The experimental criterion involves comparison of the target response before and after the intervention has been employed. All the aforementioned considerations relating to data analysis and design are relevant in employing this criterion. In addition to experimental criteria, applied behavioral investigations have been increasingly concerned with therapeutic or clinical criteria of behavior change, a procedure referred to as social validation (cf. Kazdin, 1977c). Selection of certain criteria also presupposes that the behavior selected for change is itself of clinical or social significance (e.g., eliminating elective mutism). Achieving behavior change of clinical significance offers a criterion toward which therapeutic strategies can develop and against which program outcomes can be evaluated. In the context of evaluating treatment outcome, social validation consists of two procedures (cf. Kazdin, 1977c). First, the behavior of the target subject is compared with that of his/her peers who have not been identified as problematic. In the case of mutism, several normal peers could be observed to establish an acceptable level of speech and other social skills. Second, subjective evaluations of the target subject's behavior by individuals in the natural environment are solicited. Thus, behavior changes can be viewed as clinically important if the intervention has brought the client's performance within the range of socially acceptable levels, as evidenced by the client's peer group, or if the client's behavior is judged by others as reflecting a qualitative improvement on global ratings.

Research conducted by Wolf and his associates at Achievement Place has incorporated social validity criteria in evaluating various programs for predelinquent youth (e.g., Maloney, Harper, Braukmann, Fixsen, Phillips, & Wolf, 1976). Kazdin (1977d) has also presented an excellent treatment of the topic for token economy research. Although no writers employed social validity criteria in a formal way in the treatment of elective mutism, it would be useful to employ the social validation process by demonstrating the extent to which behavior change places a subject within an acceptable verbal range when judged by the social community. It is short-sighted to assume that parents or teachers would consider establishment of a few verbalizations with a therapist a socially useful change.

2.8. Follow-Up

A final methodological issue, follow-up measures, relates to the durability of the treatment program once it is formally discontinued. Within the Stokes and Baer (1977) conceptualization, follow-up is but one feature in the assessment of generalization across time. Therefore, the strategies they proposed for facilitating generalization are also appropriate for ensuring durability. With mute subjects, perhaps the most meaningful estimate of treatment effectiveness can be obtained through accurate and reliable follow-up assessment. As demonstrated in Table 1, follow-up measures were gathered in approximately 67% of the research reported here. However, some follow-up measures are less than satisfactory. For example, at the time Munford *et al.* (1976) were proofreading the manuscript for their mutism article, a telephone call was made to the formally mute child. Williamson, Sanders, Sewell, Haney, and White (1977) conducted 2-week and 1-year interviews with teachers to obtain follow-up data. Although we can question such a strategy from such methodological perspectives as accuracy, validity, and reliability, it is probably better than not obtaining any information.

Several recommendations for obtaining better follow-up measures are suggested. Researchers should obtain a broad range of follow-up measures. Direct observation measures of the client under conditions established during the experiment proper should be used (e.g., Williamson, Sewell, Sanders, Haney, & White, 1977). Use of dependent measures in follow-up assessment similar to those used in the treatment setting will enable the researcher to assess the client's progress across time using similar measures of performance from one setting to another. This procedure would allow the researcher to assess how effective the treatment measures are in predicting posttreatment performance. Posttreatment information could also be obtained from socialization agents who interact on a regular basis with the client (e.g., parents, teachers, and peers) and from the client himself/herself. For example, if informal reports or behavioral checklist data could be obtained from parents, teachers, and peers, a more representative measure could be made, especially if added to information derived from direct assessments. Measures of posttreatment *in vivo* performance probably provide the best follow-up assessment.

Finally, frequent follow-up assessments should be made shortly after treatment termination in an attempt to detect any early relapse trends or problems (cf. Callner, 1975). In addition, follow-up assessment should be made frequently just after treatment termination and less frequently as the client becomes more verbal across a variety of situations. The importance of this is that early follow-up assessment could detect problems and thereby allow appropriate "booster treatments" to be applied to remedy posttreatment difficulties. Also important is that follow-up measures be conducted for several sessions, rather than a "one-shot" assessment. Such a strategy would promote a more representative picture of treatment efficacy.

3. Summary

This review critically evaluated the English literature reporting the treatment of childhood mutism and advanced several recommendations for future refinements. Because of the consistent methodological problems in the research to date, specific statements and conclusions about the efficacy of various approaches must remain tenuous. It is recommended that future research on the childhood problem of "elective" or selective mutism involve well-controlled $N = 1$ investigations. However, it was recommended that future studies concentrate on the need for (a) more credible $N = 1$ experimental designs, (b) more systematic variation of the treatment, (c) greater use of multiple measures, (d) greater use of and more careful observer reliability measures, (e) greater emphasis on measurement and programming of treatment generalization, (f) more careful operational definition of selective mutism, (g) more specific use of experimental and therapeutic criteria in evaluating treatment outcomes, and (h) better follow-up assessment. As a more valid, reliable, and generalizable data base of treatment information can be accumulated through well-controlled $N = 1$ research, specific treatment plans can be developed for children experiencing selective mutism.

ACKNOWLEDGMENT

The authors gratefully acknowledge Dr. Sid Bijou for his comments on an earlier draft of the manuscript and Hannelore Hennig for her assistance in translating the German references.

4. References

Adams, H. M., & Glasner, P. J. Emotional involvement in some forms of mutism. *Journal of Speech and Hearing Disorders*, 1954, *19*, 59-69.

Allen, G. J. Case study: Implementation of behavior modification techniques in summer camp settings. *Behavior Therapy*, 1973, *4*, 570-575.

Amman, H. Schweigende Kinder. *Heilpaedagogische Werkblaetter*, 1958, *27*, 209-216.

Arlow, J. A. Silence and the theory of technique. *Journal of the American Psychoanalytic Association*, 1961, *9*, 44-55.

Arnold, G. E., & Luchsinger, R. *Lehrbuch der Stimm- und Sprach-heipkunde*. Wien: Springer, 1949.

Aronson, A. E. *Psychogenic voice disorders: An interdisciplinary approach to detection, diagnosis and therapy*. Philadelphia: W. B. Saunders, 1973.

Aronson, A. E., Peterson, H. W., Jr., & Litin, E. M. Voice symptomatology in functional dysphonia and aphonia. *Journal of Speech and Hearing Disorders*, 1964, *29*, 367-380.

Axline, V. *Play therapy*. New York: Houghton Mifflin, 1947.

Babcock, M. Speech therapy for certain vocal disorders. *Journal of Laryngology and Otology*, 1942, *62*, 101-112.

Baer, D. M. Perhaps it would be better not to know everything. *Journal of Applied Behavior Analysis*, 1977, *10*, 167-172.

Bally, S. I. Ein Fall von traumatischem Mutismus. *Zeitschrift fuer Kinderpsychiatrie*, 1936, *3*, 23-33.

Bandura, A. *Principles of behavior modification*. New York: Holt, Rinehart & Winston, 1969.

Bandura, A. *Social learning theory*. Englewood Cliffs, N.J.: Prentice-Hall, 1977.

Bangs, J., & Freidinger, A. A case of hysterical dysphonia in an adult. *Journal of Speech and Hearing Disorders*, 1950, *15*, 316-323.

Barlow, R. A. A new concept of functional aphonia. *Transactions of the American Laryngological Association*, 1930, *52*, 23-34.

Barton, R. T. The whispering voice syndrome of hysterical aphonia. *Annals of Otology, Rhinology, & Laryngology*, 1960, *69*, 156-164.

Bauermeister, J. J., & Jemail, J. A. Modification of "elective mutism" in the classroom setting: A case study. *Behavior Therapy*, 1975, *6*, 246-250.

Bednar, R. A. A behavioral approach to treating an elective mute in the school. *Journal of School Psychology*, 1974, *12*, 326-337.

Bennett, P. S., & Maley, R. S. Modification of interactive behaviors in chronic mental patients. *Journal of Applied Behavior Analysis*, 1973, *6*, 609-620.

Bijou, S. W., Peterson, R. F., & Ault, M. H. A method to integrate descriptive and experimental field studies at the level of data and empirical concepts. *Journal of Applied Behavior Analysis*, 1968, *1*, 175-191.

Blake, P., & Moss, T. The development of socialization skills in an electively mute child. *Behaviour Research and Therapy*, 1967, *5*, 349-356.

Bleckmann, K. H. Mutistische Kinder. *Medizinische Zeitschrift*, 1953, *7*, 301-302.

Bolgar, H. The case study method. In B. B. Wolman (Ed.), *Handbook of clinical psychology*. New York: McGraw-Hill, 1965.

Boone, D. Treatment of functional aphonia in a child and adult. *Journal of Speech and Hearing Disorders*, 1966, *31*, 69-74.

Brison, D. W. Case studies in school psychology. A non-talking child in kindergarten: An application of behavior therapy. *Journal of School Psychology*, 1966, *4*, 65-69.

Brodnitz, F. S. *Vocal rehabilitation*. American Academy of Ophthamology and Otolaryngology, 1969.

Browne, E., Wilson, V., & Laybourne, P. Diagnosis and treatment of elective mutism in children. *Journal of the American Academy of Child Psychiatry*, 1963, *2*, 605-617.

Calhoun, J., & Koenig, K. P. Classroom modification of elective mutism. *Behavior Therapy*, 1973, *4*, 700-702.

Callner, D. A. Behavioral treatment approaches to drug abuse: A critical review of the research. *Psychological Bulletin*, 1975, *82*, 143-164.

Campbell, D. T., & Fiske, D. W. Convergent and discriminant validation by the multitrait-multimethod matrix. *Psychological Bulletin*, 1959, *56*, 81-105.

Chapin, A. P., & Corcoran, M. A program for the speech-inhibited child. *Journal of Speech Disorders*, 1947, *12*, 373-376.

Chassan, J. B. *Research design in clinical psychology and psychiatry*. New York: Appleton-Century-Crofts, 1967.

Chetnik, M. *Amy: The intensive treatment of an elective mute*. Paper presented at the American Association of Psychiatric Services for Children, 1972.

Chetnik, M. The intensive treatment of an elective mute. *Journal of the American Academy of Child Psychiatry*, 1973, *12*, 482-498.

Clerf, L. F., & Braceland, F. J. Functional aphonia. *Annals of Otology, Rhinology, & Laryngology*, 1942, *51*, 905-915.

Coates, T. J., & Thoresen, C. E. Using generalizability theory in behavioral observation. *Behavior Therapy*, in press.

Colligan, R. W., Colligan, R. C., & Dilliard, M. K. Contingency management in the classroom treatment of long-term elective mutism: A case report. *Journal of School Psychology*, 1977, *15*, 9-17.

Cone, J. D. The relevance of reliability and validity for behavioral assessment. *Behavior Therapy*, 1977, *3*, 411-426.

Cook, C., & Adams, H. E. Modification of verbal behavior in speech deficient children. *Behaviour Research and Therapy*, 1966, *4*, 265-271.

Conrad, R. D., Delk, J. L., & Willaims, C. Use of stimulus fading procedures in the treatment of situation specific mutism: A case study. *Journal of Behavior Therapy and Experimental Psychiatry*, 1974, *5*, 99-100.

Critchley, M. Spastic dysphonia ("inspiratory speech"). *Brain*, 1939, *62*, 96-103.

Cronbach, L. J., Gleser, G. C., Nada, H., & Rajaratmam, N. *The generalizability of behavioral measures*. New York: Wiley, 1972.

Davidson, W. S., & Seidman, E. Studies of behavior modification and juvenile delinquency: A review, methodological critique, and social perspective. *Psychological Bulletin*, 1974, *81*, 999-1011.

Dmitrieve, V., & Hawkins, J. Susie never used to say a word. *Teaching Exceptional Children*, 1973, *Winter*, 68-76.

Dollard, J., & Miller, N. E. *Personality and psychotherapy*. New York: McGraw-Hill, 1950.

Ehrsam, E., & Heese, G. Paedagogische Betrachtungen zum elektiven Mutismus. *Zeitschrift fuer Kinderpsychiatrie*, 1954, *21*, 12-18.

Ellis, M. Remarks on dysphonia. *Journal of Laryngology and Otology*, 1959, *73*, 99-103.

Elson, A., Pearson, C., Jones, C. D., & Schumacher, E. Follow-up study of childhood elective mutism. *Archives of General Psychiatry*, 1965, *13*, 182-187.

Fineman, K. *Developing sounds and word approximations in a deaf mute through systematic visual stimulation*. Unpublished paper, 1966.

Franks, C. M., & Wilson, G. T. (Eds.). *Annual review of behavior therapy: Theory and practice* (Vol. 4). New York: Brunner/Mazel, 1976.

Friedman, P. The phobias. In S. Arieti (Ed.), *American handbook of psychiatry* (Vol. 1), New York: Basic Books, 1959, pp. 293-306.

Friedman, R., & Karagan, N. Characteristics and management of elective mutism in children. *Psychology in the Schools*, 1973, *10*, 249-252.

Freud, E. D. Functions and dysfunctions of the ventricular folds. *Journal of Speech and Hearing Disorders*, 1962, *27*, 334-340.

Froschels, E. *Stimme und Sprache in der Heilpaedagogik*. Halle: Marhold, 1926, pp. 58-59.

Froschels, E. Method of therapy for paralytic conditions of the mechanism of phonation. *Journal of Speech and Hearing Disorders*, 1955, *20*, 365-370.

Froschels, E., Dietrich, O., & Wilhelm, J. *Psychological experiments in speech*. Boston: Expression, 1932.

Furster, E. Zur Systematik des kindlichen Mutismus. *Zeitschrift fuer Kinderpsychiatrie*, 1956, *23*, 175-180.

Geiger-Martz, D. Zur Psychotherapie bei elektivem Mutismus. *Zeitschrift fuer Kinderpsychiatrie*, 1951, *17*, 169-174.

Glass, G. V., Willson, V. L., & Gottman, J. M. *Design and analysis of time-series experiments*. Boulder: University of Colorado Press, 1975.

Gray, B. F., England, G., & Mahoney, J. Treatment of benign vocal nodules by reciprocal inhibition. *Behaviour Research and Therapy*, 1965, *3*, 187-193.

Gutzman, H. A. K. *Vorlesungen ueber Stoerungen der Sprache und ihre Heilung*. Berlin: Kornfeld, 1893, pp. 270-272.

Gutzman, H. *Vorlesungen ueber Sprache, Kunde*. Berlin: Fischer, 1912.

Hall, R. V., & Fox, R. G. Changing-criterion designs: An alternative applied behavior analysis procedure. In C. C. Etzel, G. M. LeBlanc, & D. M. Baer (Eds.), *New developments in behavioral research: Theory, method, and application* (In honor of Sidney W. Bijou). Hillsdale, N.J.: Lawrence Erlbaum Associates, 1977.

Halpern, W. I., Hammond, J., & Cohen, R. A therapeutic approach to speech phobia: Elective mutism reexamined. *Journal of the American Academy of Child Psychiatry*, 1971, *10*, 94-107.

Harris, S. L. Teaching language to nonverbal children—with emphasis on problems of generalization. *Psychological Bulletin*, 1975, *82*, 565-580.

Hartmann, D. P. Considerations in the choice of interobserver reliability estimates. *Journal of Applied Behavior Analysis*, 1977, *10*, 103-116.

Hartmann, D. P., & Hall, R. V. A discussion of the changing criterion design. *Journal of Applied Behavior Analysis*, 1976, *9*, 527-532.

Heaver, L. Spastic dysphonia II. *Logos*, 1959, *2*, 15-24.

Heinze, H. Freiwillig schweigende Kinder. *Zeitschrift für Kinderforschung*, 1932, *40*, 235-256.

Hersen, M., & Barlow, D. H. *Single case experimental designs: Strategies for studying behavior change*. New York: Pergamon Press, 1976.

Heuyer, M. G., & Morgenstern, Mme. Un cas de mutisme chez un enfant myopathique ancien convulsif. *L'Encephale*, 1927, *22*, 478-481.

Heuyer, G. D., & Morgenstern, S. Un cas de mutisme chez un enfant par la psychanalyse. *L'Encephale*, 1932, *22*, 478-481.

Howard, M. Art: A therapeutic tool. *Journal of the Oklahoma State Medical Association*, 1963, *56*, 420-424.

Hunt, J. G., & Zimmerman, J. Stimulating productivity in a simulated sheltered workshop setting. *American Journal of Mental Deficiency*, 1969, *74*, 43-49.

Jackson, C., & Jackson, C. L. Dysphonia plical ventricularis phonation with ventricular bands. *Archives of Otolaryngology*, 1935, *21*, 157-167.

Johnson, S. M., & Bolstad, O. D. Methodological issues in naturalistic observation: Some problems and solutions for field research. In L. D. Hamerlynck, L. C. Handy, & E. J. Mash (Eds.), *Behavior change: Methodology, concepts, and practice*. Champaign, Ill.: Research Press, 1973.

Jones, R. R. Conceptual vs. analytic uses of generalizability theory in behavioral assessment. In J. D. Cone & R. P. Hawkins (Eds.), *Behavioral assessment: New directions in clinical psychology*. New York: Brunner/Mazel, 1977, 330-343.

Jones, R. R., Reid, J. B., & Patterson, G. R. Naturalistic observation in clinical assessment. In P. McReynolds (Ed.), *Advances in psychological assessment* (Vol. 3). San Francisco: Jossey-Bass, 1975.

Kass, W., Gillman, A. E., Mattis, S., Klugman, E., & Jacobson, B. J. Treatment of selective mutism in a blind child: School and clinic collaboration. *American Journal of Orthopsychiatry*, 1967, *37*, 215-216.

Kazdin, A. E. Methodological and assessment considerations in evaluating reinforcement programs in applied settings. *Journal of Applied Behavior Analysis*, 1973, *6*, 1-23. (a)

Kazdin, A. E. Role of instructions and reinforcement in behavior changes in token reinforcement programs. *Journal of Educational Psychology*, 1973, *64*, 61-63. (b)

Kazdin, A. E. *Behavior modification in applied settings*. Homewood, Ill.: Dorsey Press, 1975.

Kazdin, A. E. Statistical analysis for single-case experimental designs. In M. Hersen & D. Barlow (Eds.), *Single case experimental designs: Strategies for studying behavior change in the individual*. New York: Pergamon Press, 1976.

Kazdin, A. E. Artifact, bias, and complexity of assessment: The ABC's of reliability. *Journal of Applied Behavior Analysis*, 1977, *10*, 141-150. (a)

Kazdin, A. E. Assessing the clinical or applied importance of behavior change through social validation. *Behavior Modification*, 1977, *1*, 427-452. (b)

Kazdin, A. E. Methodology of applied behavior analysis. In T. A. Bigham & A. C. Catania (Eds.), *Social and instructional processes: Foundations and applications of a behavioral analysis*. New York: Irvington/Naiburg, Wiley, 1977. (c)

Kazdin, A. E. *The token economy: A review and evaluation*. New York: Plenum Press, 1977. (d)

Keller, F. S., & Schoenfeld, W. N. *Principles of psychology*. New York: Appleton-Century-Crofts, 1950.

Kelly, M. B. A review of the observational data collection and reliability procedures reported in the *Journal of Applied Behavior Analysis*, *Journal of Applied Behavior Analysis*, 1977, *10*, 97-101.

Kent, R. N., & Foster, S. L. Direct observational procedures: Methodological issues in naturalistic settings. In A. R. Ciminero, K. S. Calhoun, & H. E. Adams, *Handbook of behavioral assessment*. New York: Wiley, 1977.

Kiml, J. Le classment des aphonics spastiques. *Folia Phoniatrica*, 1963, *15*, 269-277.

Kistler, K. Ein bemerkensweter Fall von freiwilligem Schweigen in Kindesalter. *Zeitschrift für Kinderforschung*, 1927, *33*, 2-14.

Koch, M., & Goodlund, L. Children who refuse to talk: A follow-up study. *Bulletin of the Bell Museum of Pathobiology*, 1973, *2*, 30-32.

Kratochwill, T. R. Foundations of time-series research. In T. R. Kratochwill (Ed.), *Single subject research: Strategies for evaluating change*, New York: Academic Press, 1978.

Kratochwill, T. R., & Levin, J. R. What time-series designs may have to offer educational researchers. *Contemporary Educational Psychology*, 1978.

Kratochwill, T. R., & Wetzel, R. J. Observer agreement, credibility, and judgment: Some considerations in presenting observer agreement data. *Journal of Applied Behavior Analysis*, 1977, *10*, 133-139.

Kummer, R. Betrachtungen zum Problem des freiwilligen Schweigens. *Zeitschrift fuer Psychiatrie Neurologie und Medizinische Psychologie*, 1953, *5*, 79-83.

Kussmaul, A. *Die Stoerungen der Sprache*. Leipzig: Vogel, 1885.

Landgarten, H. Art therapy as primary mode of treatment for an elective mute. *American Journal of Art Therapy*, 1975, *14*, 121-125.

Lazarus, A. A., & Davidson, G. Clinical innovation in research and practice. In A. E. Bergan & S. L. Garfield (Eds.), *Handbook of psychotherapy and behavior change: An empirical analysis*. New York: Wiley, 1971, pp. 196-213.

Leitenberg, H. The use of single-case methodology in psychotherapy research. *Journal of Abnormal Psychology*, 1973, *82*, 87-101.

Lerea, L., & Ward, B. Speech avoidance among children with oral-communication defects. *Journal of Psychology*, 1965, *60*, 265-270.

Lesch, E. Ueber einen Fall von freiwilligem Schweigen. *Bericht ueber die 4. Versammlung der Dtsch. Ges. Sprach-u. Stimmhk.* Berlin: O. Koblenz, 1934, pp. 29-31.

Liebmann, A. *Vorlesungen ueber Sprachstoe-rungen*. Berlin: O. Koblenz, 1898, pp. 20-31.

Loomie, L. S. Some ego considerations in the silent patient. *Journal of the American Psychoanalytic Association*, 1961, *9*, 55-78.

Macmahon, C. Treatment of functional aphonia. *Journal of Laryngology and Otology*, 1932, *47*, 243-246.

Maloney, D. M., Harper, T. M., Braukmann, C. J., Fixsen, D. L., Phillips, E. L., & Wolf,

M. M. Teaching conversation-related skills to pre-delinquent girls. *Journal of Applied Behavior Analysis*, 1976, *9*, 371.

Marshall, R. C., & Watts, M. T. Behavioral treatment of functional aphonia. *Journal of Behavior Therapy and Experimental Psychiatry*, 1975, *6*, 75-78.

Mash, E. J., & McElwee, J. Situational effects on observer accuracy: Behavioral predictability, prior experience, and complexity of coding categories. *Child Development*, 1974, *45*, 367-377.

Meichenbaum, D. H. Cognitive factors in behavior modification: Modifying what clients say to themselves. In R. D. Rubin, J. P. Brady, & J. D. Henderson (Eds.), *Advances in behavior therapy* (Vol. 4). New York: Academic Press, 1973, pp. 21-36.

Mitscherlich, M. Zwei Faelle von psychogenem Mutismus. *Zeitschrift fuer Psychosomatische Medizin*, 1952, *7*, 172-175.

Mora, G., DeVault, S., & Schopler, E. Dynamics and psychotherapy of identical twins with elective mutism. *Journal of Child Psychology and Psychiatry*, 1962, *3*, 41-52.

Morris, J. Cases of elective mutism. *American Journal of Mental Deficiency*, 1953, 57, 661-668.

Munford, P. R., Reardon, D., Liberman, R. P., & Allen, L. Behavioral treatment of hysterical coughing and mutism: A case study. *Journal of Consulting and Clinical Psychology*, 1976, *4*, 1008-1014.

Nadoleczng, M. *Die Sprachstoerungen im Kindersalter*. Leipzig: Vogel, 1926.

Nelson, R. O., Rudin-Hay, L., & Hay, W. D. Comments on Cone's "Relevance of reliability and validity for behavioral assessment." *Behavior Therapy*, 1977, *8*, 427-430.

Nolan, J., & Pence, C. Operant conditioning principles in the treatment of a selectively mute child. *Journal of Consulting and Clinical Psychology*, 1970, *35*, 265-268.

Norman, A., & Broman, H. J. Volume feedback and generalization techniques in shaping speech of an electively mute boy: A case study. *Perceptual and Motor Skills*, 1970, *31*, 463-470.

Pangalila-Ratulangie, E. A. Clinical treatment of a case of mutism. *Zeitschrift fuer Kinderpsychiatrie*, 1959, *26*, 33-41.

Parker, E. B., Olsen, T. F., & Throckmorton, M. C. Social case work with elementary school children who do not talk in school. *Social Work*, 1960, *5*, 64-70.

Patterson, G. R. An application of conditioning techniques to the control of a hyperactive child. In L. Ullman & K. Krasner (Eds.), *Case studies in behavior modification*. New York: Holt, Rinehart & Winston, 1965, p. 264.

Peacher, W. G. The neurological evaluation of delayed speech. *Journal of Speech and Hearing Disorders*, 1949, *14*, 344-352.

Pustrom, E., & Speers, R. W. Elective mutism in children. *Journal of the American Academy of Child Psychiatry*, 1964, *3*, 287-297.

Rasbury, W. C. Behavioral treatment of selective mutism: A case report. *Behavioral Therapy and Experimental Psychiatry*, 1974, *5*, 103-104.

Reed, G. F. Elective mutism in children: A re-appraisal. *Journal of Child Psychology and Psychiatry*, 1963, *4*, 99-107.

Reid, J. B., Hawkins, N., Keutzer, C., McNeal, S. A., Phelps, R. E., Reid, K. M., & Mees, H. L. A marathon behavior modification of a selectively mute child. *Journal of Child Psychology and Psychiatry*, 1967, *8*, 27-30.

Rigby, M. A case of lack of speech due to negativism. *Psychological Clinic*, 1929, *18*, 156-161.

Risley, T. R. Behavior modification: An experimental-therapeutic endeavor. In L. A. Hammerlynck, P. O. Davidson, & L. E. Acker (Eds.), *Behavior modification and ideal mental health services*. Calgary, Alberta: University of Calgary, 1970, pp. 103-127.

Risley, T. R., & Wolf, M. M. Strategies for analyzing behavior change over time. In J. Nesselroads & H. Reese (Eds.), *Life-span developmental psychology: Methodological issues*. New York: Academic Press, 1972.

Rosenbaum, E., & Kellman, M. Treatment of a selectively mute third-grade child. *Journal of School Psychology*, 1973, *11*, 26-29.

Rothe, C. Sprachscheue Kinder. *Zeitschrift für Ohrenheilkunde*, 1928, *62*, 904-909.

Salfield, D. J., Lond, B., & Dusseldorf, M. D. Observations on elective mutism in children. *Journal of Mental Science*, 1950, *96*, 1024-1032.

Schepank, H. Ein Fall von elektivem Mutismus im Kindesalter. *Praxis der Kinderpsychologie und Kinderpsychiatrie*, 1960, *9*, 124-137.

Shapiro, M. B. The single case in fundamental clinical psychological research. *British Journal of Medical Psychology*, 1961, *34*, 255-262.

Shapiro, M. B. The single case in clinical psychological research. *Journal of General Psychology*, 1966, *74*, 3-23.

Shaw, W. H. Aversive control in treatment of elective mutism. *Journal of the American Academy of Child Psychiatry*, 1971, *10*, 572-581.

Sidman, M. *Tactics of scientific research*. New York: Basic Books, 1960.

Silverman, G., & Powers, D. G. Elective mutism in children. *Medical College of Virginia Quarterly*, 1970, *6*, 182-186.

Skinner, B. F. *Science and human behavior*. New York: Macmillan, 1953.

Sluckin, A., & Jehu, D. A behavioral approach in the treatment of elective mutism. *British Journal of Psychiatric Social Work*, 1969, *10*, 70-73.

Smagling, L. M. Analyses of sex cases of voluntary mutism. *Journal of Speech and Hearing Disorders*, 1959, *24*, 55-58.

Snow, R. E. Representative and quasi-representative designs for research in teaching. *Review of Educational Research*, 1974, *44*, 265-291.

Sotloft-Jensen, P. Elective mutism in school psychological practice. *Skolepsy Kologi*, 1975, *12*, 3-16.

Spieler, J. Freiwillige schweiger und sprachscheue Kinder. *Zeitschrift für Kinderforschung*, 1941, *49*, 39-43.

Spieler, J. *Schweigende und sprachscheue Kinder*. Olten, Switzerland: Otto Walter, 1944.

Stern, H. Vortrag ueber die verschiedenen Formen der Stummheit. *Wiener Medizinische Zeitschrift*, 1910, *60*, 924-933.

Stokes, T. F., & Baer, D. M. An implicit technology of generalization. *Journal of Applied Behavior Analysis*, 1977, *10*, 349-367.

Strait, R. A child who was speechless in school and social life. *Journal of Speech and Hearing Disorders*, 1958, *23*, 253-254.

Straughan, J. H. The application of operant conditioning to the treatment of elective mutism. In H. Sloane & B. MacAuly (Eds.), *Operant procedures in remedial speech and language training*. Boston: Houghton Mifflin, 1968.

Straughan, J. H., Potter, W. K., & Hamilton, S. H. The behavioral treatment of an elective mute. *Journal of Child Psychology and Psychiatry*, 1965, *6*, 125-230.

Strossen, R. J., Coates, T. J., Thoresen, C. E., & Wilbur, C. S. *Extending generalizability theory to single-subject research*. Manuscript submitted for publication, 1977.

Thoresen, C. E. *Let's get intensive: Single case research*. Englewood Cliffs, New Jersey: Prentice-Hall, in press.

Thoresen, C. E., & Mahoney, M. J. *Behavioral self-control*. New York: Holt, Rinehart & Winston, 1974.

Tramer, M. Elektiver mutismus bei kindern. *Zeitschrift fuer Kinderpsychiatrie*, 1934, *1*, 30-35.

Tramer, M. *Schweigende und sprachscheue Kinder*. Olten, Switzerland: Otto Walter, 1943.

Tramer, M. *Lehrbuch der allegemeinen Kinderpsychiatrie*, Basel: Schwabe, 1949.

Tramer, M. & Geiger-Marde, O. Zur Frage der Beziehung von elektivem und totalem Mutismus des Kindesalters. *Zeitschrift fuer Kinderpsychiatrie*, 1952, *19*, 88-91.

Treidel, L. *Grundriss der Sprachstroerungen, deren Ursache, Verlauf und Behandlung*. Berlin: Hirschwald, 1894.

Truper, J. Ein Knabe mit Sprechhemmunger auf psychopathischer Grundlage. *Zeitschrift für Kinderfehler*, 1897, *5*, 138-143.

Truper, J. Ein Knabe mit Sprechhemmungen auf psychopathischer Grundlage. *Zeitschrift für Kindersalter*. Leipzig: Vogel, 1926.

Ullman, L. P. & Krasner, L. Introduction: What is behavior modification? In L. P. Ullman & L. Krasner (Eds.), *Case studies in behavior modification*. New York: Holt, Rinehart & Winston, 1965, pp. 1-65.

Van der Kooy, D., & Webster, C. D. A rapidity effective behavior modification program for an electively mute child. *Journal of Behavior Therapy and Experimental Psychiatry,* 1975, *6*, 149-152.

Von Misch, A. Elektiver Mutismus im Kindersalter. *Zeitschrift fuer Kinderpsychiatrie*, 1952, *19*, 49-87.

Wahler, R. G. Setting generality: Some specific and general effects of child behavior therapy. *Journal of Applied Behavior Analysis*, 1969, *2*, 239-246.

Wallis, H. Zur Systematik des Mutismus im Kindersalter. *Zeitschrift fuer Kinderpsychiatrie*, 1957, *24*, 129-133.

Walton, D. A., & Black, H. The application of modern learning theory to the treatment of aphonia. *Journal of Psychosomatic Research*, 1959, *3*, 303-311.

Waterink, J., & Vedder, R. Einige Faelle von thymogenem Mutismus bei sehr jungen Kindern und seine Behandlung. *Zeitschrift für Kinderforschung (Suppl.)*, 1936, *45*, 368-369.

Weber, A. Zum elektiven Mutismus der Kinder. *Zeitschrift fuer Kinderpsychiatrie*, 1950, *17*, 1-15.

Werner, L. S. Treatment of a child with delayed speech. *Journal of Speech Disorders*, 1945, *10*, 329-334.

Wildman, R. W., II, & Wildman, R. W. The generalization of behavior modification procedures: A review—with special emphasis on classroom applications. *Psychology in the Schools*, 1975, *12*, 432-444.

Willems, E. P. Behavioral technology and behavioral ecology. *Journal of Applied Behavior Analysis*, 1974, *1*, 151-165.

Williamson, D. A., Sanders, S. H., Sewell, W. R., Haney, J. N., & White, D. The behavioral treatment of elective mutism: Two case studies. *Journal of Behavior Therapy and Experimental Psychiatry*, 1977, *8*, 143-149.

Williamson, D. A., Sewell, W. R., Sanders, S. H., Haney, J. N., & White, D. The treatment of reluctant speech using contingency management procedures. *Journal of Behavior Therapy and Experimental Psychiatry*, 1977, *8*, 151-156.

Willmore, L. The role of speech therapy in voice cases. *Journal of Laryngology and Otology*, 1959, *73*, 104.

Wilson, M. S. Hysterical aphonia. *American Journal of Psychiatry*, 1962, *19*, 80.

Winkelman, N. N. Diagnosis and treatment of hysterical aphonia. *Medical Clinics of North America*, 1937, *21*, 1211-1220.

Wright, H. A. A clinical study of children who refuse to talk in school. *Journal of the American Academy of Child Psychiatry*, 1968, *7*, 603-617.

Wulbert, M., Nyman, B. A., Snow, I., & Owen, Y. The efficacy of stimulus fading and contingency management in the treatment of elective mutism: A case study. *Journal of Applied Behavior Analysis*, 1973, *6*, 435-444.

Yates, A. J. *Behavior therapy*, New York: Wiley, 1970.

8 *Neuropsychological and Neurophysiological Assessment of Children with Learning and Behavior Problems:*

A Critical Appraisal

MICHAEL FEUERSTEIN,
MARCIA M. WARD,
AND SAMUEL W. M. LE BARON

1. Introduction

The evaluation of children with learning disabilities and behavior problems has puzzled clinicians for years. In an attempt to improve diagnostic validity, a comprehensive multidisciplinary evaluation of medical, psychoeducational, and behavioral factors has been recommended (Goldstein, 1974; Ross & Ross, 1976). This evaluation at times includes neuropsychological and neurophysiological assessment, intended to determine whether some type of brain damage or more "subtle" brain dysfunction may account for the observed learning and behavior difficulties. The use of these procedures may be a result of the popularity during the last decade of the term *minimal brain dysfunction* (MBD), which was used to describe a variety of learning and behavior problems, including hyperactivity and learning disabilities. The concept of MBD assumes the presence of an underlying central nervous system dysfunc-

MICHAEL FEUERSTEIN • Stanford Research Institute, Menlo Park, California, Stanford University School of Medicine, Stanford, California. MARCIA M. WARD • Department of Psychology, Ohio State University, Columbus, Ohio. SAMUEL W. M. LE BARON • Department of Psychology, Stanford University, Stanford, California.

tion, presumably susceptible to detection by neuropsychological and neurophysiological procedures.

While the use of these techniques may be appropriate in selected cases, clinicians may refer children for these types of evaluations more frequently than is warranted. In fact, it is often recommended that the child with learning or behavior problems referred for assessment of "brain damage" be sent back to the referring psychologist for evaluation of "cognitive and behavioral" difficulties because no clear evidence of neurological damage was actually observed. For example, a recent survey of the current medical practice of pediatricians, child psychiatrists, family practice physicians, and neurologists indicated that their diagnosis of hyperactivity is based primarily on behavioral data and personal medical history, not on routinely gathered physical examinations or laboratory findings (Sandoval, Lambert, & Yandell, 1976).

This chapter will provide a critical review of the literature in the areas of neuropsychological and neurophysiological assessment of children with learning and/or behavior problems. In addition, a description of these specific assessment procedures will be presented. The chapter will evaluate the clinical utility of neuropsychological and neurophysiological assessment in differentiating children with learning and behavior problems from "normal" children and from children with demonstrable neuropathology.

2. Neuropsychological Assessment

2.1. Function of Neuropsychological Assessment

Neuropsychological assessment makes use of a variety of specific tests to determine the effects of changes in brain functioning on behavior and psychological processes. In performing such an assessment, clinical neuropsychologists measure the *level* and *pattern* of performance on a number of intellectual, sensory-motor, sensory-perceptual, verbal, spatial, and memory tests (Golden, 1978; Lezak, 1976; Reitan & Davison, 1974). On the basis of this information, inferences are made regarding the extent and type of neurological deficit and the likely location of any brain lesion(s) that may be present. Such inferences are made possible by a knowledge of brain-behavior relationships for both normal and brain-damaged populations.

The tools of neuropsychological assessment are standardized tests that enable the diagnostician to compare an individual's functioning to norms for groups of normal and impaired individuals, and to make prognostic inferences based on these data. Also, changes in individual functioning over time may be assessed by periodic retesting. In some instances, only one or two tests may be selected to measure an individual's abilities and deficits within a relatively circumscribed range of functioning. However, in order to measure the wide range of deficits associated with brain lesions, a standard battery of tests is often administered.

Many individuals are referred to the clinical neuropsychologist by neurologists or general medical practitioners for assessment of such problems as motor, sensory, language, memory, visual, or intellectual impairment. Others are initially referred by a neurosurgeon for a prognostic description of behavioral changes likely to result from neurosurgery. Neuropsychologists are also called upon to assess psychiatric patients, in order to provide objective information regarding the extent of suspected neuropathology (Buffery, 1977; Heaton, Baade, & Johnson, 1978).

2.2. Description of Specific Tests

A number of tests that have been reported to aid in the diagnosis of learning disabilities and/or behavior problems are listed in Table 1. A few of these tests have been employed in research evaluating the differences in test performance between learning and behavior problem samples and either normal controls or brain-damaged subjects. The test procedures and functions of the most frequently used techniques will be reviewed in this section.[1]

2.2.1. Wechsler Intelligence Scale for Children

The Wechsler Intelligence Scale for Children (WISC) (Wechsler, 1949) is a test of intellectual ability designed for the age range 5-15 years, 11 months. Its revision, WISC-R (Wechsler, 1974), covers ages 6-16 years, 11 months. The WISC contains 12 subtests that assess a wide range of verbal and motor skills, including breadth of general knowledge, verbal concept formation, remote and immediate memory, auditory attention, visual-motor coordination, visual recognition, and visuospatial ability. Due to the widespread use and familiarity of this test, further description will not be provided here.

2.2.2. Bender Visual-Motor Gestalt Test

Another test frequently used in neuropsychological assessment is the Bender Visual-Motor Gestalt Test (Bender, 1946; Koppitz, 1964). The

---

[1] It should be mentioned that the descriptions of the various test functions are based upon the test author's concept as to what neuropsychological function the test is designed to measure.

Table 1

Tests Used in Neuropsychological Assessment of Learning Disabilities and Behavior Problems

Test	Assessment functions
Auditory Discrimination Test (Wepman, 1958)	Auditory perception discrimination.
Bender Visual-Motor Gestalt Test (Bender, 1946; Koppitz, 1964)	Visuographic functions; integrative functions; motor and conceptual capacities.
Benton Visual Retention Test (Benton, 1974)	Visuoconstructive abilities; visual memory, spatial memory.
Frostig Developmental Test of Visual Perception (Frostig, Lefever, & Whittlesey, 1966)	Visual perception; sensorimotor, language, perceptual abilities and higher cognitive processes.
Goodenough-Harris Draw-a-Person Test (Harris, 1963)	Intellectual ability; social and intellectual maturation; ages 3-15.
Graham-Kendall Memory for Designs Test (Graham & Kendall, 1960)	Visuopractic abilities, visual memory.
Halstead Neuropsychological Test Battery for Children (Reitan, 1969; Reitan & Davison, 1974)	General battery of tests for neuropsychological assessment; ages 9-14.
Subtests	
Category Test	Abstract thinking.
Tactual Performance Test	Tactile perception; form and spatial recall.
Rhythm Test	Nonverbal auditory perception; sustained attention.
Speech Sounds Perception Test	Sustained attention; auditory acuity.
Finger Tapping Test	Lateralized fine motor functions.
Time Sense Test	Visual-motor coordination; memory.
Klove-Matthews Motor Steadiness Battery (Reitan & Davison, 1974)	Motor coordination and tremor.
Subtests	
Maze coordination	
Vertical groove steadiness	
Horizontal groove steadiness	
Static steadiness	

Test	Description
Resting steadiness Grooved pegboard Foot tapping	Motor ability.
Lincoln-Oseretsky Motor-Development Scale (Sloan, 1954)	Visuographic abilities.
Minnesota Percepto-Diagnostic Test (Fuller, 1969)	General intellectual ability; nonverbal vocabulary; ages 2½-18.
Peabody Picture Vocabulary Test (Dunn, 1970)	Manual dexterity.
Purdue Pegboard Test (Purdue Research Foundation, 1948)	Nonverbal test of intellectual ability; ages 8-65.
Raven's Progressive Matrices (Raven, 1960)	Battery of tests for neuropsychological assessment; ages 5-8.
Reitan-Indiana Neuropsychological Test Battery for Children (Reitan, 1969; Reitan & Davison, 1974) *Subtests*	
Category Test	Abstract thinking.
Tactual Performance Test	Tactile perception, form and spatial recall.
Finger Tapping Test	Lateralized fine motor functions.
Marching Test	Lateralized gross skeletal muscular function.
Color Form Test	Organizational ability; concept formation; flexibility of thinking process.
Progressive Figures Test	Abstract thinking.
Matching Pictures Test	Abstract concept formation.
Target Test	Reception and expression of visual-spatial relationships.
Individual Performance Test Matching V's Matching figures Concentric squares Star	Reception and expression of visual-spatial relationships.
Reitan-Klove Sensory-Perceptual Examination (Reitan, 1969; Reitan & Davison, 1974)	Supplemental battery to the Halstead battery.

Continued

Table 1 (*Continued*)

Test	Assessment Functions
Subtests	
Tactile, Auditory, and Visual Perception	Perception of bilateral sensory stimulation.
Tactile Finger Recognition	Tactile discrimination.
Finger Tip Number Writing Perception	Tactile recognition of numbers.
Tactile Coin Recognition	Tactile discrimination.
Wechsler Intelligence Scale (WISC) (Wechsler, 1949; Revised Wechsler, 1974)	General intellectual ability: ages 5–16 years 11 months.
Subtests	
Information	General verbal abilities, breadth of knowledge.
Comprehension	Remote memory; social knowledge and judgment.
Arithmetic	Immediate memory; concentration; conceptual manipulation.
Similarities	Verbal concept formation; general intellectual ability.
Digit span	Auditory attention; immediate auditory memory span; internal visual scanning.
Vocabulary	Verbal and general mental ability.
Digit Symbol/Coding	Motor persistence; sustained attention; response speed; visual–motor coordination.
Picture Completion	Visual recognition; organizational ability.
Block Design	Organizational thinking processes; visuospatial organization; visual–motor coordination.
Picture Arrangement	Sequential thinking; concept formation.
Object assembly	Visuospatial and organization ability.
Maze	Nonverbal reasoning; visuospatial ability.
Weschler Preschool and Primary Scale of Intelligence (Wechsler, 1967)	General intellectual ability: ages 4–6½ years.

"Bender" consists of a set of nine designs, each presented on a separate card. The subject is told that the designs will be shown one at a time, and that the task is to copy each as accurately as possible. Little beyond these basic instructions is offered so that organization of the responses is left to the individual.

It has been suggested that the Bender-Gestalt Test evaluates the ability to combine visual perception with motor ability in the performance of spatial tasks. This is a quick and easy test to administer, which may account for its wide popularity, and for its promotion by some as a valid single indicator of organic dysfunction. Indeed, Lezak (1976) states that this test has become, for some neuropsychologists, "a kind of psychological litmus paper for the detection of brain damage."

2.2.3. Reitan-Indiana Neuropsychological Test Battery for Children

The Reitan-Indiana Test Battery was designed to evaluate motor, verbal and spatial abilities; tactile, auditory, and visual perception; abstracting ability; and memory for the age range 5-8 years (Reitan, 1969; Reitan & Davison, 1974). As Table 1 indicates, this battery includes nine major subtests: *Category, Tactual Performance, Finger Tapping, Marching, Color Form, Progressive Figures, Matching Pictures, Target,* and *Individual Performance.* A brief description of these subtests is provided below.

The *Category Test* utilizes a projection apparatus for presentation of a series of figures on a screen. A response panel is provided, with which the subject is required to indicate the correct answer to each problem. Only one response per item is allowed, and a bell or buzzer sounds indicating whether each response is correct or incorrect. Before the test begins, the subject is informed that the test consists of several groups of figures, and that there is a single "principle" within each group. Thus, as the subject progresses through each group, he or she is given the opportunity to test hypotheses until the correct "principle" within the group is derived. For example, in the first group, the subject is simply required to match Arabic numerals above the answer levers with individual Roman numerals that are presented on the screen. Successful performance on the Category Test requires abstract reasoning, short-term recall, and the ability to attend to test stimuli.

In the *Tactual Performance Test* the subject is required to place six blocks of varying shapes into their appropriate spaces on a form board. The subject is blindfolded before the beginning of the test. The instructions require that the blocks be placed first with the dominant hand only, then with the nondominant hand only, then with both hands together. The time required for each trial provides a measure of relative efficiency for each hand alone, compared with both hands together.

After the board and blocks have been put out of sight, the blindfold is removed and the subject is asked to draw a reproduction of the shapes and spatial configuration of the blocks and board. This test provides a basis for assessment of tactile form discrimination, sensory-spatial abilities, motor coordination, memory, and spatial visualization.

The *Finger Tapping Test* is a measure of finger-tapping speed with the index finger of each hand using a mounted electric tapper connected to a counting device. This test permits assessment of lateralized fine motor functions.

The *Marching Test* consists of a series of circles connected by a line on both sides of five sheets of paper. The examiner records the time required for the child to "march" up the page, from one circle to another, using a crayon in either the dominant or the nondominant hand. This procedure provides an evaluation of lateralized gross skeletal muscular function.

The *Color Form Test* requires the subject to follow a sequence of figures on a page. These figures vary in terms of color and shape, and the subject must move from the initial figure to another that is similar in shape but different in color, then to a figure different in shape but similar in color, and so on, alternating throughout the test. The *Progressive Figures Test* also requires the subject to move from one figure to another on the basis of interrelated alternating geometrical shapes. The *Matching Pictures Test* consists of five pages on which the child is required to match items from the top of the page to items at the bottom. There is a progression to more complex items during the test, requiring a certain amount of ability to generalize. All three of these tests provide a basis for assessing organizational ability, abstraction, concept formation, and flexibility in thinking.

The *Target Test* and the *Individual Performance Test* are concerned with receptive and expressive aspects of visual-spatial relationships. The Target Test consists of a stimulus figure containing nine large dots in the form of a square, upon which the examiner outlines a series of patterns. The subject is required to duplicate these patterns on an answer sheet. The Individual Performance Test is comprised of four tasks: *Matching V's, Star, Matching Figures*, and *Concentric Squares*. The first, Matching V's, requires the pairing of a series of small blocks containing varying angles with stimulus cards containing the same angles. For the Star task, the child is asked to reproduce a six-sided star by drawing two overlapping triangles. In Matching Figures, the child is asked to match a variety of figures with cards containing appropriate matching figures. For Concentric Squares, the subject is required to copy a figure consisting of concentric squares. These tasks are scored on the basis of accuracy and time required for completion.

2.2.4. *The Halstead Neuropsychological Test Battery for Children*

The subtests in the Halstead Battery were adapted from the Halstead adult version by simplifying some of the components for the age range 9-14 years (Reitan, 1969; Reitan & Davison, 1974). The first three subtests include the *Category Test, Tactual Performance Test,* and *Finger Tapping Test* as described in the Reitan-Indiana Battery previously. The remaining subtests include the *Rhythm Test, Speech Sounds Perception Test,* and the *Time Sense Test.* The six subtests of the Halstead Battery are designed to evaluate abstract thinking, tactile perception, nonverbal auditory perception, sustained attention, lateralized fine motor functions, visual-motor coordination and memory (Reitan, 1969; Reitan & Davison, 1974). The three new subtests are described below.

In the *Rhythm Test,* the subject is required to differentiate between pairs of rhythmic beats that are sometimes identical and sometimes different. In addition to testing nonverbal auditory perception, this test provides some measure of the ability to maintain attention to a task.

The *Speech Sounds Perception Test* consists of a list of spoken nonsense words. The subject is required to select each spoken word from a group of four alternatives printed for each word. This test is a measure of auditory acuity and also requires sustained attention.

The *Time Sense Test* requires the subject to coordinate key depression with the sweep hand on a clock, then to reproduce the correct time of key depression from memory. This task measures visual-motor coordination and memory.

3. *Neuropsychological Findings*

A review of the literature indicates that the tests described above are the most commonly employed neuropsychological procedures for the assessment of a variety of learning disabilities and behavior problems. All of these tests have been traditionally used to differentiate children with demonstrable brain damage from normal controls. In this section, the effectiveness of each of these tests in differentiating groups of children with behavior problems and learning disabilities from normal controls will be evaluated. Unfortunately, while a substantial literature exists on these childhood problems there are few *empirical* studies on the neuropsychological assessment of children with learning and behavior disorders. In addition, with these clinical disorders the interpretability of the available research is compromised in many cases by the lack of normal control groups, the use of poorly defined clinical samples, the prevalence of case studies, and the disregard for IQ cutoff scores. In an attempt to simplify the often contradictory and confusing findings, only statistically significant results from studies that employed adequate controls will be reported.

3.1. Wechsler Intelligence Scale for Children (WISC)

A number of studies have employed the WISC to compare normal controls with groups of children who have learning disabilities and/or behavior problems (Klatskin, McNamara, Shaffer, & Pincus, 1972; Klonoff & Low, 1974; Myklebust, 1973; Palkes & Stewart, 1972; Reitan & Boll, 1973; Stevens, Boydstun, Dykman, Peters, & Sinton, 1967). Reitan and Boll (1973) used the WISC to identify differences among four groups of children. The 25 subjects in the Brain Damaged group had confirmed independent neurological evidence of cerebral damage while the 25 normal control subjects had no evidence of neurological damage or academic or behavior problems. The MBD-Academic Difficulties group consisted of 25 children with learning problems.[2] The 19 children in the MBD-Behavior Problems group were referred for school behavior difficulties. The MBD and normal subjects had WISC IQs above 80, and the mean age of all groups was 7.5 years. The results indicated that the Brain Damaged group scored lower than the other three groups on all factors of the WISC, and significantly lower on all but 4 of the 45 possible scale and subtest comparisons. The MBD-Academic Difficulties groups scored significantly lower than the control group on Full Scale IQ, Verbal IQ, Performance IQ, Information, Similarities, Arithmetic, and Coding, while the MBD-Behavior Problem group scored significantly lower than normal controls on Verbal IQ and Coding only. The MBD-Behavior Problem group performed better on the WISC than the MBD-Academic Difficulties group, with significant differences on Full Scale IQ, Verbal IQ, Information, Similarities, and Arithmetic scores. In general, the two MBD groups performed more similar to normal than to brain-damaged subjects on the WISC, but the MBD-Academic Difficulties group was somewhat more impaired than the MBD-Behavior Problems group.

Klonoff and Low (1974) compared two groups of MCD or "Minimal Cerebral Damage" children (this label was used to define a group of children with two of the following: motor, intellectual, or personality problems) with sex- and age-matched normal controls. The younger groups of 51 MCDs and 51 controls were between 4 and 9 years of age while the older groups of 44 MCDs and 44 controls were between 9 and 16 years old. For both the younger and older subjects the results indicated that the Full Scale IQ of the MCDs was significantly lower than

---

[2] At times various authors use the term MBD when describing children with learning and/or behavior problems. We will retain the use of this label only when specific sample descriptions were not provided in the original report.

their respective controls. The significantly impaired performance of the younger MCDs was evident for Full Scale IQ, Verbal IQ, Performance IQ, and all 12 WISC subtests. The older MCDs scored significantly lower than their age-matched controls on Full Scale IQ, Verbal IQ, Information, Comprehension, Arithmetic, Similarities, Vocabulary, Block Design, and Coding. When retested after 1 year, the younger MCDs and controls showed significant improvement on Full Scale IQ, Performance IQ, Object Assembly, and Mazes. The older MCD and control groups exhibited a significant improvement on Picture Arrangement and Object Assembly at the second testing. Also, it appeared that both MCD groups and their age-matched controls improved at about equal rates over the course of 1 year. But in comparing the MCD groups with their age-matched controls, the older MCDs were found to be less impaired than their younger cohorts.

Stevens *et al.* (1967) studied a group of 26 children with specific learning disabilities and/or behavior problems and a group of 26 normal control subjects. The children ranged from 6 to 12 years of age and the two groups were matched for age, sex, and socioeconomic class. Compared to the controls, the clinical group exhibited significant impairment on Full Scale IQ, Verbal IQ, Information, Arithmetic, Digit Span, and Coding. It was reported that in comparison to his or her normal scale score, the child with learning and/or behavior problems is most likely to show elevated scores on Comprehension and Picture Completion and depressed scores on Arithmetic and Coding.

Myklebust (1973) compared two groups of underachievers having minor learning disabilities (Borderline LD) or severe learning disabilities (Severe LD) with their sex, classroom, and socioeconomic-matched normal controls. A Verbal IQ or Performance IQ of at least 90 was the cutoff for all groups. The results indicated that the Borderline LD group scored significantly lower than the control group on Verbal IQ, Information, Similarities, Vocabulary, Digit Span, Block Design, Object Assembly, and Coding. The severe LD group scored significantly lower than the controls on Verbal IQ, Information, Arithmetic, Similarities, Vocabulary, Digit Span, Block Design, Object Assembly, and Coding.

Palkes and Stewart (1972) studied a group of 32 hyperactive children and 34 normal controls. The groups were matched for sex, age, grade, race, and socioeconomic class. The results indicated that the WISC Full Scale IQ, Performance IQ, and Verbal IQ were all significantly impaired for the hyperactive children.

Klatskin *et al.* (1972) compared 25 children who had learning disabilities and/or behavior problems with 25 normal controls. All children were between 7 and 12 years old with a WISC Full Scale IQ of 85 or above. The results indicated that the two groups did not differ on Full Scale IQ, Verbal IQ, or Performance IQ, but that the children with LD and/or behavior problems were significantly impaired on Coding and on the average score of Block Design and Object Assembly.

As illustrated in Table 2, these studies indicate that children with learning disabilities and/or behavior problems score lower than controls on a number of WISC scales and subtests. As would be expected, the learning-disabled children evidenced a greater number of deficits when compared to controls than did the children with behavior problems. In particular the Coding and Information subtests were consistently lower for the LD and mixed LD-behavior problem groups. It is unclear whether the consistent impairment on these subtests for the LD children reflects the true nature of learning disabilities or whether this finding is the result of poorly IQ-matched samples. As indicated in Table 2, a number of these studies reported Full Scale IQ differences between clinical and control samples. The significance of this Full Scale IQ difference is unclear given the fact that these studies tended to include a high proportion of children with above-average intelligence in the "normal" sample. Indeed, as the following studies suggest, a different clinical picture emerges when matched IQ samples are used.

Ackerman, Peters, and Dykman (1971a) tested 29 learning-disabled boys (LD) and 29 boys who reported having no academic difficulties (controls). All subjects were between 8 and 12 years old, in good physical health, with WISC Full Scale IQs greater than 90. All of the LD subjects had failed or were in the process of failing at least one grade in school. The results indicated that although the LD and control groups were carefully matched for Full Scale IQ, the LDs scored significantly lower on the Verbal Scale and significantly higher on the Performance Scale than did the control subjects. The LD group was divided behaviorally into hyperactive, normoactive, and hypoactive subgroups and also by positive, equivocal, and negative neurological findings. There were no significant differences on the WISC between any of the groups across the three levels of behavioral or neurological classifications. The authors state that the Verbal Scale depression in LD subjects is probably valid. They argue that in order to obtain groups that were carefully matched for Full Scale IQ, they unknowingly selected LDs who had Performance IQs high enough to counterbalance the low Verbal IQs. Although the LD groups reportedly evidenced less subtest score variability, the difference was not significant. In addition, only the Arithmetic subtest reliably differentiated LD and control groups. The authors conjecture that integrity in both Verbal and Performance IQ is necessary for a smooth academic career. They concluded that learning disabilities are much more frequently related to verbal deficiencies than to performance problems but that there are no characteristic WISC patterns that can accurately discriminate LD children from normals.

TABLE 2

Wechsler Intelligence Scale for Children:Findings

Type of comparison	Clinical groups	Scales and subtests[a]
Mixed Learning Disability (LD) and/ or Behavior Problem groups that scored significantly lower than controls	MCD younger (Klonoff & Low, 1974)	1 2 3 4 5 6 7 8 9 10 11 12 13 14 15
	MCD older (Klonoff & Low, 1974)	1 2 4 5 6 7 9 10 12
	LD and/or Behavior Problems (Stevens, Boydston, Dykman, Peters, & Sinton, 1967)	1 2 4 6 8 10
	LD and/or Behavior Problems (Klatskin, McNamara, Shaffer, & Pincus, 1972)	10 12 14
Behavior Problem groups that scored significantly lower than controls	Hyperactive (Palkes & Stewart, 1972)	1 3 7 11 15
	MBD-Behavior Problems (Reitan & Boll, 1973)	2 10
Learning Disability groups that scored significantly lower than controls	Borderline LD (Myklebust, 1973)	2 4 7 8 9 10 12 14
	Severe LD (Myklebust, 1973)	2 4 6 7 8 9 10 12 14
	MBD-Academic Difficulties (Reitan & Boll, 1973)	1 2 3 4 6 7 10

[a]Each numeral represents a finding from a study in which the clinical group scored significantly lower than the control group on a specific WISC scale or subtest. The various clinical groups include Minimal Cerebral Damage (MCD), Learning Disability (LD), and Minimal Brain Dysfunction (MBD). The mixed samples included groups of both learning-disabled and behavior-problem children.

1. Full Scale IQ	4. Information	7. Similarities	10. Coding	13. Picture Arrangement
2. Verbal IQ	5. Comprehension	8. Digit Span	11. Picture Completion	14. Object Assembly
3. Performance IQ	6. Arithmetic	9. Vocabulary	12. Block Design	15. Mazes

Wikler, Dixon, and Parker (1970) studied 24 children with learning disabilities and behavior problems and 24 normal controls. The clinical group (5 to 15 years of age) had no evidence of organic neurological disease and had IQs above 86. The groups were matched for sex, age, race, general social class, and intelligence. The results indicated that these "intelligence"-matched groups did not differ on Full Scale IQ, Verbal IQ, or Performance IQ, although the learning-disabilities and/or behavior-problems group did score significantly lower than the controls on the Coding subtest.

These IQ matched controlled studies indicate that very few differences exist between the clinical and normal control groups. Table 3 suggests that the clinical use of the WISC in the identification of learning-disabled and behavior-problem children must await further well-controlled investigations.

Clinically, it has been suggested that a WISC profile that shows greater than usual variability or "subtest scatter" is suggestive of behavior problems and learning disabilities (Clements & Peters, 1962). However, research that has examined subtest scatter has produced contradictory findings. Stevens et al. (1967) and Palkes and Stewart (1972) reported increased WISC subtest scatter for children with learning disabilities and behavior problems, while Ackerman et al. (1971a) and Coleman and Rasof (1963) found less variability in the WISC profiles of these same children. Anderson, Kaufman, and Kaufman (1976) report no differences in WISC profile scatter between LDs and normals. In conclusion, the available research does not endorse the use of any one WISC IQ cutoff score or pattern of subtest deficits for the assessment of these childhood problems.

3.2. Bender Visual-Motor Gestalt Test

The Bender Gestalt Test has been used repeatedly in an attempt to differentiate groups of learning-disabled and behavior-problem children from normal children. Three studies (Ackerman, Peters, & Dykman, 1971b; Koppitz, 1975; Larsen, Rogers, & Sowell, 1976) have compared learning-disabled children with normal controls; two studies (Klatskin et al., 1972; Wikler et al., 1970) have compared groups of children with learning disabilities and/or behavior problems to normal controls; and one study has compared hyperactive children to normals (Palkes & Stewart, 1972). All but one of these studies report that a formal scoring system was employed. The most commonly used scoring system was developed by Koppitz (1964) to tabulate the occurrence of 30 possible errors.

Ackerman et al. (1971b) studied 82 learning-disabled children and 34 normal controls. All subjects were 8- to 12-year-old boys with

TABLE 3

Wechsler Intelligence Scale for Children: Findings from Studies Utilizing IQ-Matched Samples

Type of comparison	Clinical groups	Scales and subtests[a]
Groups that scored significantly lower or higher than controls who were matched for IQ	Learning Disabilities (Ackerman, Peters, & Dykman, 1971a)	2 3* 6
		1
	LD and/or Behavior Problems (Wikler, Dixon, & Parker, 1970)	10

[a]Each numeral represents a finding from a study in which the clinical group scored significantly lower than the control group on a specific WISC scale or subtest; an * indicates that the clinical group scored significantly higher than the control group on that WISC scale or subtest. The various clinical groups include Learning Disability (LD) and a mixed sample which included children with both learning disabilities and behavior problems.

1. Full Scale IQ	6. Arithmetic	11. Picture Completion
2. Verbal IQ	7. Similarities	12. Block Design
3. Performance IQ	8. Digit Span	13. Picture Arrangement
4. Information	9. Vocabulary	14. Object Assembly
5. Comprehension	10. Coding	15. Mazes

either Verbal IQs or Performance IQs above 90. The LDs were in serious danger of school failure. All Bender protocols were scored using the Koppitz technique. The results indicated that 67% of the LDs as opposed to 44% of the controls scored above the mean Koppitz error score appropriate to their age. A significantly greater number of LDs than controls made errors in each of the three error categories of perseveration, rotation, and distortion. The authors warn that although the Bender score significantly differentiated between LDs and normal controls, there were many false positives and false negatives. Also, the difference in the number of *markedly* impaired Bender protocols (scored one standard deviation or more above the age norm) for LDs (24%) and normal controls (16%) was not significant.

Larsen *et al.* (1976) administered four "perceptual skills" tests to a group of 59 learning-disabled children and a group of 30 normal controls. All subjects were between 8 and 11 years old and had normal IQs; the two groups were matched for age and sex. While the Wepman Auditory Discrimination Test and three subtests of the Illinois Test of Psycholinguistic Abilities did not successfully differentiate between groups, the LD group had significantly higher error scores (scoring system unspecified) than the controls on the Bender. However, the authors warn that the difference in scores between LDs and normal controls was small and that caution is necessary when educational decisions regarding individual children are made primarily on the basis of an impaired Bender.

Koppitz (1975) compared a control group of 30 average students with two groups of 23 children with learning disabilities. One group of LDs had few or no reading skills and the other LD group had serious arithmetic, writing, concentration, and inner control problems. All children were between 8 and 10 years old with a mean IQ of 100 for the LDs and 105 for the controls. The results indicated that there were no significant differences between the two LD groups on the Bender Gestalt test, but the LDs had significantly higher error scores (Koppitz) than the controls. This suggests that the Bender Test scores can discriminate between children with learning disabilities and average students.

Wikler *et al.* (1970) studied a group of 24 children referred for learning disabilities and/or behavior problems and a group of 24 normal controls. The clinical group was composed of about equal proportions of referral for underachievement and for hyperactivity. An IQ cutoff of 86 was used and the groups were matched for sex, age, race, general social class, and intelligence. The results indicated that the Bender Gestalt test (Koppitz scoring) significantly differentiated the two groups, with the learning-disabled and behavior-problem group earning higher error scores. In addition, a subgroup of hyperactive children performed less well than did a group of nonhyperactives.

Klatskin *et al.* (1972) compared a group of 25 children who were diagnosed as having learning disabilities and/or behavior problems with a group of 25 normal controls. All children were between 7 and 12 years old with a WISC IQ of 85 or above. The results indicated that the error scores (Koppitz) were able to differentiate between the two groups. Generally, the controls scored within 1 year of their chronological ages while the clinical sample had profiles that resembled those of younger samples. The authors suggest that the Bender has diagnostic validity when used to evaluate children who have normal intelligence and minor neurologic signs.

Palkes and Stewart (1972) compared 32 hyperactive children with 34 normal controls on Bender error scores (Koppitz). The groups were matched for sex, age, grade, race, and socioeconomic class. When the Bender scores were adjusted for WISC Full Scale IQ, there were no significant differences between groups.

In summary, of the six studies reported, all but one indicated that the Bender Gestalt Test successfully differentiated between clinical and control groups. In several studies, although the differences were statistically significant, they were generally quite small. Interestingly, the one study that found no differences between groups was the only study that adjusted Bender Gestalt scores for IQ (Palkes & Stewart, 1972). While the results of the research suggest that the Bender Gestalt Test differentiates children with learning disabilities and/or behavior problems from controls, certain investigators (Ackerman *et al.*, 1971a, 1971b; Larson *et al.*, 1976) warn against overdiagnosis on the basis of the Bender score when it is used with individual children in applied settings. In addition, the information obtained from the Bender Gestalt Test is of limited value in that it does not readily translate into a treatment plan for children with these problems.

3.3. Neuropsychological Test Batteries

The Reitan-Indiana Neuropsychological Test Battery has been employed in two studies in an attempt to differentiate children with MBD from controls (Klonoff & Low, 1974; Reitan & Boll, 1973). The Reitan-Indiana Battery was also employed in a study comparing LDs with suspected brain damage and LDs without brain damage (Tsushima & Towne, 1977), and one of its subtests was successfully used to differentiate between groups of normal children and children with school problems, emotional problems, and known brain lesions (Knights & Tymchuk, 1968).

Reitan and Boll (1973) studied four groups of subjects: 25 control subjects who had no evidence of brain dysfunction, 25 Brain Damaged subjects, 25 MBD-Academic Difficulties subjects, and 19 MBD-Behavior Problem subjects (for study details refer to section 3.1.). The results indicate that the Brain Damaged group performed significantly more poorly than the other three groups. In particular, the performance scores for the Brain Damaged group were significantly lower than the scores for the control group on 23 out of 26 variables. The Brain Damaged group scored significantly lower than the MBD-Behavior Problems group on the following subtests: Target, Matching V's, Tactual Performance Test-Memory and Localization, Category, Matching Pictures, Color Form, Progressive Figures, Finger Tapping, nondominant hand Grip Strength, nondominant hand Marching Test, Tactual Performance Test, Tactile Finger Localization, left-handed Finger Tip Symbol Writing, and Tactile Finger Recognition (for a description of the associated neuropsychological functions refer to Table 1 and to section 2.2.3.). There were fewer tests that produced significant differences between Brain Damaged and MBD-Academic Difficulties groups, but those tests that did differ included Target Test, Tactual Performance Test-Localization, Category Test, Matching Pictures, Color Form, Progressive Figures, Finger Tapping, Marching, Tactual Finger Localization, Finger Tip Symbol Writing, and Tactile Finger Recognition. There were very few differences between the control, MBD-Academic Difficulties, and MBD-Behavior Problem groups. The only test on which controls scored significantly higher than the MBD groups was the Marching Test with the dominant hand. In addition, the only test that differentiated the two MBD groups was Tactual Performance Test-Memory, with the MBD-Behavior Problems group having significantly greater recall. In general, the Brain Damaged group evidenced significant impairment on most of the subtests of the Reitan-Indiana Battery while there were few differences between the MBD groups and controls.

In an effort to clarify general areas of dysfunction on which the four groups differed, Reitan and Boll analyzed the test results according to *function*. They reported that the Brain Damaged group was significantly impaired, in contrast to the control and MBD groups, on tests of motor speed, strength, coordination, problem solving, tactile perception, academic achievement, visuospatial reception, incidental memory, and concept formation. In contrast, the control group's performance was greater than the two MBD groups only on tests of coordination and the MBD-Behavior Problem group scored significantly poorer than the control or MBD-Academic Difficulties groups on tests of incidental recall.

Klonoff and Low (1974) also employed the Reitan-Indiana Neuropsychological Test Battery to compare a group of normal controls with a group of MCD children (for study details refer to section 3.1.). Since WISC IQ scores differed significantly between the MCD and control groups, intelligence level was held constant and the results of the Reitan-Indiana Battery were analyzed independent of IQ levels. The younger MCD group was significantly impaired only on the Matching V's Test and on Sound Recognition when compared to their age-matched controls. It is of interest to note that the younger MCD and control subjects improved significantly on 11 of the 31 test variables when retested 1 year later. This finding illustrates the need for attention to potential change in scores resulting from basic developmental maturation.

For the older MCDs and controls there were a greater number of differences, although the total number of tests for which differences occurred were still relatively few. The older MCDs showed significant impairment in Category, Matching Figures, Star, Concentric Squares, and Matching Pictures tests. The older children were also administered several tests of motor steadiness, and on those of MCDs were significantly impaired on the Grooved Pegboard Test with the dominant and nondominant hand. Both the older MCDs and controls improved significantly on a long list including 32 out of 42 variables at the 1-year retest.

It is interesting that when neuropsychological test scores were not corrected for initial IQ differences the exact opposite findings were reported. The younger MCD children demonstrated greater impairment than their matched controls while the older MCD children appeared less impaired in the uncorrected analysis. Given that the standard definition of children with MCD includes normal intelligence as a factor, adequate scientific control requires matching on IQ if one is to evaluate neuropsychological deficits in groups that are comparable except on the MCD behavior/learning problem dimension. However, from a clinical perspective, the Klonoff and Low data suggest that IQ scores contribute considerably to observed neuropsychological deficits in the MCD child and that this relationship interacts with age. Further developmental research on this relationship would be of interest to improve understanding of the role of age and IQ in neuropsychological deficits in these children.

Tsushima and Towne (1977) tested two groups of 6- to 8-year-old children with learning problems: One group of LDs had a history of serious illness or trauma that involved possible brain damage and the other group had no history of brain damage. Testing with the Reitan-Indiana Battery indicated that the LD group with possible brain damage was significantly impaired on Grip Strength with the dominant and nondominant hand, Finger Tapping with the dominant and nondominant hand, and Purdue Pegboard with the nondominant hand. When the four best indicators from the Reitan-Indiana Battery (Dynamometer, Finger Tapping, Tactile Finger Recognition, and Finger Tip Symbol Recognition—all performed with the nondominant hand) in addition to the WISC Picture Completion subtest were used to *discriminate between*

LD subgroups (brain damage/no brain damage), the overall accuracy of prediction was 73%. When the complete Reitan-Indiana Battery plus the WISC and Wide Range Achievement Test comprising a total of 37 variables was used, the accuracy of group identification increased to 86%. The differences between the LD subjects with questionable brain disorders and the LD subjects with no brain damage were most apparent on tests of motor ability, visual perception, and visual-motor skills.

Knights and Tymchuk (1968) employed the Halstead-Reitan Category Test for Children to compare groups of normal children with three groups of children with either school learning problems, emotional and behavior problems, or known brain damage. All groups were comprised of 40 children who were matched on age (mean = 10 years) and IQ (WISC IQ = 94). The results indicated that the normal controls had fewer errors than the children with school problems, emotional problems, or brain damage. There were no differences, however, between the learning-problem, behavioral-problem, and brain-damaged groups.

In summary, three studies have employed the Reitan-Indiana Neuropsychological Test Battery (Klonoff & Low, 1974; Reitan & Boll, 1973; Tsushima & Towne, 1977) to analyze the pattern of neuropsychological test results of groups of children with learning and/or behavior problems as compared to brain-damaged and normal control subjects. As illustrated in Table 4, there were very few critical items that differentiated children with learning and/or behavior problems from normal controls. In addition, there is no single test variable from the Reitan-Indiana Battery that proved to be significant in more than one of these studies. In contrast, Table 4 also illustrates that there were many significant differences between the brain-damage children and the control and learning/behavior-problem groups.

Reports of case studies have suggested that the Reitan-Indiana and other neuropsychological test batteries can be used to identify a profile of neurological deficits for individual children with learning and behavior problems (Reitan & Heineman, 1968; Trupin & Townes, 1976). However, the presently available research does not support the use of neuropsychological batteries as an assessment tool to aid in the identification of learning disabilities and behavior problems. To date, there are no consistent neuropsychological test "profiles" for these childhood problems.

4. Neurophysiological Findings

Evaluation of the physiologic integrity of the nervous system in children with learning and/or behavior problems has increased in recent

TABLE 4
Neuropsychological Findings

Type of comparison	Clinical groups[a]	Subtests[b]
Groups that scored significantly *lower* than normal controls	MCD younger (Klonoff & Low, 1974)	15 19
	MCD older (Klonoff & Low, 1974)	1 13 16 17 18 30 31
	MBD-Academic Difficulties (Reitan & Boll, 1973)	10
	MBD-Behavior Problems (Reitan & Boll, 1973)	10
Groups that scored significantly *higher* than the brain damaged group	MBD-Academic Difficulties (Reitan & Boll, 1973)	1 6 7 8 9 10 11 12 13 14 20 21 22 23 25
	MBD-Behavior Problems (Reitan & Boll, 1973)	1 2 3 4 5 6 7 8 10 11 12 13 14 15 20 21 22 23 25 28
	Controls (Reitan & Boll, 1973)	1 2 3 4 5 6 7 8 9 10 11 12 13 14 15 16 20 21 22 23 24 25 28

[a]MCD = Minimal Cerebral Damage; MBD = Minimal Brain Dysfunction.
[b]Each number represents a significant finding from a controlled study.

1. Category Test
2. Tactile Performance Test-dominant hand
3. Tactile Performance Test-nondominant hand
4. Tactile Performance Test-both hands
5. Tactile Performance Test-memory
6. Tactile Performance Test-localization
7. Finger Tapping-dominant hand
8. Finger Tapping-nondominant hand
9. Marching-dominant hand
10. Marching-nondominant hand
11. Color Form
12. Progressive Figures
13. Matching Pictures
14. Target
15. Matching V's
16. Matching Figures
17. Concentric Squares
18. Star
19. Sound Recognition
20. Tactile Finger Recognition-dominant hand
21. Tactile Finger Recognition-nondominant hand
22. Tactile Finger Localization-dominant hand
23. Tactile Finger Localization-nondominant hand
24. Finger Tip Symbol Writing-dominant hand
25. Finger Tip Symbol Writing-nondominant hand
26. Grip Strength-dominant hand
27. Grip Strength-nondominant hand
28. Purdue Pegboard-dominant hand
29. Purdue Pegboard-nondominant hand
30. Grooved Pegboard-dominant hand
31. Grooved Pegboard-nondominant hand

TABLE 5

Physiological Measures Included in the Assessment of Learning-and/or Behavior-Problem Children

Measure	Description	Physiologic basis	Behavioral significance
Electroencephalograph (EEG)	Scalp recording of gross cortical activity with frequency and amplitude parameters.	Synchronous and desynchronous firing of nerve cells. Reflects summation of electrical potentials produced in brain, particularly cortex.	Frequency-amplitudes related to various states of consciousness. Lower frequency-higher amplitude activity indicative of less alert/attentive states while high frequency-low amplitude activity correlated with attention and high arousal.
40-Hz EEG	Specific frequency of EEG activity (i.e., 40 cycles per second).	Same as EEG.	Increases in this response occur during periods of focused arousal/attention. It has been suggested that this response reflects cortical excitability necessary to store information in short-term memory prior to consolidation in long-term store.
Sensory averaged evoked response (AER)	Measure of cortical responsiveness to sensory stimuli. The AER is derived from the summation of a number of time-locked EEG responses to a sensory stimulus.	Same as EEG.	The duration from the onset of the sensory stimulus to the first appearance of specific AER components (i.e., latency) and the amplitude of various components in the total response are measures of the degree of cortical responsivity to the stimulus. Latency and amplitude measures are related to attention and other components of information processing.
Skin conductance	Electrical activity of the skin	Sweat-gland activity.	High levels of skin conductance are indicative of autonomic nervous system activation and its psychological concomitants (i.e., increased cognitive and/or emotional activity.)
Heart rate	Rate of heart-muscle contraction.	Bioelectric potentials produced by cardiac muscle during contraction.	Deceleration often observed during periods of attentiveness. More specifically, the typical pattern of heart-rate changes during reaction-time task is acceleration after key press at start and end of trial and "anticipatory" deceleration during foreperiod.

years. It appears that the widespread use of the term *minimal brain dysfunction* has sensitized clinicians to the possibility of an underlying physiologic dysfunction in the nervous system of children exhibiting a variety of learning disabilities and/or behavior problems. This section will review the literature on the various clinical diagnostic techniques and laboratory procedures designed to identify various characteristics indicative of a nervous system deficit in children with learning disabilities and/or behavior problems. An evaluation of the clinical utility of standard EEG diagnostic procedures will be undertaken. In addition, a discussion of certain experimental approaches, some of which have been applied at a clinical level and others which remain in their developmental stages but could emerge as additional clinical assessment techniques, will be presented.

Table 5 lists the various measures that have been used to identify physiological deficits or differences in children with behavior problems and learning disabilities. These measures include the electroencephalograph (EEG), responses derived from the EEG such as the sensory averaged evoked response (AER) and 40-Hz EEG, and autonomic nervous system indices of arousal including skin conductance and heart rate. The table should provide a general guide to the physiologic basis of the response and its behavioral significance. A number of volumes are available for the reader who is interested in obtaining further information on the physiology and psychophysiology of these measures (e.g., Greenfield & Sternbach, 1972; Venables & Christie, 1975).

4.1. Electroencephalograph (EEG)

It is well known that the EEG is a diagnostic aid in the evaluation of disordered brain function. While its use in the assessment of hyperactivity dates back to 1934 (Kahn & Cohen, 1934), the justification for a diagnostic EEG on a child with hyperactivity or learning disabilities is at present unclear. The use of the classic EEG evaluation rests on the assumption that these learning and behavior problems with their unknown etiology may be characterized by a subtle brain disorder or dysfunction that can be identified through the measurement of gross cortical activity. While it is possible for physiological differences to exist in the clinical populations, the use of clinical EEGs to evaluate such differences remains equivocal.

A number of factors may account for the contradictory findings observed in the clinical EEGs of these children. These include difficulties in defining a homogeneous clinical entity of hyperactive or learning-disabled children. In addition, the prevalence of "borderline" EEG findings in these children poses a problem in that criteria for classifying an EEG as "borderline" tend to vary, and developmental changes in the EEG often make a diagnosis of "borderline" questionable. Moreover, a substantial percent of "normal" children (10-20%) display "abnormal" EEG findings, making it troublesome to determine the discriminate validity of this procedure (Freeman, 1967). Other difficulties in evaluating the utility of the EEG in this area arise because of the variability in recording procedures. Some investigators record EEG activity during wakeful-rest periods, while others evaluate the EEG during drowsiness, hyperventilation, sleep, and/or photic stimulation. In certain studies, comparative data on normal controls are lacking, and in those reports with appropriate controls, the results are often contradictory. Only studies with normative comparison data will be discussed.

Wikler *et al.* (1970) compared 24 children (5-15 years old) referred by teachers, parents, or physicians to an outpatient clinic for learning and/or behavior problems with a group of 24 controls matched on sex, age, race, intelligence, and social class. There was no history of scholastic or behavior problems in the controls. The clinic group was further differentiated into hyperactive and nonhyperactive subgroups. The EEG findings indicated that waking slow-wave activity was significantly more apparent in the records of the clinic group than in those of the controls. However, the difference appeared to be due primarily to an excessive amount of slow-wave activity in the nonhyperactive clinic subgroup. The presence of EEG transients or sudden bursts of atypical activity (e.g., multifocal negative spikes, bitemporal repetitive spikes, 6-cycle-per-second spikes, paroxysmal spike-wave discharges, sharp waves) during drowsiness or sleep was significantly greater in the learning and/or behavior problem group than in the controls. The hyperactive and nonhyperactive subgroups did not differ from one another in presence of EEG transients.

Misurec and Vrzal (1969) reported a higher percentage of EEG abnormalities in a heterogeneous group of children (6-14 years old) with learning and behavior problems ($N = 43$) and in a group with less severe problems ($N = 29$) in contrast to a group of age-matched controls ($N = 109$). The EEG was "abnormal" in 65%, 31%, and 10% of the children with more severe problems, less severe problems, and normal controls, respectively. These investigators observed a greater relationship between EEG abnormality and behavior/learning problems in the younger age groups (8-12 years).

Werry, Minde, Guzman, Weiss, Dogan, and Hoy (1972) reported a study comparing the EEGs of 20 hyperactive children (6-12 years old; 18 boys, 2 girls) free from psychosis or major physical disease and IQ above

80 with normal and neurotic control groups matched for age, sex ratio, and socioeconomic status. These investigators found no significant differences in the frequency of EEG abnormalities across the three groups (test conditions and type of abnormalities were unspecified).

Stevens, Sachdev, and Milstein (1968) using blind ratings compared the EEGs of 120 school children with "behavior disorders" to a group of 88 normal controls. They reported that the behavior-disorder group displayed a greater percentage (47%) of moderate to severe EEG abnormalities than controls (28%). However, the general assignment of "abnormal EEG" did not differ significantly between the two groups.

Satterfield, Cantwell, Lesser, and Podosin (1972) compared the resting EEGs of 31 hyperactive children referred to a clinic with 21 normal controls. Satterfield et al. did not observe differences between hyperactive and controls on mean resting EEG amplitude, resting EEG amplitude range, slow-wave activity, or number of EEG movement artifacts. The finding of no difference in slow-wave activity is interesting in relation to the often cited observation in uncontrolled studies that hyperactive children display "abnormal" amounts of slow-wave activity in their EEGs (Dubey, 1976).

As Dubey (1976) indicated in a review of studies of organic factors in hyperactivity, the literature reporting controlled comparisons of EEGs in normals and hyperactives is equivocal. In sum, while certain uncontrolled EEG studies of the child with learning and behavior problems do indicate a predominance of abnormal slow-wave activity, the reliability and clinical significance of such a finding in these children is unclear.

The *behavioral significance* of an abnormal EEG finding in these groups is also questionable. Tymchuk, Knights, and Hinton (1970b) identified four groups of behavior-and/or school-problem children (25 per group). Three groups exhibited EEG abnormalities: (a) dysrhythmia—general dysrhythmic pattern dominated by seizure discharges, (b) spike and wave, and (c) slow-wave activity, and a fourth group evidenced normal EEG activity. The authors attempted to evaluate the relationship between specific EEG abnormalities and performance on a variety of intelligence and neuropsychological tests. In general, Tymchuk et al. reported that the normal EEG group performed best on tests of gross motor and academic ability (auditory discrimination, verbal and spatial memory) and poorest on fine motor measures. In contrast, the slow-wave EEG group performed better than the other three groups on fine motor variables, yet scored lower on academic measures. The spike and wave and dysrhythmic groups performed poorly on most variables except certain fine motor tests.

Satterfield, Cantwell, Saul, and Yusin (1974) also investigated the relationship between EEG abnormality and cognitive and motor performance. The hyperactive children with EEG abnormalities (post-hyperventilation, epileptiform, or paroxysmal abnormalities; spike or excessive slow wave) scored significantly higher than the hyperactive children with normal EEG patterns on WISC Full Scale and Performance IQ and on two WISC subtests. These subjects also scored higher on the Visual Association and Visual Closure subtests of the Illinois Test of Psycholinguistic Abilities and had fewer perseveration scores on the Bender Gestalt Test. In addition, behavioral ratings by teachers and parents did not differ between those children with or without EEG abnormalities. In sum, those hyperactive children with EEG abnormalities did not experience greater intellectual, learning, or behavior problems as measured by standard intelligence, achievement, and behavior rating scales, than the hyperactives with normal EEGs. In fact, those hyperactive children with epileptiform EEG abnormalities were found to exhibit higher intellectual performance and academic achievement and less difficulty concentrating and cooperating in class. Indeed, as Satterfield and his associates have indicated, if an abnormal EEG is used to determine eligibility for special education, those children with the least need for this service would qualify, while those most in need would not!

Therefore, the studies on clinical EEG assessment indicate that (1) the use of the procedure to evaluate brain dysfunction in children with learning disabilities and/or behavior problems is questionable, and (2) even when EEG abnormalities are present in children diagnosed with hyperactivity, scores on intelligence tests, academic achievement tests, and behavioral rating scales are similar to those of hyperactives without EEG abnormalities.

4.2. 40-Hz EEG

While the use of clinical EEGs to differentiate children with learning and/or behavior problems from normal children is controversial, more sophisticated analyses of the EEG through various computer techniques have been developed in recent years which may provide more useful information on central nervous system differences in these populations. Also, the approach to testing brain function in these children has been greatly modified. Rather than evaluating brain activity in a static test environment as is frequently done in clinical EEG analysis (with the exception of photic stimulation), *cortical response to information processing demands* has been the focus of recent efforts to differentiate these groups. One such measure is a narrow high-frequency band in the EEG, centered at 40 hertz (Hz), assumed to reflect "focused arousal" or attention.

The 40-Hz response is believed to represent the cortical excitability necessary to assist with problem solving and subsequent consolidation in long-term memory (Sheer, 1976).

Sheer (1976) suggests that certain children with learning disabilities have a primary deficit in "focused arousal," a concept somewhat similar to what others have reported as "sustained attention" (Douglas, 1972; 1974), "attentional deficit" (Dykman, Ackerman, Clements, & Peters, 1971), and "selective attention" (Kinsbourne, 1973). The clinical picture of the learning-disabled child often includes perceptual-cognitive difficulties characterized as "short attention span" and "poor concentration." Focused arousal or attention to relevant associations is critical for the normal development of reading skills. Sheer suggests that this deficit in focused arousal results in difficulties maintaining sequences in short-term memory store and stabilizing memories in long-term store. The deficit is represented cortically by a reduction in 40-Hz EEG activity during problem solving.

In order to test this hypothesis Sheer compared the 40-Hz activity during a series of problem-solving tasks in normal children with that of two groups of learning-disabled children. The LD groups were classified on degree of deficit in school performance and were matched on age (mean = 10 years) and IQ (range 94-100). Significant increases in 40-Hz activity on right and left parietal leads were observed during verbal-visual, verbal-auditory, and tactile-kinesthetic problem-solving tasks in the normal children but not in the learning-disability groups. In addition, the two learning-disability groups had significantly more errors than the control children in each of the problem-solving tasks. The two subgroups of learning-disabled children did not differ from one another on either 40-Hz activity or error rate. While these findings suggest the potential of such an approach for differential assessment and for furthering our knowledge of the etiology of learning disorders, additional research on the reliability and validity of this measurement strategy is needed. It should be noted that Sheer has not suggested the use of this measure as a diagnostic tool. These findings illustrate the potential of a more dynamic neurophysiological approach to evaluation of the child with learning disabilities.

4.3. Averaged Evoked Response

An additional measure used to evaluate presumed central nervous system deficits in these children is the averaged evoked response (AER). Cortical activity is comprised of a wide range of electrical energy varying in frequency and amplitude. This complicates the identification of transient electrical changes in the ongoing EEG that represent cortical reactivity to sensory stimulation or information processing. However, computer averaging of multiple cortical responses to repeated presentations of a stimulus results in significant suppression of the "noise" in the EEG, with consequent enhancement of the cortical response. The resulting response is referred to as the *average evoked response* (AER). The AER can be stimulated by a variety of sensory stimuli (auditory, visual, kinesthetic). Figure 1 illustrates the wave form of the AER and provides a schematic of its various components. The AER is believed to reflect the spatial and temporal characteristics of the central nervous system (CNS) and is related to sensory, perceptual, and cognitive processes (Donchin & Lindsley, 1969; John, Karmel, Corning, Easton, Brown, Ahn, John, Harmony, Prichep, Toro, Gerson, Bartlett, Thatcher, Kaye, Valdes, & Schwartz, 1977; Sutton & Tueting, 1975).

Satterfield (1973) compared the auditory AER in 31 boys with problems of hyperactivity and distractability with 21 normal subjects matched for age (6-9 years) and sex. The amplitudes of various compo-

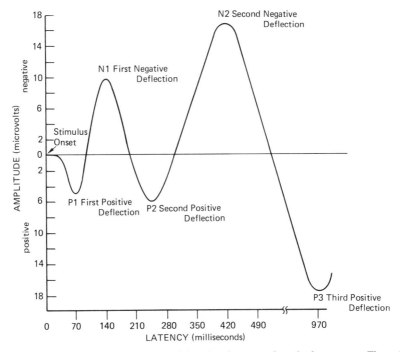

FIGURE 1. Schematic representation of the visual averaged evoked response. The values presented are approximations and are intended to provide a general frame of reference for the various AER components. Characteristics of these components vary as a function of age. As the child grows older, latencies and amplitudes tend to decrease. A positive change in electrical activity is indicated by a downward deflection.

nents of the AER wave form (N_1-P_2,P_2-N_2,P_2) were significantly lower in the hyperactive group. In addition, the latencies or the duration from stimulus onset to appearance of a specific component in the AER (refer to Figure 1) were generally longer for the hyperactive group. These latency differences were interpreted to indicate a delayed CNS maturation in the hyperactive child based on the findings that decreases in AER latencies are observed with maturation (Creuzfeldt and Kuhnt, 1967).

Shields (1973) evaluated the visual AER in children (10-13 years) with learning disabilities in processing visual information. She compared AER activity in 10 LDs with a group of 10 normal children matched for age, sex, handedness, verbal IQ, and socioeconomic status. A variety of visual stimuli were used: light flashes, pictures, designs, words, and nonsense words. The results indicated longer latencies and *greater* amplitudes of specific response components for the LD children than for normals. These findings were interpreted to suggest that LD children may require more time to process information than normal children and that their brain responses may be less mature than those of normal children. Tejral, Adler, Lichy, and Kovarikova (1975) also reported that the visual AERs of a group of 7- to 10-year-old boys with restlessness and poor concentration showed longer latencies and greater amplitudes at rest and following 3-minute hyperventilation, in contrast to matched normals.

These AER findings can be better understood following a brief discussion of normal AER activity during information-processing demands. Increased amplitudes of selected AER components are observed in normals when a stimulus is made relevant, and hence is attended to; however, in the presence of irrelevant, and therefore nonattended stimuli, amplitudes tend to decrease (Sutton & Tueting, 1975). Therefore, in the presence of irrelevant stimuli reductions in AER amplitudes are generally observed in "normal" individuals, and brain responses that continue to reflect attention to irrelevant stimuli (i.e., increased amplitudes) may reflect an information-processing deficit.

In sum, both the absence of 40-Hz activity and the persistent increased amplitudes (with the exception of results obtained by Satterfield, who monitored *auditory* average evoked responses in hyperactives) of selected AER components in children with learning disabilities may reflect this basic attentional deficit. The predominant findings suggest that children can be reliably differentiated into normals and learning-disabled/hyperactive on the basis of the AER and that the attentional deficit often described in LD/hyperactivity appears to be reflected in these electrophysiological responses. The specific implications for assessment of these childhood problems remain to be determined. Further studies replicating AER differences between clearly defined subpopulations of LD and hyperactive children would prove useful in determining the diagnostic reliability of this procedure. In addition, if consistent deficits are observed, emphasis must be placed on determining the utility of such a finding in the clinical management of these problems.

4.4. Neurometrics

A more recent electrophysiological assessment technique potentially applicable to the evaluation of neurophysiologic deficits in children with learning disorders has been developed by E. Roy John and associates (John et al., 1977). The approach is termed *neurometrics* and refers to a highly quantitative assessment of brain activity directed at obtaining information, "related to anatomical integrity, developmental maturation, and mediation of sensory, perceptual, and cognitive processes." The goal of neurometrics is to quantify a variety of brain functions and develop a series of profiles with diagnostic significance as to the structural and functional integrity of the brain. The approach is directed at providing, when appropriate, an alternative to psychometrics, one that includes information on the *underlying process* of cognition rather than its products (i.e., performance on various psychometric tests).

The neurometric test battery is based upon research in central nervous system psychophysiology discussed in Shagass (1972) and John et al. (1977). The neurometric test items include a variety of stimulus situations designed to test the brain's response to these stimuli and to provide comparisons of related stimulus conditions. Specific test items include standard clinical EEG recordings under conditions of eyes open, eyes closed, and photic stimulation. More sophisticated test items include measurement of brain activity (AER) during tests designed to evaluate sensory acuity, pattern perception, prediction of temporal order, cross-sensory modality interactions, discrimination between meaningful visual or auditory input (figure) and meaningless visual, auditory, or somatosensory input (ground), and the brain's sensory-sensory classical conditioning capabilities. For a more detailed description of the test battery refer to John (1977a, 1977b) or John et al. (1977).

John et al. administered the full neurometric battery and a number of psychometric tests to 118 normal and 57 learning-disabled male children (7.8-10.4 years). The battery required 1-2 hours for administration. John et al. (1977) reported the findings of a comparison of the neurometric and psychometric test data in the LD children. Their results indicated that the neurometric EEG measures that included only the first two conditions of the battery (1 minute each of eyes open and eyes closed) discriminated between normal and LD children to a greater extent than the most discriminating psychometric measures (including those measures frequently obtained in LD assessment). Analyses of other items in the neurometric battery indicated highly significant differences in the latencies of the AER between normals and LDs. It should be emphasized that while a number of AER studies have also reported such differences, the neurometric analysis purportedly can *localize* multiple areas where "deficits" may be occurring and thus provide a map of brain areas in which specific functional deficits are present. Prior AER procedures could only marginally provide such information. While the future utility of such a procedure remains to be determined, the ability to "map" the human cortex on a functional basis could prove useful for assessment of the "subtle" deficits assumed to be present in various types of learning disorders. That is, it may be possible to localize cortical areas that contribute to specific learning disorders. Once these areas are identified and the physiological deficit is defined, it may be possible to develop interventions to actively modify the cortical deficit (e.g., biofeedback techniques).

In the same report, John and his associates discuss a second study, which evaluated neurometric data on 533 LD children and 50 normals. Subjects were classified into seven anatomical (bilateral parieto-occipital, central, temporal, and all combinations of these loci) location categories and seven physiologic dysfunction categories (EEG frequency, EEG asymmetry, AER asymmetry, and combination of the three). In general, marked differences between the normal and LD groups were observed, with 92.6% of the LD group demonstrating some type of unusual finding and only 20% of the normal group indicating deficits. In addition, the deficits in the normal group were consistently localized to the parieto-occipital region only and were primarily in the EEG-frequency and/or EEG-asymmetry category. In contrast, the LD child displayed multiple types of dysfunction in several cortical areas. John suggested that these findings may indicate some source of "severe generalized insult" to the brain such as pre- or perinatal trauma, malnutrition, or early stimulus deprivation. John *et al.* also reported that certain abnormal patterns were apparent in children under 12 years while different structure-function deficits were noted for adolescents. They attributed these age-specific differences to a variety of possible factors such as sampling error, development lag, and/or different evaluation criteria of school personnel for different age groups. The fact remains, however, that *subtle* brain structure-function differences are observed between LD and normal children following testing on the neurometric battery. While these differences are believed to more closely reflect the underlying information-processing deficits of these children, further basic research is required to evaluate the relationship between information processing and CNS activity in children with and without learning disabilities. While neurometrics may hold much potential in the evaluation of these children, as with the other assessment procedures, the degree to which the information generated from the assessment assists in clinical or educational intervention is at present unclear.

4.5. Autonomic Nervous System Measures

An additional area of measurement relevant to the physiological evaluation of children with learning disabilities and/or behavior problems is the recording of autonomic nervous system (ANS) indices in resting states and under conditions of arousal (generally during reaction-time tasks or in response to sensory stimuli). The two measures most frequently recorded in studies that attempt to differentiate these problem children from normals on the basis of ANS indices are skin conductance and heart rate. Psychophysiological research on these measures with normal subjects suggests that increased arousal is associated with increased skin conductance (Edelberg, 1972) and that focused attention (the foreperiod of a reaction-time task) is related to heart-rate deceleration (Lacey, 1967) (refer to Table 5).

When considering ANS activity in children with learning and/or behavior problems one must first differentiate *resting autonomic levels* from *autonomic reactivity* or responsivity to a set of stimuli. While not completely consistent, the majority of studies comparing children with behavior and/or learning problems to age-matched normal controls indicate that resting levels of autonomic activity do not differ between the clinical and normal groups (Cohen & Douglas, 1972; Dykman et al., 1971; Zahn, Abate, Little, & Wender, 1975). However, a number of studies on autonomic reactivity to sensory stimuli or reactivity during performance tasks such as reaction time have reported *lower* autonomic reactivity in the clinical groups (Cohen & Douglas, 1972; Dykman et al., 1971; Satterfield & Dawson, 1971; Spring, Greenberg, Scott, & Hopwood, 1974; Sroufe, Sonies, West, & Wright, 1973; Zahn et al., 1975). Specifically, Dykman et al. (1971) reported lowered autonomic reactivity (particularly skin resistance response) in both learning-disabled and behavior-problem subjects to stimuli presented during a conditioning procedure. Sroufe et al. (1973) indicated that LD children had less anticipatory heart-rate deceleration to reaction-time stimuli. Zahn et al. (1975) reported that while hyperactive (including academic underachievement) and normal children did not differ on the frequency of skin conductance orienting responses to tones, the hyperactive group's responses were delayed, smaller, and recovered (i.e., returned to baseline) more slowly than the control group. In addition, Zahn et al. reported that the hyperactive group evidenced fewer skin conductance responses to the more "demanding" stimuli in the reaction time task.

From an assessment perspective, the ANS findings suggest that if one is interested in developing evaluation procedures to identify psychophysiological deficits in these children the assessment should not be of static activity. Rather, measurement of the individual's physiological reactivity to a set of stimulus conditions should be undertaken. If possible, measurements should be taken while the subject is performing tasks that require the use of psychological processes assumed to contribute to the clinical problem. If accurate norms could be developed on skin conductance and cardiovascular measures of arousal during a variety of these tasks, one could begin to evaluate deviations from these norms. If indeed the child was found to exhibit a deficit in autonomic nervous system arousal in either a hyper- or a hypoaroused direction, it is possible that this information could lead to clinical attempts to modify the arousal and might prove an effective intervention strategy (cf. Braud, 1978).

Considerable work must be accomplished on the clinical validity and reliability of these procedures. Recording ANS measures in conjunction with a neurometric battery may in the future provide useful diagnostic data enabling differentiation of autonomic and central nervous system deficits that contribute to the presenting problem. Once these deficits are identified it may be possible to develop integrative behavioral and psychophysiological approaches to correct such deficits.

While classical EEG assessment appears to be of limited use in the assessment of children with learning and/or behavior problems, the newer, more dynamic physiological measures of information processing such as the 40-Hz EEG, averaged evoked response, neurometric test battery, and ANS measures of reactivity may prove more useful. These newer procedures must be further evaluated on an experimental, clinical and cost-benefit basis.

5. Summary and Implications

A description and evaluation of neuropsychological and neurophysiological assessment of the learning-disabled and behavior-problem child was presented in order to familiarize clinicians with these specialized diagnostic procedures. The chapter evaluated the ability of each of these assessment procedures to differentiate clinical populations from normal children. The neuropsychological assessment approach with these problem children is directed at evaluation of the behavioral consequences of a presumed subtle brain dysfunction, while the EEG and other biologically oriented techniques attempt to directly identify the physiological deficit. Certain approaches have been somewhat more successful than others although all techniques require considerable further study prior to clinical use.

Specifically, the neuropsychological and EEG techniques are able to identify gross brain pathology; however, their utility in the assessment of learning and/or behavior problems is at present unclear. The WISC and standard neuropsychological batteries appear to identify very few deficits specific to children with learning disabilities and behavior problems, although the evaluation procedures do reveal differences between these children and children with confirmed brain damage. Also, the specific type of deficit or pattern, when observed in the learning-disabled or behavior-problem child, is not consistent across studies. While partly a function of sampling and definitional difficulties, the present literature is inconclusive as to specific reliable patterns of deficits in these clinical populations.

Contrary to the neuropsychological findings, the evaluation of physiological activity during information processing by measurement of the 40-Hz EEG, averaged evoked response (primarily visual), neurometric battery, and autonomic reactivity suggests a consistent picture. These measurement procedures indicate that the child with learning and/or behavior problems is characterized by a deficit in attention/arousal and that this deficit is reliably reflected in both CNS and ANS reactivity. While at present these assessment procedures are insufficiently developed for direct clinical application, the findings support the need for additional research in this area.

From a *practical* clinical perspective, the literature suggests that the utility of *all* these approaches for differentiating the child with learning and/or behavior problems from the normal child is limited. Additional research on larger numbers of children is necessary to further clarify the role these assessment procedures can play among the more standard evaluation protocols. To date, it appears that these time-consuming, relatively costly assessments are no more useful than what is generally completed in a standard psychological/behavioral evaluation. Nevertheless, we must not disregard the potential of these procedures as their assessment strategies become more sophisticated in the future.

ACKNOWLEDGMENT

The authors wish to express their gratitude to M. A. Chesney, Ph. D., for her helpful comments on an earlier draft of this chapter.

6. References

Ackerman, P., Peters, J. E., & Dykman, R. A. Children with specific learning disabilities: WISC profiles. *Journal of Learning Disabilities*, 1971, *4*, 150-166. (a)

Ackerman, P. T., Peters, J. E., & Dykman, R. A. Children with specific disabilities: Bender Gestalt Test findings and other signs. *Journal of Learning Disabilities*, 1971, *4*, 437-446.(b)

Anderson, M., Kaufman, A. S., & Kaufman, N. L. Use of the WISC-R with a learning disabled population: Some diagnostic implications. *Psychology in the Schools*, 1976, *13*, (4), 381-386.

Bender, L. *Instructions for the use of the Visual Motor Gestalt Test*. New York: American Orthopsychiatric Association, 1946.

Benton, A. L. *The Revised Visual Retention Test* (4th ed.). New York: Psychological Corporation, 1974.

Braud, L. W. The effects of frontal EMG biofeedback and progressive relaxation upon hyperactivity and its behavioral concomitants, *Biofeedback and Self-Regulation*, 1978, *3*, 69-89.

Buffery, A. W. H. Clinical neuropsychology: A review and preview. In S. Rachman (Ed.), *Contributions to medical psychology* (Vol. 1). Oxford: Pergamon Press, 1977.

Clements, S. D., & Peters, J. E. Minimal brain dysfunctions in the school-age child. *Archives of General Psychiatry*, 1962, *6*, 185-197.

Cohen, N. J., & Douglas, V. I. Characteristics of the orienting response in hyperactive and normal children. *Psychophysiology*, 1972, *9*, 238-245.

Coleman, J. C., & Rasof, B. Intellectual factors in learning disorders. *Perceptual and Motor Skills*, 1963, *16*, 139-152.

Creuzfeldt, O. D., & Kuhnt, U. The visual evoked potential: Physiological, developmental and clinical aspects. In W. Cobb & C. Morocutti (Eds.), *The evoked potentials. EEG and Clinical Neurophysiology (Suppl.)*, 1967, *26*, 29-41.

Donchin, E., & Lindsley, D. B. (Eds.). *Averaged evoked potentials: Methods, results, and evaluations* (NASA Publication No. SP 191). Washington, D.C.: U.S. Government Printing Office, 1969.

Douglas, V. I. Stop, look, and Listen: The problem of sustained attention and impulse control in hyperactive and normal children. *Canadian Journal of Behavioral Sciences*, 1972, *4*, 259-282.

Douglas, V. I. Differences between normal and hyperkinetic children. In C. K. Conners (Ed.), *Clinical use of stimulant drugs in children*. Amsterdam: Excerpta Medica, 1974.

Dubey, D. R. Organic factors in hyperkinesis: A critical evaluation. *American Journal of Orthopsychiatry*, 1976, *46*, 353-366.

Dunn, L. M., & Markwardt, F. C. *Manual, Peabody Individual Achievement Test*. Circle Pines, Minn.: American Guidance Service, 1970.

Dykman, R. A., Ackerman, P. T., Clements, S. D., & Peters, J. E. Specific learning disabilities: An attentional deficit syndrome. In H. R. Myklebust (Ed.), *Progress in learning disabilities* (Vol. 2). New York: Grune & Stratton, 1971.

Edelberg, R. Electrical activity of the skin: Its measurement and uses in psychophysiology. In N. S. Greenfield & R. A. Sternbach (Eds.), *Handbook of psychophysiology*. New York: Holt, Rinehart & Winston, 1972.

Freeman, R. D. Special education and the electroencephalogram: Marriage of convenience. *Journal of Special Education*, 1967, *2*, 61-73.

Frostig, M., Lefever, W., & Whittlesey, J. R. B. *Administration and scoring manual for the Marianne Frostig developmental test of visual perception*. Palo Alto, Cal.: Consulting Psychologists Press, 1966.

Fuller, G. B. *The Minnesota Percepto-Diagnostic Test* (rev. ed.), Brandon, Vt.: Clinical Psychology, 1969.

Golden, C. J. *Diagnosis and rehabilitation in clinical neuropsychology*. Springfield, Ill.: Thomas, 1978.

Goldstein, E. H. A multidisciplinary evaluation of children with learning disabilities. *Child Psychiatry and Human Development*, 1974, *5*, 95-107.

Graham, F. K., & Kendall, B. S. Memory-for-Designs Test: Revised general manual. *Perceptual and Motor Skills (Monograph Supplement* No. 2-VII), 1960, *11*, 147-188.

Greenfield, N. S., & Sternbach, R. A. (Eds.). *Handbook of psychophysiology*. New York: Holt, Rinehart & Winston, 1972.

Harris, D. B. *Children's drawings as measures of intellectual maturity*. New York: Harcourt, Brace and World, 1963.

Heaton, R. K., Baade, L. E., & Johnson, K. L. Neuropsychological test results associated with psychiatric disorders in adults. *Psychological Bulletin*, 1978, *85*, 146-162.

John, E. R. *Neurometrics: Clinical applications of quantitative electrophysiology*. Hillsdale, N.J.: Erlbaum Associates, 1977. (a)

John, E. R. *The neurometric test battery*. New York: Brain Research Laboratories, New York Medical College, 1977.(b)

John, E. R., Karmel, B. Z., Corning, W. C., Easton, P., Brown, D., Ahn, H., John, M., Harmony, T., Prichep, L., Toro, A., Gerson, I., Bartlett, F., Thatcher, R., Kaye, H., Valdes, P., & Schwartz, E. Neurometrics. *Science*, 1977, *196*, 1393-1410.

Kahn, E., & Cohen, L. H. Organic driveness: A brain-stem syndrome and an experience. *New England Journal of Medicine*, 1934, *210*, 748-756.

Kinsbourne, M. Minimal brain dysfunction as a neurodevelopmental lag. *Annals of the New York Academy of Sciences*, 1973, *205*, 268-273.

Klatskin, E. H., McNamara, N. E., Shaffer, D., & Pincus, J. H. Minimal organicity in children of normal intelligence: Correspondence between psychological test results and neurologic findings. *Journal of Learning Disabilities*, 1972, *5*, 213-218.

Klonoff, H., & Low, M. Disordered brain function in young children and early adolescents: Neuropsychological and electroencepalographic correlates. In R. M. Reitan & L. A. Davison (Eds.), *Clinical neuropsychology: Current status and applications*. New York: Winston/Wiley, 1974.

Knights, R. M., & Tymchuk, A. J. An evaluation of the Halstead-Reitan Category Tests for children. *Cortex*, 1968, *4*, 403-414.

Koppitz, E. M. *The Bender Gestalt Test for young children*. New York: Grune & Stratton, 1964.

Koppitz, E. M. Bender gestalt test, visual aural digit span test and reading achievement. *Journal of Learning Disabilities*, 1975, *8*, 154-157.

Lacey, J. I. Somatic response patterning and stress: Some revisions of activation theory. In M. H. Appley & R. Trumbull (Eds.), *Psychological stress: Issues in research*. New York: Appleton-Century-Crofts, 1967.

Larsen, S. C., Rogers, D., & Sowell, V. The use of selected perceptual tests in differentiating between normal and learning disabled children. *Journal of Learning Disabilities*, 1976, *9*, 85-90.

Lezak, M. D. *Neuropsychological assessment*. New York: Oxford University Press, 1976.

Misurec, J., & Vrzal, J. EEG in children with minimal brain damage. *EEG and Clinical Neurophysiology*, 1969, *26*, 227-236.

Myklebust, H. R. Identification and diagnosis of children with learning disabilities: An interdisciplinary study of criteria. *Seminars in Psychiatry*, 1973, *5*, 55-77.

Myklebust, H. R., & Boshes, B. A neurological and behavioral study of children with learning disorders. *Neurology*, 1964, *14*, 7-12.

Palkes, H., & Stewart, M. Intellectual ability and performance of hyperactive children. *American Journal of Orthopsychiatry*, 1972, *42*, 35-39.

Purdue Research Foundation. *Examiner's manual for the Purdue Pegboard*. Chicago: Science Research Associates, 1948.

Raven, J. C. *Guide to the Standard Progressive Matrices*. London: Lewis, 1960.

Reitan, R. M. *Manual for administration of neuropsychological test batteries for adults and children*. Indianapolis: Reitan, 1969.

Reitan, R. M., & Boll, T. J. Neuropsychological correlates of minimal brain dysfunction. *Annals of the New York Academy of Sciences*, 1973, *205*, 65-88.

Reitan, R. M., & Davison, L. W. (Eds.). *Clinical neuropsychology: Current status and applications*. New York: Winston/Wiley, 1974.

Reitan, R. M., & Heineman, C. E. Interactions of neurological deficits and emotional disturbances in children with learning disorders: Methods for their differential assessment. In J. Hellmuth (Ed.), *Learning disorders* (Vol. 3). Seattle: Special Child Publications, 1968.

Ross, D. M., & Ross, S. A. *Hyperactivity: Research, theory, and action*. New York: Wiley-Interscience, 1976.

Sandoval, J., Lambert, N. M., & Yandell, W. Current medical practice and hyperactive children. *American Journal of Orthopsychiatry*, 1976, *46*, 323-334.

Satterfield, J. H. EEG issues in children with minimal brain dysfunction. *Seminars in Psychiatry*, 1973, *5*, 35-46.

Satterfield, J. H., Cantwell, D. P., Lesser, L. I., & Podosin, R. L. Physiological studies of the hyperkinetic child I. *American Journal of Psychiatry*, 1972, *128*, 1418-1424.

Satterfield, J. H., Cantwell, D. P., Saul, R. E., & Yusin, A. Intelligence, academic achievement and EEG abnormalities in hyperactive children. *American Journal of Psychiatry*, 1974, *131*, 391-395.

Satterfield, J. H., & Dawson, M. E. Electrodermal correlates of hyperactivity in children. *Psychophysiology*, 1971, *8*, 191-197.

Shagass, C. Electrical activity of the brain. In N. S. Greenfield & R. Sternbach. (Eds.), *Handbook of psychophysiology*. New York: Holt, Rinehart & Winston, 1972.

Sheer, D. E. Focused arousal and 40-Hz EEG. In R. M. Knights & D. J. Bakker (Eds.), *The neuropsychology of learning disorders: Theoretical approaches*. Baltimore: University Park Press, 1976.

Shields, D. T. Brain responses to stimuli in disorders of information processing. *Journal of Learning Disabilities*, 1973, *6*, 501-505.

Sloan, W. *The Lincoln-Oseretsky Motor Development Scale manual*. Chicago: Stoelting, 1954.

Spring, C., Greenberg, L., Scott, J., & Hopwood, J. Electrodermal activity in hyperactive boys who are methylphenidate responders. *Psychophysiology*, 1974, *11*, 436-442.

Sroufe, L. A., Sonies, B. C., West, W. D., Wright, F. S. Anticipatory heart rate deceleration and reaction time in children with and without referral for learning disability. *Child Development*, 1973, *44*, 267-273.

Stevens, P. A., Boydstun, J. A., Dykman, R. A., Peters, J. E., & Sinton, D. W. Presumed minimal brain dysfunction in children. *Archives of General Psychiatry*, 1967, *16*, 281-285.

Stevens, J. R., Sachdev, K. K., & Milstein, V. Behavior disorders of childhood and electroencephalogram. *EEG and Clinical Neurophysiology*, 1968, *24*, 188.

Sutton, S., & Tueting, P. The sensitivity of the evoked potential to psychological variables. In P. H. Venables & M. J. Christie (Eds.), *Research in psychophysiology*. New York: Wiley, 1975.

Tejral, J., Adler, J., Lichy, J., & Kovarikova, L. Visual evoked responses and EEG in children with learning problems. *EEG and Clinical Neurophysiology*, 1975, *39*, 438-439. (Abstract)

Trupin, E. W., & Townes, B. D. Neuropsychological evaluation as an adjunct to behavioral interventions with children. *Professional Psychology*, 1976, *7* (2), 153-160.

Tsushima, W. T., & Towne, W. S. Neuropsychological abilities of young children with questionable brain disorders. *Journal of Consulting and Clinical Psychology*, 1977, *45*, 757-762.

Tymchuk, A. J., Knights, R. M., & Hinton, G. C. Neuropsychological test results of children with brain lesions, abnormal EEGs, and normal EEGs. *Canadian Journal of Behavioral Sciences*, 1970, *2*, 322-329. (a)

Tymchuk, A. J., Knights, R. M., & Hinton, G. G. The behavioral significance of differing EEG abnormalities in children with learning and/or behavior problems. *Journal of Learning Disabilities*, 1970, *3*, 548-551. (b)

Venables, P. H., & Christie, M. J. (Eds.). *Research in psychophysiology*. New York: Wiley, 1975.

Wechsler, D. I. *Wechsler Intelligence Scale for Children*. New York: Psychological Corporation, 1949.

Wechsler, D. I. *Wechsler Preschool and Primary Scale of Intelligence*. New York: Psychological Corporation, 1967.

Wechsler, D. I. WISC-R manual. *Wechsler Intelligence Scale for Children-Revised*. New York: Psychological Corporation, 1974.

Wepman, J. M. *Auditory Discrimination Test, Form I, II*. Chicago: Language Research Associates, 1958.

Werry, J. S., Minde, K. Guzman, A., Weiss, G., Dogan, K., & Hoy, E. Studies on the hyperactive child-VII: Neurological status compared with neurotic and normal children. *American Journal of Orthopsychiatry*, 1972, *42*, 441-452.

Wikler, A., Dixon, J. F., & Parker, J. B. Brain function in problem children and controls: Psychometric, neurological and electroencephalographic comparisons. *American Journal of Psychiatry*, 1970, *127*, 94-105.

Zahn, T. P., Abate, F., Little, B. C., & Wender, P. H. Minimal brain dysfunction, stimulant drugs and autonomic nervous system activity. *Archives of General Psychiatry*, 1975, *32*, 381-387.

Author Index

Subject Index